THE PRICE
OF OUR
HERITAGE

Your Obedient and Very Humble
Mary F. Clarke

THE PRICE OF OUR HERITAGE

Volume One
1831-1869
History of the Sisters of Charity
of the Blessed Virgin Mary

M. JANE COOGAN B.V.M.

MOUNT CARMEL PRESS
Dubuque, Iowa 52001

Raymond H. Schmandt

"The first law of history is to
tell the truth to tell
the truth can be
beyond all suspicion of favoring or hating
anyone whomsoever."

Leo XIII

**

To our Foundress, Mary Frances Clarke
we dedicate this work.
May her spirit,
emerging from more than a century
of obscurity,
guide us
as we move into an era
in which
women seek their true place
in the Church
and
in the world.

TABLE OF CONTENTS

Foreword

.

In this year 1975, designated International
Woman's Year by the United Nations, all persons are
being called to recognize women, their gifts and talents, their accomplishments down through the centuries. It is significant that in this Woman's Year
Sister Jane Coogan's research and able scholarship in
THE PRICE OF OUR HERITAGE bring to light the lives of
those unique women who were the first members of the
BVM Congregation. In the critical years from 1833-
1869, critical for our Congregation, for the Church,
and our country, these few women made a decided im-
pact on the lives of the early settlers in the Iowa
Territory, indeed on the lives of many in our country.
The first five women and the members who joined that
group were truly pioneers - pioneer women who looked
beyond visible horizons; pioneer women who risked,
who experienced rugged hardship, real poverty and deep
joy. They were pioneer women of faith called by the
Lord to leave everything - home, family, friends,
familiar surroundings, and to follow His call like the
Israelites of old, a call to live as pilgrims in a
new land.

Decided obstacles confronted Sister Jane in her
research: notably, the 1849 fire which destroyed
everything at St. Joseph's Prairie, our early Iowa
motherhouse and first boarding school. Coupled with
this event was Mary Frances Clarke's reluctance to
have anything written about the early days: "If all
that happened in those early days were written, no one
would believe it . . .You will know all that God wants
you to know and that will be enough."

In spite of these obstacles the book provides
enlightening background into our Dublin beginnings,
our decade of service in the city of Philadelphia, and
finally our early years in the frontier settlement of
Dubuque. There are delightful word-pictures of the
women and men, clergy and lay, whose lives were inter-
woven with those early members and whose decisions at
times influenced this young and striving community.
These word-pictures re-create those people with their
human gifts and frailties.

Some of the events sketched are familiar to many

BVM Sisters who heard of them from older Sisters or
read of them in THE EARLY DAYS. But Sister Jane has
clarified the old and added fresh insights that will
lead us to a deeper understanding of those formative
years in BVM life and ministry.

Other events are new to our knowledge and extremely significant, not only because they bring into
better focus the contributions made by these great
women of the past, but also because they help present-
day BVMs recognize a continuity with our traditions.
At the same time, the experiences of the past encourage the Congregation's members to seek prayerfully
and joyfully, new directions for the future. To high-
light just a few of Sister Jane's fresh insights: we
find turmoil within the Philadelphia Church, while our
Sisters lived and served among that city's people, a
turmoil which brought as a consequence questions regarding the vowed status of our early members; we
find an almost forty-year period (an evolving time)
when our Sisters lived with no formally approved rule,
with their religious status at times questioned; we
find the influence of the clergy and hierarchy on BVM
ministry even while Mary Frances Clarke continued to
state that we were open to meeting any needs the
people might have.

Although the individual contributions made by
our early members do not dominate the narrative,
principally because material was not recorded or was
lost, their rugged, risk-filled, sacrificing lives
emerge from the backdrop of the times. With Father
Donaghoe's death, the scene is set for full leadership
to be assumed by Mary Frances Clarke and those stal-
wart women who joined the first five.

This first volume of Sister Jane's work under-
scores the lives of BVM women of the past who identified closely with other pioneer women and contributed
significantly to the forming and shaping of our country's people. Secondly, her work is a contribution
to BVMs living today who are following the directive
of Vatican II to study the life and inspiration of
our foundress. Finally, this recording of our past
is an attempt to share our religious life and its beginnings with our families and friends who have helped
and loved us through the years.

In THE PRICE OF OUR HERITAGE insight into the lives of our first members, and into the tradition continued in BVM life today, will help our Congregation explore more fully how God wants us to live our lives here both now and in the future.

March 19, 1975

Introduction
and
Acknowledgments

In the earliest years of the Congregation of the
Sisters of Charity of the Blessed Virgin Mary, its
foundress, Mary Frances Clarke, assigned to Eliza
Kelly the office of annalist. Whatever Sister had
written before 1849 was lost in the fire which destroyed their frame motherhouse and boarding school
on the Iowa prairie in that year. Apparently a victim of rheumatoid arthritis in her later life, Sister
seems never to have recouped the loss. When, after
the death of the Reverend T.J. Donaghoe, to whom the
title of founder had come to be applied, the Sisters
begged Mother Clarke to have the Community's history
written, saying,

"Mother, won't you please have Sister Mary Joseph
write for us an account of the Community history?"
Mother's response was:
"On the contrary, I forbid her to write it. If
all that happened in those early days were written, no
one would believe it."

"But, Mother, if some of the first members do not
write such an account, we shall know nothing about
the most interesting period of our history."
"You will know all that God wills you to know,
and that will be enough," Mother responded quietly.

In reply to a plea from the Reverend John Kempker,
historian of the Catholic Church in Iowa, Mother
Clarke wrote: "I hope I do not disappoint you too
much when I tell you that upon reflection I have
yielded to a certain natural repugnance of mine to
have anything of the kind in print during my lifetime."

But Mother Clarke did not reckon on Vatican II
and its admonition to "return to the original inspiration" of our existence as a religious body, and to
accord "a loyal recognition and safeguarding of all
that gives us insight into that spirit" together with
the "particular goals and wholesome traditions which

constitute our heritage as a community."

With the time limit of Mother's repugnance long past, it is our task now to seek to "know all that God wills us to know," and in our efforts we have the blessing of the Church in consonance with the keynote of her life: "May the holy will of God be done."

Three previous attempts were made by successive secretaries general to preserve the story of the Congregation's beginnings: that of Sister M. Michael Nihill, whose efforts, save for a few scattered pages, were destroyed, by accident or design; Sister M. Pulcheria McGuire, who drew on the memories of our early members, supplemented by correspondence, and compiled in a 404-page typewritten study which she entitled Annals; and Sister M. Lambertina Doran, who published in 1911 In the Early Days, long regarded the Congregation's official history. Little investigation or organization of archival material preceded Sister's work, and there is strong evidence that Sister wrote in support of a predetermined thesis: that of Father Donaghoe's claim to have been the principal founder of the Congregation. To support the thesis, Sister chose carefully the sources used. Writing without documentation, she enveloped his memory in an aura of praise, quoted many letters of his after careful editing, and lent him prestige through citing at length letters from his friend, Archbishop Hughes of New York. Sister also included long letters to Father Donaghoe from Bishop Kenrick of Philadelphia, written in the first year or two of his episcopate, without giving any indication of a later estrangement and its serious effects on the Sisters.

Though Mother Clarke ruled the Congregation for nearly nineteen years of rapid expansion after Father Donaghoe's death, arranged for the Community's incorporation, completed the writing of the rule and made every sacrifice to gain approbation for it, one letter only, of the many letters of hers still extant, appears in Sister's work; this, despite the fact that the book quoted some thirty-six letters addressed to Mother. That Sister's published account was not consistent with her knowledge of less praiseworthy attitudes and actions of Father Donaghoe appears when we peruse her handwritten Diary and pencilled notes which remain to us. Those who knew Sister in life certainly regarded her as a woman of integrity, though of a strongly Victorian mentality. While her expressed intention of writing for the edification of the young certainly influenced her choice of details, yet even with this consideration it is impossible to believe that Sister M. Lambertina was free to write the truth impartially as she knew it. We can only conclude then that she wrote as she did under the direction of higher authority and in support of a thesis imposed upon her by those in command.

Many difficulties were involved in the search for materials necessary to a full and balanced account of the Congregation's early history. That no vital statistics were kept of Catholics in Dublin in our Sisters' day, nor of any persons in the smaller towns of Ireland, (indeed there is no record of deaths of Sisters on the Iowa Prairie through Mother Clarke's death in 1887) has proven a handicap. Within the Congregation many useful sources have been lost in the ordinary course of events, but much also has been destroyed. The care with which some members preserved correspondence and the lack of concern on the part of others make for difficulties in the production of a balanced study. In the absence of richer materials, and often at the expense of a free-flowing narrative, the writer has made use of minor details available from primary sources for such feeble light as they are able to throw on personalities and situations. Perhaps an undue amount of space has been given to the establishment of historical backgrounds. For those who find this a difficulty the writer offers an apology. The fact, however, that of the one hundred fifteen members registered by October, 1862, sixty-one were Irish-born, and forty-seven others were of Irish stock, with only nine of other nationalities, has made it seem imperative to include, at least for reference, a brief survey of the history of Ireland, the land in which their lives were rooted. This will be found in the appendix of the present volume, together with a register of those first members. The break in Irish immigration occasioned by the Civil War marked a turning point in the origins from which the membership drew.

*****

I am under obligation to many for assistance in this work. Among those are primarily the persons who labored long to gather and classify such correspondence and other materials as remained when the Congregation's historical consciousness began to awaken. Those especially responsible were three secretaries general, Sisters Mary Virginia Berry, Michael Flynn and Ethel Quinn, and all those who gave assistance to them, as well as Sister Mary Healey who established the archives on a professional basis. A substantial contribution to research, especially of the Sisters' years in Philadelphia, was made by the former Sister Mary Aquin Lally, whose extensive notes and assembled materials were left at the writer's disposal.

I deeply appreciate the untiring efforts of Ivy Embleton, genealogist of Belfast, Ireland to trace the backgrounds of the Donaghoe (Donaghey) family, the warm friendliness and helpfulness of the Joseph Farrell family in Dublin with whom I lived during six fruitful weeks of research, and the help given by the Reverend Dermot Clarke and Eileen Dunne of Dublin, uniquely beautiful and thoughtful persons.

I am grateful for the assistance of Professor Emmet Larkin, specialist in Irish studies at the University of Chicago, for his careful reading of the chapters having their setting in Ireland, and the suggestions he made in their connection; for the aid of the Reverend Hugh J.Nolan, professor of history at Immaculata college, Immaculata, Pennsylvania, and biographer of Bishop Francis Patrick Kenrick, and of John Marschall of the University of Nevada, whose dissertation covered the Baltimore years of Archbishop Kenrick, and who gave a critical reading to the Philadelphia chapters.

The many archivists to whom I owe a debt of gratitude include the Reverend John B. DeMayo of the Archdiocese of Philadelphia, the Reverend Menceslaus J. Madaj of the Chicago Archdiocese, the Right Reverend Monsignor Bernard E. Granich of the Archdiocese of St. Louis, and the Reverend John W. Dalton, vice-chancellor of the Archdiocese of Dubuque, who made the Loras files available. I owe deep thanks also to Sister John Mary of the Daughters of Charity, Emmitsburg, Maryland; to Sister Seraphia of the Chicago province of the Sisters of Mercy, and her Dublin counterpart at their generalate at Carysfort, Dublin; and to Sister Nona McGreal, archivist for the Sisters of St. Dominic, Sinsinawa, Wisconsin. I am grateful to the Reverend Thomas E. Blantz for the use of the extensive files in the archives of Notre Dame University, and to Mercedes Muenz, his assistant, for her gracious help; and to the Reverend Kenneth J. Downing, for access to the archives at Kiras College Library. My thanks to Sister Kathleen Healy, RSM, author of a recent biography of Mother Frances Warde, for her sharing of helpful research data.

It has been my special privilege to have known for many years the Reverend C. F. Griffith of St. Ambrose College, Davenport, Iowa. His generosity in giving full access to materials on the history of the Church in Iowa, gathered through a lifetime, and his interest in reading the first raw chapters of this work have been of immeasurable assistance. I thank also the Reverend Andrew Creighton of Loras College who helped me over difficult passages in the translation from the French of Father Cretin's almost illegible script in his many letters to Bishop Loras.

Sister Maryanita Cannon, BVM has given invaluable assistance in research and in the critical reading of the work in manuscript. Her unique contribution to the Congregation's history lies in the collection she has made of relics and mementoes of the early years, and their display in the Heritage room at the Mt. Carmel motherhouse. Thanks for varied services are due to many others of my Sisters in religions, conspicuous among whom are Sisters M. Michail Geary, John Thomas Hackett, St. David Carver, Ellen Clare Rinne, Margaret King and St. Joseph Dunphy.

I am grateful to the Congregation's Senate of 1972 for the authorization and encouragement of the present work, and to the members of the history board assigned its supervision: Sisters M. Joan Patricia Reilly, Rita Benz, Mary Healey, Helen Humeston, and its chairman, Sister Margaret Thornton. Their careful criticism and timely suggestions have added to its interest and reduced its limitations. I am deeply grateful to my own sister, Sister M. Philippa Coogan, for her continued encouragement, her suggestions and her long hours of typing and editing the materials contained in the work. But last of all to our eighty-one year old Sister M. Demetria Lodge goes the accolade for undertaking the heroic task of typing the entire manuscript as it is here presented.

Assistance in details of publication given with his characteristic graciousness by the Reverend John Amberg, S. J., then president of the Loyola University Press and now deceased, and by the Reverend George Lane, S. J., also of the Loyola Press, have been indispensable to the accomplishment of the present work.

Pages 417-419 give special recognition to those of our Sisters who have contributed to the many illustrations incorporated in the text, and with this there is included acknowledgement of the sources upon which they drew. I am deeply grateful for their contributions.

M. Jane Coogan, BVM

Restored parish house and chaplain's residence,
St. Joseph's Prairie. Upper view, taken from
the drive, shows lawn chairs in the winged sanctuary of the chapel. A section of the low stone
wall which marks the chapel outline is visible.
The area which was the floor of the chapel is
laid now in quarry tile.

CHAPTER ONE

The Dublin of
Our Sisters' Day-
1800-1833

Dublin Custom House beside the Liffey River

This chapter gives a picture of Dublin during the early 1800's. The gradual repeal of penal legislation by the Irish Parliament had permitted the emergence of Church institutions from attics and back alleys, resulting in the opening of religious schools and academies and the building of substantial churches. The renewal of spiritual life among the general population led to an awareness of the grave needs of the ill, the orphaned, the ignorant and the impoverished, and along with the return of religious orders, there arose new religious congregations dedicated to the meeting of those needs. The general movement toward a dedicated life of service drew together a small group of women who, after a brief experiment in community living, opened a school in 1832. Recognizing no call to any of the religious institutes then established, and realizing the unlikelihood of their securing permission to realize their hope of a congregation of their own, they were open to the urging of a priest from Philadelphia to come to America. The many needs of the poverty-stricken immigrants from Ireland pouring into that city were the basis of his appeal. In response to those needs, the little community of four set sail from Dublin on July 13, 1833, a fifth member to follow in the spring. They would be the advance guard of an army of Irish missionaries to the New World. The loss of their gold savings as they disembarked in New York, and the realization on their arrival in Philadelphia that they came as unwelcomed strangers, left them in a state of dependence. Having found temporary lodging, they provided for their immediate needs by long hours of hand sewing.

A polished nameplate affixed to a simple Georgian doorway on North Ann street, Dublin, read "Miss Clarke's Seminary." It was March 19, 1832, a busy morning for the four young women entering upon their initial apostolic project together. As the door opened to receive the first pupils and their accompanying parents, greetings were exchanged in the ample reception area of the little establishment. To the left was a single large hall or classroom, and to the right, and up a stairway, were living quarters for the teachers. It was relatively prosperous workers and tradespeople who came that day to enroll their daughters, small, tall, and middle-sized, in the new enterprise. Excitement and curiosity prevailed as the gracious-mannered women interviewed each little family group.

New arrivals from south of the school, having passed the city markets, had looked appreciatively on the Presentation orphanage and vocational school for girls at George's Hill which they passed just before they crossed Cuckoo Lane, and onto the brief but "fashionable" Ann street. Others, approaching from Little Britain street, passed the grim and forbidding walls of Newgate Gaol, doubtless casting fearful glances upward to the grisly scaffolding, scene of frequent and too recent executions.[1] Those who

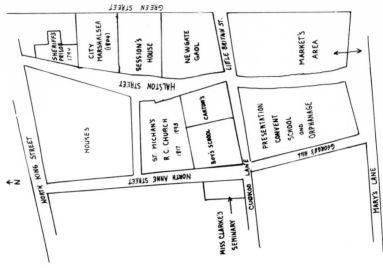

Founded by Teresa Mullaly
as orphanage and trade
school for girls. In
1789 Teresa invited the
Presentation Sisters from
Cork to take charge.

Ann street chapel, dedi-
cated in 1817. Later
enlarged to become the
present St. Michan
Catholic church

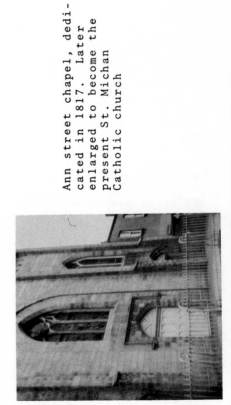

traveled Green or Halston street walked the length of
the grey and cheerless Marshalsea and Sheriff's pri-
sons for debtors, and the massive Sessions or Crimi-
nal Court Building redolent of the memories of Robert
Emmet's night-long trial and brave defense, and the
trials of many other Irish "rebels." These were glad
to find themselves in the friendly warmth and cheerful atmosphere of the little school where tradesmen
and their wives mingled with the more affluent from
Sackville, Henrietta and Dominick streets. Their
business done and their daughters safe in the care of
their teachers, many of the parents doubtless crossed
the narrow pavement to the handsome new Ann Street
Chapel,[2] to ask God to bless and care for their families and the school so much needed in the area.

What was Dublin like on that spring morning of
1832? Beautiful city that it was, with its moist,
mild climate, the broad expanse of Dublin Bay and the
mist-covered mountains in the distance, it presented
strange contrasts. Its stately public buildings,
classic in their lines, the rows of handsome town
houses that flanked its parklike squares,[3] its broad
principal streets and the several sturdy bridges
which spanned the Liffey and bound the south half of
city to the north, were worthy of the finest capitals
of Europe. Truly, "there never was so splendid a
metropolis for so poor a country,"[4] for the air of
affluence was quickly dissipated in the dark and
crowded lanes and alleys which penetrated every portion of the city, bearing with them signs of deep
poverty.[5] Yet Dublin as a capital city had seen better times in the brilliant days of the Irish Parliament.*

Wealth and leisure were then on display. Handsome
equipages with liveried coachmen rumbled over cobbled
streets, and richly ornamented sedan chairs jogged
along pathways. Compact rows of fine town houses
lined Merrion Square and Stephen's Green below the
Liffey, and Rutland Square and Henrietta and Dominick
streets above it, their wrought iron balconies and
stately Georgian doorways only hinting at the elegance within. Elaborate dinner parties, concerts and
garden parties at the Rotunda, and balls and levees
held by the viceroy in the state rooms of Dublin

---

* See Appendix for a summary of the history of
Ireland

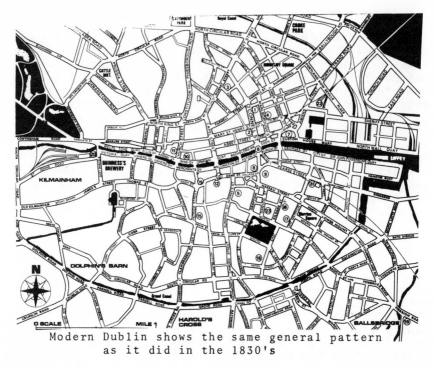

Modern Dublin shows the same general pattern
as it did in the 1830's

Castle, were occasions for bobbing plumes and rust-
ling silks. Such had been the social season in Ireland's capital city. But when in 1800, in return for
titles, sinecures and gold, its parliament had voted
its own extinction, the center of its lavish social
life had removed to London.[6] Hundreds of domestics
were turned off;[7] stores and shops, with bills for
luxuries left unpaid, closed their doors; construction of new buildings and public works came to a halt,
while unemployment reduced the Catholic masses to
even greater poverty. Crowded together in the most
squalid quarters, without fresh water or the slightest provision for sanitation, they were victims of
typhus and famine fevers. Illness meant further impoverishment, with clothing, bedding and even the
last of household furnishings sold for food and medicine. Lack of proper clothing prevented those who
survived from seeking employment or sending their
children to school where they might be prepared to
earn their bread. A contributing factor toward the
spread of disease at the time was a tax on hearths
and windows. In the poorer sections of the city,
these were therefore boarded up, with the result that
families were further deprived of heat, sunlight, and

ventilation.

Through British restrictions on trade and manufacture, the once prosperous Liberty of the Earl of
Meath,[8] where thousands of weavers had found employment, sank to the level of dangerously overcrowded
slums, the numbers of its inhabitants greatly increased as evictions and hunger drove hundreds of the
peasantry into the city. Sunk in ignorance and misery, the only release they knew from their wretchedness lay in cheap liquor,[9] and with that came deeper
degradation and immorality.

Provisions for the poor, made by the government
but supported by the uncertainties of private charity, included a House of Industry, partly intended to
clear the streets of beggars and other undesirables.
Despised by the poor, it was resorted to for relief
only in times of the direst distress, while the
Dublin Foundling Home, with its ghoulish record of
deaths and disappearances of helpless inmates and its
avowed purpose of training unfortunate survivors as
domestic servants and laborers, could scarcely be
called a charitable institution. [10]

As the penal laws were abolished, late in the
eighteenth century, and the accompanying restrictions
on religious worship and education were lifted, members of the long-submerged Catholic nobility, together with rising merchants assumed leadership.
They gave support, especially, to religious and educational enterprises made possible by the gradual return of the religious orders. A marked devotional
renewal - the use of the evening office, and the office
of the Blessed Virgin and of the dead, devotion to
the Sacred Heart and to St. Joseph, confraternities
and sodalities, third orders among the laity - encouraged and promoted by the diocesan clergy, [12] renewed
the faith of the people. Churches needed no longer
be hidden in back lanes and alleys, and the new St.
Mary Pro-Cathedral, the first Dublin church constructed along modern lines, became a symbol of a restored
hierarchy. It was followed shortly by a number of
other fine houses of worship. The "hedge schools" of
the city, hitherto confined to abandoned warehouses
and unfurnished attics, emerged in the form of "mercantile and classical" academies which would prepare
boys and young men for profitable employment,[13] and
"penny" and free schools for girls would soon be supplemented by convent academies. These gave other op-
tions to parents who, in their eagerness for some

education for their children, had only reluctantly
sent them to the proselytizing schools, set up by the
various Protestant organizations, chiefly for the
training of domestics for their own service.[14]

A severe epidemic of typhus lasting through the
years 1817-1818 brought forty-two thousand victims to
the city bospitals and emergency centers and resulted
in more than two thousand deaths. The severity of
the epidemic aroused officials to conditions in the
over-crowded parts of the city, and resulted in the
clearing out of filth, the white-washing of the tene-
ments, the establishment of a system of sewers, and
the paving of many of the mud lanes. The recurrence
of the fever in 1826, partly as a result of the poverty which followed a bad harvest, was severe, but,
with improved medical care and additional fever hospital accomodations, it was more quickly brought under control. However, each such epidemic left its
harvest of orphans, and made clear the need for a
dedicated service to the poor and the sick.

Nano Nagle had pioneered in such work when, in the
year 1775, she established the Sisters of Presentation
in Cork. Educated in a French convent and caught up
in the gaiety of Parisian social life, she nevertheless met the challenge of vocation when it came. Returning to her native Cork, Nano soon became a familiar figure in its alleys and by-lanes, its attics and
hovels. Her foundation of the uncloistered Presentation Sisters gave her the helpers she needed, but her
purpose was not to be fully realized. Such an inno-
vation was too much for the conservative Bishop of
Cork, Dr. Moylan, [15] who was not long in committing
the Sisters to cloister. The coming of the Presentation Sisters to Dublin in 1798 at the invitation of
Teresa Mulally, who had been engaged for many years
in the education of girls and their training in practical skills, doubtless had its effect in stimulating
the interest of other Irish women in a life of religious service. With the general revival of the religious spirit, it is not surprising that many young
women turned to active service for the sick, the orphans, and those for whom education was the greatest
need.[16]

A group of Poor Clare nuns of strict observance,
who had been eking out a cloistered existence on
Hardwicke street, were asked to undertake the conduct
of an orphanage. The Reverend Daniel Murray having
obtained from Rome the necessary mitigation of their

rule, the young barrister, Daniel O'Connell, undertook the purchase of a suitable location. The site chosen, at Harold's Cross in South Dublin, was at that time held by the Orange Society, who agreed to the sale of the property to "a lady with several sisters." When these "Sisters" arrived, garbed in secular attire, they took possession without protest. That was in 1804. Most of the children they received into the orphanage were suffering from malnutrition and tuberculosis. Arrangements were made to lodge large numbers of the sick children in the country, in homes of dairy farmers whose wives were willing to undertake their care. Many, however, died at the orphanage, despite the care of the Sisters. As the years went by, the Sisters at Harold's Cross convent supplemented their work with orphans by opening a school for little girls of the city. This school continues to the present.[17]

In 1817 Mary Aikenhead established the first new foundation of religious women in Dublin, the Irish Sisters of Charity. It was her plan that they should visit the poor and the sick, and open free schools for the many who could not afford even the usual penny a week tuition. Daughter of a successful physician in Cork, himself scion of a wealthy Protestant family, Mary had embraced the faith of her mother. Although she had been given every advantage of education and culture, she nonetheless found her interests centered on the poor and needy. On a visit to Dublin in 1812, Mary sought counsel regarding her vocation from Dr. Murray, then Coadjutor to the Archbishop of Dublin. It was under his guidance that her plans for a religious congregation took shape.

Having made a novitiate with the Sisters of the Institute of the Blessed Virgin in York, England, Mary established her first convent and novitiate on North William street. Vocations soon came and she was able to take over the St. Mary Training School and House of Refuge, until then in the care of her dearest friend, Mrs. John O'Brien, wife of a wealthy silk importer. On Gardiner street, the Sisters opened free schools[18] for the poor and Sunday Schools for working girls, with evening classes to prepare girls and women for the sacraments. All this was in addition to their daily visits to the poor and the sick. During the many months of the cholera epidemic in 1832, the Sisters went daily to the huge penitentiary of Grangegorman, converted into an emergency hospital. There, during three months, fifty to

eighty persons died daily, yet the little band of
Sisters survived the siege. From a foundation in the
district of Sandymount, Dublin, they courageously
battled a second epidemic in 1833 among the poor in
adjacent Irishtown. In 1835 they opened the first
Catholic hospital in Dublin - St. Vincent's on Stephen's Green - under the guidance and encouragement of
Dr. Joseph Farrell (or O'Ferrall, as he preferred to
sign himself). The first uncloistered religious in
Dublin, these Sisters were to be the first to brave a
mission in far-off Australia in 1846, there to aid in
the redemption of women confined in British penal
colonies.

Another foundation, that of the Institute of the
Blessed Virgin, or, as it was more commonly known,
the Institute of Loretto, was established in 1822 in
Rathfarnham, Dublin, by Frances Ball, younger sister
of the wealthy and charitable Mrs. O'Brien. Before
his early death, Frances' father had been a prosperous merchant, and a parishoner at St. Michan's, where
Frances tended the altar and engaged in various charitable works. Like Mary Aikenhead, Frances received
her religious training at York, where, as academy
students, she and her sister had spent some years.
At Rathfarnham the Sisters soon opened a boarding
school and a poor school for girls, and shortly
thereafter, a day school on Harcourt street. These
were followed by many other schools throughout Ireland. In 1841, a brave band of Loretto Sisters
would set out to establish the first of several
missions in India.[19]

By 1827, Catherine McAuley, a wealthy convert, had
built at her own expense, on Lower Baggott street,
the dignified and commodious structure which stands
today as a monument to her memory. It was not
Catherine's intention to make of it a convent, though
her plan was to conduct a refuge for needy women and
for orphans, and a school for the poor. To aid her
in her projects, she expected to depend on the volunteer services of lay women. A simple uniform dress
of black with cape and white cap, in the conservative
style of the day, seemed more suitable to the work
than the elaborate attire commonly worn by her
wealthy helpers. The conventlike appearance of the
new building, the uniformity of dress, and the nature
of the work, all pointed to a religious foundation,
as Catherine came to realize. Dr. Murray, now Archbishop of dublin, who had looked with favor on her
work as a lay endeavor, now came to believe that he

had been deliberately misled, and he determined to
place the institution in the hands of the newly established Sisters of Charity. When the intercession
of Dr. M. Blake, Catherine's spiritual adviser,
finally restored the confidence of the Archbishop in
her, Catherine, with two companions, was able to enter upon a canonical novitiate with the Sisters of
the Presentation at George's Hill. Her vow day, two
years later, marked the beginning of the Sisters of
Mercy. Through the dreadful days of the cholera
epidemic in 1832, the young community was called upon
to assist in the nursing of the poor in the area of
Dublin south of the Liffey, a beginning of widespread
and notable work in the care of the sick and afflicted, as well as in education.

The report on convent schools made by the Royal
Commission on Education in Ireland in 1825 spoke appreciatively of the work of religious women. It
said in part:

> We have visited many of these schools, and have
> found them conducted with great order and regular-
> ity, and the Children are in general well supplied
> with books and every School Requisite. The Nuns
> are the Teachers, and devote themselves to the Duty
> of Instruction with the most unwearied Assiduity

Mercy Convent Baggot St.

and Attention. We were much impressed with the
appearance of Affection and Respect on the part of
the Pupils toward their teachers, which character-
izes these institutions in a remarkable Degree. A
few of these Convent Establishments have also
Boarding Schools annexed to them, but in general
they are Day Schools. . .[20]

Though it was not in Dublin but in Waterford that
Edmund Ignatius Rice, a prosperous merchant, first
established the Brothers of the Christian Schools of
Ireland, he was not long in opening schools in Dublin,
the first one in 1812, for the education of Catholic
boys. Because of the strongly proselytizing efforts
in subsidized schools of the diocese of Kildare and
Leighlin, with their insistence on the reading of the
Scriptures "without note or comment," the very able
and decisive Dr. Doyle, its Bishop, had forbidden
attendance at them by the youths of the diocese. The
result was that a great number of the young were left
without any education, and with ample time to run the
streets and get into trouble. Serious concern, both
for the boys and the public, moved Edmund Rice to
dedicate his life and fortune to the establishment of
suitable schools. The first school the Brothers
opened in Dublin was situated on Hanover street,
south of the Liffey. Shortly after, Archbishop
Murray besought Brother Rice to establish a school in
the populous St. Mary parish. This he did in June,
1827, in a house at 24 Jervis street. When, in 1826,
Brother Rice and his assistants decided to change the
seat of his congregation's government to Dublin, he
procured a site on Richmond street and erected a
building there. Meanwhile the Catholic Association,
with Daniel O'Connell at its head, was concerned with
updating education in the city's rising parish schools,
desiring to see the training of their teachers under
the guidance of the Christian Brothers in the Central
Model School they were building adjacent to the monastery site. Six hundred boys from the Jervis street
school assisted at the formal opening of the establishment, at which O'Connell gave the dedicatory
address.[21]

Two personalities loom large in the Dublin of that
day. The more notable of these, Daniel O'Connell,
the first Catholic to be admitted to the bar after
the relaxing of the penal law, was by far the most
prominent of the lay leaders. O'Connell effectively
concerned himself with social problems, educational
needs and political agitation, while serving as a

formidable public defender in Catholic causes. Despite the constant harassment of the government, the Catholic Association through which he worked for reform drew the support of the Catholic population of all Ireland, whom he involved effectively through small regular payments of what came to be called the Catholic rent. The force of his powerful personality and ebullient spirit was needed to stir hopes in a people broken and disheartened by the culminating tragedy of the 1798 rebellion. Hope of winning the fight with the British parliament for complete emancipation lay in rousing them from their apathy and in gaining the support of the Catholic clergy. In his own unique way he accomplished both, and secured what might well have seemed impossible, the passage of the Emancipation Act of 1829, and with it a seat in the British Parliament from which he could plead the cause of his countrymen.

Another leader, though less heralded, was the Jesuit, Peter Kenney. Active in reestablishing the Society of Jesus in Ireland after its forty-year suppression, he was the founder of Clongowes Wood College and a preparatory school, and the builder of the church of St. Francis Xavier. In close association with the able Archbishop Murray, he gave spiritual and organizational direction to the Irish Sisters of Charity, to the Sisters of Loretto, and to Brother Rice in his establishment of the Irish Christian Brothers. An effective pulpit orator, he exerted a considerable influence in the revival of Catholic life in Dublin. Father Kenney's appointment as official visitor to the American Jesuits brought him to Philadelphia, where he made his headquarters at St. Joseph's, Willing's Alley.

It was, then, this milieu of renewed faith and rising hopes that helped form the young women who were to serve as founding members of a new religious congregation - the Sisters of Charity of the Blessed Virgin Mary. Unhappily, we know little of their personal lives and those of their families. We can only piece together the fragments that remain, endeavoring to separate fact from fancy, and resolving conflicting details as best we can.[21]

Mary Frances, born March 2, 1806, was the daughter of Cornelius Clarke and his wife, Catherine (or Elizabeth) Quartermas, who was of Quaker origin. Both parents were fervent Catholics. Described for us as "a prosperous leather merchant," Mr. Clarke dealt in harness and carriage leather, and at a time when horses were the only means of transportation, he may

well have done a flourishing business. We are told
that the family lived in a comfortable brick house on
Denmark street, and this would have made them members
of the St. Mary Metropolitan parish. One account
tells us that Mary Frances was baptized by a Franciscan father in her own home, and that to the name
"Mary," supplied by her parents, he added "Frances,"
a foreshadowing of her lifelong dedication to poverty.
There were four children in the Clarke family: the
oldest, Mary Frances, then Catherine, Martha and
Edward. They shared their home with an Episcopalian
aunt, a Mrs. Masterson, and at times, with her son, a
student at Salamanca. The Clarke children received
much of their education from these family relatives,
though Mary Frances' remark, "I never went but to a
penny school,"[23] would indicate attendance, at least
for a time, at a parish or neighborhood school. Besides the basic school subjects, the Clarke children
were trained in music and the girls in needlework, a
tradition of long-standing for Irish women. But Dublin offered many opportunities for self-improvement:
parish libraries, free lectures provided by the
Royal Dublin Society, an extensive botanical garden
at Glasnevin, a lending library and lecture hall on
Sackville, now O'Connell, street, and a zoo at
Phoenix Park. An incident recounted many years later
suggests the probability that Mary Frances spent many
hours at the botanical garden, familiarizing herself
with the common and botanical names of plants. The
narrator is Sister Mary Florence Lowery and the setting is the first motherhouse of the Sisters on the
Iowa Prairie:

> In spring along the path to the little cemetery,
> inside an osage orange hedge, were wide strips
> where many varieties of flowers were cultivated
> which in May and June blossomed in glorious ar-
> ray. Mother Gertrude sent me to gather a bou-
> quet for Mother Clarke. This pleasant commis-
> sion led me to select the most beautiful and
> colorful blooms, and the arrangement of the
> bouquet was my artistic best, and when I was
> told to take it to Mother I was highly elated.
> Mother looked the flowers over, admiring them
> and giving me the common and botanical names of
> such as grew around their convent in Philadel-
> phia, testing too my floral knowledge. In that
> visit, my love and reverence of Mother Clarke
> was firmly stamped on my mind and heart.

Instinctively, I realized the sweet, peaceful, solid spirituality of our Holy Foundress.[24]

With the Irish sense of history, and monuments of the past at every turn, Mary Frances' active mind had much to feed upon. Nor was she without business experience, for she served her father as bookkeeper and secretary. Shortly after a fire which destroyed his business, Mr. Clarke suffered a paralytic stroke which invalided him, and the settlement of his affairs fell on her shoulders. It was only when Martha agreed to take on those responsibilities, and Catherine's class of music pupils offered support to the family, that Mary Frances felt free to enter upon the North Ann street enterprise. We are told of the girls that Martha, like Mary Frances, was of a gentle, retiring disposition, while Catherine was lively and outgoing. In their mother, the Quaker tradition of charity was strong. Margaret Mann was to tell later of Mrs. Clarke's rebuke to Catherine for offering cold food to a beggar at the door as the family sat down to a hot dinner. "Would you keep the best for yourself, and give the worst to God?"

The Clarkes attended the old St. Mary chapel off Liffey street, erected in 1730. It had been made the metropolitan church by the Archbishop of Dublin, Dr. Troy, in 1797, upon his removal from the St. Francis street chapel south of the river. The church like others of the time, hid itself among a cluster of houses and could only be approached by a narrow passage leading from the pathway. Its interior was dim and cheerless, its small windows, on one side only, leaving the galleries in the gloomy dusk. Its one lovely feature was a copy of Raphael's Virgin and Child. Since the church was only half large enough for its congregation, those who could not enter crowded about it, filling up the narrow passageway to the street. It was the custom of the day for those who had carriages to arrive in state, and the clatter of hooves and the rumble of the cumbrous coaches on the approaching streets marked the fashionable midday Mass. To come in high style was regarded as equivalent to a profession of faith, and little regard was paid to the prominent person who came in modest quiet:

There was no better place, especially on a charity sermon day, for seeing the Catholics of Dublin from Liffey-street and its precincts. The Catholics of note throughout the city,

mustered in full force on these occasions. . .
Then, indeed, an inquiring stranger would have
an excellent opportunity of hearing a popular
account of the different families and learning
their genealogies. . . . An attentive listener
would not be left long in ignorance of the private worth, the commercial character, the pre-
sumed wealth of the portly gentlemen, who des-
cended with their wives in nodding plumes,
their fair daughters in silk pelisses and laced
flounces, their sons in suits of Spanish blue
and olive green, brilliant with gilt basket
buttons and proceeded to enter by the straight
way and the narrow gate.[25]

It is scarcely likely that the Clarkes arrived by
carriage, or that they waited until the last Mass of
the day. Here, though, they would have known and
been known by the Reverend Daniel Murray,[26] who for
some years served as curate, and it was here that in
1809 they would have witnessed his consecration as
Bishop of Hierapolis and Coadjutor to Dr. Troy. On
the death of Dr. Troy in 1825, Bishop Murray succeeded to the Archbishopric of Dublin, in time for
the removal to the new church which had been the
dream of his predecessor: St. Mary of the Conception
on Marlborough street. The clarkes must have shared
the joy of priests and people on the occasion of the
solemn dedication of the new Pro-Cathedral, and again
the following year when with great ceremony the Archbishop and clergy inaugurated the services of the
Jubilee year.

* * * * * * * *

Margaret Mann, born March 7, 1805, was the only
daughter of John Mann and his wife, Ann Thompson.
Margaret's father belonged to the line of Dutch weavers brought to Ireland by William III after the
"Glorious Revolution." An account in the Community
publication, Our Herald, tells us:

In his youth Mr. Mann was a Protestant and followed the weaver's trade. The terrible persecution of Catholics and especially of priests .
. .. led the young man to try to find out what
kind of diabolical religion that could be which
drew upon its professors such inhuman treatment.
The result of his investigations was the gift
of faith. He became a fervent Catholic, most
zealous in helping and protecting priests. . .

> Sister Mary Margaret used to say that it was
> from her father that she learned the devotion
> to the priesthood which was one of her charac-
> teristic virtues.[27]

A tantalizing fragment from the Doran Journal,though
certainly not wholly accurate, is doubtless correct
in linking Margaret's father with the United Irish at
the tragic time of the rebellion in 1798. Consideration of it brings the historic situation, so critical
to the families of our early Sisters, into sharper
focus for us:

> Captain Armstrong took the oath of the United
> Irishmen to get their secrets. He dined at
> Mann's the night he betrayed Lord Edward Fitz-
> gerald and three hundred United Irishmen. Mrs.
> Mann suspected him and said, "John, beware of
> that man, he has the eye of a traitor." S.M.
> Margaret was not born at that time. Three hun-
> dred men met that night to discuss plans for
> the Rising, and every one except Mr. Mann was
> put to death. When Mr. Mann was brought before
> Capt. Armstrong, the latter said, "I do not
> know this man." It is hard to tell why he was
> spared and the others denounced, for he, Capt.
> Armstrong, had accepted the hospitality of the
> Sayres [Sheares] family and denounced the
> Sayres boys.[28]

For Mr. Mann to have been in contact with the notorious Captain Armstrong, his participation in the preparations for the Rebellion of 1798 must have been
more than casual.[29] However, the Sheares were much
more deeply involved than he could have been. John
and Henry Sheares, young Dublin Lawyers, had assumed
leadership of the planned rebellion when Lord Edward
Fitzgerald was forced into hiding, and they, John
especially, had indiscreetly communicated their plans
to Armstrong, captain of the local militia, in the
hope that he and others of the company would defect
to the cause. The account is in error in attributing
the betrayal of Lord Edward to Armstrong, and probably in the execution of the three hundred men who met
that night. However, Armstrong was entertained in
the homes of the Sheares brothers, and followed their
every movement until he had obtained evidence enough
to insure for them the death sentence on the charge
of treason. The scene of their execution was Newgate
Prison, and their unmouldered coffins lie side by
side in the underground burial chambers of the

Protestant St. Michan Church, each coffin bearing the charge of treason on which they were convicted. The incident as quoted brings home to us the nearness of our Sisters' families to the national tragedy of the Rising.

An incident of Margaret's childhood is recounted for us as follows:

> When Margaret was about three years old, her baby brother died. Her mother, Ann Thompson, was then a young and very demonstrative woman. On her return from the funeral of the baby, she threw herself on her knees beside the empty cradle and cried out, saying, "Oh, my beautiful boy! Why did not God take Margaret and leave you!" The little girl, who, with her father, was standing near, understood perfectly what her mother said. Her eyes filled with tears and her little lips quivered. Her father saw this and taking the child into his arms, said, "Never mind, my darling. Mother does not mean what she says. You are all the world to me. I thank God that He has left you to me." [30]

The memory of that early hurt stayed with Margaret, and in her years as mistress of novices she tried to impress upon her young charges the care they should have of the sensitivity of even the youngest child.

Margaret was not so fortunate as Mary Frances Clarke in the matter of education. While she was a capable business woman and an able administrator, she was keenly aware of her educational limitations, and when Father Donaghoe later required her to go into the classroom, "she wept bitterly." In her later years as school administrator, her limitations were compensated for through the services of Sister M. Xavier O'Reilly, an able secretary. The millinery shop which Margaret kept in Dublin gave employment to some twenty women and girls, and helped in the support of her parents as well. As the plans of the little community matured, Margaret faced the necessity of closing the shop. She did this only gradually as she was able to find other employment for each of those who had served her.

****

Elizabeth (Eliza) Kelly was the daughter of Michael Kelly and his wife, Mary Hyland Kelly. Her father seems to have enjoyed a fairly substantial income, his employment variously given as architect, painter or decorator, and city employee. At any rate, Eliza is said to have had the advantage of a tutor. As she possessed educational advantages and something of a literary gift, she was assigned, eventually, to the position of Community annalist. Together with the daughters of O'Connell, Eliza was accustomed to visit Miss McAuley's charitable venture on lower Baggott street to give assistance in making garments for the poor. Having become a Franciscan Tertiary, Eliza was made prefect, and on December 8, 1831, she witnessed the promises of Mary Frances Clarke, Margaret Mann and Rose O'Toole as lay members of the Third Order of Franciscans on the first anniversary of her own commitment.

****

Rose O'Toole was among the younger members of a large family. Rose's widowed mother reared her family "near the strawberry beds," an area west of Dublin along the Liffey, where she grew strawberries for the local market. Mrs. O'Toole also kept a boarding house where "fine gentlemen used to go for good plain dinners." That the family was not poor is indicated by the fact that upon her mother's death, Rose was able to bring a comfortable dowry to the struggling community in Philadelphia. [31] There remain indications, however, that Rose had only the most elementary education. There is no record that she taught at any time, unless perhaps in helping little children learn their prayers.

In the course of association with one another through charitable works the precise nature of which we are not now certain, Mary Frances Clarke, Margaret Mann, Eliza Kelly and Rose O'Toole decided to rent a little cottage "in the suburbs" where they could make an experiment of community living. Here they took up their residence on December 8, 1831. It was a pleasant little home, we are told, "trim, neat and cheerful, with potted flowers in the white-curtained windows, a lovely copy of Murillo's Immaculate Conception over the mantle," and a simple oratory where they said their morning and night prayers and made their preparations for the feasts of Christmas, Candlemas and St. Joseph. [32]

Here Rose and Eliza were free to live without interruption, occupying their time with needlework,

while Mary Frances, still involved in family responsibilities, and Margaret, in her millinery establishment, found their daytime hours filled. Quiet,
steady Rose was a contrast to the pampered Eliza, who
"had a child's mind" and liked to "send out to the
store for sweets," and whose slightest indisposition
necessitated a call from Surgeon Farrell, the Kelly
family physician.[33] But piety, good will and her educational advantages were compensating factors.

It was at the cottage that Catherine Byrne made the
acquaintance of the other young women, having come one
evening on an errand for the Poor Clare Sisters regarding an order for church vestments. Margaret was
charmed by the young woman and hoped that some day she
might be one of them. Catherine had been early left
an orphan. Her father, it seems, was a confidential
agent of a large importing firm in Dublin. On hearing
of the loss of a vessel laden with rich cargo, he fell
dead. His wife died shortly after, and Catherine was
placed in the Poor Clare Orphanage at Harold's Cross
in south Dublin. Of her the orphanage records say:

> Byrne,Catherine, an orphan recommended by Mrs.
> Dwyer of Bridge Street, aged seven years, admit-
> ted the 20th February, 1813. Was confirmed the
> 16th of May, 1816, and sent to Nurse Bryan for
> the recovery of her health the 21st of the same
> month, returned to the Orphan House the 20th of
> May, 1817, and made her First Communion the
> 20th of June following. Was sent to Miss
> O'Brien on trial as a servant to the parish
> priest of Moate, County Westmeath, 8th October,
> 1820. Finally provided for.[34]

Catherine's "provision" seems to have included some
training in nursing and in pharmacy by a Dr.Farrell,
possibly the same physician who lent assistance to
Mary Aikenhead in her establishment of St. Vincent
Hospital in 1835.

Schools were perhaps the greatest need of the day,
and friends of the Kelly family urged Eliza to open
classes for their children. They soon learned of a
recently vacated building which had served as an
academy, at the corner of Ann street and Cuckoo lane,
a relatively new three-story brick building which had
been adjoined to a smaller residential structure. A
common doorway in good Georgian style served both.
The one large hall or classroom on the first floor
would meet their needs for a time, and the building

possessed the added advantage of living quarters.
The school portion had been constructed about 1810 by
a Reverend Barnaby Murphy to serve as a Mercantile
and Classical Academy, and "showed not only artistic
taste but a fine conception of space for the school-
hall."35

The little community,* honoring St. Joseph as the
patron of their enterprise, chose his feast for its
opening day, and classes were under way when the
cholera epidemic of 1832 broke upon the city. The
dark specter of it must have been threat to all they
held dear. Rose's mother fell an early victim, and
family responsibilities called Rose home. Margaret
was still involved in her own business affairs. Thus
teaching duties rested on Mary Frances and Eliza.
However, it was not long before a Mrs. Berkeley,
widow of an army officer, came to join them. Educated, refined, and possessed of a small fortune, she
was a tertiary, like the others, and was drawn to the
little community as well as to the educational project it had undertaken.

Sister Mary Pulcheria's Annals provide us with further details of those beginnings:

> More than four months had passed since they be-
> gan school, and it was thought well to give the
> pupils a short vacation, in order that the Sis-
> ters might spend a few days in recollection and
> thereby renew their fervor for the remainder of
> the year. Accordingly, they entered into a re-
> treat on August 6th, the Feast of the Transfi-
> guration, and the day appointed by the Arch-
> bishop for the celebration of Holy Mass for the
> first time in their private chapel. . .
>
> School re-opened in the latter part of August
> with an increase of pupils. The prospects for
> the coming scholastic year were encouraging,
> and the Sisters entered upon their class exer-
> cises with renewed energy, and with a confi-
> dence acquired by experience during the pre-
> ceding months. Every day, the Community had

---

* A small book of meditations preserved among the
relics in the Congregation's Heritage Room bears, in
Mother Clarke's hand, on its title page, the inscription: "North Ann Street Community, 1832."

> morning and evening prayers in common, and
> together, they made their visits to the
> Blessed Sacrament; yet, in these exercises
> there was nothing to indicate that they in-
> tended binding themselves to any particular
> rule of life. They wisely preferred to
> await further developments.[36]

Two other brief glimpses of Miss Clarke's Seminary
have come down to us. Sister M. Patricia Rocap, BVM
quotes from a family history regarding an earlier
generation: "Mother and her sisters attended Miss
Clarke's private school on Ann Street, Dublin, as day
pupils, living a few miles away, being the Glen of
Downs, Kilmurray Brae, Co. Wicklow, Ireland." The
writer, whose girlhood name was Dwyer, was the first
cousin of Sister's grandmother. Sister adds; "This
was a paragraph in which she was showing that 'the
Dwyers were not poor Irish.'" One wonders if the
rains of winter did not sometimes necessitate the
girls' boarding with their teachers, to avoid the
trip of fifteen miles or more twice a day on horseback or by carriage.

Another recollection came from Sister M. Rouina
Lee, who entered the Congregation * from St. Louis in
1890. Sister used to recount a reminiscence of her
mother, who as a child attended the Baggott street
school of Mother McAuley. On free days she and her
little friends liked to visit the school on North Ann
street, for they loved to talk to the "Sisters." Mrs.
Lee was very happy when she realized that the Dubuque
Community her daughter was entering was the same one
she had known and loved in her childhood days in
Dublin.[37]

The Annals give us further details of the little
community:

> The Christmas holidays of 1832 had come and
> gone, and the Sisters were again at their post
> in the over-crowded classroom. Something
> should be done to give accommodation to new

---

* The word "Congregation" is used to refer to the
Community of Sisters' after the Sacred Congregation of
Religious gave approbation to its constitutions in
1877. Prior to that time the term "Community" is
more appropriately used.

applicants for admission, as well as to make
more comfortable those pupils already enrolled.
. . Moreover, having lived together in community
for more than a year, they were convinced that
Almighty God had given them religious vocations;
they were anxious, therefore, to make some definite preparations for the taking of religious
vows. In the city of Dublin, there were several established and approved communities engaged in teaching, hence the Sisters feared to
mention to the Archbishop the subject which en-
grossed their minds, lest he should require
them to affiliate with one of the existing orders. In their perplexity, they had recourse
to God, who soon made known his will.[38]

The problem was a very real one. Three foundations
of religious women had been established in Dublin
within the previous two decades, and Archbishop
Murray had shown much hesitation on the occasion of
the third one. Then, too, all three had had as founders women of wealth and social position, with
friends on whom they might depend for financial support. What had the "Nuns of North Ann Street" to offer but their own poor selves? Would Dr. Murray not
tend to discourage them? or require them to offer
themselves as candidates to the Sisters of Charity,
of Loretto, or of Mercy? But it was not to any of
these that God was calling them.

In the course of the spring a young priest, Father
Patrick Costello, of the Philadelphia diocese in
America, arrived in Ireland for his health and offered to serve as their chaplain. As their acquaintance grew, he told them of the large numbers of Irish
immigrants coming into the seaport town of Philadelphia and of the dangers to the faith of their children unless Catholic teachers could be found to train
them. He described, too, the many other needs of
these Irish immigrants. Promising to communicate
with Bishop Kenrick, assuring them that they would be
received with open arms, and that he himself would
return to Philadelphia with them, he seemed an answer
to their prayers for guidance.

The decision was nonetheless a most painful one,
and the young women reached it only gradually. To
give up a work that had proven successful, to forsake
home and family and the land they loved, to face a
future filled with uncertainty - was it truly God's
will for them? After prayer and earnest consultation,
they came to their decision. They would risk all and

go to Philadelphia. Saddened patrons and much more saddened families heard the unwelcome word. Yet courageously they arranged affairs. Closing their little school and packing their belongings, they prepared their living apartments for Margaret's and Eliza's parents, who would come to occupy them.[39]

Farewells were painful, and for none more than for Mary Frances Clarke, whose ailing father suffered a second stroke only a day before their departure. Although no word had been breathed to him of his oldest daughter's plans, his little family were startled to hear him say, "What has my Mary to do with these American nuns?" Catherine would indeed do all she could to cheer him, vivacious and loving as she was. Coming in for a break in her busy day, she would throw her arms about him, saying, "How is my darling father today?" To which he would respond as best he could, "God bless my own dear daughter."[40]

Mrs. Berkeley, fearing the hazards of ocean travel, sadly withdrew from the little group, a decision which not only grieved them but also considerably reduced their resources. Rose, involved in the settlement of family affairs, found her departure delayed until the following spring, thus reducing the number to three. But,to their surprise and delight, on the very evening before their departure, they opened the door in response to the strokes of their knocker, to find Catherine Byrne on the doorstep, all packed and ready for the journey.[41]

Meantime Father Costello had returned to America without waiting for the Sisters, but had assured them that he had made all arrangements for their reception into the diocese of Philadelphia.[42] The Reverend Peter Kenrick, who would himself shortly leave for Philadelphia, said the last Mass in their little Ann Street chapel. He was much disturbed at hearing their plans, for his brother, then Bishop of Philadelphia, had confided to him the many problems facing the young diocese. He strongly urged them to alter their plans even at that late moment. But they had "set their hands to the plough and would not turn back."[43]

Mr. Kelly arranged for the passage of the "Sisters," and this caused the other passengers to identify them as the "Kelly sisters." Their fond and deeply emotional good-byes had been said in their homes, with

Margaret's and Eliza's fathers accompanying them to the quay where the ocean-going sailing vessel, the Cassandra, was tied up before the Customs House. It must have been a bustling and confusing scene, with the crowds of wretchedly poor emigrants being stowed into steerage accommodations, together with their luggage and supplies for the long journey. The four would be among the more fortunate, assigned to the upper decks. At length, on the evening of July 13, 1833, they bravely waved their last good-byes, as the vessel, released from its moorings, felt the breeze fill its sails, moving it out through the broad mouth of the Liffey into Dublin Bay. Night had fallen before the lights of Howth on the last long finger of land had slipped from sight, and their eyes turned to face through the darkness an uncertain future.

And so the first little band of Irish women to answer the call to a lifetime of dedicated service in the new nation was on its way.[44] They would share the lot of the Irish emigrant and nourish in the hearts of his children the faith and the love of learning that had ever marked his people.

* * * * * * * *

In those days the vessels were not permitted to sail directly from Ireland to foreign ports so the Cassandra headed for Liverpool. There she was to lie at anchor until July 18, and the Sisters were free to walk about the city or visit relatives and friends. Eliza, taking full advantage of the opportunity, returned to the vessel laden with gifts, not the most practical of which was a cage of birds.

Scarcely seaworthy at best, the vessel passed through a storm of near-hurricane proportions as they neared their destination,[45] both crew and passengers finding comfort and assurance in the prayers of the "Sisters." Inconveniences throughout the long voyage were many, but for the Sisters these were doubtless dwarfed by knowledge of the wretched conditions their fellow country-men were enduring in the crowded steerage below. Then, with the hope of land near, there came for all a moment of terror when the cry of the captain rang out: "All hands to the pumps!" for the vessel had sprung a leak. Although almost in the sight of land, they were still far from safety. Several hours of heavy labor were needed to lighten the sinking vessel, but with morning it was able to enter the busy harbor of New York. It was September 2, the fifty-first day after setting sail.

Having dropped anchor, the ship, rolling with the waves, awaited the harbor boats which would convey the weary passengers to the docks. The descent was hazardous, for it was made swinging hand over hand, down a rope ladder, from the rolling vessel to a rocking boat, to be caught in the arms of a sailor below. The Sisters had scarcely visualized its hazards when they decided to trust their precious horde of gold to a single satchel, which they had taken the precaution of tying to Eliza's arm as she was about to descend. Terrified as she was, dangling precariously over the waves, she slowly made her way downward. The satchel stayed with her, but not the gold, for the latch apparently catching on the rope ladder, came open, and, before the horrified gaze of those still on deck, the bright sovereigns followed one another into the swirling waters below.

It was a tragic moment indeed, and the dismay in Margaret's face moved the young church student beside her to say comfortingly, "Never mind, I have money," though she well knew the limits of a seminarian's resources. John Early, then on his way to the Jesuit novitiate in Frederick, Maryland, would many years later, when president of Georgetown University, write to Margaret in affectionate friendship, recalling their voyage together.[46]

But more precious than money was the welcome accorded to the weary travellers by Mrs. James Reilly, aunt of a second young seminarian and fellow passenger, Andrew Burns.[47] Her hospitality and home-cooked meals refreshed their spirits. It was pleasant to be in a real bed again and to feel a solid floor under their feet after weeks on a rolling boat. While they lingered, the pastor of old St. Peter's, learning of their presence, begged them to remain in New York and give their services to his school.[48] But they had pledged themselves to Philadelphia, and their tickets had been purchased to that city. They would keep their word and be on their way.

Early on the morning of September 7, the four were down at the Battery to take the ferry that would land them on the New Jersey shore. There stage coaches waited to convey the boat's passengers to a length of railroad, the Amboy and Camden Line but recently constructed and trying out its first steam locomotive

the "John Bull." After several miles of bouncing
over the bumpiest of roads in the lumbering stagecoach, they boarded the rail cars, to be drawn over
strap-iron rails to the Delaware river where a
steamer waited to carry them to their destination. A
trip of eight hours in all, it had given them an introduction to every current mode of commercial transportation.

Evening found the lonely travelers gathering their
baggage about them on the busy wharf at Chestnut
street in Philadelphia.[49] Nowhere in sight was the
Dublin chaplain to whom they had written ahead concerning their travel plans. They sought a lodging in
the vicinity of a church, and were told that St.
Joseph church was only a few squares away. Engaging
a drayman to bring their belongings, they started up
the cobbled street, and for lodging they were soon
directed to the door of a widow who kept a grocery
store and was well known in the parish, Mrs. Margaret
McDonogh, on Fourth and Spruce streets. Her daughter,
Mrs. John O'Brien, would have rooms for them, and she
lived almost in the shadow of the little church in
Willing's Alley. So night found them in friendly
hands and under a kindly roof, however limited the
accommodations.

Mass next morning, Sunday, at nearby St. Mary's,
commemorated the birthday of the Blessed Virgin, and
Mrs. McDonogh's invitation to a bountiful breakfast
honored the occasion. Dublin was the topic of much
interested converstaion, for she too had lived there
for a time; then the newcomers told of the hopes that
had brought them to the New World, and of their anxiety as strangers in the city. Mrs. McDonogh assured
them that they would find help in the person of her
good friend and former pastor, the Reverend T.J.
Donaghoe, Irish like themselves, though from Tyrone.
These were busy days for him, she explained, for he
had recently been named pastor, and was building a
new church just north of the city. He was often in
the neighborhood, however, visiting the aged Bishop,
and would be stopping in for a cup of tea.

So much, then, for the future, but what for the
present? The little silver they had on hand would
soon be gone. There were personal items of some
value which they could for a time leave with a pawn-
shop keeper. Then they were skilled seamstresses,
that is, all except Margaret, who was 'all thumbs'
with a needle. Her offer, as 'Mann of the house,' to

find employment which could give support to the rest,
Mary Frances promptly rejected. It was not for work
in shops or in factories that they had come. They
would manage, and Margaret would be their manager. A
sign "Fine Sewing Done Here" soon brought an order
for a dozen linen shirts, and for these they received
their first American income - fifteen precious dollars. It was not many days before Margaret had made
contact with the owner of a dress-making establishment, Miss S.S. Willis, at 62 South Eleventh street,
who kept them supplied with finishing work, an
arrangement which provided much of their livelihood
for the ten years of their Philadelphia sojourn.

They did not know it then, but the four young
women had come into a diocese only slowly recovering
from the effects of a long and bitter schism, with
allegiances still divided, though now the division
lay between two bishops, instead of, as formerly, between one bishop and the trustees of his cathedral.
They would not soon become fully aware of the complications involved, and it seems probable that never
more than the vaguest knowledge of Father Donaghoe's
position between the two Bishops would become available to them.

CHAPTER I - NOTES

1. ". . . there was no offense, outside those pun-
ishable by death or transportation, for which
six weeks in Newgate Gaol would not be a more
than adequate penalty. D.A. Chart, Ireland from
the Union to Catholic Emancipation (London: J.M.
Dent and Sons, Ltd., 1910), p. 216.

2. Ann Street chapel, dedicated in 1817, was built
in Gothic design of grey granite, its interior
decorated by some of the best craftsmen of the
day. In 1891, it was extended to Halston street
as St. Michan Catholic Church, a striking building even today. It was successor to the penal
chapel at the corner of Bull's and Mary's lanes,
and its baptismal records are intact from the
year 1725. There is also Protestant St.Michan's.

3. "The square [Stephen's Green] had long been a
favorite residence of the élite. Immediately
before the Union, four earls, two viscounts,
three barons, several honourables and baronets;
eighteen or twenty members of parliament; the
Protestant Primate, and the Archbishop of
Armagh; the Bishops of Ossory and of Killala and
Achonry, all Anglican, had their townhouses in
Stephen's Green. In the time of the Volunteers,
the greensward, of some twenty acres, was a favorite place for reviewing the city and county
corps. On the anniversary of the Battle of the
Boyne, and on William III's birthday, the volunteer army mustered there to fire salutes and
parade in orange cockades. . ."S.A., Mary
Aikenhead, her Life, her Work and her Friends
(Dublin: M.H. Gill & Son, 1882), p. 258.

4. Constantia Maxwell, Country and Town in Ireland
under the Georges (London: George G. Harrap &
Co., Ltd., 1940), p. 89.

5. "There were no residential quarters. The people
pervaded the whole city. The merchants lived
over their warehouses, small traders above or
behind their shops, craftsmen lived and worked
in their own homes, when the nature of their employment permitted. The streets were intersec-
ted and paralleled by innumerable lanes inhabited
by a teeming population. Neither tramway nor

railway existed. Stagecoaches and hackney cars
were the only means of conveyance in and through
the city for those whose wealth did not enable
them to run a carriage or a sedan chair."
John I. Webb, "Dublin in 1829," Catholic Emancipation Centenary Record.

6. ". . . at the Union Dublin lost her hundred or
so resident peers. This over-looks the fact
that immediately after the Union Dublin was full
of brand-new peers whose patents all bore the
shameful date of 1800. But most of these noble-
men rapidly took themselves off to the new fountain of advancement, and Dublin was well rid of
them. . . . The disappearance of resident peers
was gradual: nine years after the Union there
were still some forty with addresses in or near
Dublin, but very few of these were 'Union
Peers.'" (Maurice Craig, Dublin, 1660-1860
London: Cresset Press, 1952, p. 274).

7. Since the number of servants employed was an indication of social status, most households of
the wealthy were over-staffed, and the consequent indolence on the part of the servants led
to many disorders. With habits of sloth and
without training for any other line of endeavor,
the lot of these was especially deplorable.

8. Having served Henry VIII well and efficiently in
the suppression of the Dublin monasteries, a
certain William Brabazon had been rewarded with
the rank and title of Earl, and endowed with a
large area south of the Liffey which was to constitute a district exempt from city rule and
governed by the Earl and his council. Cf. Myles
Ronan, An Apostle of Catholic Dublin (Clons-
keagh: Richview Press, 1944).

9 Illicit liquor - poteen - was produced in stills
hidden chiefly in bogs and mountains throughout
the land. When relative safety from detection
allowed time for the malting of the grain used,
the product was generally regarded as more desirable than parliament or taxed liquor, which
made it popular enough to receive some protection from officers of the law. It was sold in
Dublin "as openly in the streets as they sell a
loaf of bread." Both the making and the selling
of poteen manifested the Irish contempt of the
laws by which the land was governed, and

contributed their share to general degradation
and even violence. Cf. K.H. Connell, "Illicit
Distillation," Irish Peasant Society (Oxford:
Clarendon Press. 1968), p. 1-50.

10. Constantia Maxwell, Dublin under the Georges,
    1714-1830 (London: Faber & Faber, Ltd., 1956).
    pp. 157-8.

11. K.H. Connell, "Illigitimacy before the Famine,"
    Irish Peasant Society (Oxford: Clarendon Press,
    1968), p. 51-86.

12. Father Henry Young was one of four priestly
    brothers, sons of a wealthy wholesale merchant
    in Dublin. James and William were diocesan
    priests and Charles a Jesuit. Of the three
    daughters, Catherine joined the Poor Clares in
    Harold's Cross, and Mary and Johanna the Ursu-
    lines in Cork. Mary was a remarkably able
    woman, writer of textbooks in history for her
    students, among them a catechism of Irish his-
    tory which became popular in other schools but
    brought angry remonstrances from the British
    Parliament. Henry, titled "An Apostle of Cath-
    olic Dublin" by his biographer, Dr. Myles Ronan,
    was the inspiration of many devotional prac-
    tices, not only at SS. Michael and John's but
    at St. Michan's, Harold's Cross and Milltown
    (Dublin).

13. Father Joseph Betagh, S.J. opened free schools
    for apprentices, servants, and other poor young
    men, instructing them in their religion, and in
    reading, writing, and "cyphering," bookkeeping
    and mathematics, to prepare them to take their
    places in industry and commerce. The number in
    daily attendance was said to be three hundred,
    and in all some three thousand students, adults
    and children, passed through his hands. Cf.
    Ronan, pp. 38-39. (The present writer is heav-
    ily indebted to the Ronan study for details of
    Catholic life and personages in this period of
    Dublin history).

14. A new plan of nationally funded schools, free
    from denominational bias, was established in
    1832. It grew out of the experience of previous
    efforts and gave much promise, inaugurating a
    system of public primary education which ante-
    dated that of England itself by seventy years.

However, the old divisions were not long in man-
ifesting themselves, born of the mutual distrust
long engendered in the land. The Christian
Brothers, feeling that the restrictions government support required of them were destroying
the effectiveness of their schools, withdrew from
the system. The Established Church would have
none of its control, and the Catholic hierarchy,
at first in favor of the plan, soon came to demand government support for exclusively Catholic
institutions, leaving only the Presbyterians
open to its best benefits, though these too protested a multi-denominational approach. The total return to denominational schools did not,
however, come until mid-century, and then, so
far as the Catholic body was concerned, through
the aggressive and authoritative Cardinal, Paul
Cullen, Archbishop of Dublin, while Archbishop
John McHale of Tuam would have none of the system at all. Cf. Donald H. Akenson, The Irish
Educational Experiment, The National System of
Education in the Nineteenth Century, (London:
Routledge and Kegan Paul,1970).

The fact that the new system made no provision
for secondary education deprived many Catholics
of an advantage that had been theirs, "for the
old hedge school masters had frequently provided
advanced education for their better pupils."
There were several flourishing Protestant schools.
However, for Catholics, religious orders stepped
into the breach. "The Christian Brothers, and
the Presentation and Mercy orders, in particular,
provided from their own resources an inexpensive
secondary education for many thousands of boys
and girls." Owen Dudley Edwards,Ed. Connor
Cruise O'Brien Introduces Ireland,"Education,"
Valentine Rice, (New York: McGraw Hill Book Co.,
1969), pp. 171-2.

15. Catholic clergy were forbidden to use any of the
titles in use for the clergy of the Established
Church. Hence the title "Doctor" was applied
to the members of the Catholic hierarchy and to
clerics of distinction. The title "bishop"
could be used only if it was preceded by the
qualifying "titular."

16. For the account of Teresa Mullaly and the foundation of the Presentation nuns at George's Hill,
see Roland B. Savage. A Valiant Dublin Woman,

A Story of George's Hill, 1766-1940. (Dublin: M.H. Gill & Son, Ltd., 1940).

17. Interview with the Poor Clare nuns, September 12, 1972.

18. The Brothers followed the Lancastrian or monitorial system of teaching, which permitted each Brother to handle a classroom of up to 150 pupils with efficiency and order. The biographer of Mary Aikenhead gives an account of the Irish Sisters' efforts to use similar methods in their newly established poor school on Gardiner street. She tells us that "Mrs.[the title 'mistress' was used for religious women because religious titles of any kind were forbidden. This doubtless seemed the one to give the greatest protection.] Hennessy's first attempt at being a schoolmistress turned out, in spite of her laboured presentation, a total failure. The schoolroom became in a short time a scene of indescribable uproar and confusion, and she felt herself powerless to control or to teach the children. "Great was the perplexity of the nuns. They felt there was no help except in humble patience and in the trust that aid would be sent them from above. Kind Providence came to their assistance by bringing them into acquaintance with the Brothers of the Christian Schools who had been recently introduced into Ireland by Mr. Edmund Rice of Waterford, and who were now conducting schools in Hanover street, on the south side of the city. The sisters from Gardiner-street being in the habit of visiting the female wards of the Jervis-street hospital, generally met there on Sundays the Christian Brothers who attended the male wards. Mrs. Hennessy determined on accosting Mr. Rice and begging him to help the Sisters of Charity in their difficulty. She did so on two occasions, but each time he turned from her, appearing to suppose she must be jesting. At last, seeing she was in sober earnest, he listened to her story of the school troubles. 'Well,' he said in reply, 'I'll send you Brother Duggan.' 'Oh!' exclaimed Mrs. Hennessy, 'is it that little boy?' 'Little boy!' rejoined Mr. Rice, 'I wish I had fifty such little boys.'

"... It was arranged that Saturdays should be

devoted to the sisters' schools, until they
should be brought into something like order. On
the following Saturday, therefore, Brother Duggan
appeared in the midst of the crowded room full
of unruly children. He had to shout and whistle
before he could command silence. At first he
took on himself the entire management of the
school. By degrees he discontinued inflicting
punishment himself, merely pointing out the
guilty parties to the sisters and leaving them to
deal with the delinquents. By degrees he for-
bore assuming any authority before the sisters,
so as to leave the children entirely dependent
on them. In the course of a few months perfect
order reigned in the schools. Besides making
these Saturday visits, Mr. Duggan came in the
evenings to teach arithmetic to the sisters, whom
he ranged round him like children and lectured
on each rule until he found it was perfectly
understood." S.A., pp. 222-223.

19. It was at Rathfarnam that Mother Teresa of Cal-
cutta received her religious formation. Today
seven hundred and fifty Missionaries of Charity
claim Teresa as their Mother.

20. T. Corcoran, Education Systems in Ireland from
the Close of the Middle Ages (Dublin: Department of Education, University College, 1928),
p. 159.

21. An interview with the director of the genealogy
department, Bublin Castle, failed to give hope
of tracing our Sisters' family backgrounds with
the very limited data at our disposal. No record was kept of the births and deaths of Catholics in Dublin at the time, and the city directories included no names of persons residing in
multiple housing. A visit to the Quaker historian, Mrs. Olive Goodbody, at the Friends' meeting house on Eustace street, proved equally
fruitless with regard to Mrs. Clarke's religious
background. Search of baptismal records in the
churches - St. Audeon, St. Michan, St. Nicholas
of Myra, SS. Michael and John, and the Pro-
Cathedral proved futile. Inquiries made at St.
Catherine's and the White Friars Carmelite
Church, Dublin, brought no response.

22. This presents some difficulty, for the St. Mary
parish was in the hands of the diocesan clergy.

The Franciscans were more active at the time
south of the Liffey, in the area in which Martha
Clarke was an active worker in her adult years.
Her address at that time was Bride street.

23. Doran Journal, p.

24. Sister M. Florence Lowery, Letter, original in
    BVM Archives.
    That botany was not the only science that in-
    trigued Mother Clarke, we learn from a brief
    though somewhat unpleasant note in a letter writ-
    ten by Father Terence J. Donaghoe to Sister M.
    Margaret Mann many years later: "Mother Clarke
    has a great taste for astronomy. It's well, for
    the other⌐ are earthly, terrestrial."

25. Op. cit. p. 131, 132.

26. Upon his graduation from Father Betagh's school,
    Daniel Murray went to Salamanca for his major
    studies, and was ordained in 1790. Stationed in
    his home parish in Arklow at the time of the Re-
    bellion of 1798, he narrowly escaped death, flee-
    ing on horseback when his pastor there was mur-
    dered in his bed. Being assigned to St. Mary's,
    he was "to labor in the midst of a multitudinous
    flock destitute of nearly all the common resour-
    ces of a Catholic community. It was enough to
    make his heart sink within him to witness the
    misery accumulated in the crowded back streets
    and lanes of the metropolitan parish, and to
    look in vain for adequate means of relieving
    their temporal distress and ministering to their
    grievous spiritual needs." S.A., p. 134.

27. Our Herald, Vol. VIII, April, 1920, p. 204.

28. Doran, Journal, p. 32.

29. A search of the United Irishmen membership rolls,
    admittedly incomplete, but preserved in the
    State Papers Office, Dublin Castle, failed to
    reveal the name of John Mann.

30. Our Herald, Vol VIII, April, 1920, pp. 203-204.

31. Rose's sister Margaret married a British army
    officer, John O'Brien. He came to New Orleans
    to consider the possibilities of life in this
    country, returned to Ireland, sold his

commission and brought his wife and son Thomas
back to New Orleans. There he entered into the
sugar business in which he was very successful.
There were born to them there Elizabeth, Joseph,
James, Mary and William. Seeing the likelihood
of war, they moved to Princeville, Illinois,
where John Henry and Theresa were born. John
Henry married Katherine McDermott and lived in
Junction City, Kansas where a son J.H. was born
March 5, 1871. The family located in Boulder,
Colorado early in 1872. The children of J.H.'s
family attended Mt. St. Gertrude Academy. One
of these, Eugene O'Brien, made a name for himself on the stage and in moving pictures. A
brother of J.H., Dr. George G. O'Brien of Harl-
ingen, Texas, graciously furnished the information given, along with family pictures. Three
of the sons of Margaret and John O'Brien, James,
William and Joseph, moved to Kewanee,Illinois,
though Joseph and William later moved to Spokane
where they died. Teresa married a man named
Potter; she died at National City near San Diego.
Thomas lived on in Princeville, and was the
town's leading banker. On retirement he moved
to San Diego, dying there. Elizabeth, unmarried,
was in San Francisco at the time of the earth-
quake and was never heard of after it. (Notes
in Files of BVM Archives).

32. McGuire, Annals (unpublished) in BVM Archives,
    pp. 3-4.

33. Nihill, Notes and Doran Journal,p. 49.

34. Register of St. Clare Convent, Harold's Cross,
    Dublin, p. 154.

35. Ronan, p. 29. With no clear evidence remaining
    of the precise location of our Sisters' first
    school, beyond that of North Ann street, the
    writer has made the assumption of this as its
    situation, based on the following circumstances:
    the street is a very short one, and could not
    have presented many possibilities; the site ac-
    cording to Father Ronan, served as an academy
    before the time of our Sisters' school, under
    the headship of the Reverend Barnaby Murphy; the
    site provided the necessary living quarters as
    well as school facilities; an historian of the
    area, the Reverend Dermot Clarke, suggested the
    very real probability of its being the scene of

their labors.

36. McGuire, Annals, p. 15.

37. Recounted by Sister M. Bertha Hayes, BVM.

38. McGuire, p. 16.

39. Doran, Journal, p. 18

40. Nihill, Notes.

41. It is related that while two of the Sisters were on an errand preparatory to the departure, as they were crossing a Liffey bridge, the span just ahead of them gave way. Startled, but safe, they were retracing their steps when an elderly man, who to their grateful hearts seemed St. Joseph himself, said to them, "Go where you will, ladies, the hand of God is over you." Sister M. Lambertina Doran, In the Early Days, Pages from the Annals of the Sisters of Charity of the Blessed Virgin Mary, Dubuque, n.p., 3rd edition, 1943, p. 14.

42. Doran, Journal, p.5.

43. Included among the treasures that would go with them to the New World was a statue of the Virgin and Child which was to survive the vicissitudes of the years and to find its place at last, together with the doorplate that had marked their North Ann street venture, among the Congregation's precious mementoes, in the Heritage Room at the Mt. Carmel motherhouse.

44. The Ursulines from Blackrock, Cork, had come to New York in 1812, but had returned to Ireland in 1815. Coming back in 1834, they disbanded in 1854, joining American groups of Ursulines. (Letter from Sister M. Paul, Archivist, Blackrock, Cork, September 3, 1973). The first Sisters of Mercy to come to the United States arrived in Pittsburgh in December, 1843.

45. The account of the voyage is taken from the McGuire Annals, pp. 22-23, and from unidentified memoirs.

46. John Early was president of Holy Cross College, Worcester, Massachusetts at the time it was

burned to the ground, July 14, 1852. He was then made president of the newly established Loyola College in Baltimore. (J. P. Marschall, _Francis Patrick Kenrick, 1851-1863_, unpublished doctoral dissertation, Catholic University, 1965, p. 63). At the time of Father Early's letter written in 1872, he was president of Georgetown University.

47. Doran, _Journal_, p. 35.

48. James A. Rooney, ed., _The Catholic Chronologist and Monthly Record of Memorable Events_, Vol. II, excerpt, no page given.

49. Details of arrival, etc., in Philadelphia, Doran, _In the Early Days_, pp. 19 ff.

CHAPTER TWO

The Man From Tyrone:
His Philadelphia Years-
1824-1843

North Ireland

In this chapter we meet three personages from County Tyrone, Ireland. One, for years a small town pastor and vicar to an absentee archbishop, would become at the age of seventy-three, the Bishop of Philadelphia. Another, after serving as a priest of the Philadelphia diocese, was destined to become New York's first archbishop. The third assumed the direction of the little Irish community on its arrival in Philadelphia and accompanied them, ten years later, to a western diocese. These three clerics were closely associated during the trying years of the schism which arose out of the trustee system. The loss of administrative authority by the Bishop as a result of his ineptitude in handling the situation, and the assignment of that authority to a young and able coadjutor, a native of Dublin, resulted in the settlement of the trustee conflict and the establishment of peace and discipline in the long disordered diocese, despite continued harassment from the deposed Bishop. It was to be the lot of the Dublin women to come under the direction of the priest from Tyrone whose loyalties lay with the retired Bishop.

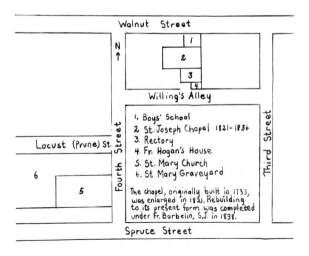

Walnut Street

N ↑

Willing's Alley

1. Boys' School
2. St. Joseph Chapel 1821-1836
3. Rectory
4. Fr. Hogan's House
5. St. Mary Church
6. St. Mary Graveyard

The chapel, originally built in 1733, was enlarged in 1821. Rebuilding to its present form was completed under Fr. Barbelin, S.J. in 1838.

Locust (Prune) St.

Fourth Street

Third Street

Spruce Street

Aughnacloy, "a fair town situated on the river
Blackwater in the barony of Dungannon, County Tyrone,"
North Ireland, is still much the same little village
it was on February 20, 1795, when Terence James
Donaghey[1] was born, save only for the addition of a
parish church and a resident pastor. It boasts a single
gle main street which, running down a hillside, is
lined with quaint stucco houses in a compact row on
each side of the street, and built flush with the
public sidewalk, occasional gateways giving access to
yards and gardens in the rear. Once a largely Catholic village, Aughnacloy was for a long period the
seat of a remnant of Catholic gentry whom the small
rural church of Killeen - "little church" - had then
served. "The day of my visit was 'Market Day,'"
writes Miss Ivy Embleton, Belfast genealogist, "and
the main street was full of stalls selling all kinds
of produce and clothing. I had the feeling that the
town had changed but little in the past two hundred
years."[2] The country round about is hilly, and divided into small fields by straggling hedges. A traveller on the main road from Dublin to Londonderry
crosses the border into troubled North Ireland just
half a mile south of the town.

The beginnings of those troubles go back nearly
four centuries. The flight of the threatened Earls
of Tyrone and Tirconnell in 1607 had left the northern six counties forfeit to the English crown.
Government officials parcelled out the land to
younger sons of English and Scotch nobility, and to
English landed proprietors, leaving the Irish Catholics who dwelt there a dispossessed people. When
Lord Wentworth, afterwards Earl of Stafford, was
named Lord Deputy of all Ireland, he resolved to make
the power of the English King absolute there. With
the country already in a chronic state of discontent,
the Catholic rebellion of 1641 broke out as soon as
his iron hand was lifted, resulting in the destruction of English plantations and settlements. The
Puritan Cromwell wreaked vengeance on the Catholic
forces, and rewarded with huge tracts of land the men,
mostly of Scottish background, who had joined ranks

with him. As a consequence, Presbyterianism became
the dominant religion of the area, and the Scottish
Moores came into possession of a vast region, including Aughnacloy. As a consequence the Catholic population became largely an impoverished peasantry and
servant class.

Small though it was, the town was significant for
its military preoccupation. The Volunteer movement
was inaugurated there in 1778-9 for defense against
foreign invasion, when British troops were withdrawn
for service against the Colonies. The Aughnacloy
Battalion and the Aughnacloy Volunteers enrolled then
under the command of Captain Thomas Forsythe, agent
to the Moore estate. By 1795, the year of Terence
Donaghey's birth, the United Irishmen, under Protestant leadership, had begun to make themselves felt,
and the area was infected with much political unrest.
That year, too, religious attitudes were crystallized
by the establishment of the Society of Orangemen in
the adjoining county of Armagh. This followed upon a
long period of harassment of Catholic residents by
such marauders as the Peep O'Day Boys, who were early
recruits of the new society. Determined to drive the
Catholics out of the area, they engaged in early morning raids, destroying the property, burning the
houses and threatening the lives of the inhabitants.
Hundreds of them were forced to flee into the barren
and desolate province of Connaught. The Catholic Defenders, with no hope of recourse to law to safeguard
the rights and lives of their people, since government officials were largely affiliated with the
Orange Society, turned to violent reprisal. In 1798
The Yeomanry Infantry Corps was raised in the town,
its evident purpose the maintaining of Protestant
control. The area had provided also a regiment of
militia, the Tyrone Fusiliers, as a part of the regular army, for preserving the power of the government
in Waterford and Galway. In the rebellion of 1798, a
Tyrone Militia, mostly composed of Orangemen and
wearing the ribbon of their party, marched to Naas,
south of Dublin, where, warned of an ambush, they
killed many of the badly armed and poorly disciplined
peasant forces. A second episode of the 1798 uprising for the people of Aughnacloy was their entertainment for a night of the captive Irish patriot, Wolfe
Tone. He, together with the French sailors was on
his way to Dublin to stand trial for treason after
the vessel "Hoche" was captured in Lough Swilly by an
English squadron. By then the rebellion had been
crushed.

Soldiers continued to be quartered in Aughnacloy for many years afterwards, and a conspicuous feature of the village was the barracks, with its officers' mess, its guard room, and in the barracks yard, stalls for their fifty horses. A hospital for the soldiers and a rifle range did service, while militia regiments or detachments quartered there in the early eighteen hundreds included in turn regiments and militias "varying from the brogue of Tipperary to the dialect of Yorkshire."

The Annals of Aughnacloy tell us that

> The Church Gate was the place of rough and ready military justice in those days, and old men used to tell of cursing and scream-ing wretches tied to the railings, while the cat o' nine tails wrote strange stories on their naked backs. There were grim tragedies too under the shadow of the stee-ple, if all be true, when martial law and a stout rope put a period to the existence of some hardy sinner.[3]

Yet, withal, we are told, it was a "gay and sporting little town," and while Methodism had somewhat re-deemed it from a state of moral laxity, its people continued to enjoy cock-fighting, races at the local course, and the clattering of horses' hoofs and the yelping of hounds in the chase. The "Moores of the Bawn," who held title to the lands of the Aughnacloy area, were a sporting family, and the "farming and labouring classes of the surrounding district were no whit behind their gentry in the love of sport." From a time perhaps as far back as James II, an annual football match had been held on Easter Monday between a team of Castledown Bawn and the local worthies.

All over the district, through most of the year, the hand-loom weaving of linen was carried on in the homes, and the Wednesday linen market netted an aver-age return of nearly five hundred pounds. A large brewery and a distillery added to the income of the town. Certainly the world was very much with the people of Aughnacloy, giving little support to spiri-tual aspirations.

While the reestablished Catholic hierarchy was restoring discipline among the clergy and people in the rest of Ireland, little had yet been effected in the North. The Archdiocese of Armagh itself had seen slight change, its absentee archbishop being supplied for by a vicar general, throughout the early nineteen hundreds, Dean Henry Conwell. He served also as pastor for the parish church at Dungannon, in County Tyrone, not far from Aughnacloy. The hostile atmosphere in which the church existed in the North had its effect on the dispositions of the clergy, tending to bring out in them an arbitrary and abrasive quality, while the lack of control by a vigorous hierarchy left them with little consciousness of the refinement of ecclesiastical law and discipline.

Terence James Donaghey, the eldest son of Edward and Suzanna McCrea(Macrea) Donaghey, was born in Aughnacloy on February 20, 1795. While the parish tithe rolls list the Donagheys as Catholics, Terence's mother, apparently a convert, came from Scotch Presbyterian backgrounds. The numerous land transactions of her family and the titles "gentleman," "esquire," and "merchant" [4] applied to them would indicate that they were people of means. There is no record of Mr. Donaghey's employment, but the record of two leases,* of rather valuable town property suggests a fair competency.[5] Terence Donaghey had at least two sisters, Mrs. Patrick McKenna, mother of Patrick, Terence and Arthur** (a priest in Nottingham, England), and Mrs. Jane Golden, possibly the wife of "George Golden, farmer," listed in the tithe rolls of the area, and mother of John Golden whose name appears years later in the rolls. There was at least one brother, for the next generation includes Jane, Thomas and Rose Donaghey, all of one family.

Terence received his early education in the local school and was probably in his teens when he met John Hughes of the neighboring village of Augher for the

---

*The Donaghey residence is described as having a gateway from the street, giving access to their own and adjoining yards and gardens. The photograph of such a residence was taken in Aughnacloy in 1972, See page 76.

**Arthur wrote his uncle from Rome on January 25, 1860, of affairs there where Napoleon was endeavoring to sieze Romagna from the Papal States, and the people were shouting for a king. He regretted that his uncle was "on the other side of the world. . . almost as on another planet," for he would wish to visit him. The letter closes with "Remember me most kindly to Aunt Jane," who was then living with the Sisters on the Prairie.

first time. Of this meeting he was to write in later years: "I have loved John Hughes from the hour when, looking up from my book, I first saw his bright handsome face as he stood for a moment in the open doorway of the little schoolhouse at Aughnacloy, on the day he came to enroll as a pupil."[6] It was the beginning of a friendship that would last until the death of New York's first Archbishop in 1864. As boys they must have shared many adventures and exchanged many tales. Among these latter may well have been John's account of his experience when "he was once waylaid by a band of Orangemen, who pointed five bayonets at his breast, so that he thought his hour had come. However, when he told them his name, they let him go, saying, 'We know his father.' His father was a quiet man who, although a strong defender of his religion, would never associate with the 'Ribbon' factions, secret societies of the nature of the Defenders, the heads of which were often the paid spies of the government that fomented divisions among the Irish so as to govern them more easily. . ."[7]

Doubtless they often philosophized about the wrongs done to their country, John recounting with bitterness the incident of his sister's burial, when the law forbade the priest to enter the cemetery to bless the grave, so that prayers could be said for her only from the graveyard gate.[8] They would ponder over the injustice, as John was to put it later, that "The rights of my birth were washed away by the rites of my baptism."

John, a farm lad, born in Annaloghan, County Tyrone, lived, later, in the little village of Augher, two or three miles from Aughnacloy. His father was Patrick Hughes. His mother, Margaret McKenna, was probably of the same family into which Terence's sister married. John was the third of seven children, and a sturdy lad, who helped with the labors of the farm. Chiefly growers of flax, the family spent the winter months spinning and weaving linen. But John's heart was in study, and farm work was irksome to him. A little less distasteful was that of gardener, when an employe on a neighboring estate took him on as a helper and taught him the secrets of horticulture. John Hughes' later bent for polemics may well have had its initiation in the local controversies on religion, each village having its champion of Protestantism and its lay theologian of the Catholic Church. The faith of such contestants was often stronger their works, and both charity and orthodoxy came out the worse for the sessions.[9]

Terence was already well-grounded in English and mathematics when, in 1812, at the age of seventeen, he began the study of Latin grammar.[10] For this he came under the tutelage of the classical scholar, Dean Conwell, pastor in neighboring Dungannon,[11] and vicar general of the Armagh diocese.

The Very Reverend Henry Conwell came from a family of some status as an Irish sept or clan, whose means permitted them to found a burse for the education of priests at the Irish college in Paris. Born in Moneymere, County Londonderry, province of Ulster, in 1748, he profited by the burse in his study for the priesthood. Ordained in 1776, at the age of twenty-eight he eventually became pastor of Dungannon and vicar general of the Armagh diocese, in which capacity he was to serve for twenty-five years. Besides having a mastery of classical languages, he spoke French fluently, and, with less ease, Spanish and Italian as well. John Hughes' biographers do not tell us whether he shared with Terence Donaghey the services of this priestly tutor. The fact that he was two years the younger would have left him somewhat behind Terence in his studies. Furthermore, the Hughes family resources would scarcely have allowed the luxury of maintaining him in the household of a priest.

When a year of bad crops was added to Patrick Hughes' heavy burdens as a tenant farmer, he and his second son, Patrick, left Ireland for America, having assigned the care of the farm to his other sons, John and Michael. The following year John followed his father to Chambersburg, Pennsylvania, where the family would shortly settle. The boyhood friends, John and Terence, were separated, not to meet again for ten years - save for one brief visit - and then as priests, subjects of the Bishop of Philadelphia, who was none other than the former pastor of Dungannon, the aged Henry Conwell.

In November, 1818, at the age of twenty-three, Terence Donaghey went to Dublin, presumably for further study. He would have a choice of Trinity, the seminary at Maynooth, Clongowes Wood, or St. Gall's. The registers of none of the three first institutions contain his name, and St. Gall's is no longer in existence. If, as we learn from the Early Days (p.227), his father opposed his plans for the priesthood, Mr.

I. Noyé
BIBLIOTHÈQUE

DE LA

COMPAGNIE DE SAINT-SULPICE

6, RUE DU REGARD · PARIS 6e.
TÉL: 548-37-91 (ou 83-26)

21 février 1972

Ma Soeur,

J'ai effectué la petite recherche que vous me demandiez, mais elle pose quelques questions. En effet, je ne trouve pas sur les registres d'inscriptions du séminaire d'Issy, ni du séminaire de Paris, le nom de Donoghoe. Mais, dans le registre des ordinations pour les années 1821-1825, il y a les inscriptions suivantes : Terentius Mac Donoghy Armaghanus, filius Eduardi et Suzannae Mavrea conjugum (né le) 23 février 1745, tonsuré le 16 juin 1821 ; prêtrise le 24 mai 1823.

Cette dernière date correspond bien à celle que vous m'indiquiez, la date de la tonsure également ; l'âge semble aussi correspondre, mais il y a divergence sur le nom de famille, et surtout l'absence d'inscription parmi les séminaristes. Sans doute le nom du père et de la mère vous permettra-t-il de voir s'il s'agit bien de l'ecclésiastique directeur de votre congrégation. Il est possible qu'il ait été, non pas au séminaire de St Sulpice, mais au séminaire irlandais de Paris et qu'il ait été seulement joins aux séminaristes de St Sulpice pour les ordinations.

Je regrette de vous donner si peu de certitudes et je vous prie d'agréer, ma Soeur, l'assurance de mes sentiments respectueux.

Donaghey's death in January, 1819 cleared the way.
However, it was not until August of the following
year that Terence went to France to enter the seminary. While it has been the constant tradition of
the Congregation that Father Donaghoe made his seminary studies at St. Sulpice in Paris, the records of
the seminary indicate that he was never enrolled as a
student there.[13] A joint ordination ceremony on May
24, 1823, with the Archbishop of Paris, Monseigneur
de Quelen officiating, included the candidates from
Picpus college, conducted by the Fathers of the
Sacred Hearts of Jesus and Mary. The record of that
college[14] includes his matriculation there in August,
1820 under the name "Terentius MacDonoghy," and the
certificatees of tonsure, sub-diaconate, diaconate
and priesthood, preserved in the Congregation's archives all bear that name.[15]

Ordained on May 24, 1823, the young priest was
assigned to the parish of St. Etienne, where he
served for a year as curate. Then, leaving Paris on
May 18, 1824, he sailed for America, though meanwhile
he probably toured the continent, for he did not
reach New York until August 18. That he did not return to Ireland for a home visit we learn from recollections of his sister Jane, who told of their
mother's grief that she would never see her son at
the altar. Since his widowed mother had met his expenses during his years of study,[16] his omission of a
home visit after his ordination seems doubly regret-
table.

Meantime great things had happened in the life of
Dean Conwell. Having served as vicar general of the
Armagh archdiocese for twenty-five years, he expected
to succeed to the see on the death in 1819 of Archbishop O'Reilly. However, the other three archbishops - of Tuam, Cashel and Dublin - petitioned
Rome for the appointment of Dr. Patrick Curtis president of the University of Salamanca, where they had
made their priestly studies. Rome acceded to their
wishes, offering Conwell, instead of Armagh, a choice
between the bishoprics of Philadelphia and Madras,
India. After some hesitation, he chose the former.
We read that "Dr. Conwell's appointment to Philadelphia was made against the protests of his own diocese
as well as to the consternation of Archbishop Curtis
of Armagh, who wrote on February 14, 1820, to Argenti,
Secretary of Propaganda, that he was 'persuaded that
the thing was almost as impossible to believe as that
he had been made Emperor of China.'"[17]

Nonetheless, Conwell, at the age of seventy-two was consecrated in London on Sunday, September 24, 1820, by Bishop Poynter, and some weeks later he started for Philadelphia, arriving there on Saturday December 2, 1820, in company with a nephew, Bernard Keenan, and at least one niece, "to rule over his palace." Keenan, who had been a student, then a teacher, in the Dungannon Protestant College, was raised by his uncle to the priesthood on January 1, 1821, in the first ordination ceremony in the Philadelphia diocese.[18] It was a new world for the elderly Conwell, in more ways than he could have anticipated. All his years of ruling the petty kingdom of an Irish pastorate and in hopeful contemplation of an absentee overlordship - for the Archbishop of Armagh did not make Armagh his place of residence until 1870 -[19] had ill prepared him for what lay ahead.

The previous May there had arrived in Philadelphia from New York a handsome young Irish priest of engaging manner, the Reverend William Hogan. His only credential was a letter of introduction from the Bishop of Limerick who, as it developed later, had taken that means of freeing himself and his diocese of an undesirable cleric. The diocese of Philadelphia had been under the direction of an administrator, the Reverend Louis de Barth, for the previous six years, following the premature death, in 1814, of Philadelphia's first bishop, the Right Reverend Michael Egan, OSF. Three successive appointees had refused to accept the assignment, involving as it did taking up Egan's battle with the entrenched trustees of St. Mary's, the cathedral church. The chief protegé of the trustees was the Reverend William Vincent Harold, OP, an able and well-educated man and an excellent speaker, but proud and assertive. The Woodstock Letters give us a survey of the situation:

> Until 1800, the Catholics of Philadelphia, with the exception of a few families, the Hayes, Careys, Ealings, Meades, Barrys, Fitzsimmons, Moylans, O'Bryans, Powells, Keefes, were not only poor, but exceedingly humble as to their social standing. During the first decade of the century, many of them had been very successful in commerce and in mercantile. pursuits, and with the acquisition of wealth, put on the airs of the parvenu. One of their greatest ambitions was to associate with the aristocratic members of the 'State Church.' These new-made ladies and gentlemen, who

thought our Divine Saviour was not up to the
age when He said, "No servant can serve two
masters," . . . called for a fine preacher.
Now Father Harold was a fine preacher...They
complained most bitterly of the lack of eloquence among the clergy, and as far as this
was concerned there was cause for complaint.
Father Hurley was brusque and unpolished.
Father O'Connell, OSA, was prolific and dry,
and Father Rossitor said, "Say your prayers,
tell no lies, mind your own business, let's
go on with the Mass . . . "[20]

The support of Harold's uncle, the Reverend James
Harold,[21] lately arrived from Australia, encouraged
the young man in his spirit of insubordination. After
a protracted struggle, the Harolds went back to Ireland, the younger in time becoming prior of the
Dominican house at Lisbon, Portugal. However, the
trustees continued to press for his return to Philadelphia, this time as their bishop.

The leaders in St. Mary parish[22] took themselves
and their rights seriously. The republicanism exercised by their Protestant neighbors in their church
government seemed to them much more suited to American Catholics than the antiquated hierarchical structure. Then too the law of the land would not recognize the right of a church as such to operate as a
corporation, for we read in the Catholic Historical
Review that

Protestant tradition of post-Reformation English law which refused to consider the Church
as a corporation and would incorporate only
specific groups of churchmen, conferred upon
the congregation and trustees broad electoral
and administrative powers which, if strictly
interpreted, could completely upset Catholic
hierarchical authority and the canon law of
administration.[23]

The board of trustees constituted the corporation
administering St. Mary's church properties, and of
this board it was required that the majority be laymen. The parvenus believed that if their church were
to continue as the élite church of the city, the pastor must have an attractive personality and be a better than ordinary speaker. The handsome Hogan met
both requisites, and when the trustees found him to
their liking, Father de Barth, the administrator, did
not stand in their way. A social favorite, Hogan was

soon enjoying his popularity, especially among
the ladies of the parish, and chose to free himself
from the restraints of rectory living, to the annoyance and chagrin of the other pastors of the city.
Some inkling of the situation had reached Conwell before he left Ireland, but he was scarcely prepared
for the tirade the young priest delivered against
Father de Barth in his sermon on the very Sunday of
Conwell's installation. When this was followed on
the next Sunday by remarks insulting to Conwell himself, the bishop rebuked Hogan for his attack on de
Barth and told him that he had had reports of his own
scandalous conduct. Hogan's answer was an open defi-
ance of the Bishop, uttered from the pulpit the following Sunday.[24]

In the light of his insubordinate attitude and
unclerical deportment, the Bishop withdrew the young
priest's faculties and began an investigation of his
status. As might be expected, the trustees were up
in arms, and there followed two years of bitter and
acrimonious struggle, with Hogan defying not only the
denial of faculties but the excommunication that had
followed, and continuing to function in the cathedral
church. Years later, Mark A. Frenaye was to write to
Bishop Kenrick:

> . . . at St. Mary's they tore down all epis-
> copal insignia, and never replaced them; . . .
> it is only since a short time that these
> Trustees called it a cathedral. Before you,
> Right Rev. Sir, they hated the title of Cath-
> edral; and, aware that a bishop was too
> strong for them they would say: "Let him go
> where he pleases, we do not want him, only
> let us have a good preacher."[25]

The Bishop and his loyal congregation were forced
meanwhile to retire to St. Joseph church, which was
enlarged to accommodate them.

The hapless Conwell, thinking to divide the allegiance of the trustees by returning to them their
former favorite, sent to Lisbon for the Reverend
William Harold, OP. The plan failed of its purpose,
though it must be said that Harold, on his return to
Philadelphia, worked hard to sustain the position of
the Bishop. Eventually, after much scandal and many
disorders, even to the public distribution of sala-
cious pamphlets and to violence within the very
church itself - all to the satisfaction of a large
Protestant audience - Hogan resigned on August 28,
1823, to the relief even of the trustees. Meanwhile

a brief of Pius VII had rebuked Hogan and his followers and had reminded the trustees of the limits of
their rights and functions, an action held by Protestant onlookers as proof that the Pope was a threat to
American republicanism.

Successive elections had brought into the board
of trustees of St. Mary's men who were no longer
practicing Catholics and who had lost all loyalty to
the Church. In their efforts to force the clergy off
the board, they had appealed even to the supreme
court of the state. Their guilt in the schism was
greater than Hogan's for, when the recalcitrant priest
had at times been ready to submit, they compelled him
to their will again.[26] Finally when the strange
choices they made of successors to Hogan failed them,
St. Mary's was left without a pastor.[27]

Such was the state of affairs in the City of
Brotherly Love when the newly-ordained Terence
MacDonoghy[28] (later, Donaghoe) arrived there in the
fall of 1824. The welcome extended by the harrassed
Bishop must have been a warm one, for his need for
support was very great. Yet even that need was over-
ridden by an urgent call for a priest at Crystal Lake,
in Susquehannah County. Given that assignment by
Bishop Conwell, Father Donaghoe took an early stagecoach to his first parish. Many difficulties attended his short stay there, and in 1825 he was transferred to Reading, much nearer to Philadelphia and
just thirty miles from Lancaster, where his friend
and fellow-priest from Tyrone, Bernard Keenan, was
stationed.

While it was certainly a long way around, before
taking up his new assignment he paid a visit to his
friend John Hughes at the Sulpician seminary at Emmitsburg, Maryland. There was much to review in that
visit. Three years had passed after the Hughes family had moved to America before John had realized his
dream of study at St. Mary's, for the Seminary was as
poor as the Hughes', and not until 1819, when it
needed a gardener, was the young man able to gain ad-
mittance. His earlier years of study then had their
reward, for he was soon relieved of his duties in
the garden, including the supervision of the seminary's two slave-hands, to be admitted to the classroom, both as a student and a teacher. As the latter, he had the Irish schoolmaster's faith in the
birch and the rule, though his students preferred
these to his verbal castigations. The young cleric

53

Bishop Henry Conwell

Reverend John Hughes

Bishop F.P. Kenrick

had much to say of Dr. Dubois, the president of the
struggling institution, and of the scholarly Father
Bruté,his theology teacher. Sharing with his friend
the satisfactions that were his as the acknowledged
college orator, he spoke proudly of the respect paid
him by his professors, and of the position he held
for a time as chief-prefect of discipline. He wasn't
at all sure that things had gone better when his superiors preferred a milder system of discipline. A well-
worn path led down the "Mountain" to the struggling
St. Joseph convent and academy conducted by the
daughters of Mother Seton. From her earliest beginnings Elizabeth Seton had sought direction from the
rector of the seminary, the Reverend John Dubois, and
the pattern became established that the little Community would look for guidance to a Sulpician Father
from the Seminary. It is altogether likely, then,
that the two friends paid a visit to the Sisters, and
prayed beside the grave of their saintly Mother.

It must have been very shortly after the Emmitsburg visit that Bishop Conwell conferred the diaconate on the young Hughes, and took him as companion on
a visitation of the diocese. To save himself the fa-
tigue of preaching, the Bishop assigned that duty to
the young deacon. Having as yet but one sermon prepared, Hughes preached it at each successive station-
his "cuckoo sermon" as the Bishop called it. This
tour of duty gave Hughes his first challenge to religious controversy and to this he responded with alacrity.

Meantime, Father Donaghoe was having an unhappy
time of it with his German congregation at Reading.
Some light is thrown on his troubles in a letter addressed to Bishop Conwell by an over-zealous parishoner. It bears the date of April 18, 1826.
Alas! poor Reading has also shown her cloven
feet - she is running after the way of Balaam
. . . she will not that Christ and his successors shall reign over them.

Since Mr. Donaghoe has resided here who it is
confessed by all has shown the most exemplary pattern of conduct, they have done nothing but cabal and intrigue amongst themselves to have him sent off and that too by the
meanest and most diabolical means, merely because they had a head to rule them and to order and regulate the church, and not suffer
Algier and his class to usurp authority and

> put the income in their purses - for having
> during the last year filched at least 200
> dollars in rent and speculation . . . and yet
> Mr. Donahoe has not received one cent from
> them.[30]

Father Donaghoe was back in Philadelphia by April 26,
1826, for his name appears as witness in the marriage
register of St. Joseph church there on that date.

Meantime, Conwell's troubles with the trustees had
continued. To defeat their claims to the ownership
of St. Mary Church and graveyard, he appealed to
Father Francis Neale, S.J., who held the deed of the
property from the days when the Jesuits had served
both St. Joseph's and St. Mary's. After Conwell fulfilled the legal requirement of naturalization, the
title was secured to him as bishop and pastor.

The principal source of contention between Bishop
and trustees had been their claim to control over the
appointment of the pastors and clergy of St. Mary's
church. Conwell's determination to maintain his position as chief pastor was a bone of contention throughout the years of the schism. Now, with no pastor to
serve their church, the trustees professed their willingness to compromise, and their desire for peace.
The Bishop had up to that time held out firmly, even
obstinately, against any compromise, and even in the
face of the trustees' threat to set up an independent
church. After a succession of meetings, however, a
contract was drawn up and signed by Conwell and the
trustees on October 9, 1826. In it the aged Bishop
surrendered all that he had so long fought for.
While the tone of the document itself was concilia-
tory, the protest of the trustees annexed to the contract in the minutes of the corporation negated its
conditions:

> The Trustees of St. Mary's Church do hereby
> declare that nothing in the preceding agree-
> ment shall be construed or intended to mean
> under any shape or form, a relinquishment or
> abandonment by them of what they consider
> their inherent rights of Presentation; i.e.,
> the right to propose names for pastor and re-
> view appointments of clergy made by the bish-
> op. On the contrary, they declare that the
> preceding agreement has been entered into by
> them solely to restore peace, and with a view
> to enable them to prosecute more effica-
> ciously their claim to the right of Presenta-
> tion practiced in all other countries. . .[31]

The second condition of their protest declared
that no future bishop could in his own right name himself pastor of St. Mary's though they would now con-
cede that office to Conwell. The third condition expressed their determination to press Rome for a de-
cree against any future bishop's being appointed without the approbation and recommendation of the clergy
of the diocese.[32] When word reached Rome of Conwell's
contract with the trustees, the Cardinals, in special
session, "altogether reprobated " his action, with
the Holy Father, Leo XII, concurring, and it was intimated in a communication to the Bishop that his retirement to Ireland would be gratifying.[33]

Meanwhile, on October 15, Conwell had ordained
John Hughes to the priesthood. Brief assignments to
St. Augustine's, Philadelphia, and to the mountainous
regions of Bedford followed. The time was not so
short, however, as to prevent Hughes' exercise of his
polemic powers against Lutheran and Calvinist settlers
at Bedford. On January 27, 1827, Conwell recalled him
to St. Joseph's and showed his predilection for the
newly-ordained priest by making him his assistant.
Further evidence of his regard is shown in the following incident, which seems to have occurred late in
1827. In that period there were three priests ac-
tively engaged at St. Joseph's - Hughes, Donaghoe,
and O'Reilly.

> Mr. Hughes was only a curate at this time.
> The senior priest, a rather dull man, took it
> into his head one day that the revenues of
> the church were not fairly divided; the three
> clergymen who composed the Bishop's household
> drew , as necessity required, from a common
> purse, "whereby," said he, "the curates get
> as much as their elders." So the Bishop and
> the three priests came together, and Father
> _____ exposed his grievance, proposing
> that the Bishop should allot a fixed salary.
> "To be sure I will," cried Dr. Conwell,"and
> I'll give Hughes twice as much as the rest of
> you. It's he that draws all the people.
> He's the only one of you that can preach de-
> cently." The question of fixed salaries was
> not mooted again, and matters remained on
> their old footing.[34]

Following the Bishop's contract with the trustees,
St. Mary's was reopened, with Harold its pastor and
Rev. Thomas Heyden his assistant. Services were re-
sumed on November 5. But peace was not to continue

Interior of St. Joseph Church until 1838.

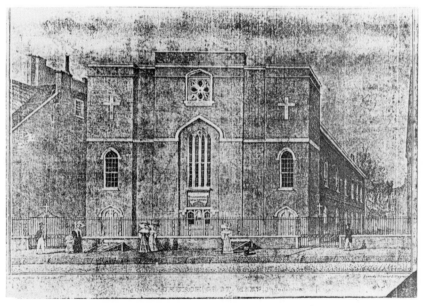

St. Mary Church in 1835. To the left is St. Charles
Seminary and the residence of Bishop Kenrick

long, and now certainly the Bishop's conduct and disposition were the most efficient causes of the strife.
The old prelate's mind "may have partially at least
given way under the strain. Whereas he had before
suspected his best friends of insincerity and disloyalty, from the date of the signature of the agreement
of October, 1826, he seemed to have suspected everybody." Looking on all as plotting against him, he
"struck out blindly against all, speaking or acting
offensively against them all without apparent cause
or motive," so that "Father Hughes seems to have been
justified when he spoke of those 'who hate the Bishop'
as having been nearly all Philadelphia."35 The one
against whom he struck out hardest was Harold, who
had been his most eloquent defender. He was now determined to take away Harold's faculties, but did not
desire the odium for such action, as Hughes' apologia,
written on May 7, 1827, to the Reverend Simon Bruté,
his apiritual mentor, indicates:

> . . . Some who think themselves his
> [Conwell's] friends wished to make tools of
> us to screen him from odium, and make us en-
> listed in his measures. For this purpose a
> paper was drawn up charging Mr. Harold with
> arrogance and domineering, &c, &c., I refused
> to sign it on any conditions whatever on the
> principle that I had nothing to do with the
> matter. It was then proposed whether the Bish-
> op had a right to ask the opinion of his
> clergy. I could not deny it. On Sunday I
> received a message requesting, or rather com-
> manding, me to attend a meeting of him and
> his clergy at St. Augustine's in the after-
> noon. I did attend when a milder form was
> presented in the words: "Resolved that in
> consequence of the very reprehensible conduct
> of Rev. Mr. Harold to his Bishop for sometime
> past we do not conceive that the Bishop would
> act improperly or uncanonically were he to
> refuse to continue Mr. Harold's faculties.
> Such is our opinion. Signed...."

But even this I refused to sign until I was
assured solemnly that this paper was never to
leave the Bishop's desk unless it would be
necessary to show his Superiors. When behold
the next thing I heard was that we had clubbed
together in a conspiracy against Mr. Harold,
and next to that, the sheriff. It seems that
the paper with several remarks on the merits
of the case had been sent to the clergymen at

a distance; some signed it, others did not.
But Mr. Dwenn gave it into the hands of Mr.
Harold and hence the lawsuit.*
Hughes adds further:
> My heart is almost breaking at the prostra-
> tion of religion in this city. . . and on ac-
> count of that Mr. Cumminsky and Mr. Harold
> are removed from the discharge of the minis-
> try, while Mr. Heyden has gone, I fear, not
> to return. The substitutes are poor - Mr.
> Donahue and Mr. Riley and Mr. Baxter and my-
> self; and to crown all, the congregation at
> St. Joseph's which was doing well is much ex-
> cited at my removal. I have been sent to St.
> Mary's.36

One of the signers of the "paper" was "Mr. Donough,"
one of a number of spellings Father Donaghoe then
made use of.

Neither Hughes nor the newly ordained O'Reilly
[Riley], who had been appointed to St. Mary's with
him, found it possible to work with the trustees, and
the two priests soon withdrew to St. Joseph's. At
this juncture, the Bishop reappointed Harold, and
with him his uncle, Father Ryan, a fellow Dominican,
who had come up from Baltimore to support his cause.37

It required three requests from Rome to secure
from Conwell the full account of his agreement with
the trustees, and two "invitations" to induce him to
go to Rome. The Reverend William Mathews, a Washington, D.C. pastor, was assigned the administration of
the diocese in his absence. In the communication from
Cardinal Cappellari, Harold and Ryan were directed to
report to the Dominican House in Cincinnati, an order
which they chose to regard as a violation of their
right as U.S. citizens to live where they wished.38
In support of their claim they appealed to President
Adams through the Secretary of State, Henry Clay,
creating a situation which caused embarrassment to
officials of both Church and State. In the end,
after long correspondence, they left for Ireland. Of
those days, Harold was to write much later to a friend:
"If I could only cancel those unfortunate days, or
make proper reparation! How my heart bleeds and my
cheeks crimson when I think of them!" 39

---

* While Harold did enter suit against Hughes,
the case was later dropped.

On July 15, 1828, Conwell set sail for Rome,
where he would remain over a year, and where he would
be accorded every courtesy. His formal surrender of
administration into the hands of the Reverend William
Mathews of Washington, D. C., was witnessed by John
Hughes, pastor of St. Joseph church, and Terence Donaghoe, his curate. The repudiation of the Conwell-
Trustees contract by Rome and the withdrawal of faculties from Harold left St. Mary church still in the
state of schism and without a pastor. The departure
of the confused and troubled old Bishop to render his
account to the highest ecclesiastical tribunal could
only have been a moment of deep sadness to the two
young clerics at St. Joseph's, as his return, dispossessed of his faculties, must have been one of equal
dismay.

The diocese was to be left for two years without
a bishop. For Hughes, as pastor, they were busy
years. Under his encouragement a meeting at the home
of Mrs. Nicholas Donnelly, the former Anne Conwell,
niece of Bishop Conwell, resulted in the organization
of a society for the support of orphans, which made
possible his founding, in 1829, the St. John Orphan
Asylum. In the same year he opened a free school on
Prune street. Both institutions were staffed by the
Sisters of Charity of Emmitsburg.

Communication of the Roman Propaganda with the
aged Conwell does not seem to have been satisfactory.
It was planned that he would go to France or England
to await orders, but the death of Leo XII left the
matter unsettled. He had been strictly forbidden,
however, to return to Philadelphia under penalty of
losing his episcopal faculties, and had been assured
a pension if he would remain in Europe.[40] By the
time Cardinal Caparelli, now Pius VIII, took possession of St. John Lateran as his cathedral, on May 14,
1829, Conwell had left the city for Paris, for he
feared to be detained by the Congregation of Propaganda. Word had reached him of the call for the
First Provincial Council of Baltimore, to be convened
in October, and he was determined to be present for
it. However, upon his arrival in Baltimore he was
denied a seat in the Council, for Father Mathews, as
administrator, had been empowered to represent the
diocese.

To the bishops assembled, Conwell seemed a piti-
able old man with very few years of life left to him
-he was well over eighty. Surely it would do no harm

to let him retain his title and remain in a degree of comfort in the Willing's Alley rectory, which had long served the clergy of both St. Mary's and St. Joseph's. And so, in a communication from the Archbishop of Baltimore, dated April 29, 1930, the announcement came that "His Holiness has restored to his grace and favor the Bishop of Philadelphia, and forgives his act, done last year . . ." It further indicated that, while the Council's choice of Francis P. Kenrick as coadjutor had been confirmed by Rome, the "honor, dignity and reputation of Dr. Conwell are consulted, the administration to be carried on as if it were spontaneously given by Dr. Conwell, who may solemnly officiate, give confirmation in public or private, confer orders on those whom Dr. Kenrick shall approve." Archbishop Whitfield added: "It would be well to keep secret (but I fear it is already known from Washington) that Dr. Kenrick's administration and jurisdiction derives from Propaganda."* [41]

While this settlement of Bishop Conwell's case left him, practically speaking, a bishop only in name, [42] Kenrick, who was made his coadjutor and administrator of the diocese, had a fixed determination to treat the aged Bishop with every consideration that circumstances would permit. Conwell, on his part, wrote to Archbishop Whitfield on May 15, 1830: "If left alone I am very sure that he and I will agree in everything, for instead of controlling him, I shall be his friend on every occasion and support his rights and dignity as he will mine." [43]

But it was going to be more than the old Bishop could accept in practice that "the boy" should be exclusively invested by the Apostolic See with Episcopal jurisdiction for the government of the Diocese of Philadelphia, for, as Conwell's biographer tells us, the unpopularity of Conwell and his peculiarities of character stood in the way of his good intentions, as he was very suspicious, jealous of his dignity, and obstinate in his views. "He had given evidence of these traits very often in the ten years of his episcopate, and began to manifest them toward Kenrick even before the latter's consecration." [44]

---

* The term "Propaganda" refers to a committee of cardinals constituting the Congregation for the Propagation of the Faith, with jurisdiction over the appointment of bishops.

Perhaps no other member of the American hierarchy
was to have so great an influence on diocesan organization or on the intellectual formation of the clergy
as Francis Patrick Kenrick. He would be advanced to
the archbishopric of Baltimore in 1851, while his
younger brother, Peter Richard Kenrick, first consecrated as coadjutor to Bishop Rosati of St. Louis in
1841, was to be raised to the rank of archbishop in
1848. That the two sons of a simple Dublin family
would have been chosen to rule two archdioceses was
truly remarkable.

The Kenrick family lived in the southern and
older part of Dublin, at 16 Chancery lane, within the
boundaries of St. Nicholas of Myra parish, where the
boys' uncle, the Reverend Richard Kenrick - sometimes
referred to for his charity as the St. Vincent de Paul
of Ireland - was pastor. His father, Thomas Kenrick,
kept a scrivener's shop, and Frank worked there beside his father.[45] Born December 3, 1796, Frank seems
to have been the only child - at least the only one
who survived - until the birth on August 17, 1806, of
a brother Peter, future Archbishop of St. Louis. The
father's situation indicates a degree of literacy
much above the ordinary in the Ireland of his day.
The mother, Jane Eustace Kenrick, was a pious and gracious woman, well worthy of the regard and solicitude
of her sons. Frank's early education was doubtless
acquired at the Classical and Mercantile Academy conducted by William Browne at 14 Chancery Lane, just
two doors from their home.

The family resources being quite limited, it was
through the interest of their priest-uncle that both
boys found themselves in a position to pursue their
studies for the priesthood. With Dr. Murray coadjutor to the Archbishop, as his sponsor, Frank was able
to secure a burse for study at the College of the
Propaganda in Rome, and there he made full use of
every intellectual and spiritual opportunity. The
years at Propaganda, in the company of men from many
nations, were a broadening experience, and one which
saved the young student from Gallicanism and Jansen-
ism, which infected many seminaries of the time.
Nearness to the heart of the Church during these formative years, and the deep respect he had for the
reigning Pontiff, Pius VII, did much to shape Frank's
ideals and allegiances. "The Holy Father thus became
for Kenrick an example of that practical administrative policy of long-suffering, the policy Kenrick was
to use in later life with a salutary effect on the

Church in Philadelphia."[46]

The death of Kenrick's father in 1817 left him anxious for the needs of his mother and younger brother, but "Mrs. Kenrick's Scrivenery Offices" at 6 York Street carried forward the father's business, and here Peter worked alongside the future Irish poet, James Clarence Mangan, with whom he formed a lifelong friendship.[47] As for Frank, his priest-uncle was quick to sense the anxiety and to reassure him, while supplying his next semester's tuition. Contacts with Nicholas Wiseman, future English cardinal, and with Paul Cullen, destined to be Ireland's first cardinal, were to provide Kenrick with the support of their friendship in later years, though he was not to share the arbitrary and aggressive spirit of Cullen, or the inconstancy toward his fellow clerics which Wiseman manifested toward the scholarly convert, John Henry Newman.

The Veto Question[48] was critical for the Irish Church during Kenrick's years of study, bringing to Rome his patron, Dr. Daniel Murray. Though coadjutor to Dr. Troy, advocate of the veto, Dr. Murray was vigorously opposed to its provisions: to confer on England's king the privilege of vetoing papal appointees of bishops for Ireland, and to agree to the payment of the Catholic clergy by the state, both measures tending to the enslavement of the Irish Church. If these were to be the price of civil emancipation, better a return to the penal days. Many influences, then, led the future bishop to adopt as his motto sentire cum ecclesia, a sentiment well-suited to temper the strong Protestant influence on both clergy and people which he would find in the young republic he was soon to be serving.

A visit to the Propaganda in Rome by the saintly Bishop Flaget of Bardstown awakened in the young Kenrick a strong interest in the Kentucky missions, and after his ordination, April 7, 1821,[49] he went to the "dark and bloody ground" where he was to serve for nine years as instructor in Flaget's seminary and to assist the clergy in their strenuous missionary labors. During his leisure hours he continued to lay the foundation of studies which would make him the foremost theological scholar in the American Church of the nineteenth century.

Flaget was a kind and prudent guide to the young priest, forming him into a true apostle, opening new

fields for his talents, and encouraging him in many
ways. First as confessor and then as director,
Kenrick was associated with the Sisters of Charity of
Nazareth, Kentucky, and in poverty and sacrifice he
shared with the other priests the work of the missions.
During the Church's Jubilee Year of 1826, a heavy
schedule of preaching left him exhausted, and he became a victim of cholera. It was thought for a time
he would not recover, and effects of the illness were
to plague him in later years. Now that his brother
Peter was in the seminary at Maynooth, and the scrivener's office in Dublin was closed, a tender concern
for the needs of his mother was with him even in the
wilderness, and Flaget, from his own slender resources,
proved a father to him in this too. The young Father
Kenrick was then a man of broad experience in pioneer
living and of deep sensibilities when Flaget chose
him as his theologian at the Council of 1829. There
he was assigned the added responsibility of secretary
of the Council sessions.

The Council having proposed the name of Kenrick
for the Diocese of Philadelphia, the aging Flaget
waited with trepidation the arrival of the bulls, and
when they came, wept openly. It was a grieving and
bereft Flaget, then, who, on June 6, 1830, consecrated the young Kenrick, Bishop of Arath and Coadjutor
to the Bishop of Philadelphia, in the Bardstown Cathedral. Conwell presented Kenrick to the consecrating prelates and performed all the offices of the
senior co-consecrator. As the two journeyed together
to Philadelphia, Kenrick wrote to Purcell, then president of Mt. St. Mary College, Emmitsburg: ". . .
you will be glad to hear that Dr. Conwell and myself
are travelling in company uno animo et corde. He pro-
fesses determination to live with me in perfect harmony, and to leave me the free administration of the
diocese. I am on my part resolved to do everything
for his honor, peace and happiness. May God grant
the union of our hearts and all our clergy by divine
Charity."50

But Kenrick's hopes of peace were short-lived.
With Conwell claiming all the perquisites of the see
and of the parish, without regard for the young Bishop, who now carried the full burden of the office,
Kenrick could write that he was "as dependent on Providence as a backwoods missionary."51 His efforts to
secure himself as the principal pastor at St. Mary's
led to open conflict with the trustees. In this he
was also challenged by Conwell, who claimed that

position for himself, and with it the privilege of
sitting on the board of trustees, while he openly con-
sorted with the lay members to secure his wish. In
this situation Kenrick took the decisive action on
April 22, 1831 of closing St. Mary's to divine service. It remained closed until he had made his point.
Compromising on the matter of salary, but determined
on his rights over the appointment of clergy, he re-
opened the church on May 28. It was his last open
clash with the lay trustees.

Meanwhile Conwell "wrote to Rome by every packet,"[52]
suggesting the transfer of his coadjutor and complaining loudly of ill treatment while he maintained,
"I am quietly bearing all these things for the sake
of peace."[53] As Bishop England wrote from Charleston
to Bishop Edward Fenwick of Cincinnati, September 22,
1830,

> In Philadelphia old Conwell plays his part
> like a fox. Your friend Kenrick was a little
> too soon for open action, but I have no doubt
> he will realize all that was expected of him.
> The Archbishop and I met them both at Phila-
> delphia and though we made some progress we
> could not get them to a full understanding as
> to temporalities. I am, however, greatly mis-
> taken if Kenrick will not make Philadelphia
> rise to its proper place, but he is yet a
> little too sanguine in his zeal - time will
> cure all this.[54]

Meanwhile the new Bishop set out for a visit to
his immense and much-neglected diocese. From Potts-
ville on September 6, 1830, he addressed a long and
friendly letter to Father Donaghoe, in which he reas-
sured Father regarding his apparent failure at Reading. A portion of the letter follows:

> My neglect of writing to you from Kentucky
> shall be compensated for by the present
> wherein I mean to give a sketch of the state
> of the Congregation wherein you formerly en-
> countered such difficulties. Several of its
> members anxiously inquired for you, and ex-
> pressed their disappointment at not seeing
> you in my company. I was about to reproach
> myself with not inviting you, but I remem-
> bered that I had doubted whether such an in-
> vitation to the scene of your sufferings
> would be acceptable, and might not appear to
> arise rather from a too great attention to
> the travelling etiquette of Bishops. It will,

however, please you to know that several still cherish your memory in Reading, and would have been happy in seeing you.[55]

On his first visitation, Kenrick fell gravely ill at Chambersburg, and Hughes, his secretary, hearing this, went immediately to his side. Though the Bishop refused to disappoint his people by postponing the scheduled confirmation ceremony, he took his illness seriously enough that on October 2 he wrote a formal document entrusting the temporary rule of the diocese to John Hughes in case of his death.[56] Thus early was the young cleric marked as one suited for episcopal responsibilities.

The life of a pioneer bishop was strenuous even for a young and vigorous man. Roads were few and stage coaches irregular, and not only uncomfortable but hazardous as well. In the Diary of his visitations, Kenrick gives fleeting glimpses of the inconveniences he experienced in seeking out Catholic families and settlements in the wilderness: "seven-mile walk through the forest," " missed the stage, a walk of fifteen miles to Somerset," "through woods by horseback to Sugar Creek," " by stage over night," "no place to preach," "preached in Lutheran church" "in the courthouse" - "in county prison." A second friendly letter addressed to Father Donaghoe, then his diocesan econome, written from Bellefonte on August 15, 1831, gave a graphic account of one of his many hazardous trips:

> On the 8th inst. I proceeded in company of Rev. J. O'Reilly and after 20 miles ride reached Squire McMullen's in Sinking Valley, where we were kindly welcomed by his lady, a pious convert. We were glad to dry and warm ourselves at a fire lighted for the purpose, as we had journeyed in the rain. I reposed most soundly during the night, the travelling in a gig over the rugged roads of Tukihoe having prepared me for the arms of Morpheus. The next day we pursued our journey to this place over roads not much superior. Ruts and rocks and stumps seemed combined for our overthrow, but a kind Providence preserved us from any serious disaster. At one time I was somewhat alarmed by a sudden somerset which my Revd. Charioteer made from the gig to the side of the road nigh a precipice. I immediately sought with some anxiety the reins which escaped from his

grasp, as he lighted on the ground. He dexterously drew in his legs as he lay on the bank, and thus rescued them from the pressure of the wheels, which might otherwise have considerably injured them. On his arising we continued our route, and reached Bellefonte the same evening. . .

It was on his return from this second visitation that Kenrick found he had been evicted from the rectory. The deposed Conwell, in the moments of his first fervor, had urged Kenrick to share with him the "episcopal palace." Being assigned a sleeping room, Kenrick had indicated his need for an office-conference room, which the old Bishop grudgingly yielded. Establishing himself there, Kenrick had replaced the original furnishings with items of his own. However, the day after Kenrick's departure Conwell wrote "it occurred to me to enter my room and to occupy it again under the protection of the civil authorities."[57]

This called for, Conwell added, the removal of Kenrick's belongings to a storage house some distance down the street. "Not long since I notified him [Kenrick] that they were forbidden to act as a priest, under pain of suspension, who did not ask my blessing before preaching the gospel."[58] To the first confrontation, the ouster from his quarters, Kenrick responded by changing his residence, but he met the latter action by issuing an opposing order, in a spirit quite foreign to his ordinary manner of acting. Father Mathews, former administrator of the diocese, in a letter to Bishop Fenwick of Cincinnati, dated September 25, 1831, expressed his reaction to the conduct of each:

> Bishop Conwell is out with his coadjutor, Bishop Kenrick, whom he invited to stay at St. Joseph's house till he procured a house, took possession of his [Bishop Conwell's] room below stairs and excluded the old gentleman. They next disputed about who should give the blessing to the priest who was about to preach. Some of the priests asked blessings of the old and some of the young Bishop, till finally Bishop Kenrick forbade any priest to ask blessing of the old gentleman - this is indeed pitiful, mortifying - as an eminent divine who preached there said - childish! When Bishop Kenrick set out on his visit to some congregations about a month ago, Bishop Conwell retaliated on him, and declared

his coadjutor shall not only not have the
room again, but shall not enter the house on
his return. The house belongs to the
Jesuits, from whom Bishop Conwell had rented
it for one dollar per annum during his life.
All good people are scandalized and grieved
at these transactions of the Bishops, and the
Trustees are delighted at these occurrences.

Although Father Mathews was not in accord with the
actions of either bishop, he had a word of appreciation for Kenrick:

I have the greatest esteem and respect for
Bishop Kenrick and hope he will conciliate
the Senior Bishop.[59]

Meanwhile, however, Kenrick was not neglecting
the real needs of the diocese. The rapid growth of
the city had brought with it the demand for new centers of Catholicity, for the first four Catholic
churches were all in close proximity to one another
in the older portion of the city. During his first
year as Bishop, Kenrick determined on the erection of
a new church which he then hoped might be worthy to
supersede St. Mary's as his cathedral. The site decided upon was Thirteenth street between Market and
and Chestnut. John Hughes was to be its pastor.
Funds were scarce, but $40,000 was advanced by Mark
A. Frenaye,[60] and the church was built. Dedication
of the new St. John the Evangelist church took place
on Passion Sunday, April 8, 1832. Kenrick officiated
with Conwell assisting. It was the last special public ceremony in which the "old Bishop" participated
before the loss of his eyesight.[61]

Kenrick was determined that the church would be
free of trustee control. Since at the time of the
land purchase he was not yet naturalized, the title
for it was vested in John Hughes as pastor. After
his naturalization on June 29, 1831, however, Kenrick
made it a regulation of the diocese that title to all
ecclesiastical property must rest with the ordinary.
This regulation applied to the new church structure.

The new pastor hoped that the sermon preached on
the occasion of the dedication would move to a spirit of generosity many of the wealthy Protestants he
had invited. The Reverend John Power of New York
blasted his hopes by delivering a highly polemic discourse on the four marks of the Church. The end result of this was to be the Breckenridge-Hughes controversy, and it was this which would launch John

Terence James Donaghoe

Hughes on a public career and become a remote cause
of his advancement to episcopal honors. [62]

John Breckenridge was a Presbyterian divine of high
standing when he issued his challenge to any Catholic
priest or bishop to meet him in religious controversy. Against the judgment of both Kenrick and
Bruté, Hughes accepted the challenge. Bruté, nonetheless responded to his call for help, as did the
erudite Peter Kenney, S.J., and, it is said, the Reverend Terence J. Donaghoe. [63] Since the controversy
was to be conducted through the press, a diocesan paper became a necessity, and with the blessing of the
Bishop, the first issue of the Catholic Herald appeared January 8, 1833. [64] The controversy continued
until September, 1833, when Breckenridge had occasion
to leave the city, but by this time Hughes had proven
himself greatly superior to his adversary in sound
argument. [65] However, like most controversies, it
abounded in personalities and recriminations, for his
share in which Father Hughes afterwards expressed regret. [66]

With the inauguration of the new St. John the
Evangelist parish, there was need for schools. Opening a small academy for boys, Hughes met the need for
the education of the girls by taking with him to his
new parish the small staff of Emitsburg Sisters who
had served his Prune Street school. An account in
the Emmitsburg archives tells us that Father Donaghoe,
having been assistant to Father Hughes, succeeded him
as pastor at St. Joseph's and as such wanted to retain a free school at the Prune street address. He
went promptly to Emmitsburg to solicit teachers and
would not depart without a promise. The Sisters' St.
Joseph Academy was flourishing at the time and teachers were at a premium, but four Sisters were finally
appointed for the Sacred Heart school at the Prune
street location. Among these was "a Sister but fresh
from the academy and sent along by Father Hickey to
teach and 'to see the world.'" Then "Mother Augustine
and the Council named Sister Ann Gruber, 'who was a
dear soul but never knew anything about teaching.'"
The account continues:

> The first week every seat was filled. Many
> offered to pay for their children's tuition.
> Sister Olympia, who had been a teacher in the
> world before she came to the Community, had
> over one hundred little boys between six and
> ten years of age. Father Donaghoe was
> charmed with her good order and management.

> Sister Aloysia had over one hundred large
> girls, and Sister Rosina [the aspirant] a
> class of about the same number of smaller
> ones. Sister Ann a class of A B C's.
> This school disappears from our list of
> establishments in 1837.

Meanwhile, however,

> . . . everything went prosperously. The Sis-
> ters never knew what it was to want, the peo-
> ple were so generous. Every once in a while
> Father Donaghoe would ask the young Rose, "Do
> the Sisters have enough to eat?" "Oh, yes,
> Father! - but if we had a little ham!" And
> ham would surely come. "But," adds Sister
> Rosina,"the Sisters never knew why the hams
> were always coming."

It was to this institution that Bishop Kenrick referred in a long and friendly letter to Father
Donaghoe, written from Pittsburgh, November 19, 1832,
in which he said: "I have reason to regret my absence from the City when sixty-two innocents approach
for the first time the divine table; but duty called
me to other places where, amidst less gratifying
scenes, I was still favored with many unmerited con-
solations."

Since his school could provide for only a portion
of the Catholic children, many of whom were compelled
by necessity to work in factories,[67] Father Donaghoe,
in an effort to have these children instructed, at
least in the truths of their faith, chose five young
men, members of his choir, as teachers. After a
three months' course of instruction, he opened a Sunday school in a room on Prune street between Fifth and
Sixth, where a Mr. Boylan kept a school for boys. By
the third Sunday the attendance had grown so large
that classes were moved to St. Joseph church. Later
when Father was made pastor of St. Michael's his Sunday school faculty went with him, serving there until
Mary Frances Clarke and her companions could take up
the work. John E. Norman,[68] one of the young men,
was to have many later contacts with Father Donaghoe
and the Sisters.

But through it all Kenrick's problem with his
aged predecessor continued. Complaining "that he had
been deprived of the juridical power over 'his diocese,'" Conwell endeavored to intimidate Propaganda
by suggesting that he still had the civil courts of
Pennsylvania as a refuge in case it was necessary to
assert his prior rights over the young bishop."[69]

And in this there was truth, for, having been permitted to retain his title of Bishop of Philadelphia, he
would be so recognized by law. His frequent references to "his friend, President Jackson" were them -
selves implied threats. Yet "the old Bishop . . .
was surrounded by those who faithfully clung to him
in his struggles, overlooking minor mistakes in the
feeling of the duty they owed his position . . . .
They were willing to submit to the new administrator,
but little enthusiasm could be expected while the old
man, around whom they had rallied, was in their midst,
dissatisfied and complaining."[70]

A major financial problem presented itself to
Kenrick, for Conwell, still holding the title of Bishop of Philadelphia, was able to procure the grants of
money allotted to the diocese by the three European
missionary aid societies, and to solicit funds on his
title in England and Ireland. "In fairness to the
aged bishop," Kenrick's biographer tells us, "it must
be said that there is no evidence that he ever misap-
propriated funds so acquired."[71]

It was not until September 17, 1831, that a brief
from the Holy Father gave Kenrick permission to publish throughout the diocese that all jurisdiction had
been entrusted to him alone.[72] His authority having
been established with the trustees, Kenrick determined now to set up norms for the conduct of affairs
in the diocese, calling a synod for which he had been
preparing for the previous two years. It convened
May 13, 1832, with John Hughes as secretary. The
nineteen statutes proposed by the Bishop, embodying
modifications suggested by free discussion, were
adopted and promulgated, laying the cornerstone of
ecclesiastical discipline in the diocese. The eighteenth statute dealing as it does, with religious
women in the diocese, especially concerns us:
> That undertakings begun rashly may not end in
> failure, we decree that in the future no or-
> phan asylum, or school, under the care of the
> Sisters of Charity, or of other Virgins dedi-
> cated to God, be established in this diocese
> without Our previous written permission, with
> due regard, however, to the privileges of
> Regulars.[73]

The need for such a regulation had been brought
home to Kenrick by an unpleasant situation he had experienced shortly before. Two French-speaking "reli-
geuses, Les Dames de la Retraite,"[74] had prevailed

Map of Old Philadelphia

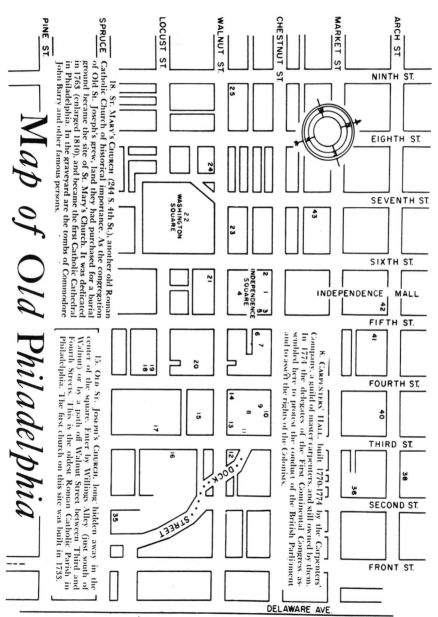

18. St. Mary's Church (244 S. 4th St.), another old Roman Catholic Church of historical importance. As the congregation of Old St. Joseph's grew, land they had purchased for a burial ground became the site of St. Mary's Church. It was dedicated in 1763 (enlarged 1810), and became the first Catholic Cathedral in Philadelphia. In the graveyard are the tombs of Commodore John Barry and other famous persons.

8. Carpenters' Hall, built 1770-1774 by the Carpenters' Company, a guild of master carpenters, and still owned by them. In 1774 the delegates of the First Continental Congress assembled here to protest the conduct of the British Parliament and to assert the rights of the Colonies.

15. Old St. Joseph's Church, long hidden away in the center of the square. Enter by Willings Alley (just south of Walnut) or by a path off Walnut Street between Third and Fourth Streets. This is the oldest Roman Catholic Parish in Philadelphia. The first church on this site was built in 1733.

PENN'S LANDING PROJECT

DELAWARE AVE.

DELAWARE RIVER

on Bishop Kenrick to finance a select academy for
young ladies in the so-called Gothic Mansion, an ar-
chitectural monstrosity which came later to serve as
an orphanage. After publishing their venture in the
Catholic Directory and Almanac, for circulation in
1833, they shortly took 'French leave,' much to the
Bishop's inconvenience and chagrin.

Despite straitened circumstances, Kenrick's next
venture was the establishment of a seminary. Having
for peace' sake removed himself from the St. Mary
rectory, he opened the upper rooms of his house at 92
South Fifth Street to five young church students.
Placed under the patronage of St. Charles Borromeo,
this first seminary was to make several moves before
it would find permanent quarters in its present site
in the suburb of Overbrook.

Bishop Kenrick had urged his brother Peter, even
before his ordination, to come to Philadelphia, but
the latter's concern for their mother led him to remain near her, at Maynooth. Ordained March 6, 1832,
Peter briefly cooperated with his classmates in the
establishment of a secondary school in Dublin, the
initial move toward the founding of the Lazarist Fathers there. His mother died during that summer, and
Peter, knowing the wishes of his elder brother, came
to Philadelphia in 1833, with the blessing of Archbishop Murray. He was soon established as teacher
and director of the St. Charles seminary. To this
responsibility were added those of assistant pastor
at St. Mary's, member of the editorial staff of the
Catholic Herald, and, finally, vicar general to his
brother.

A scourge of cholera struck the city during the
summer of 1832. As the death rate mounted, many fled
in terror to the country, leaving appalling conditions behind them. For fear of contagion, the dead
were left for weeks unburied, and the stricken left
untended.[75] The Bishop's request made of the Sisters
of Charity for assistance met an immediate and heroic
response, thirteen nuns coming at once from Emmitsburg to nurse the sick in the almshouse. The Bishop
himself stayed in the city, visiting the hospitals,
comforting the afflicted, administering the sacraments and preparing many for death.

Father Donaghoe was acting pastor at St. Joseph's
at the time. Mr. J.J.E. Norman, one of his five Sunday School teachers, wrote of him much later:

Few of us will forget the advent of the cholera in Philadelphia in 1831 [sic]. Notwithstanding every precaution, the pestilential
breath of this disease swept into eternity
scores of souls. The ministerial services of
Father Donaghoe were called into requisition
by the very first victim, a man living in
Franklin Place, a street running from Chestnut to Market, between Third and Fourth, and
on the following evening a girl living on
Fourth below Shippen, the writer of this accompanying him to the latter place. From
this out, until the disappearance of the cholera, there was little leisure or relaxation
for him; night and day he was at his post of
duty; a fresh horse and gig stood constantly
ready at the gate in Willing's Alley, and
while a large number of evangelizers and deacons were hiding in the country or in imagin-
ary security, he was ministering to the dying
and despairing, and receiving many into the
true faith who before were bitter in their de-
nunciation of it . . . [76]

There were 2314 cases reported, and of these 785 died
during the three months of the siege.[77] Among the
victims was Dr. Columbus Conwell, nephew of the Bishop and a resident at St. Joseph's. He had been a
Greek scholar of distinction, and one of the most
brilliant writers of his day, a man remarkable too
for his generosity.

Kenrick's concern for a seminary was a measure of
his concern for Catholic education in general, and he
made many efforts, successful and otherwise, toward
securing teaching sisterhoods for a parochial school
system. He was scrupulously careful to assure equi-
table treatment of the Sisters employed, drawing up
contracts which would protect their interests as well
as the interests of the schools involved.[78]

Early in 1832 the Very Reverend Francis
Dzierozynski, S.J., vice-provincial of the Maryland
Province, wrote to Bishop Kenrick, requesting the
return of St. Joseph church and rectory to the Jesuits.
The original St. Joseph church, the first public
place of worship for Catholics in Philadelphia, had
been built by the Reverend Joseph Greaton, S.J., in
1733. At the suppression of the Society of Jesus in
1773, titles to Jesuit properties had been placed in
the hands of individual Jesuits, who then assumed the
status of diocesan clergy. St. Mary's, the daughter

church, built by the Jesuits in 1763, continued to be
their property. But because of its disturbed state,
and because it was still officially Kenrick's cathedral, the Society did not ask for its return. Bishop
Kenrick readily granted the request for St. Joseph's,
asking only that Father Donaghoe's appointment as pastor be respected until his new church of St. Michael,
in the early stages of construction, was ready to receive him. The Jesuit Fathers, Peter Kenney, acting
visitor of the Society in America, and Louis
Dubuisson,[79] took up residence in Willing's Alley in
April, 1833, just one hundred years after its founding by Father Greaton. Father Donaghoe, officially
assigned as pastor to St. Michael's on May 1, took up
his abode in the basement of the partially completed
church, "to the great edification of the Catholics,
not only of Kensington, but of the whole city."[80]

Bishop Conwell was aging rapidly, and in August,
1832, he became blind, and so stricken he never after-
ward celebrated Mass. But the vigor with which he
clung even to the shadow of episcopal power continued
undiminished. No longer able to discharge even the
least of its functions, he laid claim still to its
emoluments. When the Jesuit Fathers took up residence at St. Joseph's, the old Bishop was permitted
to retain his rooms, these being promised to him for
life. There was no move on his part to reduce his
entourage of relatives, a fact which complicated the
lives of the Jesuits, as they tell us:[81]

> The Rt. Rev. Bishop Conwell, with his nephew
> Henry McKeon and an indefinite number of
> nieces remained at St. Joseph's. Our Fath-
> ers, Kenney and Dubuisson, who in October
> were joined by Father James Ryder, were al-
> lowed to have a stove placed in the kitchen,
> where their cook and maid-of-all-work pre-
> pared their meals; they had the use also of
> one of the ground floor rooms, as parlor,
> dining-room and confessional, and of the sac-
> risty and three attics; the rest of the house
> was occupied by my Lord and his numerous
> relatives.

> The good Bishop, from their very arrival,
> treated our Fathers in a kindly manner, but
> his relatives regarded them in the light of
> intruders; and with a view to the purse, gen-
> erally had some one posted near the door, so
> that when a baptism or a marriage arrived, the
> party might be conducted to uncle's room,

where the Sacrament was administered in the most expeditious manner.[82]

The new parish of St. Michael, north of the city, lay in the Kensington-North Liberties area. The church under construction was situated at the southeast corner of Second and Jefferson streets. It was a rapidly growing area, with mills, factories, shipyards, carriage shops, paper mills, iron works, breweries and potteries springing up against a skyline of masts along the Delaware river. All this promised steady employment and a prosperous future. While a considerable portion of the area was being settled by Irish Catholic immigrants, a large part of its population consisted of Irish Protestants with Orange affiliations.

The blessing of the cornerstone of the new church took place on Monday, April 18, 1833, in the presence of a large gathering, Bishop Kenrick officiating. Father Boyle said of the new pastor, T.J. Donaghoe:

He was not a rugged man, not one suited apparently, either in physique or habit, for the kind of duty here demanded of him. There was the fragility of the saint and the scholar about him, an air of refinement which made one associate him with a mellowed civilization. He was in fact a very holy and a very learned man. But, though not of robust build, he was not at all sickly, and like most men of his type had an indomitable spirit, which was capable of astonishing endurance.[83]

Such then was the man from Tyrone, and such the Church in Philadelphia, when the "Dublin ladies" entered upon the scene on September 7, 1833.

Recent snapshot of the gateway type of house in Aughnacloy leased by the Donaghoe family

CHAPTER II - NOTES

1. Sometimes spelled "Donaghy." Later, in Philadelphia, after passing through several other spellings, it became "Donaghoe."

2. Letter, dated October 10, 1972, BVM Archives.

3. Annals of Aughnacloy, p. 23. The writer is indebted to The Annals of Aughnacloy and of the Parish of Carnteel not only for the direct quotation but also for the data contained in the background materials concerning the town of Aughnacloy. The copy used was a xerox of the first 37 pages of this study, but bibliographical data were not included.

4. Data furnished by Ivy Embleton, genealogist, Belfast, in a series of communications with the writer, from the 1825 Tithe Book, Aghaloo Parish.

5. On January 16, 1796, Edward Donaghey leased from Thomas Findlater a house with its outbuildings, yard and gardens, and in February of 1804 signed a lease for a second house, with "Back Houses, Yard and Garden thereunto belonging, and now in his possession," with the provision that he allow free passage through the adjoining gateway to the owner, Robert Miles, and his other tenants. The annual rental of the latter, ₤11.7.6., indicated a substantial property. Registry number 559, p. 271, 110, 373976, Registry of Deeds, King's Inn, Dublin.

6. Our Herald, Vol. IV, p. 14.

7. Rev. Henry A. Brann, D.D., Most Reverend John Hughes, First Archbishop of New York, (New York: Dodd Mead & Co., 1892,) p. 17.

8. Ibid., p. 18.

9. Ibid., p.10.

10. Sister M. Pulcheria McGuire, BVM, Annals (Unpublished), p. 35.

11. Interview, Rev. Louis O'Kane, October 12, 1972.

12. Chronology, Father Donaghoe's handwriting,
    BVM archives.

13. Letter of I. Noye, Library of St. Sulpice Semi-
    nary, Paris, February 21, 1972. The letter
    gives the names of Father Donaghoe's parents as
    Edward MacDonoghy and his wife Suzanna Macrea.
    (His letter, and the official certification of
    tonsure in the BVM archives both have it
    "Mavrea," but the genealogist consulted declares
    that there is no such name in that area, but
    that there were many Macreas or McCreas, and
    conclude that it was a misreading of the letter
    "c.")

14. Letter of R.P. Oswald, Superior of the Fathers
    of the Sacred Hearts, or the Picpus Fathers,
    March 12, 1973. It reads: Je suis vous confir-
    mer que le jeune MacDonaghy se trouvait deja au
    Seminarie des Pères de Picpus, au mois d'aout
    1820. En effect, il est fait mention dans nos
    archives d'une lettre pour lui adressée au Père
    Cummins, Prieur de la maison, en provenance de
    Monseigneur Patrick Curtis, Archeveque d'Armagh.
    La chose n'est past etonnante, car il y a, a
    cette epoque, plusieurs Irlandais, venus simple-
    ment y faire leurs études. Quelques uns sont
    restes dans la Congregation, mais les autres
    sont retournés dans leur diocese d'origine.
    C'est le case, evidement, du Père Terence.

15. English law had long forbidden the prefix "Mac"
    or "O" before Irish names, and it may have been
    in a spirit of national pride that the young man
    chose to restore the name to what he believed to
    have been its ancient form. (Mac) Donaghy is
    given as a variant, in Tyrone and Derry, of
    MacDonagh. (Edward MacLysaght, Irish Surnames,
    p. 72.

16. Sister M. Lambertina Doran, BVM, In the Early
    Days, St. Louis: Herder & Herder, 1911, p.227.
    (This publication will hereafter be referred to
    as Doran, Early Days.

17. Records of the American Catholic Historical Soc-
    iety of Philadelphia, Vol. 38, p. 329,1927.
    (The Records will hereafter be referred to as
    RACHS).

18. Keenan spent the next two years at St. Mary's
    College, Emmitsburg, Maryland, studying and tu-
    toring, until in 1823 he was assigned to St. Mary
    church, Lancaster, Pennsylvania, upon the death
    of its pastor. Here he was to survive several
    admonitions about uncanonical procedures, and
    even Kenrick's threat of dismissal (see original
    letters in Kenrick's Journal of Correspondence)
    from the diocese. He acquired in time, however,
    the status of vicar general and continued as pas-
    tor for the remainder of his 97 years. RACHS,
    "The Catholic Church at Lancaster, Pa.," Vol. V,
    1895, p. 333.

19. Letter, Rev. Francis Lenny, Secretary to the
    Archbishop of Armagh, April 26, 1972,
    BVM Archives.

20. Woodstock Letters, Vol. II, No.3, 1872. p. 180.

21. The Reverend James Harold, Pastor of Kilcullen
    in Ireland, had only recently been freed from
    the penal colony at Botany Bay, Australia. Prior
    to the outbreak of rebellion in 1798, he had
    urged his people to shun disorder and discord.
    During the fighting he had rebuked the yeomanry
    and military for their barbarities, and this won
    him disfavor. He remained concealed in the home
    of a Protestant for some time, but was finally
    taken into custody on his way to say Mass. On
    a writ from Lord Kilwarden, he was detained on
    the prison ship, "Lively," lying in the harbor
    at Cork. After several months of detention, and
    without further trial, he was transported on the
    convict ship "Minerva" to Botany Bay, the first
    priest-convict in Australia. Conditions on such
    ships were appalling, for each was "a floating
    dungeon of disgusting filth." A trip of eight
    months, chained to the deck or in the hold, al-
    lowed only a pint of water a day and wretchedly
    poor, unwholesome food, and without a change of
    clothes, they landed emaciated and vermin-ridden.
    The brutalities to which they were subjected
    there caused many of them to ask for execution
    rather than undergo them. From these Father
    Harold was excused, but only to be forced to
    witness floggings which laid bare the bones and
    entrails of some of the victims. After ten
    years in various prison camps in Australia and
    Tasmania he was given permission to return to
    England. However, stopping at Rio en route, he

changed his course and came to Philadelphia. Cf.
T.J. Kiernan, The Irish Exiles in Australia.
Clonmore & Reynolds, 1954, and "Reverend James
Harold, the Botany Bay Irish Convict Priest of
Philadelphia," RACHS, Vol.   p. 17, et passim,

22. The term "parish" cannot be accurately applied
in a country still having missionary status.

23. "Trusteeism in the Atlantic States, 1785-1863,"
The Catholic Historical Review, Vol. XXX, July,
1944, p. 140.

24. Rev. Eugene F.J. Maier "Matthew Carey, Publicist
and Politician," RACHS, Vol. XXXIX, p. 144,
June, 1928.

25 Frenaye to Kenrick, Dec. 31, 1837, (Kenrick-
Frenaye Correspondence,) (Philadelphia: Catholic Historical Society, 1920.) p. 12.

26. The subsequent career of Hogan was not a happy
one. He reappeared in Philadelphia on July 1,
1824, having preached in a number of Protestant
churches. He offered himself to again serve as
pastor of the St. Mary's congregation if it
would call itself the American Catholic Church,
as he was tired of the doctrine and discipline
of the Roman Catholic Church, which required
celibacy and fasting. His appearance caused
great consternation among the schismatics. After
ordering his second successor, Father O'Meally,
out of his house and bringing judgment against
him for bed and board, he left for Wilmington,
N.C., "accompanied by his servant." There he
married a wealthy widow. After various esca-
pades, including efforts of the government to
deport him, and the marriage to a second rich
widow, he died unreconciled to the Church, having sunk to the level of Maria Monk in his calumnies against her. Cf. Martin Griffin, "Life
of Bishop Conwell," running serially through
RACHS, Vols. XXIII-XXIX, 1914-1918, Vol. 27, 1916
pp. 360-380.

27. Of these successors, the Reverend Angelo Inglesi
was the most conspicuous. The young adventurer,
after a Canadian marriage, had sought ordination
from Bishop Dubourg of New Orleans, with claims
of prior studies interrupted by an auspicious
army career. Bishop Dubourg, much impressed by

the young man, proceeded with his ordination,
contrary to the provisions of canon law. As further proof of his confidence, Dubourg sent him on
a tour of the capitals of Europe to seek funds.
Returning to the States after a supposedly successful venture (during which, however, he had
been ordered out of Rome for unclerical behavior)
he stopped off in Philadelphia and offered his
services for the healing of the schism there.
Harold, as vicar general, refused him faculties
and threatened him with excommunication if he
dared to celebrate in St. Mary church. Hearing
of these many involvements, Bishop Dubourg, in
remorse over his indiscretion in ordaining
Inglesi, resigned his diocese and returned to
France. Cf. F.G. Holweck, "Contribution to the
Inglesi Affair," St. Louis Catholic Historical
Review, Vol. V, 1923, p. 14-39 and Joseph L.J.
Kirlin, Catholicity in Philadelphia from the Ear-
liest Missionaries Down to the Present Time,
John J. McVey, Philadelphia, 1909. p. 238.

28. The spelling of Father Donaghoe's name presents
an interesting study. Ordained under the name
MacDonoghy, he refers in memoranda to his family
under the spellings Donaghey and Donaghy. The
Reverend William J. Boyle, in his history of old
St. Michael's, p. 25, comments that "He seems to
have been uncertain about the correct form of
his name for it is signed differently from time
to time, but he finally settled on Donaghoe."
A study of the Commission of Historical Research
says: "This clergyman seems to have displayed a
rather singular fashion, not, however, so unusual
in former days, of writing his family name. We
have seen his signature frequently thus: 'T.
O'Donoughhoue, then Donoughou, and Donoghoue.'"
We find Margaret McDonogh's daughter, Ann O'Brien,
writing to her son, John O'Brien, then at West
Point, under date of October 25, 1832: "Grandmother, the Bishop and Rev'd Donoghue send a
thousand loves and blessings to you." The present
writer has come upon other forms used in addres-
sing or referring to him, including: Donough,
Donohue, Donahoe, Donaghue, and O'Donoghue.
Real estate records for the family in Ireland
seem confined to Donaghy and Donaghey.

29. Father Donaghoe's Chronology.

30. Original in a scrapbook, <u>Conwell's Letters,</u> Archdiocesan Archives, Philadelphia.

31. Kirlin, pp. 250-251.

32. <u>Ibid.</u>, p. 251.

33. John Gilmary Shea, <u>History of the Church in the United States,</u> (New York: n.p., 1856,) p. 258.

34. J. R.G. Hassard, <u>Life of Most Reverend John Hughes,</u> (New York: D.Appleton Co., 1866,) p.57.

35. Griffin, <u>RACHS,</u> Vol. XXVIII, 1917, p. 245.

36. <u>Ibid.</u>, p. 251.

37. <u>Ibid.</u>, p. 319.

38. <u>Ibid.</u>, p. 335.

39. <u>Woodstock Letters,</u> Vol. XIV, 1874, p. 20.

40. The <u>United States Documents in the Propaganda Fide Archives,</u> first series, Vol. 3, contains the precis of correspondence with reference to Bishop Conwell, under the title "Lettere E Decreti. . . S. Congreg." Precis 2208 reads:
    Prop. Fide to W. Matthews, Philadelphia,1829, September 17, Rome.
        Towards the end of August Bishop Conwell left Paris secretly, and it is very likely that he is on his way to Philadelphia. If this is so, he is acting against the express orders of the Holy See, and in virtue of this present letter Matthews should make it known throughout the diocese that Conwell, by apostolic decree, is ipso facto suspended from the exercise of all episcopal jurisdiction. Matthews should do this "prudenti providaque ratione." In the meantime he is to perform the offices of a vicar general until further notice.

    Précis 2209 reads:
    Prop. Fide to Bishop J. Yorke Bramston, London. 1829, September 19, Rome.
        This letter deals with Bishop Conwell, and the theme of it is similar to that of Letter 2207 supra. If Conwell arrives in London, Bramston should let him know the

instructions given to Matthews in Philadelphia. If, however, Conwell remains in Europe
and gives a written undertaking not to return
to America without the permission of Prop.
Fide, he will be granted an annual pension of
720 scudi.

41. Ibid., p. 171.

42. Ibid., 172.

43. Ibid., p. 173.

44. Ibid., p. 173

45. For biographical details, except as noted, the
writer is indebted to Hugh J. Nolan, The Most
Reverend Francis Patrick Kenrick, Third Bishop
of Philadelphia, 1830-1851, (Philadelphia: American Catholic Historical Society, 1948.)

46. Ibid, p. 19.

47. John McCall, "Jottings on the Kenrick Family,"
RACHS, Vol. IX, 1878, p. 459.

48. The English government sought to have assigned
to the King the right to veto appointments of
the Holy See to bishoprics in Ireland.

49. George E. O'Donnell, St. Charles Seminary,
Overbrook, 1832-1943,)Philadelphia: Jeffries
and Manz, 1943.)

50. Ibid., p.3.

51. Griffin, RACHS, Vol. XXIX, 1918, p. 177.

52. Ibid., 170.

53. Ibid., p. 250.

54. Archives, Notre Dame University. Indexed under
"England," "Fenwick", and "Conwell."

55. BVM ARchives.

56. Nolan, p. 133.

57. Griffin, RACHS, Vol. XXIX, 1918, p. 250. No
address given.

58. Ibid., p. 251.

59. Archives, Notre Dame University, indexed under "Matthews," " Fenwick," and "Conwell."

60. Mark A. Frenaye, a refugee from the French Revolution and later from the slave uprising in San Domingo, became the confidential agent of four bishops. In 1842, a synodal letter issued by Kenrick announced his official appointment as econome of the Philadelphia diocese. In the course of the years he served as confidential agent for Peter Kenrick of St. Louis, Joseph Flaget of Bardstown and John E. Neumann, successor to Kenrick in Philadelphia. From the early 1830's until shortly before his death in 1873, Frenaye lived at St. John Rectory. "Marc Anthony Frenaye," RACHS, Vol. XXXVIII, 1927, p. 135, and Nolan, P. 126 n.

61. Cf. I.J. Griffin, "St John the Evangelist," RACHS, Vol. XX, 1909, p. 364.

62. Cf. Nolan, p. 161.

63. Woodstock Letters, Vol. III, No.1, 1874, pp. 20-21.

64. Several letters which remain, addressed to Father Donaghoe, apply for subscriptions to the Herald, which seems to associate him with its circulation.

65. Cf. Nolan, p. 163.

66. Hassard, p. 143.

67. In 1816, Matthew Carey, an outstanding figure in early Philadelphia and in St. Mary parish,instituted Sunday schools for the teaching of elementary school subjects to the young factory workers, with sessions in morning and afternoon. The long hours that the children worked during the week, however, left them too exhausted for regular attendance and the effort was finally abandoned. (Cf. Lawrence F. Flick, ed., Pioneer Parochial Schools of Philadelphia, "Minute Book of St. Mary's Church, Catholic Historical Society Records, Vol. IV, p. 258.) As a young man, Carey had been sufficiently active in the cause of Irish freedom to have been forced to leave his

native land for France. There he was for a time
in the employ of Benjamin Franklin, continuing to
serve him on his return to Philadelphia. Subsequently setting up his own publishing house in
Philadelphia, Carey was able to list Scott, Dickens, Cooper and Irving as "Carey's authors." The
firm continues today as Lea (Carey's daughter married a Lea) & Feliger, probably the most respected publishers of medical books in the country.
Cf. Nathaniel Burt, The Perenial Philadelphians,
(Boston: Little, Brown & Co., 1963), p. 405.

That Carey's Sunday School project was not the
first of its kind inaugurated in Philadelphia we
learn from What a Modern Catholic Believes About
Women, by Sister Albertus Magnus McGrath (Chicago:
The Thomas More Press, 1972), p. 91. "In 1808, a
group of Philadelphia women got the Superior court
of the State to recognize them as citizens of Pennsylvania. Armed with this legal standing, they
went on to secure a charter of incorporation for
their Union Society, a union of several Protestant
denominations. They took as their work the teaching of poor girls to read, write, sew and memorize
passages from the Bible. They held annual public
exhibitions at which they condicted examinations
and gave prizes, chiefly for biblical knowledge.
Thus humbly began the Sunday School movement."

68. An account of the Norman children is given to us
in the Doran Journal, pp. 64-65: John J. Norman,
his brother Edmund and a young sister were orphans who had learned little of religion. John
appealed to Father Donaghoe for instructions and
was given a catechism with directions to return
when he had it memorized. To Father's surprise
the lad was back in two days. The three children
were eventually baptized. John thought for a time
of entering the priesthood and attended St. Mary
college and seminary in Emmitsburg with that in
mind. However, he did not persevers, but went
west, first to Bardstown, Kentucky, then on to
Dubuque. There Bishop Loras employed him to conduct a school for boys and to play the church
organ. It was through Norman that Bishop Loras
learned of Father Donaghoe and the Sisters.

The Hoffmann account of Loras college gives further information regarding Norman. (pp. 46-47).
Settling in dubuque in 1841, he conducted a school
for boys in the Bishop's house and was Latin
teacher for three young men studying for the
priesthood. His advertisement in the weekly

Miner's Express in the early fall of 1841 refers
to the school as an "English, Classical and Mathematical Academy." indicting that Norman had had
many years' experience as "Disciplinarian and Prefect of Studies in the College of Mt. St. Mary at
Emmetsburgh, Md., Cincinnati, and St. Joseph's at
Bardstown, Ky." In the new school "the various
branches of useful and refined English, Classical
and Mathematical education will be taught with
vocal and instrumental music, and etc.," while
"Ladies or Gentlemen who wish to receive private
lectures will be attended to before or after
school hours. Terms made known on application at
the school or at his residence near the Washington Hotel."

After severing his connection with the Bishop's
school in 1843, Mr. Norman continued his interest
in educational work in Dubuque. The next year he
became the secretary of the newly created Dubuque
school board, and served for many years on the
later established board of education. During the
Civil War period, he became one of the leading
Union Democrats of Iowa. From 1863 to 1873 he
held the office of Dubuque county superintendent
of schools. Norman met his death when he was
thrown from his buggy, on a steep grade near Cascade, Iowa.

A letter in the BVM archives from Mrs. Jacques
Marchais Klauber of Jacques Marchais, Inc., New
York, dated April 25, 1941 and addressed to
Sister M. Lambertina, stated that the father of
the three Norman children was Captain Sir John
Norman of England, organist in the King's
chapel under George III. Sir John was a barrister, but interested also in commerce, owning
ships trading between the Orient and the New
World. The three orphans lived with a half-
brother, Henry Rittenhouse and his wife.

69. Nolan, p. 110.
70. Ibid., p. 130.
71. Ibid., p. 189.
72. Ibid., p. 136.
73. Statutes Drawn up and Promulgated in the First
    Diocesan Synod of Philadelphia on the 15th of
    May, 1832 by Right Reverend Francis Patrick
    Titular Bishop of Arath and Coadjutor of the Right
    Reverend Henry Conwell, Bishop of Philadelphia, and
    Administrator of the Diocese of Philadelphia.
    (Archdiocesan Archives.)

74. Madame Hery du Jarday had been a member of the
    order in France, the house of which had been de-
    stroyed during the Revolution. She was an adven-
    turesome and unstable person and had left her
    community, coming to America in September, 1831.
    In New York she had given the habit to another
    French woman and admitted her to vows, and the
    two had then come on to Philadelphia. Their
    school there, with its high tuition of $300.00 a
    year, failed in less than six months, and the two
    betook themselves to Charleston, N.C. Bishop
    England accepted them on condition of letters
    guaranteeing their rightful standing, but none
    came. On November 27, 1835, he offered a letter
    of recommendation to Madame du Jarday if she
    would leave his diocese,with her community. On
    May 6, 1836, she asked the Archbishop of Bordeaux
    for permission to go there because of the "perse-
    cution of religious orders of women in the
    United States." Receiving no answer, they went
    to St. Augustine. There is no word of them
    thereafter. Cf. Peter Guilday, Life and Times
    of John England, Vol. II, pp. 142, 150.

75. Cf. Nolan, p. 157.

76. J.J.E. Norman and Rev. Doctor Middleton, OSA,
    "The Very Rev. T.J. Donaghoe," RACHS, Vol.
    XXIII, June 12, pp. 69-70.

77. Joseph Jackson, "Catholic Burial Grounds in
    Philadelphia," RACHS, Vol. LVI, 1945, pp78-79.

78. Contract as proposed by Kenrick in connection
    with the establishment of St. Mary parochial
    school:
    "The Board of Trustees entrusts to the Sisters
    of Charity the entire direction and management
    of the School of St. Mary's, reserving to them-
    selves, however, the right of admitting the chil-
    dren; and the Sisters agreeing to receive such
    children as the Trustees shall admit, and the
    Sisters shall be able to instruct. No boy shall
    be admissible after he shall have attained the
    9th year of his age. The Trustees shall be in-
    vited to all the stated Examinations of the
    Children. The house destined for the school
    shall be exclusively devoted to that purpose; no
    room thereof being reserved as a room of deposit
    for any benevolent society, or as a place of
    meeting."

"The Board will hold itself responsible for the annual sum of fifty dollars for each Sister, payable to the Emmitsburg Institution or to any person authorized by the Superior of St. Joseph's to receive it, as an indemnification for the clothes of each Sister.

"As the Sisters are liable to be removed at the direction of the Superiors, the Board is responsible for the travelling expenses of such Sisters as shall from time to time be sent to take charge of the School.

"The Board will exonerate the Sisters from all attention to pecuniary concerns, and all responsibility; and will provide for the Sisters'.support and house expenses, as also pay the Rent of the House. The Board and Sisters shall mutually be at liberty at any time to rescind this agreement on reasonable notice, but shall strictly adhere thereto until it shall be rescinded." Kenrick's handwritten Journal of Correspondence, 1830-51, February 7, 1833, Archdiocesan Archives, Chancery Office, Philadelphia.

A report from the School Committee for the year 1833 indicates that they had "rented a house in 104 Fifth Street, to serve for the Sisters at $280 per year." RACHS, Vol. III, 1892, p. 96.

79. Cf. Woodstock Letters, Vol. III, 1874, No. 1, p. 94.

80. Ibid., No. 3, p. 95.

81. Griffin, RACHS, Vol. XXIX, 1918, p. 361.

82. The marriage register for the parish for the years 1826-36 as given in RACHS, Vol. XX, 1909 ("Francis X. Reus, p. 290 et seq.) presents an interesting study for the years after the coming of the Jesuits. Of seventy-nine marriages listed for 1833, Bishop Conwell, blind and in slippered ease, officiated at 35. In 1834 he did not fare so well, performing only seventeen out of the sixty-four listed. In 1835, he is recorded as performing twenty-two out of twenty-nine, and in 1836 he had a perfect score, nineteen out of nineteen. That was, however, the last year in which he administered the sacraments. As witnesses to the marriage ceremonies

at which he officiated, we find the names of various Conwell relatives, but the most persistent name was that of Mrs. Elizabeth Johnson, his housekeeper.

83. Rev. William Boyle, The Story of St. Michael's, 1834-1944. (Philadelphia: Jeffries and Manz, 1934,) pp. 26-27.

St. Joseph Church, Willing's Alley as it appears today. It was rebuilt in 1838 by the Reverend Felix Barbelin, S.J.

A Decade of Deferred Hopes-
1833-1843

Chapter three is concerned with the problems of the Irish immigrant in Philadelphia, the reaction of the Protestant population to the great Catholic influx, and the perpetuation in the New World of the age-old conflict between the Orange and the Green, which would lead eventually to arson and bloodshed. It deals too with the labors and frustrations of the little community of women who are the focus of our study. Believing themselves properly constituted a religious institute, with the blessing and permission of the lawful Bishop, they were dismayed to find themselves, after six years, in an extra-legal status from which they could not free themselves. They were provided by their reverend-superior with an academy-convent two blocks south of his parish church. There they conducted a small boarding school and taught the parish children, though without the status of religious. In 1842, they were invited to send four or five of their number to the young diocese of Dubuque, Iowa. Its Bishop was to arrive in Philadelphia in the spring to accompany them west. However, on his arrival, their priest-superior insisted that the Bishop must receive into his diocese the entire community, which by then had grown to nineteen members. Despite the difficulty this presented, the Bishop acceded, on condition that the priest accompany the Sisters and commit himself to service in the frontier diocese.

Sisters present for erection of plaque in St. Joseph Church, summer, 1959, commemorating 125th anniversary of our foundation. However, the Emmitsburg Sisters had been in Philadelphia since 1814. Further, our Sisters were never canonically recognized there.

Philadelphia, in the early nineteenth century, resembled in many ways the Dublin the Sisters left behind. It was an old city, by American standards, with historical sites and traditions. Like Dublin, it was a busy seaport at the broad mouth of a river. And its glory as a nation's capital, like Dublin's, lay behind it. But unlike Dublin, it had never known great poverty or grave religious oppression. A city proud of its historical significance in the New World and of the dignity lent it by its share in Old World culture, it had known affluence, and its older inhabitants had settled into a comfortable and complacent conservatism.

But Philadelphia was also a rapidly changing city. The poor and the distressed were beginning to pour into it. Weather-racked and unseaworthy sailing vessels were disgorging daily from their steerage decks hundreds of soiled, ragged, half-starved families from the sod houses of the Irish countrysides and the crowded slums of Ireland's cities. The sick, the old, the orphaned would soon be city charges. Even relatively strong and healthy immigrants came with empty pockets and with a debt of service to pay for their passage. Largely unprepared for the amenities of urban life and untrained for any but unskilled labor or domestic service, they showed themselves often a reckless and turbulent element in a staid, self-conscious city.[1] Their numbers were greatly added to in the thirties, but the floodgates would open in the forties.

St. Joseph's church was a beacon to the wretched and travel-worn, and its Emigrant Society did what it could to meet their needs. Situated between Third and Fourth streets, St. Joseph church was approached through a narrow passageway beside the Quaker Almshouse on Walnut street. But in 1746, the wealthy merchant Thomas Willing - the first American to send a trading ship to china - built a mansion on Third street, and it was he who opened a carriageway to Fourth street which came to be known as Willing's Alley. The red brick rectory[2] which served St.

Joseph's and its eldest daughter, St. Mary's, was
then a two-and-a-half story structure, set well back
from the Alley. It was not until 1851, when the
Jesuit Fathers shared their quarters with St. Joseph
college, that the rectory was extended forward to the
public sidewalk, and upward through four stories as it
stands today. But that was after Father Barbelin, S.
J., had replaced the original church in 1838, with
the present historic shrine, and, renewing faith and
love among the young, had brought a second spring to
the parish.

St. Mary church, built in 1763 to meet the need
for larger quarters, is situated between Fourth and
Fifth, just beyond Willing's Alley, and half surrounded by a burial ground. Few who tour Philadelphia
today fail to visit the quaint old cemetery where lie
buried Commodore Barry, father of the United States
navy, General Stephen Moylan of General Washington's
staff, and other notables. St. Mary's and St. Joseph's were both under the care of the Jesuits - Sunday Masses at St. Mary's, weekday Masses at St. Joseph's, - with the one rectory serving both. At the
time of the suppression of the Society of Jesus in
1773, the title to these properties was assigned to
one of the Jesuit Fathers, who, with most other members of the Society, then identified himself with the
diocesan clergy.

The four "Dublin ladies," who had arrived in Philadelphia on Saturday evening, September 7, 1833, found
living accommodations in Willing's Alley. They attended Sunday Mass at St. Mary's, breakfasted and
spent much of the day with Mrs. McDonough.[3] Monday
was taken up with unpacking and arranging their belongings to the best advantage, while Tuesday doubtless was spent in getting acquainted with the city
which was to be their home, and in considering together the problems that faced them. It was Tuesday
evening, while Catherine was puzzling over her many
unsuccessful attempts to start a grate fire, that Mrs.
McDonough's friend and former pastor, the Reverend
T.J. Donaghoe, paid his first call. After witnessing
Sister's futile effort to apply to the Pennsylvania
hard coal the methods suited to the light and spongy
Irish turf to which she was accustomed, he quickly re-
arranged the contents of the grate and soon had a fire
blazing. The Sisters talked with him of their homeland and the hopes of service which had brought them
to America, while he told them of his present involvement in the opening of a new parish north of the city,

two or three miles away. It would be some time before
he could have his parish thoroughly established and
could build a school there, where he hoped they would
help with the teaching. However, some arrangement
could be made in the meantime, by way of a beginning.
The evening passed quickly; before his departure, the
priest made them an offer of money which they graciously refused. With heightened hopes they busied themselves through the days that followed with orders of
sewing which soon came their way.

Father Donaghoe had been paying rent on a building at 520 North Second street, which he now lent to
the Sisters for a small select school. Classes were
in session by mid-October, when Father set out for
Frederick, Maryland, to make his annual retreat at
the Jesuit novitiate.

Father Donaghoe had been considering for some
time the possibility of becoming a Jesuit, but the
coming of the Sisters now presented him with an alternative. If he remained in the diocesan ministry, he
would be free for the direction of this promising
group of young women. He hoped the retreat under the
able Father Francis Dzierozynski[4] would help him make
a decision. Having explained to his director that he
had been training the members as religious teachers,
and that it would be his wish to dedicate them to the
Blessed Virgin conceived without sin, he sought assurance as to his decision and his method of proce-
dure. The Jesuit requested the prayers of a novice,
Brother Faye,[5] for the special intentions of "a certain retreatant," and, as the story comes down to us,[6]
toward the close of the eight days the Brother returned to Father Dzierozynski with the message:
"Father, tell that person he is not to become a Jesuit.
This will greatly disappoint him; but tell him for his
consolation that the far west will one day resound
with the praises of the children of Mary." Taking his
director's word as God's will, Father Donaghoe did not
seem to think it necessary or suitable to consult the
wishes of the Sisters. On his return to Philadelphia,
the account tells us, Father went immediately to confer
with "the Bishop," and obtain his blessing on the new
venture. However, it was not Bishop Kenrick, the authorized administrator of the diocese, but the deposed
Conwell, whose blessing he sought.[7]

Then, on the eve of All Saints, after his two
weeks' absence, Father Donaghoe called on the Sisters.
Assuring them of the "Bishop's" approval and blessing,

he announced that on the following day, November 1, he
would receive them formally into the religious life.
He would be their director and reverend-superior, and
it was his wish that the capable and efficient
Margaret Mann should act as Mother. To this Margaret
could not agree. Mary Frances had been their acknowledged leader from the beginning, and Margaret refused
to supplant her. Father Donaghoe acquiesced, conferring on Mary Frances the title of Mother, and assigning to Margaret the positions of assistant to Mother
Clarke and of mistress of novices. Further arrangements included Mass at St. Joseph's for them in the
morning, at which they would receive Holy Communion.
On their return to their little "convent," they would
make an act of consecration, and he would instruct
them in the duties of the religious life.*

    If Mother Clarke experienced a certain uneasiness
at the abruptness of it all, with no time for consultation or for immediate preparation by way of recollection or retreat, she may have reminded herself that
they had been making a remote preparation for two
years. The assurance of the "Bishop's" approval, her
own eagerness for a realization of their hopes, and
their indebtedness to Father Donaghoe for his assistance in arranging for their school were weighty considerations. To these were added her native respect
for the sacred character of the priesthood, and the
consciousness of her own limited experience in such
matters.

    Father Donaghoe's own preparation for assuming
the directorship of a congregation of religious women
was meager. His early years had given him no opportunity of observing the work or life patterns of such
a group, for there was no such institution in County
Tyrone in that period. His years of seminary training in Paris could have offered him little opportunity

-----

*
    (The account as given by the author of In the
Early Days tells us that "In their private oratory on
that memorable morning the Sisters received the religious habit from the hands of Father Donaghoe." But
the author does not indicate by what system of leger-
demain he produced overnight four religious habits,
or the Sisters established a "private oratory" under
the   living conditions that must have been theirs
at the time.)

for such associations. The only religious women he
had known at first hand were the Sisters of Charity
of Emmitsburg who served his Prune street school, and
his contacts with them would have been confined to
school administration. That they had a priest-superior he knew, but of the purpose and limits of that
office he apparently had little knowledge. His reading had brought him into touch with the ascetical writings of St. Francis de Sales, and it was apparently
from these that he drew some inspiration. But religious life in the France of St. Francis' day was far
removed from that of the Sisters he planned to direct.
While Francis' own days were spent in incessant labor,
he had had opportunity to observe the comfortable and
leisured regimens of choir religious in the endowed
convents of his time, where all the menial tasks of
the household and garden fell to the lot of the lay
Sisters.[8] Regarding this as less than an ideal arrangement, he contemplated the establishment of a
community of religious women where all shared in the
toil necessary for their own support. It was to the
plan of this ideal community rather than to the realities that faced the community he was to direct that
Father Donaghoe turned for guidance. The following
excerpt from the writings of St. Francis is contained
among his notes:

> An institution established for instruction
> by females whose livelihood shall depend on
> labour.
>
> What would be my consolation if I could see
> before death an establishment of devout Fe-
> males who would carry with them no other
> provision to the community but that of a
> good and ready will, and whose habits of in-
> dustry would secure them a support from the
> labour of their own hands.
>
> To effect this desirable object they should
> have no other choir than a Labour Hall where
> all united should participate in that happi-
> ness of which the prophet speaks: "You shall
> be blessed if you eat of the fruit gained by
> the labour of your hands."
>
> Oh, my God, how great is the consolation to
> eat one's bread by the sweat of their [sic]
> brow and to be able to say with the great
> Apostle St. Paul, "My hands have not only
> furnished me with things necessary but also

to bestow·on those who suffer from necessity."
Such poverty as this is more agreeable before
God than all the treasures of the earth.
This manner of living can be called properly
and truly evangelical poverty such as our Divine Redeemer practiced during his life,
while his Blessed Mother, St. Joseph and the
Apostles abandoned all and after his example
supported themselves by their labours either
corporal or spiritual.[9]

On November 1, after the Mass and the act of consecration, Father announced to the Sisters that their
religious title would be Sisters of Charity of the
Blessed Virgin, and confirmed his decision that Mary
Frances would thenceforth be known as Mother Clarke.
The other three Sisters would retain their Christian
names, with the prefix, "Sister Mary." His exhortation to the Sisters, with its emphasis on labor, was
in part as follows:

The love of God is the great principle that
has established communities, that has increased and sustained the members of them.
Communities in the earlier ages of the
church made labor an essential part of their
rule because man since the fall had been
condemned to it and by fulfilling it as a
duty he complied with the law of his God...

Other communities may have by large fortunes
rendered it unnecessary to toil for their
support, still they had to have recourse to
labor in order to fulfill an obligation that
is so indispensable to religious life.

In making these observations it is evident
that employment is necessary for all and
more especially for those who cannot associate together without it. Since in this little association we now contemplate commenc-
ing, we know that whether we eat or drink or
whatever else we do we must do all for the
glory of God - it will greatly console its
members that the workroom can be considered
their choir, and that the purity of the motives that employ them will also ascend and
find acceptance before their divine master
who loves to see them fervently working in
his vineyard.[10]

Having concluded his discourse, he gave the Sisters the following simple horarium, preserved today in his handwriting:

1. The hour of rising shall be at the first dawn of day light, and that of retiring to rest shall be so regulated as to allow from seven to eight hours of sleep.

2. Morning prayers shall be said in common, concluding with the Angelus -

3. The points of meditation that have been slowly read before retiring to bed, shall be recalled to memory by each or at least some leading thought of it, reflecting on it on their way to the church to hear Mass -

4. The hours of meals can be disposed of at convenient hours -

5. The labor of the day to be offered to the greater honor of God and in union with the actions that Jesus Christ performed when on earth for the love of us - the conversation may sometimes be of the meditation and the thoughts may be more profitably on it, drawing from it affections and resolutions -

   The Angelus again about noon and also about seven in the evening - After dinner and supper retire before the crucifix and in silence each return thanks for five minutes only, unless when Sister Superior shall judge it proper to read or have read a consecration or a few aspirations to Sacred hearts of Jesus and Mary - concluding with night prayer and reading very slowly the meditation for the ensuing day -

* * * * *

On September 28, 1834, the Sisters witnessed the solemn dedication of St. Michael church, by the Rt. Reverend Bishop Kenrick and the blind and enfeebled Bishop Conwell.[11] Father Donaghoe celebrated the solemn high Mass, with the Reverend Edward McCarthy, S.J. as deacon, and, as sub-deacon, to their surprise, the Reverend Patrick Costello, the priest whom they had met in Dublin, and who had induced them to come to

America. Father John Hughes preached the sermon on the occasion and the collection was a handsome $500.00. The church was "considered an excellent specimen of the Gothic architecture of the twelfth century," according to the newspaper reports of the time, though the centennial account of the parish is somewhat less commendatory:

> There was really no distinctly Gothic feature to the exterior of the church. It was a building of plain walls and round arched windows and doors. Were it not for the crosses - there was a small one over either side angle of the pediment, and a large one at the apex - it might almost have been taken for a simple auditorium. In this locale of small homes and low, sprawling mills, it was imposing, but it would really be too much to say it was beautiful.[12]

Nevertheless, in the eyes of those who had sacrificed to make it a reality it was doubtless a many-splendored thing. The congregation could be proud of the altar-piece of St. Michael the Archangel by Guido Reni, once the property of Cardinal Fesch, given to St. Michael's by the Charles Bonaparte family, who had long held a pew in St. Joseph Church. But there was a debt of $22, 028.00 to worry about, and some of the obligations were pressing. Father Boyle writes:

> In the United States Gazette of March 18, 1835, there appeared a notice that St. Michael's R.C. Church and its lot would be sold by the sheriff on May 4. The announcement was the result of a certain O'Toole's having recourse to the Law because his bill for plastering had not been paid -- one would judge by his name that he was Catholic, and by his action that he was the type of Catholic who would sell his religion at any time for personal gain. However, Mr. O'Toole got his money and the advertized auction was never held.[13]

The debt was a large one for Father Donaghoe to pay by door to door collection. The possibility of his having become the beneficiary of Propagation of Faith funds coming to the diocese through Bishop Conwell is a real one, for not only was the debt reduced to $10,000 by 1844 but many improvements had been made in the meantime.[14] The problem of trustee control was

solved for the new parish by a decision of the Pennsylvania Supreme Court which placed the choice of the
trustees in the hands of the bishop of the diocese.

While it might have been anticipated that when
the St. Michael free school was opened after the completion of the church, it would be manned by the little company of which Father Donaghoe had made himself
priest-superior, this did not happen. The new school
continued there through 1837. Mother Clarke and her
small faculty maintained the independent select school
on North Second street for two years after the opening of St. Michael's, and the Sisters continued to
reside at Willing's Alley.* Then both school and residence were moved into a large house at Second, opposite Laurel. Soon a second and adjacent residence
was added. Through the years the Sisters supported
themselves and their school on such tuition as they
were able to collect, and on their own needlework,
though they rendered semi-annual accounts to Father
Donaghoe of all receipts and expenditures.[15]

* * * * * * * * * * * *

Meanwhile Philadelphia was having various troubles, many of these resulting from its administrative
pattern. As each new area was settled, it had set up
its own local administration, twenty-nine such governmental units then constituting the area now comprised
in the City of Philadelphia. To escape apprehension
for a misdeed, a culprit had often only to cross a
street. He would then be in another jurisdiction,
and thus free from arrest. Law enforcement officers,
largely volunteer, were untrained, ununiformed, and
unarmed. In some areas law enforcement was left to
the volunteer fire companies. In earlier times,
these had been made up of public-spirited, often professional, men, but in the course of the years they
had been largely supplanted by ruffians, with much
rivalry existing between companies. A fire call responded to by two or more of these companies often
resulted in a battle royal over jurisdiction, while
the fire blazed on. Loving the sound of the firebell
and the clatter of their engines, the crews took delight in night calls, real or imagined. For an Irishman, to be a 'fire laddy' in a volunteer company was

---

*For a brief time the Sisters moved to a brown-
stone house near a graveyard, but "nocturnal disturbances" caused them to return to their earlier quarters.

the height of his dreams.

Unemployment was widespread among the immigrants, especially for those in the construction trades where there were seasonal periods of idleness. The search for diversion resulted in the forming of bands of young rowdies who prowled the city. Many times during the 1830's and 1840's gangsters terrorized the town. As a result, Philadelphia came to be known as a rough and lawless place.

The causes of racial violence in Philadelphia were two-fold: the struggle over abolition, with Quakers lending help and protection to the Negro in a city whose business interests were largely southern, and the competition for unskilled jobs, which pitted the Irishman against the freed Black man. Riots were frequent, and it was often difficult to determine which motive prevailed. On August 12, 1834, a meeting house frequented by Blacks, located near the Wharton Market, was torn down, and many Black people were assaulted and their homes sacked. In October occurred the Robb's Row riots. Blacks suffered in another riot in July, 1835, when many of their homes were burned. They were victims again on August 1, 1842, when Smith's Beneficial Hall, dedicated just three days before by the Pennsylvania Society for the Abolition of Slavery, was destroyed by fire. This was followed the next day by more trouble, when Irish laborers in the coal yards on the Schuylkill attacked a band of Black laborers, and the militia had to be called in to quell the riot. In his study of The Irish in America, Wittke observes:

> In Philadelphia, where antagonism between the two groups was great, to be called an 'Irishman' had come to be almost as great an insult as to be called a 'nigger.' Frederick L. Olmsted referred to the contempt with which Negroes regarded Irishmen who carried hod for colored masons in the South. He pointed out that Negroes were considered to be worth more than "Paddies," and therefore needed to be spared from the most unhealthful and dangerous tasks.... "My Master is a great tyrant," a Negro slave is supposed to have commented in 1850, "he treats me badly as if I was a common Irishman." 16

Other riots in Kensington found Catholic and Protestant weavers in conflict over jobs as machinery was beginning to replace hand-labor.

Nor did religion contribute to the city's peace, subject as it was to political overtones. A large majority of the residents in the western section of St. Michael parish were Irish, and these were divided into two religious factions. Old world animosities had lost nothing of their virulence when the Orange and the Green found themselves neighbors and competitors for jobs in the new land. The Irish immigrant was aggressive about his religious affiliations. To the Irish Catholic, all things Protestant were anathema, and every Protestant was an Orangeman. The former's love of celebration, expressing itself in St. Patrick's day and Fourth of July parades and fiery orations, was responded to by an equally spirited celebration on July 12 of Orangeman's Day. As a result, the Battle of the Boyne was fought over and over again in the streets of Philadelphia. As they gained in numbers and prosperity, there were days of glory for the sons of St. Patrick, when the voice of "Ireland's King" * was heard across the waters, and they responded with the kinds of celebration that set the teeth of Protestants on edge. Such was that of July 4, 1841, when the Irish took the occasion to stir up enthusiasm for Daniel O'Connell's efforts to repeal the Act of Union and restore a separate parliament to Ireland. A pamphlet of the times gives the following account of the rally:

Friends of Ireland in Philadelphia

"The American Cock crowing at
the other side of the Atlantic
shall awaken Ireland from her
distressing slumbers, and bid
her arise to enjoy a day of
light and happiness." Daniel O'Connell.

Monday was indeed a proud day for the friends of Ireland! Never did the American cock crow louder or more cheerfully. Lively as this great city usually is on the anniversary of Our Independence as a Nation, never did it exhibit so much spirit, so much joy, as on

---

Daniel O'Connell

that day on which was celebrated that glori-
our event.... At one o'clock the line of
march was formed and the procession proceeded
up Chestnut street, the Hibernia Greens...
and Irish Volunteers [17] with their fine bands
of music playing, Hail Columbia, Erin Go
Bragh, and other such soul-stirring airs....
The whole streets were lined with spectators,
while every window was filled with ladies
waving their handkerchiefs as the procession
passed by. What Irish heart did not beat
with emotion at the glorious spectacle and
its reception by the fair daughters of America? ... Then came in soldierly movement,
the Philadelphia Repealers, in sections of
four, and numbering two thousand well-looking,
highly respectable men, having their repeal
badges on their left breast.

The Chief Marshal and his aides, as well as
the other Marshals, wore green and gold
sashes surmounted by a blue rosette, which
added much to the effect of the scene. Nothing can be imagined finer than those sashes.
Rich with gold bullion and spangles, they
were admired by all....

Having arrived at a theatre, there followed a succession of fiery speeches on repeal, together with the
reading of the Declaration of Independence, the celebration lasting until

at a quarter past 6 o'clock the Association
adjourned . . . with nine cheers for Old
Ireland, O'Connell, and Repeal, waving their
handkerchiefs and clapping their hands,
speaking in a language which cannot be mis-
understood, the unanimous voice of America -
Erin! oh Erin! thy winter is past,
And the hope that lived through it
shall blossom at last.[18]

Having been stirred to political awareness by the
eloquence and invective of O'Connell, the Irish immigrant was seeking early naturalization. Scorned by
the more exclusive Whigs, he joined the receptive
Democratic party in which his natural aptitude for
politics would soon make him a power. As Wittke
writes:

Irishmen felt the lure of American politics
much as they were attracted to the sociability

of the saloon, and it was no accident that the saloon and the political club were closely allied.... Irish peasants had been tools of their landlords; it was not very different to become the tools of political bosses, who marched them in groups to the polls and cemented the allegiance with free liquor. . . . But the Irish immigrant had a tremendous advantage over other new-comers - he knew the English language and could enter American politics without first hurdling a difficult language barrier . . . . In many places there were no registration of voters, no secret ballot, and naturalization was easy. Before elections, agents of local machines scoured the cities to bring in aliens to get citizenship papers from political judges who asked few or no questions . . . . Youths under age were naturalized; little attention was paid to the period of residence in the United States; citizenship papers were handed out in saloons; and fraudulent signatures were unchallenged.

But, given time,

The same genius for organization which made the Irish so successful as leaders in the Church and in the field of labor helps account for their success in politics. To all three fields, warmhearted, sociable Irishmen brought a human touch that proved most important.[19]

Proud as he might be of his American citizenship, no true son of Erin was ever expatriated from the land of his birth. An internal solidarity set the Irish apart and their dedication to the cause of their country's freedom from England's control never lagged.

The great influx of Catholic immigrants in the 30's and 40's led to a panic among the settled Protestant population, reviving all the old fears of plots and intrigues on the part of Rome and Catholic nations. A wave of hysteria spread over the country, and with it, determined efforts to save American institutions from "insidious Jesuitical workings," from the Pope, "the man of sin," and from the Church, "the whore of Babylon." Small local societies provided forums for the expression of anti-Catholic sentiments, and from these grew national organizations - among them, the

American Protestant Union, with Samuel F. B. Morse at
its head. With Lyman Beecher, the Protestant minister, Morse led the controversy over the reading of
the Bible in the public schools, declaring that the
aim of Catholics was to control the nation's educational facilities, and subjugate the country to the
power of the Pope. There was a deluge of debates and
controversies, often acrimonious in spirit, together
with a flood of scurrilous pamphlets, newspaper articles and books. The sale of these was enormous. Before the Civil War, 300,000 copies had been sold of
the Awful Disclosures of Maria Monk,[20] with its horror tales of immoralities and of strangled infants in
a Canadian convent from which the author claimed to
have made her escape. The book's popularity gave rise
to many similar calumnious and inflammatory publica-
tions. Then, noting a revulsion on the part of high-
minded Protestants, against such tactics, the promot-
ers of the crusade turned for a time to a "loving concern" for the souls of Catholics, in which efforts
were concentrated on the conversion of "Papists to
Christianity" through a wholesale distribution of
Bibles.[21]

Education was a paramount need among the Irish,
but even when it was free it was not available to all,
for the low wages earned by parents had to be supplemented by their children's earnings in factories. It
was for such children that, in 1816, Matthew Carey
had established Sunday schools, to supply them with
at least the rudiments of education. However, these
were not so successful as he had hoped. Undernourish-
ment and the long hours of labor during the week left
the children with little enthusiasm for Sunday classes. Catholic schools were too few to meet the needs
of the growing population, though Bishop Kenrick's
goal was a free school in every parish. The necessity of charging tuition for private ventures put them
beyond the reach of laboring men's children. The aim
of the state was free public education for all, and a
fairly adequate system of elementary schools was
built during the 30's and 40's. But for the Irish
Catholic, the requirement that the King James Bible,
"without note or comment," be a part of the daily curriculum classed these schools with the proselytizing
schools of Ireland, which had operated on the same
principle. Catholics protested also the daily singing of Protestant hymns in the classrooms, but their
most serious complaint was against the anti-Catholic
texts and reference books supplied the pupils, and
the ungracious treatment of the Irish children by

their teachers and fellow students. All this brought
protest from Bishop Kenrick. While he did not regard
the Bible as a suitable textbook for young children,
if it was to be required, he requested that the Catholic Bible should be available to Catholic pupils.
His request led to a hostile reaction, with the hue
and cry that Kenrick sought to exclude the Bible entirely from the public schools. Holding this to be a
Protestant country, with the reading of the Bible the
one source and sign of their faith, militant Protestants were loud in their protestations. The feeling
stirred up against Kenrick was such that his house
was bombarded with rocks, and he actually feared for
his life.

Under these circumstances it is not surprising
that the activities of the anti-Catholic forces, given
direction and leadership by the Native American Party
formed in Philadelphia in 1837, would lead to open
violence, as it was to do in the Riots of 1844. Although its avowed purpose was the protection of the
young country against foreign influence, its animus
was directed almost wholly against the Irish Catholic
population, leaving Protestant and German Catholic
immigrants unmolested.

The City of Brotherly Love was, then, scarcely living up to the promise of its name, and it is not difficult to understand why Mother Clarke and Margaret
Mann were bitterly disappointed with their first experience of America.[22] The disorders they witnessed
and the unfriendliness they felt were combined with
the frustration of their religious hopes. To these
were added the privations of poverty, for even the
low tuition charges was often uncollectible, and the
number of free scholars they provided for was ruin-
ously high.[23] The Sisters sewed "for sundry persons,"
"for boarders," but principally for "Miss Willis,
dressmaker." For her the work would seem to have
been the finishing of the lined, whaleboned, bead-and-
sequin-trimmed and braided garments of the day. That
much of it was done by artificial light - candle or
grease lamp - may be inferred from the note: "Father
Donaghoe let the Sisters use very severe penances.
They rose at three and sewed, then their health
failed."[24] Apparently early rising was not their
only mortification, for "Dr. McNeill, nephew of Bishop Conwell, and a later member of the staff of St.
Jsoeph hospital, told Father Donaghoe he was too aus-
tere and rigid, too strict about fasting; the Sisters
couldn't stand it."[25]

The pressure of their daily stints of sewing left
the Sisters little time for study or for the reading
and preparation of lessons so essential to successful
teaching, and less time still for the visiting of the
sick and the families of their pupils. The arrival
of Rose O'Toole in the spring of 1834 brought a welcome dowry of a hundred pounds and helpful household
items. Then, since Rose was not equipped for the
classroom, she could give relief with sewing and
household chores, and could be available for nursing
care among the poor of the neighborhood. There was
little time or opportunity for private prayer, and
with the church at a distance, quiet contemplation in
the presence of the Blessed Sacrament was a rare privilege. The luxury of an annual retreat was quite beyond their reach.

While the Sisters lived at Willing's Alley, Fathers
Kenney and Dubuisson were very kind to them and they
could assist at Mass at St. Joseph's, but their school
was a mile away, and Sunday school classes at St.
Michael's meant a walk of over two miles each way.
Moving farther north, where school and convent were
combined, their walk of several blocks to Mass at St.
Michael's took them through an unfriendly area.
Father Donaghoe thought it best that they be accompanied from convent to church and back, and he sent
as escort young Denis Mahony, whom he was tutoring in
Latin in preparation for the seminary, and who was in
residence at the rectory. Another resident there was
John Mann, Margaret's father, who had come to Philadelphia after her mother's death. His eysight, affected by his years of close work at the weaver's
loom, was still sufficient at that time for him to be
about, and both he and Denis were proud to accompany
the Sisters.

Those were days when it was not safe for women to
appear on the streets of Philadelphia in a religious
habit. The Sisters chose a simple black or brown
dress, gathered at waist and cuff, and a short cape
with a soft linen collar. A frilled lace bonnet,
commonly worn by women of the day, was both conservative and becoming.

But the unaccustomed cold of winter and the heat
of summer, and the muddy footpaths they travelled,
their long skirts wet with rain or snow, were sources
of hardship and discomfort.

Meanwhile Bishop kenrick was earnestly seeking

for religious congregations to undertake the various
works of the diocese, especially education. When the
small group of Irish Ursulines from Cork passed through
Philadelphia late in 1834, on their way to Charleston,
South Carolina, Kenrick urged them,unsuccessfully, to
stay in his diocese.[26] The Sisters of Charity of Emmitsburg were, at that time, teaching at St. Joseph's,
then later at St. Michael's, under the direction of
Father Donaghoe, and at St. Mary and Holy Trinity parish schools, as well as conducting the orphanage
Father Hughes had founded. It would take a long
search and much correspondence, with the offering of
buildings and building sites, before the Bishop could
secure the services of the Good Shepherd Sisters, the
St. Joseph Sisters of Carondelet, the Ladies of the
Sacred Heart, the Sisters of Mercy, of Notre Dame,
and of the Visitation, but by 1848 he had accomplished
all that.[27] However, his "Report on the Condition of
the Church of Philadelphia to Our Holy Father, Pope
Gregory XVI, made June 1, 1838"[28] when the Sisters'
Sacred Heart Academy on Second and Phoenix was nearing completion, made no mention of the religious who
were to occupy it. After listing the two Jesuits in
residence at St. Joseph's, the Sisters of Charity of
Emmitsburg in their several institutions, and the
convent of St. Clare near Pittsburgh, the report said:
"We have no other pious foundations under any other
title." [29]

* * * * *

The years had been hard ones for Kenrick, with
the large influx of Catholic immigrants and the consequent need for churches, schools and clergy, in the
face of the growing anti-Catholic spirit, and with the
tremendous financial strain, crucial in depression
years. Shea tells of the situation in the panic year
of 1837:

> He[Kenrick] found Philadelphia sunk in the
> depths of one of the worst financial panics
> it had ever experienced. The disaster which
> began in 1834 with the increase of unemploy-
> ment, the decrease of wages, and the sharp
> liquidation of debts, was now at its worst.
> Business houses long established in the city
> were failing; new enterprises had stopped;
> wage-earners, particularly the immigrant
> laborers who made up the bulk of the Cath-
> olic laity, were discharged by the thousands.
> Parish incomes slumped to the point where
> they were no longer sustaining. Money

became scarce, especially as a result of
President Jackson's order through his secretary of the treasury, Levi Woodbury, that
only gold and silver should be accepted as
payment for the public lands which had been,
and were being sold at the time at a great
rate. The demand for specie on the eastern
banks was consequently large. Interest was
raised to an exorbitant rate.[30]

Added to all this there was Kenrick's loss of John
Hughes to the New York diocese, leaving the new church
Hughes had built under a heavy debt of $40,000. The
course of Hughes' relations with Kenrick had deterior-
ated through the years. When in 1835 Kenrick proposed
the division of his diocese, he named Father Hughes
as his choice for the bishopric of Pittsburgh. Then
later, when he himself considered requesting a transfer from Philadelphia, he recommended Hughes for the
Philadelphia see. Learning, however, that cowardice
was imputed as his reason for leaving the diocese, he
withdrew his request for a transfer,[31] a decision
that caused a temporary breach with Hughes. When the
bulls arrived on November 30, 1837, naming Hughes coadjutor to the aged Dubois, bishop of New York and
friend of Hughes' seminary days, a further misunderstanding arose. Hughes had unfortunately publicized
Kenrick's half-formed plan to make St. John's his
cathedral, a point which Kenrick had been unable to
clear with Rome. Hughes pressed for the carrying out
of the Bishop's intention, withholding for a time his
signature which would release to Kenrick the title to
the church site. It is evident from the following
that certain of his letters to the Bishop were not
notably friendly for Kenrick's response, recorded in
his Journal, to an invitation to Hughes' consecration
reads: "The terms of your letters must be my apologies
for not being present at your Consecration; but I wish
you with all my heart all the blessings of an Apostolic Bishop. Your affectionate Brother in Xt." *

On the other hand the close bond which had existed between the Donaghey and Conwell families in
County Tyrone, was to find added strength through
associations in the New World. Father Donaghoe's

---

*Later Kenrick yielded, however, for an entry in
his Diary (p. 156) indicates that he had just returned
from the Hughes' consecration.

youthful years as student under Dean Conwell had led
to a friendship with Bernard Keenan, Conwell's nephew,
the first candidate to be ordained in Philadelphia
after Bishop Conwell's installation. Records remain
of Father's visit to his friend Bernard when the latter was pastor in Lancaster, Pennsylvania, and of
their presence together in the parish of Father
Patrick Kenney. Evidences of other associations between the families are given in the following letters,
addressed by Father's niece, Jane Donaghey, and his
nephew, Patrick McKenna, to Bishop Conwell. Jane had
apparently just completed a visit to Philadelphia,
during which she had spent some time at the bishop's
rectory, no doubt as the guest of his nieces:

> Liverpool, Nov. 8, 1837
>
> Right Rev. Sir:
> With grateful affection I return you my
> sincere thanks for your great kindness to me
> while under your hospitable roof. I had a
> pleasant passage of 23 days. My Brother-in-
> law received your letter, so he had a look
> out for me. I gave my sister Rose a pleas-
> ant surprise as my brother Thomas has gave
> [sic] me this morning after his arrival in
> Liverpool to see me; it is I think so strange,
> he wishing me to go home that I have not the
> most distant thought of home . . . .
> Mr. McKenna has the picture. Please tell
> Mrs. Donnelly [Conwell's niece] I walked
> through Paradise Street at length but have
> not seen Mrs. Heart. Remember me to Mrs.
> Johnston and to Henry. I remain, my Lord,
> with love, regard and esteem,
> Your humble servant
> Jane Donaghey 32

The second letter indicates something of the Bishop's
determination still to be involved in diocesan affairs, despite his infirmities and his situation as
a retired bishop:

> 78 Dale St., Liverpool
> Nov. 8th, 1837
> Right Rev. Sir:
> I take the present opportunity of send-
> ing these few lines to your Lordship, hoping
> you will receive the same in a short time;
> together with the small parcel I enclosed, I
> send you 12 of Riley Catechisms, also two of

the English laitey's [sic] Directory &
Brown's union Dictionary; the other part
of your order I shall send early in Jany,
'38. Jane was 23 days on her passage.
The present you sent to your native parish
has been committed to my care; it has cost
me about £2 and three days labour, and if I
was not up to the Custom House laws and I
will say a little bribery it would be little
short of 100 duty, but, thank God, I have it
safe. I have sent the Rev. C. O'Brien a letter and told him he must find some trusty
friend to take it home.

I am sorry to hear your Lordship has lost
the use of your sight but pardon me if I
humbly crave your prayers in the old Irish
fashion, viz. your beads for my Dear Wife
and little family, also for

Your obedt sert.,
Patrick McKenna [33]

*   *   *   *   *

We have but few glimpses into the convent life of
the Sisters during these years, although a somewhat
idealized account of the Congregation's beginnings
tells us that

At the close of each day it was their custom
to sing a hymn and to their great joy they
frequently heard a charming voice blending
its strong rich tones with theirs. So delightful was it and so sweet a consciousness
of God's presence did it impart that they
felt a foretaste of Heaven, but as soon as
they attempted to enjoy the pleasure of
merely listening, it ceased. . . . The voice
seemed to emanate from a picture of the
Blessed Virgin, a little print of no intrin-
sic artistic value, yet priceless to the little group of choristers singing their loved
Mother's praises.[34]

An undated interview among the pencilled notes of the
Reverend J.F. Kempker, Iowa Catholic historian, re-
veals that the same Denis Mahony we met as Father
Donaghoe's Latin student had been for a time a pupil
of the Sisters and had also served as a kind of errand boy for them. He adds that Denis, present with
the Sisters one evening, "listening enraptured, heard

a heavenly voice from a picture of the Madonna which joined in their singing."35

Another incident of Sister M. Lambertina's telling is somewhat modified by notes in her Journal. Her published account reads:

> One who, light-hearted and merry, loved recreation well, playfully sought to extend the time by stopping the clock. While they were in the midst of their enjoyment, suddenly they heard at the customary time, the little bell ring clearly and distinctly, the signal for the cessation of recreation and for night prayers. Now the bell was in the accustomed place on a shelf in the entry; no human hand was near it, no Sister was absent from the room, it was altogether inexplicable. A strange feeling overpowered them, and they felt intimately and understood admirably the value of obedience.36

We learn from Sister's Journal that the "light-hearted one" mentioned above was none other than the same Denis. Finding the lad at recreation one evening, Father Donaghoe expressed his displeasure, indicating that Denis was "too old for that kind of thing," and ordering that "he should never come again until he had the cap and cape, meaning never." A few evenings later Denis arrived, decked out in cap and cape of his own devising. As it was then late, he feared he would have too little time to spend with the Sisters, so it was he who had stopped the clock.37 The Kempker notes tell us that the ringing of the bell "frightened Denis very much."38

Regarding the new academy Father Donaghoe had long planned for the Sisters, we read:

> It is almost incredible that with all his duties and financial worries in connection with his church, Father Donaghoe should have gone about soliciting funds for the erection of a convent. But he really did this; he began it even before the church's dedication. What is more, he did it successfully. Well-to-do Catholics of the city were impressed by his fervent pleas and responded generously. Ground was purchased at the southeast corner of Second and Phoenix [Thompson] Streets, and the convent of the Sacred Heart was built

at a cost of a trifle over six thousand dollars. The trustees of St. Michael's were
invested with the legal title, for Father
Donaghoe did not wish it to be held in the
name of an individual, and the community itself was not capable under the law of possessing property.[39]

According to Pennsylvania law, Father Donaghoe could
not himself hold the title for the convent, since he
was not a naturalized citizen.[40] The regulation that
the title to all such property should be in the name
of the local bishop seems to have been disregarded.
On several occasions Kenrick had clearly indicated
his position with regard to the holding of ecclesiastical property. "In one instance, September 11, 1831,
the Bishop was present to bless St. Paul's Church in
Pittsburgh when he learned that a group of laymen
were legal possessors of the property. He refused to
go on with the ceremony until the deed was made out
in his name."[41]

Work was progressing on the convent and academy
when, in August, 1838, Father Donaghoe went to Frederick, Maryland, to make his annual retreat. From
there he wrote to the Sisters on August 15, giving
assurance that he was remembering them in the exercises of the retreat. His return trip would take
another eight days, as he was coming back by way of
Emmitsburg, Georgetown, Washington, and Baltimore.
His concern was for the religious education of the
children, for he said: "Oh, the catechism, the catechism! Premiums only for memory; encourage the lazy
ones. Tell them I will meet them on Sunday week -
my poor little pearls!" Then his mind turned to the
academy under construction, for he added the hope
that the Venetian blinds and the doors had been hung.
Greetings to Mrs. McDonogh closed the letter.

That Father Donaghoe had serious difficulty in
arriving at a philosophy of education which would extend beyond religious instruction becomes evident
from his hand written notes found in the Congregation's archives.

What is the leading object of the Society?
It consists in teaching young persons of
their own sex in honor of the Sacred Childhood of Jesus Christ, 1st the practice of
every virtue, 2nd the knowledge of religion
and 3rd to form their hearts to the love of

God. Will the parents of these children require nothing else? Yes, they do, and generally insist upon the secular instruction of
their children more than the knowledge of religion which alone can make them good members of society. What are the Sisters to do
when parents give or appear to give the preference to secular knowledge? Sisters must,
nevertheless, cherish their love to honor the
Sacred Childhood of J.C., by endeavouring to
possess as also to inspire their pupils with
this Divine love. What then have they to do
with the secular learning? The Sisters sanc-
tify their secular studies by prayer, and
recommend themselves by the ability they
show and the industry they use in the advancement of their pupils and thereby attract
the parents & children to serve Jesus Christ
which is the true way to honor his Sacred
Childhood in young persons of their own sex.

He closed the above with the remark: "I intended to
give a comment on the rule - O God, - O Mother!"

In November, 1838, the Sisters had the joy of moving into their new Sacred Heart academy, just two
blocks south of St. Michael church, though no evidence remains of a dedication ceremony. By that time
they had welcomed two postulants - Mary Lawlor, from
King's County, Ireland, on June 16, 1835, and Maria
Lalor * from the same county, on August 15, 1837.
Mary had served for a time as housekeeper for Father
Donaghoe, when her brother, suffering from a scrofu-
lar condition of the knee - King's evil they called
it then - had become an added member of the rectory
household.[42] Maria, like Catherine Byrne, had been a
resident at St. Clare orphanage at Harold's Cross,
Dublin, and the Register there gives the following
data:

Lalor, Maria, whose father is dead, aged
eight years, recommended by Mr. John Lynch,
No. 6 South Earl Street, who promised to sub-
scribe annually during her stay in the Orphan House £7.10.0 as her mother is living

---

* Given as "Lawler" in the Congregation's
necrology.

but totally unable from infirmity of sight
to provide for her. She has also friends
who will provide for her when fit to be
placed out. Admitted into the house the 17th
of September 1824. Sent to Rush to Margaret
Ford for the recovery of her health, who is
to be paid at the rate of Ł 6 per year for
her diet and lodging, in November, 1829.
Maria Lalor sent on trial 1st August 1832 to
Miss O'Connor, Furrier, Grafton Street to
learn the trade, and was bound August 9th
1832.

Later relatives brought Maria to America and here she
sought out Catherine Byrne, and so became acquainted
with the Sisters.

* * * * *

Six years had passed since the arrival of the
four first Sisters in Philadelphia, years of puzzled
waiting since they had made their act of consecration
on that memorable November 1 in 1833. It had all
been done with the consent, Father Donaghoe had told
them, of the Bishop. Yet since that time there had
never been the slightest sign of recognition from
Bishop Kenrick, in whose hands lay the sole administration of the diocese. Why, when Mary Lawler completed her two-year novitiate, was her little vow
ceremony on May 22, 1837, so strictly private, with
none but the Sisters and their chaplain to give witness? Why had not the Bishop been invited to dedicate their new academy? Indeed, why had he never
been witness to a public vow ceremony for even the
five founding members? Each time they had raised
with Father Donaghoe any of these questions, he had
put them off, indicating that Bishop Kenrick's experience with the two French Sisters [43] had put him on
his guard against any but duly established religious
communities, even prejudicing him to the extent that
from that time on he had refused to hear the confes-
sion of any religious. [44]

Among the unpublished notes of Sister M. Michael
Nihill there is an effort to explain the Sisters'
unusual situation:

The good Father,[Donaghoe] well knowing the disposition of Bishop Kenrick for new foundations, gave it as his opinion that the present was an unfortunate time to petition for approval, counseling them to defer it until a later period when they should be better organized. Being in Philadelphia at the time of the young Bishop's appointment to the coadjutorship of the diocese, he witnessed the complete failure of an attempt on his Grace's [sic] part to establish a house planned on a grand scale after which the disaffection of the Prelate for any essay of a like nature became most pronounced.

Then the account seems to indicate that Father Donaghoe was withholding from the Sisters the reality of their situation, lest knowing it they would not persevere:

Fearing to deter them from prosecuting the wearisome journey they had begun, the amiable and trusty guide added that the future would prove more promising, adroitly withholding from their expectant gaze the uninviting prospect that lay before them. To reassure them that the arduous undertaking they had but commenced had long been the uppermost thought of his mind and its completion would be as great a source of comfort to him as to them, "God works slowly," he said, "let us prepare ourselves a little longer that we may become fit instruments in his hands for the fulfillment of his divine behests."

Regarding the second cause of their concern - their desire for a chapel in their own convent - the account continues:

Acting on the advice of their vigilant pastor they abstained from soliciting the privilege of having the Blessed Sacrament under the same roof with them, a precaution taken to avoid giving those who were said to be unfavorably disposed toward the new foundation an opportunity for captious questioning.

The division among the clergy in their allegiance to one bishop or the other was the principal source

of what "captious questioning" there might have been,
on that and other subjects. The struggle to maintain
a loyal stance with reference to Father Donaghoe and
yet analyze the Sisters' situation continues:

> Notwithstanding the implicit trust placed in
> their conservative guide, it[the denial of
> Mass and the Blessed Sacrament in their con-
> vent] was looked on with disfavor, the pri-
> vation of Our Lord's presence being viewed in
> the light of a bereavement. Distances from
> church made a return the same day impossible,
> especially when a multiplicity of pressing
> duties required close attention and prompt
> execution. Resigning themselves to the in-
> evitable . . . they endeavored to supply in
> part the want and the ommission by anticipa-
> ting the hour of the holy Sacrifice of the
> Mass, in order to spend a few minutes in si-
> lent communion with the Prisoner of Love.
> How they must have longed for the privacy of
> the first religious home. . . . With what
> affectionate regret did they not recall the
> prized appellation by which a reverent Cath-
> olic people addressed them in the cradle of
> their institute where they were designated,
> "The Nuns of North Ann Street." Here they
> were unknown to outsiders except as Father
> Donaghoe's Sisters. . . .

The Sisters recognized the debt of gratitude they
owed Father Donaghoe for building their commodious
academy, and for providing a home for Margaret's father and Mary Lawler's brother. Perhaps they only
needed to be patient and wait a little longer.

Then the mail on an early October morning brought
a letter bearing the seal of the diocese, and addressed, in a clear masculine hand, to "Miss Mary
Clarke." Opening it, she read:

> Respected Miss Clarke,
> As several persons have spoken to me of
> you and the ladies associated with you as a
> Religious Community, I feel bound to inquire
> into the nature of your institute, the laws
> of the Church forbidding the establishment
> of any religious institution in a diocese
> without the sanction of the Bishop. I re-
> quest, therefore, your attendance on Monday
> next at 10 o'clock at my house, to explain

this matter, and beg of you to come furnished
with such documents as may be in your possession to prove your claim to be considered a
religious community, in case you wish to be
regarded as such. I also wish to be informed
what interest you claim in the house now ac-
cupied by you. I remain with respect

                        Your Father in X
        October 2,1839. Francis Patrick + 45

It is not likely that Mother Clarke was aware at that
time of an interview with the Bishop to which Father
Donaghoe had been called. Its date is not certain,
but it would seem to have preceded Mother Clarke's,
the second interview having been sought to gain information which the first did not supply. The account of Father Donaghoe's interview with the Bishop
reads:

>   Some priests not too friendly with Father
>   Donaghoe told the Archbishop[sic] about Fr.
>   Donaghoe's new sisters; the Archbishop said,
>   "I never gave my sanction." He sent for Fr.
>   Donaghoe and said: You have a new community
>   I hear.
>   Fr. Donaghoe: I have some ladies employed.
>   In establishing my new parish they are of
>   great assistance.
>   Archbishop: Haven't they a religious rule?
>   Fr. Donaghoe: They go to the sacraments.
>   They visit the sick and help in many ways.
>   Archbishop: Aren't they religious?
>   Fr. Donaghoe: They keep the commandments.

The account continues:

>   Hence the Sisters were called the Sisters of
>   the Decalogue. Father Donaghoe once said as
>   if it slipped, "He (meaning Bishop Kenrick)
>   had not the courage to tell me to disband
>   them." 46

    The incongruities in the report of this interview
would make it seem incredible if there were not evidence that the strange title, "Sisters of the Deca-
logue," persisted. A letter from the Reverend
Benedict Cowles, OCSO, dated July 3, 1884, preserved
in the Community archives, quotes one written by Brother Hillarion of the New Melleray Abbey, Dubuque, to
Abbot Bruno Fitzpatrick, under date of April 12,1850.

It reads: "The Sisters of the Ten Commandments are very kind. Their goodness to us is astonishing. You would scarcely believe me were I to tell you, but God will reward them." Father Benedict adds: "This is the first time I ever heard the BVMs referred to as the Sisters of the Ten Commandments."[47] It is worthy of note that in the course of his interview with the Bishop, as reported, Father Donaghoe made no reference to the Sisters as religious or as teachers, or to the school in which they were employed.

While it would have been quite out of character for the Bishop to have shown Mother Clarke anything but the greatest kindness and consideration,[48] it is equally unlikely for her to have failed to respond with complete openness to any inquiries Kenrick would have made. With no account available of the inter - view, its subject matter is open to conjecture. It seems a fair presumption that the Bishop presented to her two possible lines of action, if she and her companions seriously planned a religious career: 1) that she would make a canonical novitiate in a recognized religious institute, as Catherine McAuley had done, then would direct her Sisters along the lines in which she had been trained, while she was composing a rule subject to his approval; or 2) that the entire group would enter the familiar congregation of the Sisters of Charity of Emmitsburg, or another of their choice.

The former plan, besides the disruption of school arrangements and the probable expense involved, would have constituted them a diocesan congregation, while in the latter their identity would have been lost, as would have been the case if they had been willing to follow a similar plan in Dublin. Either arrangement would have involved a breaking of relations with Father Donaghoe. The fact that four years later, when the Sisters left Philadelphia for Dubuque, they were still without canonical status would indicate Mother Clarke's own unwillingness to see her little community bind itself to a single diocese, or submerge itself in a religious body to which the members did not feel themselves drawn.

The question might well be asked whether Mother Clarke ever informed Father Donaghoe of her interview with the Bishop, or discussed with him the matters it involved. It is altogether probable that she conferred long and thoughtfully with Margaret Mann, but since an account of the meeting to the other Sisters would have involved an exposure of Father Donaghoe's subterfuges in their regard, and would thus have made more difficult obedience to his directives, she may well have kept the entire matter in confidence. Meanwhile there was nothing to prevent continuing the plan of private vows, and so of a dedicated life, for those received into their ranks. The future lay in God's hands and he would make his will known to them, in his own good time.

Only fragmentary accounts remain of the Community's Philadelphia years, and of the young women who entered its ranks there, but there is interest in such data as have survived. The name "Miss Adele Hamelin" appears among the boarding students of the academy in 1843, the only name to merit the title "Miss," a concession evidently granted to her as a postulant and a woman of years, for she entered the Community June 2, 1842, at an acknowledged age of thirty-five. It would be necessary to add at least three years to that figure, however, if we are to credit the following account of her origins, for the last of the slave uprisings in San Domingo took place in 1804, and by 1805 all the whites had disappeared from the island, either through massacre or flight, and the country had become a Black republic. The account comes to us from the Doran <u>Journal</u>:

> Sister M. Ignatius (Adele) Hamelin was the daughter of a rich planter in San Domingo. Mrs. Hamelin died shortly before an insurrection of the negroes in which Mr. Hamelin was killed near his own door. A faithful negress, a servant, put the two children into a basket and covered them with her wearing apparel. When the fierce negroes burst in and rifled the house, she knew it was useless for her to speak, but when they went to seize the basket she coolly said, "Hands off, that's mine." They left it untouched. When the slave saw her chance, she took the basket on her head and went down to the wharf. She succeeded in getting the children to their aunt in Philadelphia, whither she had gone several times with Mrs. Hamelin. When S.M. Ignatius was sometimes depressed, Father Donaghoe would cheer her, saying, "Where is my old friend - we were friends long before we ever heard of those," pointing in fun at the Sisters.[49]

→ Die Solem donipis ad Mariam Crawin, quæ prima est inter forman

Miss Maria E. Alminele communicate.

Respected Miss Clark. As several persons have spoken to me
of you and the ladies associated with you as a Religious Community, I feel bound to inquire into the motives of your Institute,
the laws of the Church forbidding the establishment of any Religious
institution in a diocese without the sanction of the Bishop. I request
therefore, your attendance on Monday next at 10 o'clock at my house,
to explain the matter, and beg of you to come furnished with such
documents as may be in your possession... in case you wish to be regarded
considered as a Religious Community, in case you wish to be regarded

as such. I also wish to be informed what interest you claim
in the house now occupied by you. I remain with respect.
Your bishop in
† Francis Patrick Kenrick

Phila. Octr 8. 1839.

123

Brief accounts remain regarding several of the other young women who entered the community in Philadelphia. Of Sister Mary Aloysius O'Leary, who entered June 21, 1839, there is the following record received from the Poor Clare nuns, Dublin:

> Bridget Leary was an orphan aged seven years when she was recommended by Mr. Simon Farrell, South King Street, admitted in 1805, received First Holy Communion, 1809, received Sacrament of Confirmation 4th May, 1810. Was sent on trial 13th January, 1820 to Miss Fulham's shop, Moate, Co. Westmeath, and provided for. Returned to Harold's Cross at her own earnest request in capacity of caretaker of the children, 1828.

The account is supplemented as follows:

> The above is a copy of entry re Bridget Leary in register of that period. You will notice that it is 'Leary' the prefix 'O' was unlawful at that time. . . .[50]

The "Miss Fulham" who kept the shop in Moate was doubtless one of the three Fulham sisters who inherited from their Protestant father stores "where they sold material for vestments." It was in one of these in Dublin that Margaret Mann first met Catherine Byrne on an errand for the convent at Harold's Cross. One of these stores was burned the "night of the big wind," a hurricane that struck Ireland in February, 1839. Possibly it was the store in Moate, County Westmeath, for Teresa Fulham [Fullam] and her mother left Moate for Philadelphia about that time, Teresa entering the community in 1840. Of her there remains the following description, written many years later:

> Small, delicate, fine dark eyes, manner of gentle sweetness. Skilful in herbs. Her cheerful manner and tender sympathy were a solace to the sick. Special aptitude for office of Infirmarian. Her very presence like pure air and sunshine brought refreshment to the poor invalid languishing on a bed of pain. . . . The members of the community were the first objects of her care, but her charity was extended without measure to all in affliction. No matter what might be the state of her own health she was ready to visit the sick and the dying. This

admirable woman was not less skillful in
ministering to the needs of the soul than in
healing the ills of the body.[51]

Moate featured in the life of Catherine Byrne, also,
for it was there that she served for a time as housekeeper for the parish priest. We have seen that
Bridget O'Leary was apprenticed to the Fulham store
there, and in Mother Clarke's accounts, under date of
August 15, 1843, we find the item, "Clothing from
Moate, $102,00."

One of the young women who became members of the
community in Philadelphia was to succeed Mother Clarke
as superior-general. Eliza Regan[52] was born January
5, 1827, in Cork, Ireland. Her father was William
Regan, a weaver by trade, and her mother, Mary Lane,
daughter of a master weaver. Eliza, the fourth of
six children born in Cork, was about five years old
when the family came to America, settling at Pratt
Court and Second street in Philadelphia. Here five
more children were born. The father, unfortunately
"had a weakness," and the family resources were consequently extremely limited. Eliza attended the public school with the other children until she was eleven years old. At that time the Sisters transferred
their school to the new academy building, near the
Regan home, and the child begged her mother to permit her to go to the Sisters' school. On September
24, 1841, she joined the ranks of the Sisters a few
months before her fifteenth birthday.

Three O'Reilly girls, Frances, Eliza and Catherine,
from Cavan County, Ireland, entered in the years 1839,
1840, and 1842, to become Sisters Mary Francis, Joseph,
and Veronica. Their mother, Catherine O'Reilly, and
their sister Jane followed them to Dubuque, where Mrs.
O'Reilly served for a time as Bishop Loras' housekeeper, and Jane joined her sisters in religion, as
Sister Mary Xavier. The only other member of the
family, a brother, was a doctor in Kentucky.

Mary Austin Baker, (Sister Mary Lucy) from Shrop-
shire, England, was a young widow at the time of her
entrance. During Mr. Baker's last illness, Mother
Clarke and the other Sisters visited him frequently
at his request. On one of these occasions, Mary,
kneeling at her husband's bedside, took Mother
Clarke's hand, asking if, in case her husband was taken from her, Mother would admit her into their little Community. When Mother Clarke assured her she

would gladly do so, the sick man expressed his relief
and happiness that his young wife would be safely
provided for. Shortly after Mr. Baker's death, Mary
became a postulant in the Phoenix street convent,[53]
where she would remain when the other Sisters went
west, detained by the settling of her husband's business affairs, and the care of the convent property
until a buyer could be found.

Eliza Mullen was at the early age of fifteen, the
first American girl to enter the Community. The
daughter of a successful Philadelphia merchant, she
was for a time a student at the Sisters' academy
where she proved herself an earnest and able scholar.
Her special aptitude for music had been cultivated by
excellent teachers. Notes in Sister's personal file
describe her as a pleasing personality, with a beautiful face and manner and a gentle reserve. "She
treated the smallest child with a respect that. . .
she would have shown to the most distinguished man or
woman. . . She could not be discourteous to anyone."
As Sister M. Philomena she taught music in the academy on the Iowa Prairie, and for a time acted as superior of the motherhouse there. Death claimed Sister on September 13, 1854, at the early age of twenty-
nine.

Sarah Cole (Sister M. Magdalen), who joined the
Sisters in Philadelphia January 1, 1842, attributed
her conversion to the faith to a scrap of paper she
had picked up as a child on which was written the
triple prayer to Jesus, Mary and Joseph. It had a
strong appeal for her and she used often to repeat it.
On one occasion, having wandered into a wooded area,
she lost her way, and, becoming frightened, she began to shout the prayer aloud. She quickly found a
clearing and saw on the road ahead of her a couple
with a small child. As the story was told to Mother
Gervase many years afterwards, she followed the trio,
trying to catch up with them, yet she never could,
though they looked back from time to time to see that
she was following them. Assured in her own mind that
they were the three holy persons to whom she had
prayed so earnestly, she did indeed reach home safely.
As an adult, Sarah sought baptism from Father Donaghoe
at St. Joseph church,[54] though she did not enter religion until some years later, at the age of thirty.

Sister M. Camillus came to the Sisters from the
Emmitsburg Sisters of Charity, having entered there
as Mary McNulty on July 21, 1829. As Sister Seraphine,

she was one of four Sisters sent to Philadelphia in
1830 to staff St. John asylum and school, and after
some time there, spent a year's leave with Mother
Clarke's Sisters, where, taking the name 'Camillus,'
she taught in the school. Apparently she then returned to her former community and served for some
time in a German orphanage in Cincinnati. Her second
departure from that community took place from a Baltimore house in 1846, probably from Mount Hope Retreat.[55]
From there Mary McNulty went to Wisconsin, where she
taught briefly in a district school in the vicinity
of Sinsinawa Mound. In 1847, she was accepted as a
candidate by the Reverend Samuel Mazzuchelli, OP, and
shortly became the first prioress of his young congregation, having chosen again the name Sister
Seraphine.[56]

Only the merest fragments remain regarding the
Sisters' days in Philadelphia: that Mary Baker's
aunt, Mrs. Hunt, taught music to the children and
gave private lessons to Sisters Mary Francis and
Ignatius; and that Mother Clarke was teacher of arithmetic and "set the copies" for writing, while "a man"
taught the boys, and a Mrs. O'Connor, who later moved
to the Dubuque area, was also among the teachers.
Then there was Mother Clarke's "butter and egg boy"
whose memory of her gentle kindness included recollections of a weekly bonus of homemade cookies.

While Mother Clarke now felt secure in the good
will and understanding of Bishop Kenrick,[57] Father
Donaghoe's position had evidently become uncomfortable, as a letter to him from Father Francis
Dzierozynski, S.J., dated April 25, 1841, indicates:

> Yours of the 20th inst. came to hand on the
> 23d. I lose no time in answering your pious
> request. My opinion now, is the same as for-
> merly, that you had better remain where you
> are, first on account of the difficulties
> you experience - these are real blessings -
> we have Our Lord's word for it. Blessed are
> the poor, etc. blessed are they who suffer,
> etc. Our Lord took you up to the Cross, for
> him, persevere in carrying it. Secondly, on
> account of those pious ladies, who have now
> established for themselves a character, who
> are making themselves useful to Religion.
> Were you to remove them, this might not be
> the case, and it would expose you to censure
> from a wicked world. Other reasons might be

suggested, but these in my opinion are sufficient to keep you where you are clinging
fast to the Cross which our Dearest Redeemer
has destined for you. I would request you to
be particularly kind and respectful to your
good Bishop, although he may not reciprocate,
still he is to you in the place of Christ.

A second letter from the same priest in September of
that year throws light on the first:

When you wrote me last, the same difficulties existed, and no greater than now - the
same pressing invitation from New York as
now without greater reason for it. My advice is consequently the same as it was before - that is, remain at your post under
the protection of St. Michael and the holy
Virgin Mother whose sufferings we commemorate. . .

Though Bishop Hughes, now administrator of the
New York diocese, continued to urge Father Donaghoe
to settle in New York, the latter followed the advice
he had sought and received from Father Dzierozynski.
For this the Sisters were later to be most grateful,
when Hughes' policies became apparent in his dealings
with the Emmitsburg Sisters. His determination that
he would have no religious institute of women in his
diocese who were not subject directly to his rule
forced those Sisters to decide between their allegiance to their own institution and their concern for
the children who were their charges in the New York
orphanages.[58]

Meanwhile Bishop Mathias Loras, in his new diocese in the West, was seeking a religious congregation of women.[59] John Norman, whom Father Donaghoe
had befriended and trained as one of his Sunday
School teachers, was then engaged in teaching the
boys of the Cathedral parish in Dubuque. When the
Bishop heard from him of the Philadelphia Sisters, he
wrote at once to Father Donaghoe. Before reaching a
decision, Father and the Sisters made a novena to St.
Joseph, and on its closing day, March 19, 1842, the
Bishop's petition was reinforced by the arrival of
John Norman. Father's decision then was that it was
God's will that some of the Sisters be sent to the
West. It was his wish that the feast of St. Joseph
be kept as a holy day in the Community as a token of
gratitude for the answer to their prayer. For that

reason also the new home in the West was to be named St. Joseph's.

On May 28, Bishop Loras wrote from Prairie du Chien, expressing his gratification at Father Donaghoe's ready decision to place three or four of the Sisters at his disposal. He explained that for three years he had tried in vain to secure a religious institution in his diocese, and while he had received some promises, none had come as speedily as Father's. While Loras was not in a position to receive the Sisters at once, he promised to visit them in Philadelphia on his trip to Baltimore for the Council the following spring, when he would complete arrangements and conduct the Sisters to Dubuque. The Bishop added:

> In the meantime I feel confident that you will not forget your promise and that you will prepare some good Sisters either for our Indian missions, or for other purposes. I would like very much to have among them one who could speak French and another one Deutsch, although I should be satisfied if they were only English scholars.
>
> I would be thankful if you would suggest to your Superioress the propriety of writing to me in a few months to let me know if they are always in the same dispositions, and if they have any desire for devoting themselves to the Indian missions, after the example of the ladies of the Sacred Heart of St. Louis.

* * * * *

The aged Conwell had been failing for some time. Now at the age of ninety-four, after twelve years of retirement and nine of blindness, death claimed him on April 22, 1842. Those who had observed the eccentricities of his conduct during the troubled years of conflict had learned to regard with sympathy his patient acceptance of his helpless condition and death. Bishop Kenrick celebrated the Requiem Mass in the church of St. Joseph, in the presence of nearly all the priests of the diocese, the seminarians, and a great concourse of laity.[60] His death left Kenrick with undisputed claim to the title and perquisites, as well as to the burdens, of the Bishop of Philadelphia. A long-drawn-out law suit was to follow, however, over the title to the 'Bishop's burial ground,' which Conwell's various nieces and nephews claimed as his natural heirs. When the Board of Health forbade additional burials in the cemetery at 13th Street below Spruce, Conwell had purchased in his own name, at Passyunk and Washington Avenue, a burial ground, with funds solicited for a Catholic graveyard. Regarding this, Bishop Kenrick wrote to the Holy Father, during the lifetime of the aged Bishop:

> The Bishop Conwell declares that he bought this land out of money that was personally his own, excepting a small sum that was given to him for the purpose by some of the people. Others insist that almost all the money came from the offerings of the faithful. The Bishop, however, protests that after his death he intends to leave it by will to the future bishop.[61]

All this came at a time when Kenrick was feeling the weight of his office, for he assured the Holy Father that he deplored the honor that had come to him, and would gladly go back to the forests he had left.[62]

Conwell's will, which he had committed to the care of Father Donaghoe as his executor, bequeathed the St. Joseph cemetery to the Jesuit Fathers. However, a week before his death, the aged Bishop asked for the document, promising to return it in a day or so. This he failed to do, and after his death no trace of it could be found.[63] After long litigation, the Court of Equity, assisted by Father Donaghoe's testimony regarding the contents of the will, decided in favor of the Jesuit Fathers. The end did not finally come, however, until Kenrick issued the reminder that excommunication was the lot of those who would take to themselves properties belonging to the Church.[64]

A letter from Father Donaghoe's director, postmarked "Georgetown, September 1842," seems to indicate that after the death of Conwell matters eased between Father Donaghoe and Bishop Kenrick, and that Father would be shortly on his way to his annual retreat. In the letter, Father Dzierozynski expressed pleasure that Bishop Kenrick had invited Father Donaghoe to accompany him on a trip to Charleston, South Carolina. He viewed the invitation as an indication of improved relations. He rejoiced that the Sisters were "being called to the vineyard of the red men," where he thought of them as future "Angels to the Children of the forest," adding, "Better for you

than all the honors of the Church or riches of the
state, the share you will have in the missionary labors of your Children in Xt."[65]

A visit to the Sisters in the fall of 1842 by
Father Pierre J. DeSmet, the renowned Jesuit missionary to the Indians of the Northwest, stirred their
spirits and turned their thoughts to the Red Men of
whom they had long heard in tales of America, and
whom they now were impatient to see. Then in November came a second letter from Bishop Loras, addressed
to Father Donaghoe, in which he expressed deep satisfaction regarding the willingness of Mother Clarke and
the Sisters for any of the various works of which his
diocese had need.

> I have offered my thanks to Almighty God for
> the favorable dispositions He has put into
> the hearts of your excellent Sisters, whom I
> shall soon call mine, at least a good portion
> of them. Their devotedness for every kind
> of good work, even among the children of the
> forest, is truly admirable and promises a
> plentiful harvest in the field of the Lord.
> I am preparing the way for them and I am
> sure they will not disappoint me.

Then followed a plea that Father Donaghoe accompany
the Sisters to the "poorest diocese of the Union,"
indicating that he himself would go East immediately
after Easter, and would then settle all things properly.

For the Sisters, the winter months were filled
with dreams and hopes and fears. The thought of the
parting was painful and the question of who would be
chosen to go and who would stay was never far from
their thoughts. Father Donaghoe, at long last, announced the decision: Margaret Mann would be superior of the five on their great venture, and with her
would go the once-pampered Eliza Kelly, the lovely
young Francis O'Reilly of the beautiful voice, and
her talented sister, Joseph, together with the pious
but rough-hewn Patrice Caniff from Connaught. Sewing
and planning and packing would make their busy days
busier still, until the time of departure. Meanwhile,
some slight misunderstanding must have risen among
them which occasioned a letter of admonition from
Father Donaghoe. In it he admonishes the Sisters to
observe the Community regulations faithfully, indicating that where difficulties arise in connection

with their observance, a Sister should go to her superior for direction. He reminds the Sisters that
one who refuses to act in this way usually confides
her troubles and imparts her discontent to a Sister
who is herself a weakling, instead of going for advice to one remarkable for strict observance. He
continues:

> Oh, my dear childern [sic] when you find one
> troubled, point with your index finger the
> road to the murmurer, tell her the remedy is
> not with you, pray for her but never indulge
> her -- I am sure you will, my dear children-
> - Oh! it is this evil that made and makes so
> much havoc in other communities. May our
> blessed Lord preserve you from it who have
> the honor of being properly called a commun-
> ity. Love one another, try to be truly hum-
> ble for this is the Virtue of all virtues of
> our Blessed Lord. May it be yours, my dear
> children, and pray that our good Lord will
> give it to your
> affectionate Father in Christ.

In response to Bishop Loras' urging, Father Donaghoe wrote that he would accompany the first party to
the West, though later his plans were changed. In
reply to Father's letter, the Bishop wrote from Dubuque on March 8, 1843, not long before setting out for
the Council in Baltimore, assuring him of the consolation his promise had given. The Bishop spoke also
of the satisfaction Father's plans were to John Norman and his wife, and of their intention of writing
the Sisters to give helpful suggestions for their
travel and their needs in the West. The letter
closed with a listing of

> our little band of excellent clergy, twelve
> only, but devoted, pious and equable, viz:
> Rev. J.C. Alleman, Jas.Causse, Jos. Cretin,
> L. Galtier, A.Godfert, Jno. Healy, Anthony
> Pelamourgues, T.C. Perrodin, Remigius
> Petiot, Augustin Ravoux,

adding only, "I intend to buy a printing establishment in order to issue in Dubuque a small Catholic
paper. Be so good as to prepare the way for me."

The new Dubuque see was suffragan to that of St.
Louis, and it was of the latter archdiocese that
Peter Kenrick had been made coadjutor on November

30, 1841. Under that date the elder Kenrick, bishop
of Philadelphia, had written in his Journal, "My
brother was consecrated Bishop in St. Mary's Church
by the most illustrious and Reverend Joseph Rosati,
Bishop of St. Louis," and on December 1, he, whose
brother had served him so well, added touchingly,
"Early in the morning my brother went away." 66

To serve as his theologian at the Council, Loras
chose the remarkable Italian missionary, Samuel
Mazzuchelli, who was the lone priest in the Dubuque
diocese at the time of its creation. The two traveled by steamboat to St. Louis, then past Cairo and
up the Ohio to Cincinnati, a journey of four days and
nights. Taking a third steamer to Wheeling, they
then "traveled by stage one hundred and twenty miles
in twenty-two hours, to take the railroad at Cumber-
land. This mode of traveling seems to have attained
the last limit in speed," Mazzuchelli observes in
his Memoirs,"for in eight hours, including the stop-
pages at different stations, we reached the city of
Baltimore, a distance of one hundred and twenty-five
miles."67 At the close of the Council, Mazzuchelli
set sail for his native Milan, while the Bishop went
to Philadelphia. Little did Bishop Loras think then
that his faithful missionary was not to return to his
diocese.

Loras had something of a rude awakening when he
met Bishop Kenrick at the Council in Baltimore and
learned that the "religious" Father Donaghoe had promised him were without canonical status. Evidently
believing that Father's lack of candor in their regard freed him from the arrangement of receiving them
into his diocese, Loras decided to make another of
several attempts to secure the services of the Sisters of Charity of Emmitsburg. He hoped this time to
be successful. Setting out by stage for a fifty-mile
trip to Emmitsburg, he was disappointed to find
Mother Xavier Clarke away, a fact which occasioned
the following letter:

Baltimore, May 20,1843
Mother M. Xavier, Superior -general of the
Emmitsburg Sisters,

Respected Mother,
Having been deprived of the satisfaction of
seeing you at St. Joseph's last week, I take
this opportunity to let you know the principal object of my visit. Since Divine Providence has entrusted me with the administration of the diocese of Dubuque, I have always

had the desire of admitting into it your excellent Sisters. For this purpose I have
bought next to the Cathedral's garden a good
lot which does not measure less than 160 by
300 feet; and I have built on it a large and
commodious house which is to be soon completed.
I wish to organize there a day school of about
50 girls, and as soon as possible a little
orphan asylum. I am willing to give a deed
to the Sisters for that valuable property in
order to establish them in my diocese in a
lasting manner. I shall pay for their journey from here, and comply with all the rules
of the order concerning their support.

Be so kind, respected Mother, as to let me
know if you can give me some of your Sisters
whom I might accompany myself to Dubuque.

In the expectation of a favorable answer I
recommend you and all your community to God
Almighty   and I remain, respectfully and
devotedly, dear Mother,

                    Yours in Christ
                    +Mathias, Bishop of
                    Dubuque.68

    Mother Xavier's inability to furnish Sisters left
Loras with little choice if he was not to be deprived
of essential help. The original plan, to provide him
with the services of five of the Sisters, was adequate
for the immediate needs of his diocese, and would
have sufficiently taxed his resources. That Dubuque
received, within the year, the entire community of
nineteen Sisters calls for some explanation, the only
possible source of which lies in Father Donaghoe's
confidential letter to his friend, Bishop Hughes
written after the entire Community was settled in Dubuque. The first portion of this letter indicates
that there has been an estrangement of some nature
between the two friends, the explanation for which
Father Donaghoe is trying to search out, as he lays
his case before Bishop Hughes. Without knowledge of
the context in which the letter was written, the
meaning of the contents is not entirely clear. However, it is apparent that Father Donaghoe is also in
some difficulty with Bishop Kenrick, the resolution
of which may call for an exercise of power on the
part of Hughes. This portion of the letter gives insights into Father's tendency toward introspection

and his dependence on Hughes' good will and affectionate understanding. The second portion of the letter,
that with regard to the expenses involved in removing
the second group of Sisters to Dubuque, seems to be
rather a bid for sympathy than a statement of facts.
The heroic sacrifices Father claims to have made to
provide for the Sisters on their journey seem to have
no basis in fact, for the letter from Bishop Loras,
written from Dubuque on July 5, 1843, only shortly
after his return to his diocese with the first five
Sisters, gives no hint of pressure for funds, and as-
sures Father Donaghoe that he has no cause for concern in that regard. Loras' letter reads in part:
"You say in the 2nd place that you ask carte blanche
for the traveling and winter's expense, and all is
right. Come, therefore, as soon as convenient with
our dear 14 children of Mary, who are all as devoted
as our 5."

December 27th, 1843
Right Revd & Dear Bishop, [Hughes]
        The Festival of the Apostle St. John has
more than usually stirred up many an association connected with this day.* It may be
that it is because I find myself on this
side of the great Mississippi - no, that is
not it. It is something altogether different. But to the point. I have labored under the impression that you were entirely
displeased with me; at least these three
months past.** To the letter I wrote you on
the day that I obtained permission from Bishop Kenrick to go to the far West, and made
known to you on the eve of your going to Europe, I attribute your displeasure. When letters were received by others, I expected one
to drop in for me; when accused by some of
concealing it, I answered that I supposed
that you concluded that I must have already
set out for the West. I fancied that myself
- I arrived safely at Dubuque on Tuesday
morning, the 8th of October. I read of your
arrival in the beginning of November. My
first impulse was to write & tell you my many

---

* The Bishop's patronal feast.

**   This would have been about the time he left
Philadelphia for Dubuque with the fourteen Sisters
who went West after the closing of their school.

adventures. The thought crossed my mind of
your displeasure & I concluded to wait, but
now delay is unnecessary. I am convinced of
what I apprehended! Could I do otherwise?
You saw and knew my difficulties in Baltimore.
You knew my repugnance. On this side of N.Y.
all had been heretofore determined, except in
case I might stand in need of your power as
well as friendship. I had resolved to abide
faithfully at my post, devoted to my little
community. I had not been many days in Philadelphia before the Council, when by and
through those who hover around the White house
I knew that my ordeal of trial was very far
from being ended. I then looked on all sides.
I saw no alternative. Bp. Loras could get
none from E'burg. He asked me for five, I
told him I would give all or none. He agreed
if I would come myself. The interview with
Bp. Kenrick I told you, I think, in my letter of the 5th of June. He departed with 5
of the best Sisters on Wednesday the 7th and
in ten days I rec'd a letter from him - of
his fears of not having rec'd his allocation
from Lyons, etc. - poverty & his cathedral.
I had already commenced to prepare for the
fall as agreed. Judge of the stroke this
was to me - I had but $80 - yet, I wrote to
him that if money was the only obstacle "in
the name of God keep it for the wants of his
diocese - that I would do all and support
the Sisters there for the winter - if he approved to send me his consent and Benediction. I received it. I pledged my furniture,
vestments, type - all except my books - and
thereby I was able to carry out my purpose.
My mind is warmed by all the recollections
and I cannot think if you condescend to weigh
my difficult position, that you can remain
displeased, or punish by a silence that is
worse than any other chastisement. I have
done. I can think of nothing else. It is
now for you to treat me as you please. I
will, however, remain
                    Your devoted Donaghoe till death.

On the eve of the Sisters' departure for Dubuque,
Mother Clarke submitted to Father Donaghoe the following recap of receipts and expenditures for the Sisters'
ten years in Philadelphia:

EXPENDITURES		RECEIPTS	
Housekeeping from		Sundry Receipts	
1833 to 1843	9020.40	from 1833-1843	652.82
Clothing - Wood-		Deducted from	
Rent- Coal . .	4228.26	Clothing.	. 189.42
Trimmings -Bot		By cash . .	. . 152.85
[bought] . .	120.08	Sale of books	. . 625.88
Books -Bot . . .	563.79	Work done by	
Returned to Mary		Sisters .	.4263.99
Nolan	50.00	Boarding and Day	
Paid to Mrs. Hunt		School	. .2579.90
for lessons. .	. 60.00	Do [ditto] by	
To Rev. Father		Boarders	2557.71
returned . . .	1215.68	From Rev. Father	3674.34
	15258.27		14696.91
		From Rev. Father	561.36
			15258.27

> The expenses of Buildings, traveling &c are
> not included in the above. The above is a
> full acct. of receipts and expenditures from
> our commencement in Philadelphia, Nov.1st,
> 1833, to our leaving for Dubuque Sept. 12th,
> 1843, as entered in this Book. See large
> Book with old receipts and Bills. The Books
> of particular accts. were burned.[70]

A careful study of the above statement indicates that
the Sisters supported their school and themselves for
the first five of their Philadelphia years. On the
completion of the Academy in 1838, the Emmitsburg
Sisters withdrew from St. Michael's, leaving the academy Sisters to care for the free school pupils as
well as their own boarders and paying day students.
The net amount the Sisters received from Father
Donaghoe, $3020.02, would scarcely have covered more
than the parish contribution to the instruction of
the free students for the years 1838-1843.

In marked contrast to the above account is the
page of assembled items which constituted Father
Donaghoe's financial record for the same years.
Made up, as it seems, from loose memoranda, most of
the items are without dates. Those having dates were
not set down in chronological order. All entries,
written in a single column of a two-column page -
receipts, expenditures, moneys due, and "bad debts"-
are listed without differentiation. Items include
$90.00 due me per my mare," and $131.25, either due

or received or owed or paid out for the stereotype of
a child's prayerbook he had compiled. The accounting
can scarcely have been complete in any respect.*

But the ten years were at an end, and a new life
lay ahead.

Rev. T. J. Donah___ ?

Journal

138

1834 title due Mr Fox. myself ~~~~~~ in 10 00
1835. Apr 6 Paid Saml Joseph & Flander (Emmittsburg) for oister . 535 62 also
1832 Mr Fugeray's 1 bile for stores & coal . 149 42
x Mr Fugeray 2 bile, rd Son ———— 114 —
1833 Paid Revd for supply to McBride . 58 "
1836 Chappel B B Grolly for Nails & Pd 9 67
1835 Fillean for myself dues . 5 25
1836. paid R R Robb postage Feb 3 22d . 15 91
(made by Bishop)
no charge
1834 & Making of the Vestments & Linen Com cloth —
-34 Paid Manchester Linen bile . 40 00
Engraving S H . 11 75
& Charity home rent . 57 55 Probably B M's
Paid on Cath Companion 100 "
Draft on Mechanicks & Johnston 75 72
due me for My three by P Green 90 " pd 50 "
paid Campbell for E Norman . 30 "
Do Eagle . 5 75
due me Mrs Coffry & Monaghan 12 50
Revd Dr Hurley & O Donnell — 123 "
Salembier French — sopie - 50 & 30 130 "
- Other bad debts viz . Monaghan 5-Kelly 12-
-50 Tucker girl R. McDonnel 25 - Brt Ths Moore 10
Mr Harper 5 Fed OBrien 8 Barry 15- Furnan 25
Moyne 10 Mrs N Coffry 12.50 " — 138 "
Recd from L Lalor . viz

CHAPTER III -- NOTES

1. "They would in time constitute the bulk and back-
    bone of Kenrick's laity, and it would be diffi-
    cult for him to find a more faithful and gener-
    ous body of Catholic people." Nolan,p. 106.

2. On a visit to Philadelphia many years ago, the
    writer noted on the old brick structure next to
    Willing's Alley rectory a marker indicating that
    there Evangeline has discovered the dying Gabriel.
    The building has since been demolished, and
    there is no present memorial of the exiled Aca-
    dians. It is interesting, though, to recall
    that:
    "On 19 and 20 November, 1755 three vessels ar-
    rived at Philadelphia with more than 400 Acadian
    exiles. Their arrival at the time when the
    French had gained victories in the Western Penn-
    sylvania filled the inhabitants with alarm. . . .
    After a long delay the exiles were allowed to
    disembark, and fear of them gave place to pity
    at the forlorn state of these poor, heartbroken
    exiles, half-naked and starved and worn out from
    the hardships of their cruel journey. Temporary
    quarters were made for them in tents on the va-
    cant land on the north side of Pine street be-
    tween Fifth and Sixth streets. The pastor of
    St. Joseph's,Father Harding, and members of the
    Society of Friends led by Anthony Benezet minis-
    tered to them from their private funds, and se-
    cured public aid for them. . . . The kind offi-
    ces of those interested, however, were not pow-
    erful enough to soften the mental sufferings of
    the Acadians, the disappointment at their re-
    peated efforts to secure justice, or save them
    from disease, especially the small-pox, so that
    more than one-half of them succumbed and were
    buried in . . . the Catholic portion of the
    Stranger's Burial Ground. . . .Of those who sur-
    vived some were sent to France, some to other
    colonies to rejoin lost relatives, and the rest
    melted imperceptibly into the population of the
    city. Today there is no trace in Philadelphia
    of the sojourn of those exiles; no monument yet
    marks the hallowed earth at Sixth and Locust
    streets where lie the dust of so many hundred
    Catholics who died in a strange land, exiled and

martyred for their stanch[sic] adherence to their creed." J.L.J. Kirlin, Catholicity in Philadelphia (Philadelphia: John Jos. McVey, 1909), p.84.

3. While Mrs. McDonogh lived a number of years after the above incidents, the following account, written after her death, may be of interest:

> Among the recent deaths in our city, we notice, with no ordinary feeling, that of Mrs. Margaret McDonogh. . . . A tribute of respect to her memory is peculiarly due. Independently of her personal claims to it, as one who in every way and at all times was a lady, a beautiful specimen of Christian character, gentle, kind and beneficent, she merits it as the mother of Lieutenant Patrick McDonogh, who sacrificed himself so nobly at the storming of Fort Erie, and as the grandmother of Capt. John P. O'Brien, who acted so bravely and efficiently at Buena Vista. . To this explosion which destroyed the magazine of Fort Erie, about to be taken by the British in the War of 1812 the enemy attributes their failure. How happened it? Some refer it to accident; but other officers relate"that Lieutenant McDonogh, not having been removed after his several wounds, from the foot of the bastion and being exasperated at the determination which he saw in the conduct of the enemy's troops to show no mercy to the vanquished soldier, resolved upon devoting himself to stop the progress of their inhuman career, and to this end threw a lighted match into the chest of ammunition, which, by its immediate explosion, produced those tremendous effects which restored the bastion to the Americans, and terminated the conflict. No monument, as yet, designates the burial spot of this self-sacrificing soldier." (RACHS, Vol. pp. 312-313).

> His mother "fancied that her beloved son was probably not justified in taking his own life, even though in so noble a cause, - in a word, that his act might have been in a measure suicidal," which accounts "for her life-long grief and the silence in regard to her son which was rarely broken in after years, even to her family and most intimate friends. Monument, public demonstration,

plaudits of the multitude, - of what value
these to the broken-hearted mother? Early
one August morning that devoted mother went
forth from her home, in all probability to
attend Mass at Old St. Joseph Church. In
the city's streets she found little knots of
people gathered, saw and heard on every side
the excitement and exultation of her fellow-
citizens over the news, just received, of a
victory gained by the Americans over the
British at Fort Erie . . . Those ringing
cheers of a nation's rejoicing were for that
startled mother but the sad wailing of a
death-knell, for then and there she learned
that the life-blood of her son, her only son,
had helped pay the price of that victory."
(Ibid., p. 315).

4. The Reverend Francis Dzierozynski, S.J., a native
of Poland, entered the Society from White Russia
in 1779, during the years of the general suppression. Associated during his novitiate and schol-
asticate with many of the surviving Fathers of
the old Society, he was an important link con-
necting them with the young society after its
restoration, both in Russia and in the States.
Possessing talents of a high order, he was to be
distinguished for both holiness and learning.
After the expulsion of the Jesuits from Russia in
1820 and his coming to the States, he succeeded
Father Charles Neale in the office of Superior
or Visitor of the Mission of Maryland, which at
that time directed the activities of all Jesuits
in the States, an office to which Father Peter
Kenney succeeded in the year 1830. Filling the
positions of professor of theology and philosophy, of novice master, provincial, spiritual father, and finally, confessor to the Visitation
Sisters at Georgetown, he also carried the responsibility for founding both St. John College,
Frederick, Maryland, and the College of the Holy
Cross at Worcester, Massachusetts. He was well
loved and deeply respected, but he was especially regarded for his sanctity. Father Dzierozynski
died September 11, 1850, at St. John College, in
his 73rd year.

5. Brother Faye died of consumption within the year,
just after making his vows. (Eleanor Donnelly,
A Memoir of Father Felix Joseph Barbelin, S.J.
Philadelphia: n.p., 1886, p. 83).

142

6. McGuire, Annals, pp. 61-62.

7. The Catholic Chronologist, a Monthly Record of
    of Memorable Events, Ed., James A. Rooney,
    Brooklyn, N.Y., Vol. II, November, 1914.

8. The Bishop of Belley, in his Spirit of St. Francis
    de Sales, quotes from the works of Francis in
    this connection: "I must acknowledge that con-
    gregations employed in teaching please me above
    the rest, because they really support themselves
    by their own labors." (translated from the
    French of Bishop Camus, by "a clergyman of Mas-
    sachusetts," New York: P.O'Shea, 1867).

    The religious institute for women of Francis'
    day was ordinarily well endowed, and open only
    to women of wealth, even of nobility, able to
    bring an ample dowry and accustomed to a life of
    leisure, with the labors of the convent house-
    hold performed by lay help. The ardent desire
    of Francis, whose own life was one of almost in-
    supportable labors, to see an institute of dedi-
    cated women leading more useful and productive
    lives seems quite understandable. To him,
    teaching was a labor to which they might well
    have looked for their support. Unfortunately, as
    we shall see later, Father Donaghoe's application
    of the principle of labor to our Sisters failed
    to regard teaching as worthy of remuneration,
    expecting rather that they should make provision
    for their own livelihood through the labor of
    their hands beyond the hours of the school day.

9. Spirit of St. Francis de Sales, Vol. 2, Chapter
    21.

10. Doran, In the Early Days, pp. 32-33.

11. "When the aged prelate was told to spare himself
    the fatigue of the long ceremony of dedication,
    he said, 'My son's church is being dedicated to-
    day: I must go and bless it.'" (Doran, Early
    Days, p. 251.)

12. Rev. Wm. J. Boyle, The Story of St. Michael's,
    1834-1943. p. 31.

13. Ibid., pp. 34-35.

14. Ibid., p. 35.

15. It is significant that Catholic Directories from
    the years the Sisters served in Philadelphia

contain no mention of our Sisters. A reference
to "St.Michael's free school" in the care of
three teachers was made in the directories of
1835, 1836, and 1837. In that of 1838, both enrollment and the number of teachers are omitted,
while the 1839 directory lists an enrollment of
160 pupils with no accounting of the number of
teachers. Where the school is referred to it
seems to be associated with the Emmitsburg Char-
ities. Such may well have been the case, for
their school on Prune Street under Father Donaghoe's direction may have been removed from the
St. Joseph parish to his own and continued until the opening of the Sacred Heart Academy on
Second and Phoenix. The fact that "This school
disappears from our list of establishments in
1837" (see p. 66, Chapter 2) would indicate that
such might have been the case. The school kept
by our Sisters previous to 1838 was probably regarded merely as a "select school" under lay direction.

16. Carl Wittke, The Irish in America, (Baton Rouge:
Louisiana State University Series,1956) p. 125.

17. Before the Civil War practically every immigrant
group had its militia companies, for the foreign-
born were not welcome in the military organizations of native Americans. The Irish loved uniforms, parades, and ceremonial and convivial occasions. Irish military units before 1860 included the Emmet Guards, Irish Rifles, Napper
Tandy Light Artillery, Hibernia Greens, etc.
They were conspicuous in Fourth of July and St.
Patrick's Day parades, but they also marched on
other occasions on the slightest provocation.
Cf. Wittke, op. cit., pp. 52-54.

18. Pamphlet, ORATION delivered by the Hon. Robert
T. Conrad at the CELEBRATION of the ANNIVERSARY
OF AMERICAN INDEPENDENCE by the PHILADELPHIA RE-
PEAL ASSOCIATION at the ARCH STREET THEATRE,
July 5, 1841.

19. Wittke, pp. 103-104.

20. The supposed writer was a wretched girl who
after a shameful career had been placed by
her mother in a Magdalen asylum in Montreal
from which she was dismissed or escaped through
the aid of a male friend. She was induced to
write her "awful disclosures" as though she had

144

been a nun in the Hotel Dieu, where she supposedly
witnessed immorality, cruelty, and infanticide.
Harper Brothers were willing for the profit but
not the ill repute connected with such a publication, so issued it under the names of two of
their employees. The book was greedily received
and read perhaps more widely than any book ever
before published in the country. Those involved
in the plot of wholesale defamation quarreled
over the profits from it, while the wretched woman sank lower and lower and finally died in a
city prison. William L. Stone, a man strongly
prejudiced against the Church, obtained permission to visit the convent, and, book in hand,
visited every room and closet there, publishing
as his conclusion that Maria Monk was an arrant
impostor who had never been a nun and had never
been inside the convent mentioned. He described
the "disclosures" as "either the vagaries of a
distempered brain, or a series of calumnies un-
equaled in the depravity of their invention, and
unsurpassed in their enormity." Cf. Gilmary
Shea, History of the Church in the United States
(New York: n.p. 1856) Vol. III, pp. 500-512 and
Ray Billington, The Protestant Crusade, 1800-1860,
p. 108 et passim.A Study of the Origins of American Nativism, (Chicago: Quadrangle Books. 1964.

21. The sources for the above material, except as noted, were : Ray Allen Billington, The Protestant
Crusade, 1800-1860,the Rev. Hugh J. Nolan, The
Most Rev.Francis Patrick Kenrick, Third Bishop
of Philadelphia, and the microfilmed doctoral
dissertation of John Joseph Kane, Irish Immigrant
in Philadelphia.

22. Doran, Journal, p. 49.

23. There is a listing of the names of twelve boys
and twenty-five girls as free scholars for the
school year 1836-37, in a school that could not
have been large.

24. Doran, Journal, p. 14.
25. Ibid., p. 28.
26. Nolan, p. 292 n.
27. Ibid., pp. 498-499, also Kenrick-Frenaye
Correspondence.
28. RACHS, Vol. 38, p. 209.
29. Ibid., p. 213.
30. Shea, pp. 216-217.

31. Cf. Hassard, p. 167.

32. Griffin, RACHS, vol. 29, p. 368. Mrs. Johnston was the aged Bishop's housekeeper. A nephew, Henry McKeon, was residing at the rectory at that time.

33. Ibid., p. 369. The name "Mary Donagher" appears as a member of the Conwell household during the elderly Bishop's last years. Other names, occurring in marriage records at St. Joseph's and making use of one or other of the spellings Father Donaghoe seems to have used at various times are: Hugh and Mary Donaghey, Mary Donoughoo, Mary Donahoe, Patrick and Susan Donaghoe, James, Arthur and John Donaghy etc. It is impossible to know now whether any of these were relatives of Father. RACHS, "Marriage Registers at St. Joseph's Church, Philadelphia, Penn., 1824-1836," Francis X. Ruess, Vol. 20, 1909.

34. Doran, Early Days, p. 58.

35. The Reverend C.F. Griffith, former history professor at St. Ambrose College, Davenport, Iowa, collected through many years items of Iowa Catholic history. Among these are random notes of the Reverend J. F. Kempker, historian of the Catholic Church in Iowa, taken in the course of interviews in the process of research. Father Griffith placed his extensive files at the disposition of the writer. It is hoped that they may be eventually incorporated in a central archives and properly classified for general research.

36. Doran, Journal, p. 46.
37. Griffith files.
38. Ibid.
39. Boyle, p. 34.

40. A communication from the United States Immigration and Naturalization Service, Philadelphia, dated November 6, 1972, says that "no record relating to Reverend Donaghoe can be found."

41. Nolan, p. 38.
42. Doran, Journal, p. 10.
43. See Footnote 74 Chapter II above, for full account of this episode.

44. This last assertion, made in the Doran Journal,
    p. 11, is subject to serious question. In re-
    sponse to the writer's inquiry of September 15,
    1973, the Reverend Hugh J. Nolan, biographer of
    Bishop Kenrick writes:
    > I never saw any evidence that would prove or
    > even indicate that Bishop Kenrick might re-
    > fuse to hear confessions of religious. In
    > fact, that would seem to be totally out of
    > character for him, whose cause the diocese
    > once contemplated introducing for canoniza-
    > tion. By nature, he was gentle and kind,
    > even though a contemplative scholar.

    John Marschall, whose doctoral dissertation was
    a study of Kenrick's Baltimore years, writes on
    September 19, 1973, in the same vein: "I cannot
    imagine his refusing the sacrament to anyone.
    He was far too conscientious and pastorally ori-
    ented for that!"

45. This letter is contained in Bishop Kenrick's
    handwritten Journal, where it bears the super-
    scription: "Oct. 2, 1839 Die eodem scripsi
    Miriam Clarke, qua prima est inter feminas pias
    prope Ecclesiam St. Michael commorantes. "It
    was the Bishop's custom to retain in his Journal
    of correspondence copies of communications re-
    garding significant matters. The Journal is
    preserved in the archives of the Philadelphia
    archdiocese.

46. Doran, Journal, p. 11. No indication is given
    as to the source from which the account came.

47. Original in BVM archives.

48. This conclusion was confirmed in person by both
    the Reverend Hugh Nolan and John Marschall, whose
    letters concerning the Bishop have been quoted
    above. Both men used Bishop Kenrick's career as
    the subject of their doctoral dissertations, and
    both kindly granted interviews with the writer
    on this subject.

49. Doran, Journal, pp. 74-75.

50. "As the Orphanage in Harold's Cross did not open
    until 1806, Bridget Leary must have been in the
    Hardwicke Street Orphanage which originally was
    opened by a group of Catholic laymen led by James
    Auger in 1801. The upkeep and education posed a

perpetual problem to James Auger and his friends,
and as the Poor Clare convent was situated at
that time in Dorset street (adjoining Hardwicke
street) the nuns agreed to assume care of the
children." (Note appended to the record quoted
for Bridget.)

51. Doran Journal, p. 61.

52. In a small notebook, Father Donaghoe has listed
the members of the Regan family as follows:
Regan, William, Pratt's Ct. No. 1. Mary, wife,
Timothy, Ellen, Mary Anne, Elizabeth, Patrick,
Dennis, William, John, John his brother." It is
difficult to know how to interpret the "John his
brother," unless it could mean that the first
John died and the next child born was given the
dead boy's name. We cannot be certain, either
that the above listing includes all the children,
or only those of school age. BVM archives.

53. Doran Journal, p. 69.
54. Unidentified memoir, BVM archives.

55. Letter, dated May 4, 1972, signed by Sister Mary
Ellen, Provincial Secretary, Daughters of Charity,
Emmitsburg, Maryland, in BVM archives.

56. Sister's subsequent history is of great interest.
As a candidate, Sister had met Mary Routtan, who
had served with her in the Cincinnati orphanage,
and from there had gone to St. Louis, where, until her secularization in 1847, she served as
nurse in the Sisters' hospital. Father Mazzuchelli had great hopes of these two young women in
his plans for an educational institute. On the
feast of St. Dominic 1847, he invested both with
the white scapular of the Dominican order. Both
took again the names they had borne as Sisters of
Charity, Sister Mary Seraphina McNulty and
Sister Mary Ermeline Routtan, and adopted a
black habit similar to the one they had laid
aside. Sister M. Seraphina's first assignment
was to a small school-house, just built, at New
Diggings, Wisconsin, eight miles from the Mound,
and to her teaching assignment was added the office of prioress. After the retreat in the summer of 1848, the thirty-eight year old Seraphine
and the twenty-six year old Ermeline, still novices, returned to their missions. Early the next

year, Sister Ermeline, attired as a laywoman,
left the convent and later appeared as a choir
member in a local church. "The Sisters' first
trial was climaxed before January had ended when
the prioress, Sister Seraphine, made a startling
announcement: It was no use struggling any
longer against poverty and a lack of members to
carry on the increasing work. The wise thing,
the sensible thing to do was to disband!" (Sister M. Paschala O'Connor, OP, Five Decades
(Sinsinawa Press: Sinsinawa, Wisconsin, 1954).
Sister Seraphine shortly left Wisconsin to enter
the Ursulines in New Orleans.

57. Bishop Kenrick's saintliness is amply attested
to by John Marschall, Ph.D., in the closing
chapter of his study of Kenrick's Baltimore
years - p. 373 ff. In this the author indicates
that had the cause of his successor in the see
of Philadelphia, the Venerable John Neumann,
CSSR, not been introduced so promptly, that of
Kenrick himself might have received that distinction. Kenrick's kindness and mildness, and, as
Marschall suggested in an interview with the
writer, his special predilection for a fellow
Dubliner, would have combined to make his manner
with Mother Clarke one of gentleness itself. He
could not have failed to sympathize with her
situation and to have taken her measure as a
woman of vision and principle, and as such to
have regarded her with great respect.

58. Cf. Rev. Joseph B. Code, "Bishop Hughes and the
Sisters of Charity." Of Father Donaghoe's de-
cision, the Doran Journal tells us: "Sister M.
Gonzaga said today (May 17, 1909) that Arch-
bishop Hughes made the separation in Mother
Seton's order and that he wished Fr. Donaghoe to
bring our Sisters to New York to join his order.
That while Mother Gertrude and Sister M. Joseph
liked Archbishop Hughes very well, they never
could sanction his action in regard to Mother
Seton's order. Father Donaghoe did not let our
Sisters go to New York because the Sisters of
Charity were already there and Bishop Hughes
would have the groups joined in one community.
Father Donaghoe did not want that but that we
should be independent and separated from others."
We gain some insight in the Hughes' manner of
dealing with those not in accord with his way of

thinking and acting from the following letter to
Sister Rosalia, Visitatrix, Sisters of Charity
Emmitsburg, dated Feast of St. Bartholomew, 1846:

Dear Sister,
I believe all the changes have been made
among the Sisters of Charity under my jurisdiction, which it was the purpose of the
Council to make, on the principle that in
such matters the bishop of the diocese was
not to be consulted.
This kind of business has gone far enough.
Be assured then that I mean no disrespect
when I communicate to you a message which
must seem rude, addressed to a Christian and
a religious lady, viz: that I wish, and request, and require that you shall leave the
diocese of New York with as little delay as
possible.
I shall tolerate no officer of a religious
community, male or female, exercising without my previous advisement and consent, powers of disturbance and embarrassment, such
as have been exercised, conscientiously, no
doubt, in my diocese of late. (Quoted in
the Code study identified above.)

59. Copy of Letter in Archives of Daughters of Charity, Emmitsburg, Maryland, from Father DeLuol to
Mother Rose White.

Baltimore, June 5, 1839
Monsignor Loras, Bishop of Dubuque, wrote to me
sometime ago to beg me to urge his claim on your
mercy to have soon some Sisters. Certainly the
good prelate deserves attention and commisera-
tion, but I don't want you to break your necks
going too fast. It has been done already too
often. But at the same time I have no doubt
that you will help him as soon as prudence al-
lows it.
Letter Book #34 Archives of St. Joseph College,
Emmitsburg, Md.

60. J.L.S. Kirlin, Catholicity in Philadelphia
(Philadelphia: Joseph J. McVey, 1907), p. 296.

61. Griffin, RACHS, Vol. 38, 1927, p. 215.
62. Ibid., p. 217.
63. Woodstock Letters, Vol. III, p. 110.
64. Griffin, RACHS, Vol. 29, pp. 378-379.

65. Original in BVM Archives.
66. Kenrick, Journal, p. 201.
67. Mazzuchelli, Memoirs, p. 313.
68. Original in the Archives of the Daughters of Charity, Emmitsburg, Maryland.
69. Photostat from Hughes Correspondence, Catholic University, furnished by Rev. Henry Browne.

70. The account book into which Mother Clarke's recap has been pasted contains the page of Father Donaghoe's entries as indicated. It also includes fragmentary school enrollments, a listing of free students for the school year 1836-7, an itemization of boarding school receipts for a brief period, as well as a semi-annual accounting of receipts of "Work done by the Sisters" and of expenditures for the school-convent complex, for the ten years of their residence in Philadelphia. The initial date for such accounting was November 1, 1833.

On The Banks of The Mississippi- 1843-1846

Chapter four tells of life and conditions in the frontier town of Dubuque where a largely Irish congregation were resisting the rule of their French Bishop. The principal instigator of the discontent was an elderly Irish priest who had been dismissed from both the Philadelphia and the St. Louis dioceses, but had been given an opportunity to redeem himself by the Bishop of Dubuque. The Sisters came in for a share in the general displeasure. Their countrymen found it hard to accept the idea of religious without habit or cloister, and when the priest let it be known that they were without canonical status, their problems increased. Their priest-superior had returned to the east to close affairs in Philadelphia, and long delay there left them in deep poverty from which the Bishop could give them but sparing relief. The small day-and-boarding school provided little in the way of their support, with the result that the public regarded them as more of a burden than an asset. The vicar general, in the repeated absences of the Bishop from the city, made heroic efforts to meet their needs with the limited means at his disposal, and to win for them support from an unfriendly congregation. It was he who gave them the first opportunity for a religious retreat in their nearly twelve years in the States.

Gravesite of Julien Dubuque on a
bluff above the Mississippi

The lead "diggings" that pocked the hills of Mt. Carmel,[1] the round stone tower crowning the neighboring bluff - the mecca of generations of novices on Sunday afternoon hikes - take us back to the days of antique Dubuque, and to the personage who gave the city its name.

The lead deposits in the Dubuque and Galena area had been discovered by the Indians in the early 1700's, and formed a source of ammunition for the British in the French and Indian wars. A French-Canadian, Jean Marie Cardenal, had worked the mines in the Dubuque area in the 1760's, travelling down the river to market the ore. (The records speak of him and his Pawnee wife having had their marriage blessed and their eight children baptized on May 30, 1776, in the log church which later became the first St. Louis cathedral). But the prospector for whom the town was named, Julien Dubuque,[2] did not come into the lead-mining region until 1788. Winning the confidence of the Fox Indians, he learned that a rich lead deposit discovered by Peosta, wife of a Fox chief, was located on the west bank of the Mississippi, near the mouth of Catfish creek, just below Mt. Carmel. He acquired a claim to a huge tract of the land on the west bank of the Mississippi, extending southward to the Maquoketa river. Establishing a trading post on the site of present Dubuque, he named his entire holdings the "mines of Spain," for Spain then claimed sovereignty over the territory. Twice a year lead ore was carried down the river to St. Louis by flatboat, and goods, tools, guns and trinkets were poled upstream to his trading post. As trappers were added to his patrons, valuable pelts were added to his downstream cargo, and trapping needs were supplied by the return trip.[3]

Dubuque gathered about him white men who had found their way into the area, many of whom had married Indian women. White influence with the Fox tribe was thus increased, and Dubuque was able to set up smelting furnaces, operate a mill and cultivate an extensive farm at the mouth of Catfish creek. He conducted his mining operations all along the bluffs and ravines of the Iowa shore, and a few miles inland, then, across the Mississippi along the Apple and the Fevre rivers. For mining, he used old men and squaws, with young bucks to tend the smelting furnaces. The Spanish governor at New Orleans gave ready recognition to Dubuque's land claims, regarding him and his associates as the welcome buffer against possible invasion from Canada.

After the area came into the possession of the United States in 1803, the tide of fortune turned against Dubuque. Having become indebted to the powerful merchant and financier, Auguste Chouteau of St. Louis, he was forced to make heavy land transfers to satisfy his obligations. A succession of serious illnesses compounded his difficulties, and death by pneumonia came on March 24, 1810, at the age of forty-eight. The Indians interred his remains with solemn rites on a hilltop overlooking the Mississippi. They planted a cedar cross above his grave, inscribing it "Julien Dubuque, Miner of the Mines of Spain."[4]

The Black Hawk war in 1832 marked one of the darkest pages in American history. As a result of it the peaceful Sacs and Foxes lost their cornfields and villages along the Rock river in the Illinois territory, and their hunting grounds in Iowa. The troops being transported from the east by way of the Great Lakes to do battle with the Indians were stricken with cholera and the disease spread death among the pioneer population in the Mississippi Valley. It was then, a troubled General Winfield Scott who met with a band of Indian warriors and their venal chief, Keokuk, on September 21, 1832, for the signing of a treaty of peace, while their proud chieftain, Black Hawk, was held a helpless prisoner. The Black Hawk Purchase which followed gave the United States six million acres of the best wood and farm land of eastern Iowa, at a price of nine cents an acre.

On June 1, 1833, the Indian title to the lands of Iowa expired, and before dawn there waited at the three ferries opposite Dubuque, Burlington, and Rockingham - a few miles south of the present Davenport - long lines of covered wagons, impatient to reach the Mississippi's western bank. The land was obviously intended to be settled and they were there to settle it. That the government had not extended its administration or the reach of its laws to the new region did not deter them. On June 28, 1834, these Iowa homesteaders were redeemed from the status of

outlaws when the Black Hawk Purchase was adopted by
the Territory of Michigan. When it again became a
political orphan by the admission of Michigan into
the Union, President Jackson, on April 20, 1836, approved an act creating the Territory of Wisconsin,
which then included it. A territorial convention and
a legislature, both held in Burlington in November,
1837, sought separate recognition for the Territory
of Iowa, presenting their memorials through the Honorable George W. Jones, then delegate to Congress
from the Territory of Wisconsin. He was able to cir-
cumvent the opposition of the slave-minded, and on
June 12, 1838, to add to the free North another territory. Eight years later, the new land attained the
full dignity of statehood. The transition from Indian
hunting grounds to a place among the States of the
Union was therefore a rapid one, and the name of Iowa-
"Beautiful Land" - had taken hold to stay.

Even before the area had been recognized as the
Territory of Iowa, it had been given a bishop, whose
diocese extended to the borders of Canada, and included the vast stretches of land between the upper Mississippi and the Missouri rivers. Mathias Loras [5]
was chosen for the see. Then vicar general of Alabama and the Floridas, under Bishop Michael Portier,
he had founded and presided over Spring Hill college
and seminary of Alabama, and had taken strenuous missionary journeys into the wilderness of swamps and
woodlands of the diocese. He was, then, no stranger
to the hardships of a missioner's life.

Jean Mathias Loras, born in Lyons, France on
August 30, 1792, at the height of the revolutionary
horrors, was the tenth of eleven children. His family were people of culture and substance, having for
five centuries dealt in the development and sale of
fine seed grain.[6] When the Lyonese troops sought to
defend their city against the excesses of the revolution, M. Loras, one of the city's eight councillors,
was apprehended, and, despite the pleas of Madame
Loras, met death on the guillotine, as did two of his
brothers and two sisters, the sisters for harboring
priests. In all, seventeen members of the Loras family lost their lives in the course of the disorders.
With execution came the confiscation of the family
properties, and Madame Loras and her family were left
penniless. Young Gilbert Tallon, a nephew whom M.
Loras had received as a son in happier times, returned
to them, and with the aid of Madame Loras, a capable
business woman, was able to reopen the family

establishment. Tallon also served as tutor to the
younger Loras children, When Father Charles Balley
opened a school near Lyons, Mathias met there Jean
Marie Vianney, the future Curé of Ars, and they became fast friends. Confirmed in 1807 by Cardinal
Fesch, uncle of Napoleon Bonaparte, the young Mathias
entered the "grand séminaire" of Lyons, where he had
for a teacher the future archbishop of Baltimore,
Ambrose Marechal, and as classmate, Marechal's successor in that high office, the English James Whitfield. During his diaconate, Loras taught in the
minor seminary, while preparing for his ordination on
November 12, 1815. It was an exciting time, with
Austrian troops occupying Lyons as Napoleon battled
for return to power in the crucial Hundred Days.

Two years later, Father Loras was made superior
of the minor seminary at Meximieux, where he had as a
pupil Joseph Cretin, son of a well-to-do innkeeper
and proprietor of a public bakery. Cretin's family
suffered as bravely as the Loras family through the
days of the terror in Lyons. His own mother was imprisoned for a time, and an uncle, a Carthusian monk,
was guillotined. Members of the Cretin family risked
much by frequently sheltering fugitive priests.
Cretin received his early training for the priesthood
in the home of the Abbé Desnoyel, a scholarly priest.
Attending major seminaries at L'Argentiere and Alix,
Joseph spent his vacations at home with his parents,
an elder brother, and a sister, Clemence. The last
was deeply devoted to her seminarian brother, and later, when his needs as a missionary were great, a
family inheritance permitted her to give him much assistance. His excellence in studies resulted in his
assignment to the great seminary of St. Sulpice in
Paris, where he was ordained deacon in May, 1823 by
Monseigneur de Quelen. Cretin's ordination followed
in December of the same year. The deacons from Picpus college, Paris, Father Donaghoe among them, were
ordained by Monsiegneur de Quelen at St. Sulpice on
May 24, 1823, probably on the same occasion as that
on which Cretin was raised to the diaconate.

At the age of thirty, Michael Portier, who had
studied with Loras in Lyons and had served for eight
years under Bishop Dubourg in the diocese of New
Orleans, became vicar-apostolic of Alabama and the
Floridas. Returning to Lyons, he sought the aid of
the Society of the Propagation of the Faith, and
tried to enlist helpers to replace the only two
priests who had been serving the region and who had

been recalled to Europe by their bishops. Cardinal
Fesch helped financially, and Father Loras, accepting
the challenge to a missionary career, set sail with
Portier from Havre for America on November 1, 1829.
Eight years later, in April, 1837, the Third Provincial Council of Baltimore created the see of Dubuque
and proposed the name of Loras as its bishop. Upon
confirmation of his appointment, Loras appealed to
Bishop Rosati of St. Louis for information about his
frontier see. Learning to his dismay that it was attended by one priest only - the missioner, the Reverend Samuel Mazzuchelli, O.P. - he hastened to name
the young Dominican his vicar general and the administrator of the diocese until he could assume his duties there. The newly consecrated bishop set out for
France toward the end of December, 1837, seeking both
recruits and funds. He hoped he might secure an
Irishman, a German, and three or four French priests
or seminarians for his mission. Visiting the Abbé
Cretin, at the time pastor at Ferney, home of Voltaire,
he found his former student conducting a school for
boys and reawakening in his people a faith that had
slumbered since the Revolution. Urbane, tactful, and
charitable, a seasoned pastor and educator, Cretin,
by his decision to accompany Loras to the new world,
provided the bishop with a valiant missioner and a
valuable co-worker. St. Paul, Minnesota, would claim
him as its first bishop in 1851.

Loras' tour of the French seminaries had borne
fruit, and embarking with him and Cretin were the
Reverend J.A.M. Pelamourgues and four subdeacons:
Augustin Ravoux, Lucien Galtier, Remigius Petiot, and
Jacques Causse. Leaving Pelamourgues in Baltimore to
improve his English and familiarize himself with
church management in this country, Loras placed the
four seminarians at St. Mary college in Emmitsburg,
Maryland. Cretin remained in New York to acquaint
himself with his new land. The two planned to meet
later in Pittsburgh and travel by boat to St. Louis.
Having arrived in the smoky city, they counted eighty
steamboats in the Pittsburgh port, and, as they moved
down the Ohio, a hundred at Cincinnati - signs to them
of the country's burgeoning commerce. Travelling on
the steamer Fremont, as they moved into the Mississippi
they passed several thousand Creek Indians from
Georgia, being transported from their homelands to
territories beyond the Missouri. This puzzled Cretin.
In a land dedicated to the principles of liberty, he
was surprised also by the sight of many negro slaves
working in the fields along the Ohio and Mississippi

rivers.

The two missioners did not reach St. Louis until
November 27, where their meeting with Bishop Rosati
was a source of mutual joy. Already the upper Mississippi was frozen over and there was no hope of Loras'
reaching his new diocese until spring. To the great
satisfaction of Rosati, they busied themselves giving
retreats, conferences and missions in the St. Louis
area. Mass on the feast of St. Francis Xavier in the
chapel of St. Louis University and on December 8 at
the Visitation Sisters' convent in Kaskaskia were
privileged occasions. When spring broke, the first
boat from up the river brought the impatient missionary, Father Mazzuchelli, to conduct the long-awaited
bishop to his see city and partially completed cathedral. Loras' installation in full pontificals on
April 21, 1839 was an impressive occasion for his new
flock, who filled the unfinished cathedral to over-
flowing. Mazzuchelli's sermon was brilliant. No
doubt the one the new Bishop preached at the gathering
for vespers that afternoon was also, but his new subjects, largely German and Irish,7 "anxious to receive
from his mouth the words of truth," would never know,
for he delivered it in his native French.

What manner of man was the youthful, slight-built
missionary whom the devoted Irish knew as their
"Father Matthew Kelly"? Samuel Charles Mazzuchelli,
born of aristocratic parents in Milan, Italy on November 4, 1805, was an ordained priest at the age of
twenty-four, and already on his way to Mackinac Island as missioner to the French-Canadians and the
French-Indians, under the assignment of his fellow
Dominican, Bishop Fenwick of Cincinnati. He was to
spend nine years in largely futile efforts to convert
and civilize the red man - the Ottawa at Old Arbre
Croche near Sault Ste. Marie, the Winnebagoes around
Green Bay and the Menominees at Mackinac. Extending
his ministry to the fur-traders and the voyageurs who
gathered at the trading posts during the summer
months, he built for them the first Catholic church
in the Wisconsin territory. Frustrated in his efforts to secure government funds for the school he
had built for the Catholic tribe of the Menominees,
he was helpless to lay a solid foundation among them.
The corrupting influence of liquor and the rapacious-
ness of whites in their transactions with the unlet-
tered Indians seriously hampered his efforts. At the
same time, the need for priests increased among the
fast-growing white population to the south. The lead

mines about Dubuque and Galena and the southern areas
of the Wisconsin Territory were attracting hundreds
of Irish, German and French settlers - prospectors,
miners, mechanics, roustabouts - many with their families. With them came second and third generation
Americans who hoped to build their fortunes in the
new west by way of law, real estate and trade. Young
doctors who came were sure of a practice. Contract-
ors for docks and roads and bridges, carpenters, masons,
and budding politicians saw hopes of a bright future
in the fast-building towns, while the farm population
was growing steadily.[8]

Appointed "pastor" to the whole of "Wisconsin," a
vast territory subject to the dioceses of Detroit and
St. Louis, Mazzuchelli arrived in Dubuque in 1835.
He was received warmly, especially by the Irish, and
found living space on the upper floor of the log house
Pat Quigley had built for his growing family. Along
with preaching, catechising and ministering sacrament-
ally to Catholics in an area covering hundreds of
square miles, he soon had a stone church "on the drawing boards," himself serving as architect and quarry
worker. Despite all these varied labors, the church
of St. Raphael was under cover by winter. St. Michael's
in Galena followed shortly, and through the generosity
of the French-Indian, Antoine LeClaire of Davenport,
St. Anthony's church-school-rectory complex became a
reality in 1838. Hastening from place to place on
horseback or snowshoes, by boat or, on the frozen river,
by sleigh, Mazzuchelli slept where he could and ate
what he was offered, visiting cabins and lumber camps
from Prairie du Chien to Burlington and numerous points
between. Then, twice a year he traveled the five hundred miles to St. Louis to confess his sins![9]

In 1838 a colony of Irish from Cork and Limerick
arrived in the area, settling on the Maquoketa river,
twenty miles south of Dubuque. Early records refer
to the site as Maquokiti, but eventually a young Irish
schoolmaster, Denis Mahony, from Garryowen, in County
Limerick, would stir the pride of his countrymen.
Lately come from Philadelphia, and presiding over the
settlement's one-room "academy" with the pride of
place accorded the Irish schoolmaster, he sought to
replace the Indian title with a good Irish name.
Sister M. Candida Williams, BVM, whose people were
among those early settlers, tells of the succession
of spirited and spirituous discussions on the subject
of the name which took place in the back room of the

local grocery store and grog shop. Sister's grand-
father, somewhat the worse for the final afternoon's
meeting, was walking home along the bluff when he was
hailed from below by Father Perrodin, the parish
priest. "Well, Pat," called the priest, "what's the
name you've settled on?" "Sure, I'm in no state to be
spakin' to your riverence, Father, but the name is
Garryowen," came the reply.

Though the Irish who came west to settle on the
land in the pre-famine days had been relatively prosperous at home, holding leases of perhaps thirty
acres, they were the exceptions among their people.
The Irish immigrant was not a frontiersman by instinct
or by choice. He preferred to settle in the urban
areas, for the Celt loved people; he wanted to be near
his church and to enjoy the pleasures of companionship
with his peers. He hated great distances and was a-
fraid of the lonely prairie. We hear the plaint of
an Irish farmer who had done well in Missouri and was
duly appreciative of the democracy of American society,
yet wrote home in 1821 to say how much he yearned for
his native Ireland: "I could then go to a fair, or a
wake, or a dance . . . I could spend the winter's
nights in a neighbor's house cracking jokes by the
turf fire. If I had there but a sore head I would
have a neighbor within every hundred yards of me that
would run to see me. But here everyone can get so
much land . . . that they calls them neighbors that
live two or three miles off."[10] However, coming in
a colony, the people of Garryowen brought their sociability with them. Visited by Mazzuchelli and encouraged by Bishop Loras with a gift of six hundred dollars from the Propagation of the Faith, they soon had
a sizable log church which attracted others to the
settlement. By 1841 the parish had a resident pastor,
the scholarly, gentlemanly Father Perrodin, [11] who had
come from France to aid Loras in his missionary labors. Garryowen was by then an entirely Catholic
settlement.

In 1839, the Iowa Territorial Legislature, meet-
in in Burlington, determined on a site in Johnson
county for the capital of their projected state.
Situated on the Iowa river, it would be called Iowa
City. At that time a wilderness, it was quickly
"laid out with broad streets and squares, sites for
the Capitol building or State House, churches, public
gardens, etc." Within a year, so Mazzuchelli's
Memoirs tell us with some exaggeration, "it contained
a thousand inhabitants, with hotels, post office, a

Rev. Samuel Mazzuchell

Bishop Mathias Loras

Rev. Joseph Cretin

line of stage-coaches, dealers of every kind, workmen, houses of brick and stone, Courts of Justice, also lawyers, doctors, Protestant ministers with their churches. , . . "12 The capitol, built with elegance and taste, and situated on an eminence above the river, serves today as administrative center for the University of Iowa.13

Yet that year Loras had written in a moment of discouragement to Bishop Rosati in St. Louis:

> ...all Iowa hasn't another congregation be-
> sides Dubuque and Davenport, and the latter
> has only four Catholic families. Mr. Mazzu-
> chelli is leaving for Burlington, where I am
> told there are none at all. Blessed be God.
> This diocese will have to be closed in the
> course of time. In the meantime we are go-
> ing to strive not to die of starvation. This
> winter flour costs $10 and other things in
> proportion. It isn't a small thing to keep
> up a house like ours.14

When land was made available for church purposes in the new capital, Mazzuchelli hastened from a church-building enterprise in Burlington to claim one of the lots and to make plans for the early building of a church, as the arrangement required. On December 10, 1840, he celebrated the first Mass to be said in Iowa City, and by 1842, St. Mary of the Assumption, a two-story structure intended as church, school and parish house, was ready for service. It was attended by Father Pelamourgues, one of Loras' first French recruits, then pastor of St. Anthony's, Davenport. The Dominican missionary, Father John G. Alleman, the unconventional but heroically self-sacrificing pastor of Fort Madison and surrounding missions, came when he could to minister to the German people.

Those were busy years for the Bishop and his vicar general. In the brief time before Mazzuchelli's de-parture for Milan in 1843, he had cooperated in the building of St. Gabriel church, Prairie du Chien; St. Thomas, Potosi, Wisconsin; St. Paul's, Burlington; St. Mathias, Muscatine - or Bloomington, as it was then called - and churches or stations at Bellevue, Illinois, and Shullsburg, Mineral Point and New Dig-gings, Wisconsin, besides St. Raphael's in Dubuque, St. Michael's in Galena, St. Anthony's in Davenport, and St. Mary of the Assumption, in Iowa City: twelve churches in all.15 Such haste was motivated by the

easy terms available on lands purchased for church
use. Through the financing of these, Loras was laying
a firm foundation both for the diocese of Dubuque and
for its three future suffragans in Iowa.

In the late winter of 1843, illness interrupted
Mazzuchelli's strenuous labors, and recovery was slow.
Loras' desire to provide a change which would aid in
the complete recuperation of his missionary, and his
own need for a theologian at the coming Council in
Baltimore prompted him to arrange for their trip east
together. After the Council session he would see
Mazzuchelli off to Milan for a home visit of several
months. Little did he realize when he bade his vicar
farewell that their ways were parting, not just for a
year but for always.

The Council over, Loras accompanied the two Kenricks and other clerics to Philadelphia where, in a
visit to the Sisters at the Sacred Heart academy, he
made the acquaintance of the young community. Travel
arrangements were quickly decided upon, and after
tearful farewells and a call on Bishop Kenrick to receive his parting blessing, Loras and his five new
missioners were on their way. They were pleased to
learn that the coadjutor-bishop of St. Louis, dignified and remote Peter R. Kenrick - the same Father
Kenrick who had said the last Mass in the little Ann
Street chapel in Dublin - was to be a fellow traveler.
Father O'Connor, soon to be bishop of Pittsburgh,
accompanied them as far as that city, where he was
then serving as parish priest, and vicar to Kenrick.
A trip of eighty miles by rail took them to Columbia,
Pennsylvania, beside the Susquehanna river. There
they boarded a canal boat bound for Pittsburgh, a
barge-like structure with a box-shaped cabin covering
most of its surface. The canal, a large one, meas-
ured forty feet broad at its surface, but at its four-
foot depth of water, the canal bed had narrowed by
  twelve feet. Dragged through the water by mules
walking the tow path beside the canal, the boat was
limited to a "speed" of three miles an hour, for a
faster pace tended to agitate the water and cause
erosion of the canal wall. All comers were taken,
regardless of the limited space for passengers, and
after the narrow berths with their straw-filled ticks
were all claimed, the extra passengers slept on the
floor. A curtain dividing the men's compartment from
the women's gave a modicum of privacy; in the circumstances, though, undressing involved little more than
the removal of hat and shoes. In good weather, the

cabin roof was a pleasant place to sit, though it
was not without danger, for when the call, "Bridge
ahead," rang out, those on the roof were obliged to
lie flat on the floor, hence the old canal song:

Low bridge, everybody down,
Low bridge, we're going through a town.

At the foot of the Alleghenies, passengers, boat and
mules were placed on cars of the Portage railway to
be drawn over the succession of mountain ridges ele-
vated as much as a thousand feet, and slowly lowered
down the western slope. From thence the trip continued
by canal to Pittsburgh, where the party of bishops and
Sisters arrived on June 10, the fifth day of their
journey. There was much that was pleasant in the experience, as an appreciative traveler has described it-
"... the bold and striking scenery of the Allegheny
mountains, the lazy motion of the boat, the silver
tones of the horn on approaching the villages, and the
pleasant ripple of the waters at night, as we glided on
noiselessly through mountain gorges and past dark
forests." [16]

The Sisters found a welcome with the Emmitsburg
Sisters at their Pittsburgh orphanage, while Father
O'Connor, soon to be bishop of Pittsburgh, provided
for his fellow ecclesiastics. On the following Monday, June 12, the party took passage on an Ohio river
steamboat, destined for Keokuk. The shoreline, filled
with craft of every kind, provided a preview of scenes
that lay ahead: flatboats laden with produce; house
boats with clotheslines hung with family wash; freight
steamers, unloading boxes and bales come up from the
ocean port of New Orleans; passenger steamers with
excursion parties; coal barges; fishing craft; it was
a lively scene to be many times repeated. On the upper deck small staterooms offered privacy, with wash-
room facilities at opposite ends of the boat. A spacious main cabin, taking up the central portion of
the deck, served for lounging and visiting until meal-
time approached, when negro servants set up tables
for the serving of bountiful meals. The lower deck
offered quite a different scene, with the red glare
of the furnaces, the bales and boxes of freight piled
high, the ship's crew busy with the shifting and sort-
ing of cargo and the feeding of voracious wood fires.
Crowded in with their poultry, live stock, farm equipment and luggage were dozens of immigrant families,
seeking new home sites in the west. These would shift
for themselves for food, and sleep on their luggage or

on the bare deck floor, open to the chill of the night.

Three days brought the travellers to the beautiful
city of Cincinnati. Even here they would see hogs,
cattle and market wagons milling through the unpaved
streets along the water front. Here again was a busy
scene and the taking on and discharging of passengers.
As they moved on down the river past dense woodland
with occasional stretches of open prairie, their vessel scattering flocks of water birds, they found company in the many boats that passed them, and the frequent stops at landings to take on wood for fuel and
supplies of butter and eggs, fresh fowl and garden
produce. And always there were the barefoot urchins
who raced down to the levee at the familiar tone of
the ship's bell or the pitch of the steam whistle.
There was fascination in the widening wake of the boat,
churned up by the creaking paddle wheels, and in the
thump of the great engines, as well as in the ever-
shifting crowds of fellow-passengers. Yet the English
novelist, Charles Dickens, who had preceded them just
the year before across Pennsylvania and down the beautiful Ohio, had proven himself "a strangely incurious
traveler, heedless of the past and bored with the present." [17] There was truth, however, in his sardonic
observation that "western steamboats usually blow up
one or two a week during the season." [18] Many others,
caught on snags, joined their fellows in the river's
depths, while others burned to the water's edge, in-
cinerating cargo and passengers as well. The record
was a bad one. Few steamers outlasted five seasons,
but they were quickly replaced, usually with larger
and better ones.

At Louisville the party was met by the aging Flaget, pioneer bishop of Kentucky, who invited them to
celebrate the feast of Corpus Christi in his new cathedral. He had regretfully left Bardstown for Louisville when the growing population of the river city
had made it the logical site for his see. The Sisters
were guests of the "white cap" Sisters of Charity of
Nazareth[19] at their Presentation academy near the
Cathedral. All were on their way again that evening,
but the memory of the Sisters' warm and gracious welcome lingered. It is perhaps not surprising that
when the Sisters assumed a distinctive dress, in 1853,
the form chosen bore a striking similarity to that of
the Nazareth Sisters' - a long, full skirt of serge,
black, with a full-length apron, a cape with a white
collar - though ours was to be closed in front -
large and small sleeves, and a rosary and crucifix of

identical pattern with the Nazareths'. The white sun-
bonnet adopted for our postulants, to be worn in chapel and parlor, was reminiscent of the trim, white
starched caps of the Kentucky Sisters.

The marshy lands about Cairo, threatening malaria
and ague, were soon passed. Pushing on up the Mississippi, the boat was met at Cape Girardeau, Missouri
by a gathering of priests from the St. Louis diocese.
They were there to welcome their bishop-administrator-
Rosati was away on a papal commission to the island
of Haiti - and claiming him for a visit. Stopping at
the busy river port of St. Louis, the Sisters saw a
thriving city. Bishop Rosati's cathedral was near at
hand, and the equally stately and handsome public
building somewhat farther up from the river's edge.
Sister Angela Hughes, of the Emmitsburg Sisters of
Charity and sister of Bishop Hughes, came to the landing to greet the Bishop and Sisters, hoping to retain
them for a visit and to acquaint them with that western outpost of culture. A truly Catholic city it was,
with academies, orphanages, a hospital, a medical
school, a seminary and a university. These various
institutions were staffed by the Sisters of Charity,
the Visitandines, the Religious of the Sacred Heart
and the Sisters of St. Joseph, and by Jesuit, Via-
torian and Vincentian Fathers. It was a far cry from
Dubuque, where they would be the first women religious.
Another year, however, would bring flood waters, covering low-lying areas for miles around St. Louis.
Failure to solve the drainage and sanitation problems
which followed, would leave the city an easy prey to
the cholera epidemic of the summer of 1849, which
would carry off its hundreds. That catastrophe would
follow the fire of May 7 of that year, which would
wipe out a full mile of waterfront docks and warehouses, together with river craft of every kind.

But there was to be no delay in St. Louis, for
Bishop Loras was eager to get back to his labors and
his people. Soon they would be passing the beautiful
site of Nauvoo, Illinois, home of the Latter Day
Saints. Bits of the story of that strange new religion doubtless came to them, and of the persecutions
its adherents were experiencing. These, they would
learn, were the result of their aggressive evangel-
izing and the fears engendered in the public by the
radicalism of Joseph Smith, their founder and ruler,
who planned Nauvoo as the capital of his projected
kingdom. Changing boats at Keokuk, the party took
the smaller packet, the "Dubuque," putting in at the

villages of Burlington, Bloomington, Davenport, Lyons
and Bellevue, exchanging passengers, loading and unloading cargo at each stop. As they moved up the
river the traffic grew heavier, with vessels carrying
upstream their load of passengers, household goods,
farm animals and machinery, but bearing also blasting
furnaces, hoisting equipment and rude carts for trans-
porting metal ore from the lead mines around Galena
and Dubuque. Returning vessels were burdened with
heavy cargoes of lead. Galena was at that time a
thriving city of some 6000 inhabitants, situated a
few miles up the Fevre river, then a broad and easily
navigable stream. As their steamer nosed its way
gingerly up that stream, they must have watched with
interest the lusty, sweating, swearing roustabouts
loading the pigs of lead onto the decks of nearby
vessels. Little wonder that as their boat strove to
pull out of its close quarters, one of the side
wheels struck a projecting pier. The damage delayed
their arrival at the more open port of Dubuque until
Friday morning, the feast of the Sacred Heart.

The Bishop had planned to surprise his people
with a bell for their cathedral which he had purchased

in St. Louis. This he had mounted on a stand, so that as they approached their busy little port the sound of the Angelus rang out. Morning tasks were forgotten as hundreds of tradespeople, miners, housewives with tousled children clinging to their skirts, swarmed down to the wharf to welcome their Bishop and the little band of Sisters. It was a motley procession the Sisters led as they left the boat in the wake of the Bishop, and gathered their skirts about them for the sandy uphill trek to the simple stone cathedral. Their Mass of thanksgiving in honor of the Sacred Heart was too quickly over, yet they were eager for what lay ahead.

The large two-story structure intended for the Sisters, at the corner of Bluff and third streets, was not yet completed, so the Bishop graciously betook himself to the sacristy of his cathedral and left his house to them. They accepted his courtesy for three weeks, but then insisted on moving into their still-uncompleted home, making themselves as comfortable there as possible. Doubtless letters were soon traveling back and forth between Dubuque and those left behind in Philadelphia. Though none written to or by the Sisters remain, one addressed by Bishop Loras to Father Donaghoe was soon on its way with instructions for the second group of travellers and word of those already settled in their new home.

Dubuque, July 5, 1843

Rev. T.J. Donaghoe
Rev. & dear Friend in Christ

After reading your letter written on Corpus Christi day, after praying, making others pray, offering the Holy Sacrifice, & applying to our dearly beloved Virgin Mother, & even consulting the dear children of Mary, I most willingly give my assent & say with the crusaders: <u>God wills it</u>.

You have, dear Sir, plainly perceived that among my objections 2 were prominent: 1 of which interested the Sisters and 1 me personally. You say that the locality will suffice. As it is perfectly well understood that you will come yourself with them, we will soon fix them tolerably well before the winter. You say in the 2nd place that you ask <u>carte</u> <u>blanche</u> for the travelling &

winter's expenses, and all is right. Come,
therefore, as soon as convenient with our
dear 14 children of Mary, who are all as devoted as our 5. You speak of Buffalo, it is
perhaps because you intend to come by the
lakes. I think it is better to follow the
road which we have proposed via Pittsburgh
and St. Louis [an illegible phrase.in Latin].
The Reverend D. Ryan has arrived in Dubuque
the day before yesterday by the lakes. But
he paid for himself and his niece $25 from
Boston to Chicago, and $20 from Chicago to
Dubuque, 180 miles. Try to consult and do
for the best. Our Mississippi is in good
stage of water & still rising. It is a good
omen for the health of our place next fall.
The Ohio must be pretty high owing to so much
rain.

We have arrived in Dubuque most luckily. Our
Sisters are so far very much pleased & in
perfect health, they sigh after nothing else
but the arrival of the principal colony. The
people are highly pleased with them. They
commenced their school this morning and expect to have it soon large. I expected to
receive some boarders, but I shall not do it
in order to leave all the space for the balance of the family. But if we are smart people we will soon raise some additional building for that purpose, even before the winter.

I have to speak to you now, Dear Sir, on an
important subject which will confirm my sentence: God wills it. The Right Rev. Bishop
Provenchere of Red River will send persons
to St. Peter, Iowa, next August to take &
accompany 3 or 4 Sisters of Charity of the
Blessed Virgin to establish a school near
his cathedral & I hope I shall be able to
let one of my priests go as far as that distant country to take care of them. I shall
say to you more on this subject viva voce.

But it will be right to mature this affair
with our dear Mother Clarke & prepare the
way to that great new mission - I believe
that some other establishment will soon be
solicited. What a grand prospect for the
glory of God in our far west!

We forgot to bring some writing paper & different articles which the Sisters will mention. But remember that heavy articles
ought not be brought to St. Louis, but must
be bought there. The freight from St. Louis
is actually only 90¢ per 100.

Do not forget your good piano, nor some good
paintings, etc. Sister Mary Francis practices
at the organ very well. I give them all their
tasks for reading and studying grammar, history, etc., so that they may soon be great
scholars. Postulants will not be wanting; an
excellent young lady, who teaches by herself
at St. Louis a large school & well, & who is
very pious, has made an application as soon
as she saw me in St. Louis. Another one, a
convert of Galena, did the same last Sunday.
In my opinion we must be quite prudent in
receiving new members. Excuse me for speaking to a person of so much experience. I
feel confident that the house will be disposed
of to advantage as well as the heavy furniture,
so that our dear children will sooner arrive
in our poor territory, where so much good can
be done with the assistance of God & of our
Blessed Mother. In the anticipation of seeing you on our shores, which will be yours
for life, I remain, dear Sir,

> Your most affectionate svt. in Christ
> Mathias Bp. of Dubuque

The means at the Bishop's disposal for the financing of such an enterprise would come from European
missionary societies. For the years 1838-1848, Loras'
account book shows the following receipts:

Propagation of the Faith, Lyons	89,042
Ludwig Missionsverein, Munich	65,765
Leopoldine Society	2,395
	$157,202

The Annals of the Propagation of the Faith indicate
that it alone had contributed to the Dubuque diocese
$199,390 by 1866. All this Bishop Loras used for the
purchase of land for future development, the support
of his clergy, the building of churches and of his
seminary at Table Mound, and the encouragement of
educational and charitable institutions.

St. Raphael's Cathedral and Bishop's House
Dubuque, Iowa 1835-1839
N.W. Cor. Second and Bluff Streets

Floor Plan
Scale: 1/8" = 10'

This postal picture was made from a city plate and buildings of Dubuque, Iowa, engraved in 1852 and preserved to this day in the office of Judge D.J. Lenehan, 9th and Main Streets. The stone church of St. Raphael was the first Catholic Church built in Iowa. It was commenced 1835, brought under roof 1836 and completed 1837; and was 40 by 77' in size and had a basement room.

The Bishop's House, built by direction of Rt. Rev. Mathias Loras in 1839 was 40 by 48' in size, of brick, two stories, and basement and garret. Both were built by the Very Rev. Samuel C. Mazzuchelli O.P., L.G.

May 10, 1919

Rev. John F. Kempker
St. Mary's Church
Dubuque

Loras' request for a good piano when so many basic
needs were unsupplied strikes one as strange, but similar demands had to be met by the Sisters of Providence in their Indiana wilderness. Stopping over in
Frederick, Maryland, on their way west in 1841, at a
"fine academy" conducted by the Sisters from Emmitsburg, they wrote later of the school there:

> They teach the various sciences scarcely
> known in our French schools, but they excel
> in music which is an indispensable thing in
> this country, even for the poor . . . . No
> piano, no pupils. Such is the spirit of the
> country - Music and Steam. At Frederick, of
> the five Sisters, three teach piano and guitar.[20]

The matter of Sisters for Bishop Provenchere's
Red River mission was soon settled when it was learned
that none of the Philadelphia community spoke French.
Ursulines would come from Canada, and later the
French-founded Sisters of St. Joseph from Carondelet,
Missouri, would serve the southern portion of the area
when Bishop Cretin established his see at St. Paul in
1851. As for the possible candidates of whom the
Bishop spoke, we hear no more. While Loras had
planned to keep space in the large frame structure for
the second group of Sisters, he was apparently prevailed upon to permit the admission of boarders, so
that the arrival of the fourteen in October called for
much crowding and inconvenience, and for the hurried
building of a log house. By spring the house was
ready, and a small brick school-house was completed
by December of 1845.[21]

The academy in Philadelphia had been closed and a
part of its furnishings sold. Mrs. Baker was forced
to delay her departure for the west by the settling
of her husband's estate, and with her was left a second postulant, Elizabeth Sullivan. Sharing living
quarters with them were two others, Mrs. Hill, niece
of Mrs. Baker, and Jane O'Reilly, youngest of the four
O'Reilly girls. She would shortly follow her sisters
to Dubuque. Father Donaghoe, with fourteen Sisters,
left Philadelphia September 12, 1843, to the sorrow
of patrons and friends, many of whom accompanied them
to the station. In keeping with the advice of Bishop
Loras, they followed the route of the first colony.
At Pittsburgh, they were met by a group of Father
Donaghoe's friends who had moved there from Philadelphia, and at Louisville, Father Badin came on board
to extend greetings, and wish them a safe journey.

It was a quaint message which Bishop Kenrick sent to
inform his brother, Peter Kenrick, coadjutor to
Bishop Rosati of St. Louis, of their plans:

> To the Bishop of Drasa - the Bishop of Phil-
> adelphia, Greeting
>
> Yesterday left here the priest Donahoe, pro-
> tector on the way to the devout women who
> are going to the city of Dubuque. In the
> course of the journey they will visit you,
> and expect to remain a short time as your
> guests. He has in mind to return here, un-
> less he finds a home more to his taste. . ?22

The "devout women" included Mother Clarke and Sisters
Mary Rose O'Toole, Catherine Byrne, Alphonse Lawler,
Clare Lalor, Aloysius O'Leary, Bernard Murray, Theresa
Fullam(Fulham), Philomena Mullen, Gertrude Regan,
Magdalen Cole, Ignatius Hamelin, Veronica O'Reilly,
and a postulant, Julia Donavan. Accompanying them,
besides Father Donaghoe, were Denis Mahony, now a law
student, and his wife, formerly Father's housekeeper;
T.P. Norman, brother of the J.J.Norman who had first
acquainted Loras with the Sisters; and, apparently,
Mrs. Catherine O'Reilly mother of the Sisters M.
Joseph, Francis and Veronica. The trip from St. Louis
to Dubuque occupied a week, and on October 8, 1843,
the five members of the first group received them with
joy. The arrival is recounted in the Catholic Tablet,
published in St. Louis, and issued in November, 1843:

> Nineteen Religious Ladies under the name
> "Sisters of Charity" but distinct from those
> (of the same name) connected with the mother-
> house of Emmetsburg, Md., have arrived in
> Dubuque from Philadelphia. Dubuque, Daven-
> port and Burlington are said to be among the
> places in which they intend to take charge
> of charitable institutions.

Dubuque and the surrounding area had a population
of not more than three thousand persons at the time
of the Sisters' coming. Log houses mingled with frame,
while a few buildings were of local brick. The sandy
river bank made steamboat landing difficult, and in
bad weather the mud streets were almost impassable,
though a few board sidewalks served pedestrians.
There were still remnants of the dispossessed Indians
in the area, for a record remains of Father Donaghoe's
baptism of three Winnebagoes in the Dubuque jail on

October 17 and 18, 1843.

From the time of Loras' arrival in Dubuque in the
spring of 1839, he and Mazzuchelli had worked as one,
sharing the same goals and undergoing the same hardships. That the older man operated at a disadvantage,
despite the authority of his position, is perhaps not
surprising. The young Dominican had been highly popular from his first coming into the frontier settlement. Language seems never to have been a barrier
for him. While always priestly, he was somehow at
one with the people he served. Refined and cultured,
he was nevertheless at home with the roughest; slight
and seemingly fragile, he put many a bigger man to
shame with the work he could accomplish and the distances he could travel. Firm and exacting though he
was, his admonitions only drew him closer to his people. An Italian aristocrat, he was to the Irish their
"Father Kelly," loved, respected and responded to.
Then Loras came, French to the core, a practical and
pedantic man, much more at home with figures and properties than with people. Steeped in a rigorism that
knew little compromise with human weakness, he was a
stranger to the casual, free-wheeling spirit of his
flock. Though he was heroic in his self-sacrificing
service, a model of virtuous living and anxious to
win his people to virtue, he never came fully to terms
with the Irish, and to them he was a poor substitute
for the loved missionary who was theirs no longer.

To add to the problem of personality there was
also Loras' interpretation of his role as bishop.
The Irish, as Cretin describes them, "so yielding in
Ireland under the absolute and often arbitrary rule
of their highest clergy," found it hard to understand
a bishop who dealt with them in any other way, certainly not one to whom Cretin could offer the advice:
"I think that a father ought never to excuse himself
before his children, nor give them protestations of
devotion and affection when he continually shows them
sensible and palpable proof [of his concern for them]
by his conduct."[23] Their recollection of a bishop
was of one "who knew his place and kept it," a man
of cloth, and good cloth at that, a judge of horse
flesh, and one who sat well on the best mount. It
was easy to bow one's head and tip one's cap to such
a bishop, but quite a different matter to yield obedience to a mud-spattered cleric returning afoot from
a journey of two or three miles in the country, even
though he had been on an errand of mercy; or, side by
side with the village carpenter, nailing rough shingles

on a church roof; or, dust-covered, in a worn soutane,
travelling across country in a farmer's wagon or a
lumbering ox-cart. His interdiction of their social
center, the grog shop in the rear of a grocery, even
if it did sell liquor on Sunday or operated too close
to the church, was an offense sure to rouse a true
Irishman's ire, however much need there was for re-
buking the prevailing intemperance and the disorders
which accompanied it. Frustration drove him often
from his see city, leaving the congregation there
largely in the hands of others, while he sought more
congenial situations in other parts of the diocese.

If the Irish found it hard to understand their
Bishop, they were equally hard put to accept as religious this sudden influx of women whom they couldn't
take to wife, yet who wore no habit and kept no cloister. Nor were they sure that these simple, unprepos-
sessing women were the able teachers they ambitioned
for the education of their children.

His Irish parishioners at the cathedral were not
the only problems Loras faced. Heroic in his own
self-sacrifice, he expected as much from his priests,
while they, suffering the hardships of pioneer living,
often frustrated by the lack of response they received
from their scattered flocks, lonely and discouraged,
were cut more deeply than he ever could have intended
by letters of remonstrance and rebuke from their Bishop.
His correspondence tells many tales of the kind, containing also frequent requests for release from the
diocese. Such came from Petiot, Causse, Galtier,
Poyet, Perrodin - his own compatriots - and from others, too, as the years went by, but the deepest hurt
to the Bishop himself was occasioned by the loss of
Mazzuchelli. A missioner during all his early years,
the Dominican priest returned in 1844 after his visit
to Milan, this time as an organizer and administrator,
not in the interests of the diocese as such, but in his
role as a religious, with authorization to establish
in the area he had evangelized a Dominican provincial-
ate, and with the hope of claiming for his purpose at
least one of the churches he had labored to build.
The divergent goals of diocesan and religious clergy
caused a rift that seems never to have healed.

The Baltimore Council of 1843 had proposed the
need for new dioceses in Wisconsin and Illinois, and
Rome acceded to the proposal, naming John M. Henni to
the former see and William J. Quarter to the latter,
with Milwaukee and Chicago their respective diocesan

cities. Loras was thus relieved of care of the areas he had been serving centered in Galena and Prairie du Chien. The spring of 1844 would see the new prelates consecrated. Meanwhile, however, Father Remigius Petiot who had been one of the four seminarians Loras brought to his new diocese, and was now pastor of St. Michael church in Galena, was seeking both his exeat from the Dubuque diocese and Sisters for the parish school.

As early as August 22, 1839, Bishop Loras had written to the Propagation of the Faith that even the Protestants of Galena were eager for Sisters to train their children, indicating that a convert from Episcopalianism, Mme. Farrer, had offered herself and her home for the work, and that the wealthy Mr. Dowling and others had made offers of substantial assistance. It was his hope then that he could bring Sisters from Emmitsburg back with him on his return from the Council the following summer.[24] However, the Bishop's hopes had failed of realization. Now, in 1844, when Father Donaghoe set out for Philadelphia to arrange for the sale of the academy there and to obtain his exeat from that diocese, the prospects were bright that some of the Sisters whom he had brought from the East would soon be established in Galena. In a letter to Loras from St. Louis on March 17, he told of a stop-over at Galena, where nothing had as yet been arranged for the Sisters. Mrs. Farrer had proposed, indeed, that they live with her but Father wrote:

> . . . when I found she had two children who depended on her -- besides that she was still in expectation she would have Rev. Mazzuchelli with her on his return -- at any rate I changed my own plan and told him to secure a house and pay the rent for one year and the Sisters would run the risk to make their own support. [emphasis ours]. It would never do to have an extern in the same house with the Sisters, unless as a boarder. . . .

His next stop was Burlington, where he called on the Bishop's local agent, a Mr. Postlewait, who took the opportunity to petition for Sisters. Father continues:

May 11. 1846

Rt Rev'd Father in Christ

Mother Clark.

(Notation by Bishop Loras)

> I told him by the time of my return to the
> west, that they might expect me to go down
> to make the necessary preparations. Their
> [the Sisters'] support would be precarious
> unless they taught music -- to do this a <u>new</u>
> <u>piano</u> and a boarding school would be neces-
> sary. [!]

Then he added apologetically:

> Our poor children, though good, are unexpe-
> rienced. What a burthen I feel I have im-
> posed on you, but you do it for the love of
> God.

And finally,

> I parted with the Revd. Mr. Haly [Healy] in
> Burlington.

Meanwhile the Sisters were making their plans for a
beginning in Galena, for Mother Clarke wrote to the
Bishop on May 11, 1844:

> Rt.Rev. Father in Christ
>   As it is left to me to send the Sisters,
> I have been considering of it. As to consult
> the Sisters in matters of this nature, I have
> never done so, nor would I wish to do it for
> their own sake.
>   Less than 4 I would not wish to send, and
> two of them experienced. If you permit me
> to send Sisters Mary Margaret and Mary Joseph,
> for even a short time, with them; then what-
> ever time you think proper they can be re-
> called and two others sent in their place.
> If you do not approve of this, I think it
> would be better, no matter how advantageous
> it may be for the community in the present
> state of things, to decline sending them un-
> til Rev. Father's return, or at least until
> I write to him and receive an answer.
>
>   I am with the greatest respect
>   Your very Humble
>   Mary Clarke

But their hopes for the mission were short-lived, as
we see from Father Petiot's letter to Bishop Loras of
May 24:

I am really surprised at receiving this morning a letter from the Rt. Rev. Bishop Quarter
by which he tells me that he was not apprised
of the coming of the Sisters to Galena, particularly after the letter of Mr. Donaghoe,
and your letter in which you told me posi-
tively you had received the authorization.
Here are his words: "Painful as it is to me,
I wish and hereby forbid their introduction
until I have first visited the place and until I am made satisfied that they are calculated to take charge of the religious instruction of the female children in that section of the diocese." He will be here himself on Wednesday or Thursday of next week,
if the weather permits, and I hope everything
will be satisfactorily settled.

Subsequently Bishop Quarter made an unsuccessful attempt to arrange a meeting with Loras in Galena, no
doubt on this and other matters, and in the end nothing further is heard of the Galena school situation
until in 1846 when the school was assigned to the
Sisters of Mercy from Chicago. Father Donaghoe attributed the loss of Galena to his refusal of the offer of an honor which Bishop Quarter had made to him
when they met in Baltimore in the spring. After a
thanks to Loras for according him the honor of making
him vicar general of the Dubuque diocese, Father continued at some length to list other opportunities that
had come his way:

You urge me not to attend to the offers of
my worthy friends, I have not, because I was
always impressed with the conviction that
providence had the whole of what related to
me and my poor community. Last January I
received a letter from Bishop Hughes inviting me to take charge of some of the New
York congregations as the Rev. Gentlemen had
all accepted though their bulls did not at
that time arrive, & to draw upon him for
what sum I stood in need of and come if possible immediately - I wrote him to let me
not delay him in his arrangements, that my
purpose was fixed and determined to remain
with my Community.

Then as regards Bishop Quarter he wrote:

On my way to Philadelphia when I got out of

the cars at Baltimore I was saluted by Bp.
Quarter and found we had been travelling together from Frederick without knowing it.   I
spoke then and afterwards in Philadelphia
about my arrangements with Mr. Petiot by your
permission. He urged me to engage myself
with him at Chicago. I told him I could not.
He then offered to make me president of his
contemplated College as also to take my Community where alamode of the mountain[25] I
could attend to both -- My answer was that I
was unfit for the president and that for his
goodness I would when I went west do if it
lay in my power what I could for him.[26] I
told this all &c to Bishop Hughes. He told
me I did right. ... The Community brought me
out to Iowa, it's the cause of my return, and
to its prosperity or otherwise will my con-
tinuance be prolonged which I trust in God
may be all the days of my life.

Since Quarter's rejection of the Sisters was apparently based on some report he had heard of their inadequacy, could it have been that Father Donaghoe's tendency to speak deprecatingly of their abilities lay
back of his action in the matter of the Galena
school?[27]

We are told that Bishop Loras left Dubuque about
the time of Father Donaghoe's departure, placing the
Sisters in the care of Father Cretin, who promptly
gave them the privilege of having the Blessed Sacrament in their home.[28] He came every Sunday evening
to give them instructions, but since his life was a
very busy one, the Sisters were troubled lest they
were taking too much of his time. They deeply treasured his response that it was a "pleasure to come here
to the chosen portion of the flock of Jesus Christ."
To their great sorrow, on the Bishop's return the
privilege of having the Blessed Sacrament in their
home was withdrawn, as Loras did not regard their
cramped quarters a suitable place for Its repose.
Father Cretin had occasion at times to bring Holy
Communion to Mother Clarke in the attic of the log
house, and both he and the Bishop are recorded as having the greatest reverence for her. We learn also
that Denis Mahony, by then a grave and studious young
man, shared with the Sisters the results of his education, holding classes for them, especially in the
field of English.

The failure of the Galena project was a very real disappointment, for it was awkward to have nineteen religious women occupied with serving one small school in a pioneer settlement. The pressure on the struggling young townsmen of carving out a future for themselves and providing for growing families was too obvious for members of the congregation to fail to observe. That they were not above speaking their minds on the subject, we find from Mother Clarke's letter of May 27, 1844 to Bishop Loras:

May 27, 1844

Rt. Rev. Father in Christ,
I bow and submit to the holy will of my God. Dear as the Community is to my heart, my constant prayer is that it may be dissolved if it exists contrary to his holy will, or that it should act against his glory or the sacred character of religion. As to the future prospects of the Community, it is in the hands of God. But as to the Community benefitting by the public sympathy, I am decidedly opposed to it, not from foolish pride or independence, but for the sake of religion, the Community and the public themselves. If their charity lead them to decide on carrying out the plans which they contemplate to their own interest, then the Sisters will benefit by it as far as their services may render them useful to the public. Let an hospital or an orphan house be established, then the Sisters shall take shelter under their roof and partake of their fare, and render their duties of charity to the proper objects.
We have heard the remarks of the people of Dubuque already. They said it was a shame for Revd. Father to leave such a charge on you to provide for. What would they say if they had to provide for us themselves? I have received a letter from Revd. Father. He is well. He is in New York with Bishop Hughes. I will write to him a statement of all.
I am, with the greatest respect,
Your very humble
Mary F. Clarke

To reassure her, Loras sent with his reply a gift of money. Her response was:

In the name of the Community I return grateful

thanks for your kind present this morning. But we are sorry to deprive you of
the money, as we do not want [for] it.
I have some of the gold Revd. Father
gave me when he was going, which, I think,
with economy, will last until his return.
. . . We return our humble thanks to you
for your kind solicitude in our behalf.
We feel bound to pray for you and your
Diocese. I wrote Revd. Father yesterday.
I urged his return, then all will be
well.

Little did Mother Clarke think then that Father
Donaghoe would not return for a whole year. When
he reached Philadelphia the bitterness against
the growing Catholic population was at the kind-
ling point. When the Nativists, in a spirit of
antagonism, held a mass meeting on May 6 in the
heart of the Catholic district in the Kensington
area, their inflammatory speeches were a bid for
trouble. It took only a minor incident to touch
off the anticipated conflagration. Armed mobs
quickly attacked Catholic homes, ransacking them,
breaking up furniture and tossing it into the
street, and then setting fire to the houses. The
occupants had to flee in terror. The mob then
moved to the Sisters' academy, clamoring for the
destruction of the "Irish nuns." Setting fire to
the high board fence surrounding the property,
they threw rocks and fire brands at the building.
Living in the convent at the time were Mary Baker
and Elizabeth Sullivan, postulants, Mrs. Hill
(Mary's niece), and the fourth O'Reilly sister
Jane. The dauntless little Mrs. Baker, certain
that none could be so savage as to wish to burn
helpless women alive, opened the door. But the
moment she did so a brick or rock, thrown with
deliberate aim, struck her on the head and she
fell back senseless. An angry crowd of Irishmen arrived just in time to drive the mob off and
rescue the frightened women. At least, in the
darkness and confusion, they thought they had
rescued them all. Bishop Kenrick gives an account of the affair in a letter to his bishop-
brother in St. Louis:

...The Irish who had made no resistance
thus far, now armed with guns, drove
them off carrying the frightened women

Burning of St. Michael Church, Second and
Jefferson streets, and of Sacred Heart
Academy, Second and Phoenix (Thompson)
streets, during the Nativist Riots of 1844.
From old engravings.

to a place of safety. Two at least of the
Nativists were killed. This prevented the
firing of the house and the church of St.
Michael. But the next day the Nativists
planned revenge. They met in the place
called Independence Square, armed with weapons and firearms, and after hearing an ha-
rangue they moved off to the place of the
fight - four thousand men fully. They carried the American flag before them. All day
they kept the flag raised bearing the placard,
a lie, that the Irish and Papists had trampled on it. They shouted death to the Irish
. . . at length the military which had refused the day before to give aid to the County officer known as the sheriff, arrived on
the scene . . . and St. Michael's church
was placed under military guard.

On the feast of the Apparition of the Archangel [May 8] the Rev. T.J. Donahoe celebrated
Mass in the church; later he went to visit
some parishioners and came also to see me,
leaving at home the Rev. Mr. William Loughran.
He [Loughran] gave the keys of the church to
the military commandant and made his escape
with difficulty, as the mob, which had made
frequent attempts upon the lives of the
priests, was pressing on. The officer in
command did not prevent the firing of the
church, as it appears, and in a short time it
was destroyed.[29]

The rectory also was soon enveloped in flames, while,
to the crackling of the flames and the shouts of the
mob, anguished parents were burying their child in the
church-yard. As the cross on the burning church fell
blazing to the ground, a band struck up the tune,
"Boyne Water." All this Father Donaghoe watched from
the belfry of St. Augustine church, which was to be
reduced to ashes that same evening. Bishop Kenrick's
account continued:

During the night the church of St. Augustine,
the Library and the house*were burned. The

_____
* The monastery of St. Augustine had been turned over
to the care of cholera patients during the epidemic of
1832, housing in all 367 patients of whom only 48
were Catholics.

Nativists gave expression openly of their delight. Right after this the mob moved on to the Cathedral church [St. John's] but the soldiers had reached there a quarter of an hour ahead of them and the Governor in the city proclaimed what is called <u>martial law</u>. The next day was a day of dread for the Catholics. They feared, following the repeated threats that were made that all the churches would be burned, and all the priests, myself first of all, would be publicly hanged. Therefore most of them, counseled by their friends, changed their apparel so as to avoid recognition.

Many of the clergy, including the Bishop, left the city for a time and the churches were closed to services. An item in Kenrick's visitation diary states that "A large wooden image of the All-seeing Eye of God would not burn in the fire of St. Augustine's and the morning after the fire it stood out among the ruins as a powerful reminder to the culprits." He added that "A chapel [of brick and frame] was erected, and opened on the second day of June in a place near the ruins of St. Michael's church. It required four days only, or hardly four, to build it; but to the consolation of the faithful, Mass was celebrated there on the reast of the Most Holy Trinity, the result of the efforts of Father Donaghoe."

According to a community account,

When Fr. Donaghoe said his last Mass in St. Michael's the rioters were in the basement and some in the back part of the church. He was obliged to hurry the last part of the Mass and taking a little bronze statue of the Blessed Virgin, he commended himself to her keeping, and walked out through the Know-Nothings [sic] unharmed. On the street the confusion was terrible.[30]

While witnesses of any exciting event will differ in their accounts of it, the sworn testimony of Mrs. Baker leaves us in a quandary, for it has always been supposed that there were four young women residing in the academy at the time of its attack by the rioters, and that all four were taken to a place of safety by their rescuers. What purports to be the sworn statements of a number of witnesses to various incidents includes the following account of the attack on the

Sisters' academy:

Mrs. Mary Baker,[having been] sworn, said -

On the 6th and 7th of May last I lived at the
corner of Second and Phoenix streets, in the
dwelling part of the Catholic schoolhouse; I
knew nothing of any circumstances till eight
o'clock on Monday evening; I was informed by
a boy that they were about to attack the
house; I fastened up the shutters and doors,
but had no idea they would put their threats
into execution; between eight and nine they
came to the house, tore down the fence, and
continued firing and beating against the
doors and windows; they fired with balls
against the house; when they came to the back
part, the rabble splintered the door and put
fire within the house; I came out and told
one of them to let me go out before setting
fire to the house; he took a rock stone and
knocked me down; I was knocked insensible,
and when I came to, I found there was no person there; I then took a candle and went out,
and remained away until four in the morning;
the people who came in the evening were thousands; I can't say what language they used,
it was low and abusive; it was abusive of the
Pope and the Catholic Church; there were no
arms or weapons about the house; the next day
all the doors were open, and I tried to remove my furniture.

Cross-examined: They remained two hours
there; I saw a firestick put into the entry;
about four men were at the back door when I
went and requested one of them to let me go
out, and he knocked me down; the firing was
from all sides of the house, and the balls
struck everywhere; stones came into the windows; I went out the side door; I had charge
of the house; it is now in ruins, being
burned the day following.[31]

In omitting any mention of the other three women
believed to have been present, was Mrs. Baker hoping to
spare them the necessity of testifying? Was she possibly unwilling to expose them to public criticism
for having gone to safety, leaving her behind? Did
they and their rescuers, in the darkness and confusion,
believe that all had been provided for? Would the other

three have been separated from each other in such a
way that until they returned to the academy when morning came they would not have realized that Mrs. Baker
had been left behind? These are questions that cannot
now be answered.

Letters giving word of the tragedy went immediately
to the Bishop and the Sisters in Dubuque, but they apparently did not arrive until early June. Loras' response to Fr. Donaghoe's report is dated June 7,1844,
and in it he pressed Father to return to the diocese,
where, he said, Father's two rooms in the Bishop's
house "are as white as snow and are painted elegantly."
He asked Father to tell him if, when, and for how long
he planned to serve in the Dubuque diocese, as other
arrangements would depend on his plans. Then, regarding the Sisters, he wrote:

> The Rev. A. Pelamourgues of Davenport who was
> not at first favorable to a school for the
> Sisters at Davenport writes thus: "June 1st.
> All persons, Catholics and Protestants, are
> very anxious to see some of the Sisters come
> down. I have no doubt now, they will do well
> here, and they will have a large school. But
> they must try to be here in September, and
> commence their school in November. If the
> intended house is not ready, we can rent one
> for a time."

A letter from Father Donaghoe from Philadelphia,
dated August 15, 1844, brought disturbing word to
Loras, whose notation on the back of the letter read
bluntly: "Cold comfort, Mazzuchelli." Father wrote:

> After I celebrated Mass I observed a trunk in
> St. Joseph's with Galena, Ill., on it - lo,
> it was the arrival of the Revd. Mazzuchelli.
> I saw him and he expects to settle in Galena
> with ulterior views regarding the arrival of
> others to establish his order &c. He gave
> me cold comfort about our success, &c. ...

In his letter Father Donaghoe expressed pleasure over
the Davenport prospect. He then continued with details
of the Philadelphia situation and his plans for going
west:

> I must now look out for my expenses to go
> west - I must have it. Its mortifying to me
> to do it, but no compensation can or may be

soon expected. I have entered suit against
the County & will have my part arranged by
the 1st of September. The 2nd battle delayed
all, yet its effects in favor of religion I
know will be good. Converts already are coming in. They admire our forbearance & indeed
it was admirable!

Mother or Sisters know nothing of all the
above as its always time enough to let them
know my anxieties when all is over. It
strengthens their confidence afterwards, and
saves troubles of mind in the meantime. Tell
the good Mr. Cretin I will attend to his commission about the type, and with the help of
God we will all be great people out there,
which may many lengthened years afford you
the pleasure to witness. Kind remembrances
to all, especially to my dear Childern [sic].
I am yours very devoted and affectionately
                    Terence J. Donaghoe
This closes a day on which my ever blessed
Mother complacently looks down on the labors
of the Bp. of Dubuque.

Cretin had written to Fr. Donaghoe on July 10 from
Dubuque, where he was supplying for the Bishop, then
in Iowa City. Loras had withdrawn him from the pastorate at Prairie du Chien, since that station now
belonged to the Milwaukee diocese. His letter assured
Father Donaghoe that "all your dear Sisters, the
Mother excepted, are well, and sigh for your return."
He asked Father to purchase various kinds of type for
his printing press, and to bring with him the plates
of a small prayerbook, the Catholic Companion, which
Father Donaghoe had compiled. The Sisters added their
request that he bring them a chest of black tea.

There was to be a long wait, however, for the fulfillment of these commissions. While Father Donaghoe
had made plans to return in the early fall, affairs in
Philadelphia required that he remain close at hand.
Thinking that he might have departed from Philadelphia,
and that a letter would catch up with him in Pittsburgh,
Bishop Hughes wrote him there on October 10, 1844,
urging him to spend the winter in New York. The letter read in part:

I read with regret if not surprise in your
letter of the 6 that you were about to start
for the west. If letters can accomplish it,

I hope yours will oblige you to stay till the
affair in Philadelphia is settled. I hope
also that you may come to New York - for in
truth, besides other reasons, I stand much in
need of one additional priest at this time.
Even for the interests of that Community to
which you are so thoroughly attached, this
would be desirable. I will give you a situation which you can quit when you will, but
which in the meantime will enable you to do
something for them. I do not know that you
ever took my advice in any matter appertain-
ing to yourself. Neither do I think that
strange. But in this particular instance,
try it. I do not think you will have an occasion to be sorry for doing so. Write soon,
and tell me that you are coming to spend at
[least] one winter with your old friend.

A second letter from Hughes, addressed to Philadelphia
on November 30, settled the matter , and Father Donaghoe accepted his invitation, remaining with his friend
until spring.

Meantime the Sisters had undertaken the school at
Davenport, and Mother Clarke had accompanied Sisters
M. Eliza Kelly, Philomena Mullen and Patricia Caniff
to their new home. Arriving by boat, the Sisters were
escorted to a partially completed three-story brick
building, the property of the diocese, in the 200
block on Second street, which was to serve as an academy. To it they gave the name of St. Philomena, probably
with recollections of the incident on the Dubuque prairie. During the interim between Father Pelamourgues'
request for Sisters and the establishment of the academy, fortune had taken a turn for the worse in Davenport, for his annual report of January 5, 1845, indicating a population of only 2000 persons with just
250 Catholics among them, added:

> The congregation of Davenport which had in-
> creased for sometime very fast, had decreased
> of about one third during the last summer.
> But it is probable that it will not decrease
> any more as most of the families live on farms.
> The members of the congregation are in gen-
> eral very poor, and can neither contribute
> for the support of the priest, nor send their
> children to school for want of decent clothes.
> The Sisters of Charity of the Blessed Virgin
> have commenced a school, but it has not been

patronized till now, it is hoped, nevertheless, that the number of pupils will increase
when the Sisters are better known.

In Dubuque, Father Cretin, as vicar general to
Loras, was involved in many problems, while the Bishop,
in a kind of self-imposed exile, was residing in the
recently established capital, Iowa City. A principal
concern of Cretin's involved the Sisters, who were
only too anxious for ways in which they could be of
service and thus earn their own support. Of the nineteen, not more than five or six could have been needed
for the St. Mary school, even with the boarders it was
admitting. While the others might have found some
employment in visiting the sick and caring for them,
they were without definite assignment and so had little means of livelihood. Cretin's second concern,
dear to his heart, was the Winnebago Indians in the
area about Fort Atkinson on the Turkey river. In the
hope of solving the problems of both groups, he wrote
the Bishop requesting that he visit the Governor in
Iowa City in the hope of arranging for an appointment
to the government-supported school maintained for the
Winnebagoes. Cretin wrote:

Dubuque, Nov. 2, 1844
. . . I am going to write to the agent to be
informed as to the best conditions that he
offers for one to take charge of this school.
It is indispensable that we know on what we
can count - to know the number of Sisters and
of teachers that I can bring, and I shall require travel costs. It will be a good thing
for the Sisters. They cannot live here in
the large number, and it is perhaps the only
place in this mission or any mission they
could be supported easily.

Regarding their financial status, he wrote:

I have taken in twenty piastres*... but I have
been obliged to lend 15 to the Sisters who
have absolutely nothing. They are always
without news of Father Donaghoe.

Then, as though the Sisters had been caring for a little orphan girl, he said:

---

* The Spanish dollar.

The child at the Sisters regarding whom the doctors have disagreed so openly has recovered.

However, in a footnote three days later - the stage to Iowa City went only two or three times a week - he added:

The little girl of the Sisters has been buried. Always without a word of Father Donaghoe.

Then, as a hint of troubles the Sisters were having in the matter of school enrollment, he continued:

No child has come to school besides those that you know. The most devoted - John Ragan, Mr. Power - have sent their children to the other school, not coming to catechism which I have at one p.m. for everybody.

Cretin's hopes were raised by the Governor's approval of his nomination, a first step in his securing the assignment to the Indian school. His letter of November 13, in view of his own likely departure, advised the Bishop to return to Dubuque rather than send another:

. . . if I absent myself I presume that you yourself will return here, and that you will not send M. Healy. This would yield entirely in some respects, the field of battle to the hopes of the opposition which would manifest itself. Some fox has already interpreted your departure to a sort of spite or of fear. They consider it as a forced retreat. I do not believe the better Irish susceptible to this sort of malice against their proper pastors. . . . The more that is granted to them [the dissidents] the more they increase their demands and their audacity. When one has . . . taken the means which he believes in conscience to best secure their spiritual well being, then one ought not to be disquieted by their approbation or their opposition. . .

Daniel Brodie, an Irish teacher in the boys' school and a resident of the Bishop's house, in a letter to Loras, August 3, 1844, indicated that the trouble the Bishop was having with the Irish had as its instigators "north country Catholics tinged with a little orangeism" who are "at all times troublesome to the clergy."

Father John Healy, whom Bishop Loras had included
in his list of "devoted clergy," and whom Cretin hoped
the Bishop would not send to Dubuque, had had a check-
ered career before coming to the diocese. Listed for
a time in the diocese of Charleston, South Carolina,
he appears to have gone from there to Philadelphia,
where his record was less than savory.[*] Dismissed
from there, he made his next stop at St. Louis, and
from there, he was soon on his way again, this time to
Dubuque. A handsome, grey-haired man and an able
speaker, he had been assigned by Bishop Loras to Burlington, where he remained for several months. From
there he addressed several letters to the Bishop, telling of problems with the German parishoners -- their
refusal to contribute to the support of the church
and other difficulties. Bishop Loras knew the German
language, so, thinking to solve a double problem, he
went to Burlington, and despite Cretin's warning, sent
Healy to deal with the troublesome Irish of Dubuque.
The exchange was probably made in early November, 1844.

Cretin's letter of November 13 continued, speaking next of the financial problems of the Sisters:

> The Sisters have been very disappointed at
> the non-arrival of Mr. Donaghoe. They await
> him especially for financial relief. They
> find themselves without a single piastre[**]
> for bread or shoes. I lent them at once the
> money that you sent for Mr. Causse and Mr.
> Mazzuchelli, besides $50 personal money that
> I had on deposit. It is unfortunate that
> some in the village know of their distress.
> They would not have been able to borrow where
> you had indicated to them. I pray you, then,
> Monseigneur, to have the charity to advance

---

[*] It was this John Healy of whom Bishop Kenrick had
written in his _Visitation Diary_ on June 4, 1837: Having received an account referring to the Rev. John Healy,
I wrote him, also to my brother [stating]that I would
recall his faculties."(p.137. It is not surprising then
that when Healy later appeared in the St. Louis diocese,
the Coadjutor of that diocese, Peter R. Kenrick, in a
letter of early February, 1842 would indicate that he
was giving dismissorial letters to three clergymen,
among them mentioning J. Healy.
(Rothensteiner, Volume I, p. 800.)

[**]Cretin uses the coin "piastre" for its close
equivalent, the dollar.

to them two hundred piastres. They will return to me the fifty of the deposit, and
they will return all later. The draft of
$400 which you left with me can serve to sup-
ply their needs and those of any who may
receive your assistance.

Loras' crisp note on the back of the letter reads:
"Told to tear the $400 draft." Later the Bishop did,
however, assist the Sisters on the receipt of a letter
from Mother Clarke.

But November 21 brought bad news to Cretin, a letter from Iowa Governor John Chambers, stating that the
Indian school for which he had applied was to be left
in the hands of the Protestants. In his letter to
Loras, Cretin quoted the Governor in full, adding:

Your Lordship can see from the tenor of the
letter that there is little to hope for.
Nevertheless they speak of an approaching
change of governors. He is happy that I had
counted on nothing as certain, regarding my
departure and that of the Sisters, who appear more indignant than I over the disappointment.

Then, referring to the needs of the Sisters, he indicated that some relief had come by way of payment for
sewing they had done.

I have received, Monseigneur, your three letters of exchange. One only has been negotiated. I shall make a good account of them.
You can subtract $30 from the sum that you
regard as advanced to the Sisters. The sum
of 15 piastres of silver left each for Mr.
Causse and Mr. Mazzuchelli is the same sum
which I had dispensed in your name and which
they [Causse and Mazzuchelli] gave voluntar-
ily in virtue of some work of sewing [done by
the Sisters]. I shall tell them [the Sisters]
tomorrow to write you themselves if they have
need of something. You ought to know that
Mr. Donaghoe will not come before next spring.

School problems in Dubuque had come to a crisis
again, but Cretin could report that "the girls have
returned to the Sisters' school, and the catechism is
better attended." But there were other problems in
regard to which it would seem Loras had acted with

more haste than prudence, for Cretin took the liberty
of withholding a letter which Loras had intended for
the "Sister Superior," returning it to him on November 21 with a caution and veiled explanation of the
situation which had occasioned the Bishop's hasty letter. His remarks against calumniators in his Sunday
sermon give some hint of the problem:

>   Only wicked and corrupted men speak against
>   their neighbors. Because they are corrupted
>   they think all others like them. If calumny
>   be bad it is much more so when it attacks ir-
>   reproachable persons, &c, &c.

Sister M. Lambertina's Journal may throw some light
on the subject, for it indicates that Father Healy
had induced the Sisters to join the cathedral choir,
and that the very attractive Sister M. Francis O'Reilly,
possessed of a fine voice, had become an object of his
attentions, not only in the choir associations but in
the course of her assistance of her mother with the
household tasks in the Bishop's residence. The situation had not gone unobserved, and as a result there
was some show of disrespect by the people toward the
Sisters. Father Healy's stay in Philadelphia had no
doubt made him aware that the Sisters had no canonical
status, a fact which he seems to have communicated rather widely. He used this information also in an effort to induce Francis to leave the community, with
some promise of providing for her support. She seems
to have responded to what she regarded as fatherly solicitude and to have shared the idea with Sister M.
Gertrude Regan, who rejected it peremptorily, and with
Sister M. Margaret Mann, who was much troubled by it.
A priest cousin of Sister M. Joseph tried to induce
her also to leave, and for the same reason. As a result, some of the Sisters became discouraged for a
time, Sisters M. Vincent, Joseph, Veronica and Philomena being tempted to return to Philadelphia. This
they might have done had not their friend Denis Mahony,
a cousin of Sister M. Vincent, persuaded them to stay
on in the hope of better days. All this made the matter of public vows imperative, though Bishop Loras
seemed to think it best to hold to a full two-years
of "novitiate," to insure, as Kenrick may have suggested, the validity of their vows.

However, other problems were involved with the
choir, for it seems apparent that the convert-organist,
Norman, who conducted the choir, chose unauthorized
(Protestant?) hymns, which the Sisters refused to sing.

However, "with their consent and even their entreaty," Father Cretin wrote the Bishop,"I have permitted Mr. Norman to reappear at the organ. He has made ample and satisfactory apology for the past." When Norman promised to make use only of hymns approved by either the priest or the Bishop, peace again reigned, and the Sisters returned to the choir.

Mother Clarke may not have been aware of all this at the time, for her letter to Bishop Loras, written November 27, 1844, indicates that she had spent the previous weeks with the Sisters in Davenport, where the needs were greater than she had the means to supply. Her letter accounted to the Bishop for money he had given her, and laid out the situation of the Sisters at the Davenport academy, indicating the pressure she was under for funds.

> Right Rev. Father in Christ,
> By direction of Revd. Mr. Cretin I write to you. I would not presume to write without your permission unless I had something very important to treat about. I have troubled you through him for some money, which he tells me you cannot give except $50 which he has already given.
>
> It must be the holy permission of God for my trial that I did not know in time that Revd. Father would not come this winter. If I did know, I would have written and told him that his money was out since last September; and that I had to provide winter clothing for the Sisters, wood and provisions for the winter. I know if he could get it in the world he would send it. He has sent on with Mrs. Baker and Elizabeth Sullivan who arrived on the 8th, a new piano with other articles. Letters followed him from Philadelphia to Pittsburgh which obliged him to return.

Apparently it was of the Dubuque boarding school - St. Mary's - that Mother next spoke, for there is no indication of boarding students attending St. Philomena's at that time:

> We cannot take another boarder for want of room; some of those we have, their pension hardly clears their expense. Others who are more profitable, their payments are so tedious and uncertain that it is an inconvenience.

Still there is no excuse on our part. Their
table must be provided, their beds and bedding, washing and every other necessary. I
will write to Revd. Father for some money; I
know he will send it if he can. I received
from you $25 before I went to Davenport. I
laid it out for clothing for the Sisters who
were going, but three dollars I left with
Sister Mary Catherine. I brought some money
with me, thinking we might want something in
a new place, although I expected there was
tea - coffee - sugar - flour - beds and bedding at least. To my surprise there was nothing but four cots with mattresses and two
stoves - neither pillows - bed clothes - nor
provisions.

Although the people were very kind, it could
not be expected that they could provide.all
that was absolutely necessary. As far as I
had means, I got what answered the present
wants, in preference to eating our meals out
of the house for some days, as Revd. Mr.
Pelamourgues proposed. He did not think, of
course, that we could get them. The $25 you
gave me in Davenport I laid out $15 with the
Sisters there. The remainder I kept to bring
me home. I was nearly four weeks there; during that time they did not receive in the
school but one dollar in cash, and one dollar's
worth of wood, as payment for tuition.

I heard from the Sisters this week; they were
well, and doing better. I wished very much to
have spoken to you when I saw you on the boat,
but I had no opportunity. Three or four of
the Sisters have been ill with bad colds, but
they are now better. I have trespassed too
long on your precious time.

> I am with the greatest respect
> Your very humble
> Mary F. Clarke   32

A notation in connection with the above letter reads:
"Endorsed by Bishop Loras. Sister M. Clarke promised
75 besides 25. Proposed the establishment of Potosi.
Told to write to Father Causse herself." 33

Obedient to the Bishop's directive, Mother Clarke
arranged with Father Causse for the Potosi mission,and

Sisters M. Theresa Fullam, Veronica O'Reilly and Magdalen Cole, opened school there in 1845. In 1846 Sister M. Theresa was called to the motherhouse where she would serve as infirmarion, while Sister M. Gertrude Regan replaced her as superior, continuing in that position until the mission closed in 1848.

In late October of 1844, Father Donaghoe had written from Pittsburgh explaining the necessity for his returning to Philadelphia in order to defend himself against serious charges in connection with the riotings of the previous spring. He had come that far on his way west when letters reached him urging his return. The little party he was accompanying would proceed westward.

> I have arrived at Pittsburgh with Mrs. Baker and Miss Elizabeth Sullivan [and Jane O'Reilly] also a young man for St. Joseph's Indiana, and one[?] for the Visitation, St. Louis. The water is so low that we cannot go unless by giving 20 dollars to St. Louis or 10 to Cincinnati. I have dry goods, etc. I have equipment which will be a great curiosity at Dubuque. But of all I have, nothing is equal to the splendid new pianno[sic], one of Low's best. These with my own clothing have cost me 700. I believe I would not have purchased the pianno only I did expect compensation would have been made for the burnt Seminary.
>
> I gave fees to lawyers and had they been able to reach it before that hurry of the election I had strong hopes that I would be successful. As it is, it is deferred until the November term, where it's necessary that I should attend, my lawyers have insisted on this. Bishop Kenrick wished me to stay with him at St. John's in the interim, until the Supreme Court shall have adjudged the affair. The defense that is in preparation - and for this they had 22 witnesses subpoenaed - had the case been reached, consists in this that the priest had armed men in St. Michael's who went down to the School-house and killed Wright and Ramsey on Monday night. I was 14 miles distant on Monday and during that night, of course, the priest (Donaghoe) can prove an alibi, by many witnesses. I wish Rev. Mr. Loughran could do the same. The object is that I should be in court, so that the owner

of the property may be identified, if they
dare to give evidence to that effect, and
confound by rebutting the evidence that I was
not in the city on that night or day. The
Lawyers say I must not allow such a stigma to
rest on me. I care little about that, if I
could go without allowing the interest of my
poor Community to suffer the loss. It is
very painful to me to be separated from the
mission that I have chosen amid so many con-
flicts. I hope all goes on well with you.
I am much pleased that Mr. Cretin is in
Dubuque. . . .

Then, turning to the affairs of the Sisters, he wrote:

I hope that the house at Davenport now contains 3 or 4 of the Sisters, who will reli-
giously cultivate their own Territory before
they think of foreign soil. May it not be
that our Blessed Mother has given what lies
beyond the Father of Waters to her own childern[sic], that there they may teach the be-
nighted the greatness, the power & the influence of their Mother and their Queen? My
confidence is nourished with the thought,
neither am I depressed by the inadequacy of
the members, since I know that God chooses
the weak things of the world to confound the
strong.

Mrs. Baker will entertain you with a detailed
acct. of all the disasters of Kensington. I
admitted her now after two years' application
and the more so because she escaped Martyrdom.
She is an English lady of respectable family,
simple and prudent -- She will, when her affairs are arranged, have about 800 dollars.
I made her leave the power of Attorney with
one in whom I can confide -- This will be one
of my first attentions when I return to Philadelphia.

I will send the stereotype of C. Companion,
which fortunately was with Luhan[?] whom I
owed some money when I went west last year.
Bishop O'Connor has asked me for an edition
of it -- I now enjoy his hospitality. Console Mother Clarke and her Sisters. It is
admirable how she keeps them together and yet
appears able to do nothing. I am your ever
devoted servant   T.J. Donaghoe

Entrance date for Mary Baker and Elizabeth Sullivan is given as November 11, 1844, while Jane O'Reilly entered on August 15, 1845, at the age of sixteen.

Father Cretin's letter of January 3, 1845 brought New Year greetings to Bishop Loras:

> . . . Be assured, my Lord, that you have the greatest share of my wishes and the wishes of the Sisters, the first day of the year; they ended on that day a week-long retreat by a general communion. I have had them say five paters and five aves for your intention. They have been very edifying.

A small leaflet printed by Cretin on his hand press was the treasured memento of the first retreat the Sisters had experienced since the one in Dublin in 1832. It listed the names of all present, that is, the entire Community, save the three Sisters then at St. Philomena academy in Davenport - Sisters M.Eliza, Philomena, and Patrice.

Cretin's letter continued with an exhortation to the Bishop to have confidence, and a plea for his return to Dubuque. Cretin was disturbingly discreet in his references both to the Sisters and to Father Healy in his communication to the Bishop.

> I would persuade your Lordship to return as soon as possible. Be assured, Monseigneur, that you are more able to do good here than any of your priests, and you know that I have never had the bad habit of flattery. The great majority await you with pleasure and certainly all understand you better than Mr. Healy. You have enough condescension for it. God will aid you in all difficulties. I had thought that I would be able to take it upon myself to suspend all changes in spite of your orders. I had recommended the greatest silence to the Sisters to prevent any troublesome disturbances, and to protect their reputation. In all that, Mr. Healy has been very imprudent, and has blamed me exclusively before Mr. Godfert who has since then become very audacious. All was calm apparently. All would have disappeared in silence. It seems that someone has informed the public. . . . Mr. Mazzuchelli has been here for four days. He is not the man to reestablish peace. . .

Loras commented strangely on the back of the letter:
"Nous avons perdu la confiance en nos pastours."

Writing on January 8, 1845, Cretin gives a clearer
picture of the resistance of the Irish parishoners,
which seemed to manifest itself largely in their refusal to support the church and the clergy:

> . . . After the Mass I asked the members
> of the association to remain a moment in
> the church. I made some observations to
> them very calmly and I thought very reason-
> ably, to destroy some prejudices which
> they had on the subject of us . . .[This
> portion is largely illegible.] Mr. Quigley
> wished to respond. I did not permit them
> to speak in the church. I invited all
> the members to go down to the chapel.
> There Mr. Quigley and Mr. Corkery rose
> up with force against two French names
> which were found on the list * declaring
> that these people had not given a sou.
> Some wished to speak with very much ir-
> reverence against Monseigneur. I imposed
> silence. The greater number disapproved
> of what was said. Most finished by pay-
> ing and very many promised to pay at the
> first opportunity. . . . Johnny Sullivan has
> fallen from the roof and he is still very
> poorly, if he escapes death. . . They will,
> I think, in superstition, regard this acci-
> dent as a warning from heaven, which can make
> many of the people return to themselves.
> These gentlemen were the principal opponents.
> . . All the tumult is dissipated. They com-
> mence to repent of the wrongs. Peace is made
> with Mr. Quigley. . . but I perceive that
> episcopal authority is very little respected
> among the laity and the ecclesiastics.

From the earliest days in Dubuque, Pat Quigley had
been among the staunchest supports of the Church.
Judge Corkery and he had joined in the first appeal
for a Bishop for the territory. They had both worked

---

* of subscriptions which he had printed and
placed in the pews, having given full warning of
his plan to do so, a warning to which only one
member responded by making payment.

loyally with the Bishop, Corkery especially having
furthered in every way Loras' efforts to bring Catholic
immigrants into the diocese. This spirit of rebellion
on their part was quite out of character for them. It
seems likely to have had its source in the pervasive
influence of Fr. Healy. Fortunately, it did not last
long. Both men were prominent in the politics of their
day, and both were able and disinterested civic leaders,
so that even their temporary defection was serious.

Cretin's letter continued:

> Mr. Donaghoe has written that he will not be
> able to be here before Easter, That is vex-
> atious. He would have done much here during
> lent, expecially if your Lordship is not here.
> It is said that your Lordship plans to depart
> in the springtime for Europe to get money for
> the new cathedral, and three German priests
> and two Irish. . . .Mr. Mazzuchelli . . . has
> assured me that the people here decided to
> give nothing [for the building of the cath-
> edral] if your Lordship takes part in it.
>
> As soon as I shall be able to return to the
> savages, I shall go there with great pleas-
> ure. If you absent yourself for six months,
> you will be able to depend with great assur-
> ance on Mr. Donaghoe for the whole diocese.
> On an invitation from you he would be able
> to come quickly. I doubt that Mr. Healy is
> able to meet your expectations for that sit-
> uation. The prayers of the Sisters will be
> very useful. It seems to me they are true
> ladies. They do not have any cause to blame
> themselves.

And on January 25, he wrote in deep concern for the
strenuous labors and privations of the Bishop, and of
his own desire to be supportive:

> The last letter of your Lordship under date
> of the 16th of this month is a powerful mo-
> tive for me to redouble the zeal and the
> fervor in the prayers that I address for you
> to heaven. I see with a very sensible pain
> all the fatigues and the privations to which
> you subject yourself to do good for the
> flock confided to your pastoral solicitude.
> I would wish to be able to sweeten them. I
> regret very much that you should not be better

> seconded. I am completely ready to give
> place here to the first that comes. It will
> be very easy for me to find a little retreat.
> . . I am going to visit every Sunday some
> station ten or fifteen miles from Dubuque,
> which I leave entirely to the care of Mr.
> Healy. Many families have not appeared here
> at church for eight or ten months. I shall
> go to see them. . . .

Father Healy was continuing to give trouble, but the
spirit of the Sisters was a source of encouragement,
as we see from Cretin's account of the Dubuque situation:

> Mr. Healy . . . ought very much to repent for
> having shown me so much injustice. . . . I
> have done everything to always keep the great-
> est peace with Mr. Healy - that he would be
> dangerous to disaffect because of the nation-
> al prejudice . . . Those who would so unjust-
> ly speak calumnies have themselves lost coun-
> tenance by their imprudence and their kind of
> mischief-making. . . .

> The Sisters are happy. It proves how good
> and simple they are, and it is this goodness,
> this simplicity, that I admire in them, and
> that can do very much to make their estab-
> lishment effective for the good of the dio-
> cese. I have confidence that this house will
> one day be your greatest consolation. All
> the Sisters, without exception, have very
> much the spirit of their state. They are in
> peace in spite of the attempt [illegible] of
> division which people have sought to sow
> among them as far as to speak of diverse ex-
> pedients for establishing [themselves] in the
> world.

At last, on May 25, 1845, Father Donaghoe returned
from his sojourn of fifteen months in the East. Learning at once of the complications in which Father Healy
had involved the Sisters, and of the talk that had
been stirred up against them, he rebuked Sister M.
Margaret Mann with much harshness as the one on whom
he had depended to watch over the younger members.
With her usual directness she responded: "You might
have warned us," for Father Donaghoe can scarcely have
failed to know something of Healy's background and his
Philadelphia record. The letter of June 5, 1845, which

Father received from Bishop Loras, then in Burlington, can have given him little comfort under the circumstances. It would be some months before the two could meet to discuss their mutual problems. The letter read:

> Please, respected friend, to accept the title and the faculties of Vicar General of the Bishop of Dubuque, because I am sure that you will render me important services. The Revd. J. Healy has a copy of the extraordinary faculties which he was directed to remit to you.
>
> Your favor of May 30 . . . afforded me both sorrow for your indisposition and great pleasure for your arrival among us. . . .
>
> I beg you, Revd. friend, to take in my absence, the management of the spiritual affairs of Dubuque and in the absence of the very Revd. J. Cretin [who had at last departed to his beloved Winnebagoes] the care of the temporal ones. It grieves me very much to be deprived of the pleasure of seeing you until the beginning of Aug. but the interest of Religion in the southern part of the diocese does not permit it sooner.
>
> It is customary that a clergyman from Dubuque should visit Holy Cross on the third Sunday of every month. Suppose you take M. Corkery[*] & old Tom and the gig, and go there on the 3rd Sunday of June, if you are well enough then, and also in the following month. Would it not please you & give you an agreeable vacation. If so it be, do it and I shall be thankful to you.

Father Healy left the diocese in early fall. His had been a harvest of tares. On the occasion of his dismissal, Loras wrote to Bishop Blanc of New Orleans, July 30, 1846 that he had been "compelled by sad necessity and only to prevent scandal and a kind of schism," to give Healy his exeat.

---

[*]
There was a workman of that name as well as Judge Corkery in Dubuque at the time.

Loras, back in Dubuque, was desirous of restoring peace among his people, and with this in mind, suggested to the Sisters that they make a gesture of friendship to them. Sister M. Lambertina's Notes tell us that "When Bishop Loras wanted the Srs. to go at New Year's to call on the people who were unfriendly & thus 'make up' with them in the Fr. manner, Fr. Donaghoe made Mother Cl. write to Bp. Loras in these words: 'I will never permit my Srs. to enter those abodes of vice and iniquity. . . .'" The Notes continue: "S.M. Michael said that the organist, Mr. Luttinger, of the Cathedral, who was a convert, was on Fr. Healy's side in the controversy. Later he went to California, but before going, he went to Old St. Joseph's and on his knees begged pardon of Fr. Donaghoe for all he had said against the Srs. and for all the trouble he had caused."

Fr. Cretin laid at Healy's door the loss of vocations on the part of a number of young men in the diocese. In his letter to Bishop Loras, April 25, 1845, he wrote: "If Mr. Healy had not been in Dubuque you would have perhaps five or six young men on whom you could be able to count." Mentioning by name three who had not persevered, he suggested there were others.

The subsequent history of Father Healy is sad. In October of 1845, the Bishop sorrowfully dismissed him, providing him with ten dollars for travel and fifty as a parting gift. He was next found at St. James church, Charleston, Wisconsin, where some years later he died at the altar. Loras sent two priests to represent him at the funeral. In passing through the rectory they noticed the Lutheran housekeeper quietly cutting up a set of vestments for the material they contained, and on inquiry they were told, "My husband gave them to me."[34]

The Bishop's position was most difficult, subject as he was to blame on every side. For instance, W.H. Postlewait, his agent for church properties, wrote to him from Burlington concerning Father Healy and other problems of the diocese. We quote in part:

> June 17, 1847
> I heard you make a solemn promise at my table once to Mr. Healy(about the time you sent him to Dubuque to bring about a better feeling between you and the Catholics of your place) that he should remain at Dubuque the remainder

of his life if he wished. He remarked with
tears in his eyes that he was satisfied to
remain here but he was getting along in years
and wished to be settled at some place. Did
not want to be tossed about to and fro. Well,
Bishop, where is he now? at Dubuque? No, Wisconsin, in another diocese. Why? I don't
know, but I have heard the blame laid at your
door. You have no Irish, no Catholics in
your diocese. Only a few at least, and all
the foreign emigration is to Wisconsin. Is
it our country, soil, or climate which is the
cause of keeping Catholics away from us?

The accusation must have been especially bitter to the
Bishop, after all his efforts through the years to
help Irish immigrants find homes on the land, and to
furnish them with the consolation of their religion.
The letter continued in the same harsh spirit:

You will hear in the mouth of every Irish
emigrant - ask him, are you going to Iowa?
No, no. Why? Oh, there is no churches there,
they say Bishop Loras can't keep a priest in
his diocese no time, they won't stay with
him. This I can hear in the mouth of foreign-
ers. Now, Bishop, is it for the want of means
to support priests that you can't keep them?

Here the letter made an accusation, the result of a
calumny spread widely by a "wandering priest" apparently Father Healy, 35 whom Loras had found it necessary to dismiss him from his diocese. It regarded
mission funds Loras was supposed to have improperly
lent out at interest in St. Louis:

Have you not got more funds at your command
than any other Bishop in the west, now lying
in St. Louis? Yes, and have had all the
time, and now throw-up to the Catholics here
that you have spent upwards of $5000 now to
build a church. What have we to do with
that? What is it worth now? Not more than
$1500 or $1200 at the outside and going to
rack because the Catholics won't support a
priest. I have turned back to your former
letters and I find you have mentioned the
subject of $5181,75 in no less that 4 or 5
of your letters. Is this not taunting me
enough? If not for me, is it not enough for

all? I hope not to hear of it again. I wish
you had not spent one cent here. The money
would have done a great deal more good kept
in St. Louis, in safe keeping, or was it sent
to you to keep up missionary priests and
build churches in Iowa, I would like to know
anyhow. If you have made a bad investment of
it you have not me to blame or any other Catholic in this place. It was all done under your
own direction.

Now Bishop, I will tell you the real cause
why a priest cannot be supported here. All
know how changeable your mind is, and they
don't know how long is to remain. You take
them away unexpectedly and you send one back
when it suits you. For my part, I hope you
will not send a priest here at all. No one
likes to give much for the support of a
priest unless they are satisfied he is to
remain some time.

I think I have written enough, so I will end
it until I hear from you again.

Your W.H. Postlewait

And as a parting fling he added:

Bishop, did our Savior vote against the use
of intoxicating liquor when he wrought his
first miricle [sic]?

Loras' cryptic comment on the back of the letter read:
"False statements. M.H. the pest of the diocese."

It was a lonely and beset Bishop, then, whose vicar general Father Donaghoe had become. It was a
factious congregation Father was to serve. Despite
Cretin's esteem for the Sisters and his efforts to
give them support, there was little friendship for
them in the town. Father Donaghoe's one hope was to
put a distance between them and the people of Dubuque
and at the same time provide a refuge for himself
when the pressures grew too great.

FOOTNOTES - CHAPTER IV

1. Site of the present motherhouse of the Sisters of Charity, BVM.

2. Dubuque was born in Trois Rivieres, Canada, January 10, 1762.

3. The writer is indebted to M.M.Hoffmann's Antique Dubuque, 1673-1833 (Dubuque: Telegraph Herald, 1930), for the account of Julien Dubuque's years in the area.

4. In 1897 the citizens of Dubuque erected the picturesque stone tower which now marks his burial place. As for the lands forfeited to Chouteau, the courts eventually disavowed Chouteau's claims and the titles reverted to the Indians.

5. Biographical data on Loras and Cretin have for their principal source M.M. Hoffmann's Church Founders of the Northwest (Milwaukee: Bruce Publishing Company, 1937).

6. Booklet "1440-1940, 5^e Centenaire de la Maison Loras, Lyon: n.p., 1940" commemorating the fifth centennial of the Loras business enterprise, and preserved in the archives of Loras college, Dubuque, Iowa.

7. It is apparent from lists of names available from this early period that two-thirds of the early membership in the cathedral church were Irish, a fact not easily accounted for.

8. By 1841 "The number of his [Mazzuchelli's] parishioners rose to 3,500, the greater part of Irish origin, while there were many French, Germans and Americans. They often dwelt in rude cabins which had for the most part neither windows nor floors. In the very humble dwellings of one or two rooms the family cooked and slept and ate on the same table where the missionary preached, heard confessions and administered the sacraments." Soeur Rosemary Crepeau, OP, Un Apostre Dominican Aux Etats-Unis. Le Père Samuel Charles Gaetan Mazzuchelli (Paris:n.p.1932).

9.   Samuel Charles Mazzuchelli, Memoirs, Historical
     and Edifying, of a Missionary Apostolic.(Chicago:
     W. F. Hall Printing Company, 1915.) The details
     given are drawn chiefly from this source.

10. Carl Wittke. The Irish in America.(Baton Rouge:
     Louisiana State University Press, 1956.) p.62.

11. (note on Father Perrodin as given.)
     Father J.G.Perrodin spent the years 1842-1851 as
     pastor of Garryowen, living in a log house and
     serving a log church. He attended also the con-
     gregations of Bellevue, Sabula, Templehill and
     Cascade, making the trips by horseback, a mode
     of travel which he found particularly difficult.
     His request for a"gig" the Bishop did not find
     himself in a position to grant. Perrodin was
     more of a scholar than a pioneer, spending his
     spare hours translating the French treatises on
     apologetics, and at one time delivering a ser-
     ies of lectures in Iowa City. He suffered much
     from the lack of means for scholarship and from
     the bitter Iowa winters. His one-room "academy,"
     presided over for some years by Denis Mahony, was
     supported from public funds, as were the other
     schools of the diocese, doubtless because pub-
     lic schools were not yet available. As pastor,
     Father promoted temperance and strove to help
     his people raise their standard of living. In
     1849 he caught the gold fever and asked his
     exeat for northern California, hoping that Cretin
     would accompany him there. Being disappointed,
     he continued on in Garryowen until 1851, when
     he returned to France where he would find cir-
     cumstances more favorable to the priestly per-
     fection to which he aspired. On his departure
     Perrodin wrote touchingly to the Bishop of his
     pain in leaving "a place where I spent the nine
     best years of my life," and where"the kindness
     of my good people literally brought tears to my
     eyes." (Centennial booklet - Saint Patrick's
     Parish, Garryowen, Iowa, 1840-1940.)

12. Mazzuchelli, p. 271.

13. The question of who served as architect for the
     new capitol has long been argued. The picture
     it presented of old world culture on the Iowa
     frontier certainly suggests the influence of
     one familiar with the dignified and graceful
     beauty of structures in the great architectural

centers of Europe. The tabernacle carved by Father Mazzuchelli in the form of the capitol's turret, and the spiral staircase he designed into the residence of the first Iowa bishop suggest that the dream of the capitol plan was his. That it was executed by the professional architect, John F. Rague, who was responsible for the dignified but less beautiful capitol building in Springfield, Illinois, seems to be a matter of history.

14. The fact that this letter is found in the Dubuque Archdiocesan archives suggests that it may never have been sent.

15. It is interesting to note that the three small churches of Muscatine, Bellevue and Shullsburg were "pre-fabs," built by expert workmen at Prairie du Chien and sent by way of the river to be assembled by local workmen. The one at Muscatine is preserved as an historic shrine as a part of the parish plant. It is located picturesquely on the summit of a hill to which it was moved after the building of the present church.

16. Sister M. Borromeo Brown, The History of the Sisters of Providence of Saint Mary-of-the-Woods (New York: Benziger Brothers, 1949), p. 122.

17. Walter Havighurst, Voices on the River, the Story of the Mississippi Waterways (New York: Macmillan Co., 1964), p. 83.

18. Ibid., p. 81.

19. The Sisters of Charity of Nazareth, Kentucky were established in 1812 by the Reverend John David, later Bishop David, under the guidance of Bishop Flaget. Mother Catherine Spalding was their first Mother General. They followed the modified rule of the Sisters of Charity of Emmitsburg insofar as it met their needs, but had no direct ties with that, the earliest of the American foundations of religious women. (Elizabeth Seton had established her sisterhood under the direction of the Sulpician Father Dubois at Emmitsburg, Maryland, in 1809, adapting to their need the rule of St. Vincent de Paul.) The Sisters of Loretto at the Foot of the Cross were founded the same year - 1812 -

by the Reverend Charles Nerinckx, a Belgian
priest, serving also under Bishop Flaget. It is
remarkable that a third institute of religious
women was founded in Kentucky ten years later,
that of the Order of St. Dominic, at St. Rose,
under the direction of the Dominican Fathers of
the priory there. European foundations, chiefly
French - the Sisters of Providence, of the Holy
Cross, of St. Joseph, the Religious of the Sacred Heart, the Visitandines and others - early
penetrated the wilderness, bringing religion and
culture even to the frontier. The first foundation of the Sisters of Mercy was established
in Pittsburgh in December, 1843. Save for early
establishments in New Orleans during its years
under French and Spanish rule, the Sisters of
Charity, BVM were second only to the Religious
of the Sacred Heart to come from overseas and
make a permanent establishment in the United
States.

20. Borromeo, op. cit., p. 160.

21. Loras' original gift to the Sisters was a 120-
foot lot, valued at $1000.00, and the frame
house on it, costing $1200.00. This gift, to-
gether with other contributions to their needs
through 1849, amounted to $3617.14. This in-
cluded the cost of the small brick schoolhouse-
$336.02. See Loras' account book, in the Arch-
diocesan archives, Dubuque, p. 53.

22. The Kenrick-Frenaye Correspondence, 1830-1862,
selected, arranged and annotated by F.E.T. (Philadelphia: Wickersham Printing Co., 1920), p.171.

23. Cretin to Loras, November 13, 1844. Dubuque
Archdiocesan archives.

24. Hickey Collection, Archives, Loras college,
Dubuque, Iowa.

25. "Alamode of the mountain" has reference to the
arrangement in Emmitsburg where the Sulpician
Father Deluol, acting as director of the Sisters
at St. Joseph's, resided at the St. Mary Seminary - the "Mountain."

26. The Reverend M.J.Madaj, archivist for the Archdiocese of Chiacgo, writes on May 27, 1974:
"There is no evidence either in Bishop Quarter's

diary or in the Archdiocesan Archives that
Father Terence J. Donaghoe was offered the presidency of the University of St. Mary of the Lake.
Father Jeremia Kinsella was appointed to that
office even before he was ordained a priest.
There do not seem to have been any other candidates for the position." This, however, is not
conclusive, for an oral discussion which bore
no fruit might have failed of record.

According to Bishop Quarter's Diary, he was consecrated on March 10, 1844, and left for Chicago
via the Lakes on April 18, arriving there May 5.
His Diary, makes no mention of a trip from
Frederick to Baltimore, but since it may have
been made on the return from a retreat at the
Jesuit novitiate in Frederick, he would not have
included it in an official record. The Diary
is included in the Catholic History of Chicago,
compiled by the Reverend James J. McGovern, D.D.,
as a souvenir of Archbishop Feehan's silver jubilee in the episcopacy, (Chicago: n.p., 1890).

27. When in 1856 Bishop O'Regan wished to withdraw
the Mercy Sisters from Galena, and requested
our Sisters to replace them, his request was not
honored. The O'Regan letters and one communication from the Galena pastor, the Reverend P.J.
McElhearne, are retained in the BVM archives.

28. Pencil notes of Sister M. Lambertina Doran remain in the BVM archives. Secretary General of
the congregation for many years, Sister was the
author of In the Early Days, but in that account
of the Congregation's history Sister failed to
include some items of interest from her notes
and also from what has come to be called her
Journal, a collection of episodes and recollections, largely communicated to her by Sister M.
Michael Nihill. Where the writer has been able
to verify these, or where there seemed no reason
to question their validity, they are included
in the present work.

29. Kenrick-Frenaye Correspondence, p. 188ff

30. Doran Journal, p. 12.

31. Quoted from a pamphlet: The Warnings of Thomas
Jefferson: or A brief Exposition of the Dangers
to be Apprehended to our Civil and Religious

Liberties from Presbyterianism, Justin E. Moore
(Philadelphia: Wm. J. Cunningham, 1844), p.25.

32. Bishop Loras' account book, pages 56 and 139,
lists the value of his Davenport lots as $1425.00
and the cost of the building assigned the Sisters
for their academy as $3120.00. Furnishings he
had provided came to $34.83. A gift of $50,
plus tuition for poor girls to the amount of
$57.50, completed the endowment of the school
provided by the diocese during the Sisters' two
years in Davenport. As for the property itself,
that remained in the ownership of the diocese.

33. Unclassified note in Griffith file.

34. Doran Journal, pp. 32-33.

35. Bishop Loras wrote the following to the Propagation of the Faith in justification of his position:

> A priest who had been interdicted twice was
> received on trial in my diocese by an excess
> of bounty on my part: he did not change his
> ways and tried to hinder our missions by
> calumnies. He said to one or more bishops
> of the United States that he was certain
> that I had at St. Louis at interest 25,000
> piastres. Atrocious calumny! I have never
> let a penny to anyone. It has been believed
> and repeated. I have not actually 1500 frs.
> for the needs of 27 priests and of the whole
> diocese."
> There is much evidence that the priest re-
> ferred to was Father Healy.

The Home On The Prairie-
1846-1853

First structure on the Prairie

In chapter five we have the account of the Sisters' admission to canonical vows on August 15, 1845, and, in the following spring, of their removal to a site on the Prairie, eight miles from Dubuque, where somewhat over a square mile of land awaited the plow. Here they were to suffer all the hardships of pioneer living and the labors of operating a boarding academy under the most primitive conditions. A fire in May, 1849 wiped out their rock chapel and the frame structure which served as motherhouse and boarding school. Only a parish house of rough limestone and a large log church where the priest-superior served the settlers of the area as pastor were left standing. Then, in November, 1850, with the rebuilding in mid-course, the priest joined his boyhood friend from Tyrone on a voyage to Rome where the latter was to receive the pallium as the archbishop of New York. The arrival of a small band of Trappist monks from Ireland in the summer of 1849, and their situation three miles distant from the Sisters' prairie home gave hope of assistance both physical and spiritual. Meanwhile a small group of charitable men came one by one, to the assistance of the Sisters, entering upon a community life and taking private vows under the direction of the priest. Three of these would survive him and share the labors of the Sisters. The summer of 1849 brought with it also a severe epidemic of cholera, with the Sisters sharing in the care of its victims. In early 1853, the Sisters were required to assume a religious dress.

School house and bell tower on St. Joseph Prairie, adjacent to Motherhouse.

The federally funded Military Road from Dubuque
through Cascade to Iowa City had not been greatly improved since Lyman Dillon of Cascade marked its path
with a breaking plough and five yoke of oxen some
three years before. By 1845 many sections of it had
been made useless by washouts which had carried the
simple bridges away, and only in March of that year
were contracts let for new bridges and general road
improvement. It was along this rough road that Father
Donaghoe set out in early June of 1845 on horseback
or with "Tom and the gig" to find a site well away
from the city of his troubles, where he might plan a
home for the Sisters. Perhaps he had heard of the
broad stretch of prairie the eccentric John Walsh was
holding, with the aid of a long-range rifle, for a
group of religious women that he had dreamed up in his
own odd way. But was it odd? For the oratorical ef-
fusion with which Walsh told that he responded to the
maiden of his vision was scarcely of the mystical order. We have the story as Sister M. Raphael Barry
claims she heard it from the lips of Father Donaghoe:

> John Walsh had a fine physique, with an erect and
> soldierly bearing. Like many among the early set-
> tlers, he was a unique character, and by some was
> regarded as a trifle eccentric. A fervent Cath-
> olic, he received Holy Communion every Sunday,*
> had a good education and was said to be the best
> mathematician that had ever come to the lead
> mines. He was engaged in the dry goods business,
> but was a splendid horseman, and not infrequently
> slung a rifle over his shoulder, mounted a spiri-
> ted pony and rode like the wind over the bound-
> less prairie.
>
> On one of these expeditions he said that he saw
> a young girl of marvellous beauty, who said to
> him: "Good sir, I am Philomena, martyr for Christ,

---

* A practice quite unusual at the time.

and I have come to bring you a message." He said,
"Sainted maiden, to the best of my knowledge,
this is the first time I have heard your name,
but I am, I boast, a loyal son of Holy Church.
All her saints are dear to me, and if you are one
of them, you have only to command me and I will
listen with all respect to your words." Then the
young girl told him that one day a community of
nuns would come to Iowa; they would build a convent here, and that through their means many souls
would be brought to heaven. She pointed out a
tract of land which she told him to hold until
the Sisters came. And that he might know them
when they did come, she bade him look toward the
east and he would see a Sister advancing. He
turned and saw, near enough to see her face dis-
tinctly - a nun. He turned again to his companion but she had disappeared.[1]

There is further evidence that Walsh was indeed an
eccentric, for once being invited with his wife to
Sunday Mass in the convent chapel, which was shortly
built on the land he had held for the Sisters, he was
angry when he found that another guest had had the
temerity to be present also. Then there was the matter of a gift to him in the form of an address of welcome, over which some Sister had labored long. It
was, we learn, "embroidered on white silk, surrounded
by an ornamental border, and surmounted by a slanting
cross."[2] When two of the Sisters made the presentation, he received them kindly, thanked them for their
intention to do him honor, but, looking critically at
the cross, said: "Ladies, as a Roman Catholic, I
adore only an upright cross. You will please take
your address away." and the offending gift was promptly
consigned to outer darkness. We hear no more of the
good man save that, some years later, he met his death
on the prairie on his way to new ventures in California.

But to go back to the June of 1845. Once Walsh had
surrendered his preemption right to Father Donaghoe,
matters moved quickly. The tough prairie sod was soon
broken on an acre or so of land, sufficient that
Father Donaghoe could write on October 10, to the Sisters at Potosi, Wisconsin: "John Walsh's potato patch
gave me about 150 bushels for the children and we have
hay for the cattle." Legal titles to eighty acres
each in sections 32 and 33 came into the possession of
Mary Frances Clarke, Margaret Mann, Rose O'Toole, Mary
Baker and Bridget O'Leary when the government opened
the lands for sale in 1847 at $1.25 an acre. More

purchases would follow, including 244.96 acres of woodland, filling up the total of John Walsh's quit claim to 724.96 acres.

With the first small harvest over, Pat Clarke a neighbor, broke ground and sowed winter wheat. Construction went forward quickly, as we see from a letter which came from Michael McGill, Father Donaghoe's Philadelphia agent, addressed to "My best and dearest Friend," and dated November 27, 1845:

> . . . You inform me that you are engaged in making improvements on the farm and that you intend by next spring to have at least commenced on the Territorial Road on St. Joseph Prairie, a house to be called the Motherhouse. I trust it will be made for the comfort and convenience of those pious Sisters that so providentially escaped with their lives out of the hands of the Natives of Kensington. May their useful lives be spared long, and your industry and enterprises be crowned with success. . . .

The first building constructed on the newly acquired land was a log house, lined with wooden planks and having a wooden floor. It was intended as a temporary shelter for Father Donaghoe and as a residence for the workmen needed for farming, fencing and construction. In the course of its construction in August, Father preached a retreat for the Sisters in preparation for the great event of their first canonical profession. The feast of the Assumption was the day chosen, when Bishop Loras, assisted by Fathers Donaghoe and Cretin,* officiated with all the pomp of a pontifical ceremony. In the presence of a large and curious congregation, the Bishop asked of each Sister in turn, as she knelt before him, the canonical questions which would give assurance that each was acting in full freedom and in consciousness of the obligations she was assuming. The Bishop's sermon which followed explained the significance of the occasion and the nature and obligations of the religious state. Then, at the Communion of the Mass, the Sisters filed, two by two, into the sanctuary, and each pronounced the formula of vows, and, pledging herself to service

---

*
The vestments worn that day had been the gift of Cardinal Fesch of Lyons, France, "to the poorest church in America."

1835 ~ Nov 1st

Entered	Names	Age	Residence	Register Commenc.	No Rec'd	Name in Religion	Profess.	Left	Death
1835 Nov 1st	Mary Clarke	27	Dublin Ireland		1	St Mary Frances			1879 Decr 1st
" " "	Margaret Kinsea	25	"		2	" Margaret			1875 Christr
" " "	Rose McCl	24	"		3	" Rose			1890 Decr 11th
" " "	Eliza Kelly	25	"		4	" Eliza			
" " "	Catharine Byrne	24	"		5	" Catharine			1866 Octr 1
1835 June 16	Mary Lawler	25	Kingston Ireland		6	Alphonsa	1837 Augst		1858 July 25
1837 May 15	Maria Lawler	21	"		7	Clara	1838 Decr 3		1861 May 9
1839 June 21	Bridget DeLacy	35	Dublin		8	Aloysia	1841 Jany		1861 Decr 3
" 24	Frances Reilly	15	Kildare		9	Frances	" Decr 26		1845 Octr 16
1841 Aug 16	Catharine Mowray	25	Dublin		11	Bernard	1843 Aug		1865 Feby 21st
1841 June 19	Eliza Reilly	24	Kildare		11	Joseph	1842 May		1857 May 1st
" June 26	Eliza Fallon	30	Meath		12	Teresa	" June 19		1888 Octr 28
1841 Augt 1st	Eliza Mullen	15	Philadelphia Penn.		13	Philomena	1843 Sept		1864 April
" Aug 8	Anne Connell	21	Galloway Indiana		14	Patricia	" June 8		June 1867
" Aug 24	Eliza Ryan	15	Philadelphia Penn.		15	Gertrude	1842 Decr 3		
1842 Jany 1	Sarah Coda	30	"		16	Magdalen	1843 July 2		1876 July 22
1842 June 2	Adel Hamlin	35	"		17	Augustine	1842 Octr 9		1857 June
1842 Decr 7	Catharine Reilly	18	Co Cavan Ireland		18	Veronica	1843 Decr 8		1861 Octr
" 24	Julia Donavan	19	Cork		19	Vincent	1846 Novr		1872 June 10th
1844 Octr 11	Mary Baker	40	Shropshire England		20	Lucy	1846 Augst		1849 Octr 19

First page of Mother Clarke's community register.

in the diocese of Dubuque, sealed her pledge by the
reception of Holy Communion at the hands of the Bishop.
Deeply grateful at last for the security of their status
as religious, Mother Clarke and her Sisters returned
quietly to their places, conscious of a new courage,
and of a new acceptance on the part of the attentive
congregation about them.

The following formula used by the Community for
many years, was doubtless the one the Sisters made use
of on that day:

> I, Mary_____in the presence of
> God and the whole court of Heaven, renew the
> promises of my Baptism, and take a simple vow
> of Poverty, Chastity, and Obedience, for one
> year, to serve in the Diocese of Dubuque, and
> to engage in all the duties pointed out by
> our Rule, in the Community of the Sisters of
> Charity of the Blessed Virgin. To fulfill
> these engagements, I beg the assistance of
> my crucified Savior and His Blessed Mother;
> moreover, it is my intention to renew these
> engagements annually during the remainder of
> my life. Amen.

The BVM archives contain three community registers.
The first, a simple grade school notebook, without
cover or title, contains in Mother Clarke's handwriting records of the years 1833-1868. The second begins
in the distinctive hand of Mother Clarke's sister,
Sister M. Josephine, whose short span of religious
life extended only from May 25, 1852 to April 29, 1855.
Upon her death, Mother Clarke took up the record, carrying it to 1867. The third register is apparently
one kept by Mother Cecilia Dougherty. Its list of
entrants begins with the first four members on November 1, 1833, and continues through the "set" of July 2,
1919. Mother Cecilia died September 7, 1919. Mother
Clarke's register shows no dates for the reception or
profession of the first five members. It does, however,
provide vow dates from May 22, 1837 for Mary Lawler,
(Sister M. Alphonse), through December 8, 1843, for
Catherine O'Reilly (Sister M. Veronica), shortly after their arrival in Dubuque. For Julia Donavan (Sister M. Vincent), who was a postulant when the Sisters
came west, it gives the date of November 21, 1845.
Sister M. Josephine's register is, in these regards,
identical with that of Mother Clarke's, save that
hers has been defaced. The last column of page one,
in which were listed profession dates, has been torn

off in two separate tears, quite evidently with the
purpose of obliterating those dates. The third register,
Mother Cecilia's, lists no reception dates at all, but
assigns August 15, 1845 as the day of profession for
all the first nineteen Sisters, save only Mother Clarke,
for whom she gives no date at all. The vows the Sisters made in Philadelphia, when no recognition had been
given them as religious, could have had the force of
private vows only.

All this presents us with a mystery. In what light
did Mother Clarke view her own religious commitment and
that of her earliest companions? Did she regard them
as having been clearly and finally committed when they
left home and country behind them? To her, were the
Sisters' and her own spoken vows, necessary as they
were for canonical status, merely giving public evidence of a covenant long since registered in heaven?
It is not for us to know, but after the public ceremony in Dubuque on August 15, 1845, Bishop Loras could
then be satisfied that the canons had been fulfilled;
likewise the people of Dubuque could no longer question
their status as religious.

The rule to which the Sisters engaged themselves on
that August morning of 1845 Father Donaghoe had written
in his own exquisite hand and entitled the "Regulations
of the Society of the Sisters of Charity of the Blessed
Virgin." * In its first chapter - "Of the ends of the
Society and the virtues peculiar to their state," -
he defined their "principal end" as "the honor of the
Holy Family" for which purpose "they will consecrate
the labor of their hands in imitation of the hidden
and laborious life of the Holy Family." Its "secondary
end" was to honor the childhood of our Lord, through
the teaching of "young persons of their own sex,"
while the "principal object " would be their own perfection, as the "latent spring of all their endeavors."
Therefore, the "first thing they must inviolably observe was to place the salvation of their own souls
above every other consideration and to spare no pains
to keep themselves in the state of grace. To obtain
of God the grace necessary for this purpose and to secure the rewards that our Lord promises to those devoted to the service of his little ones, they must use

---

* The inclusion of "Mary" in the title seems to have
been a growing practice made definitive only when the
Community was incorporated in 1869.

their utmost endeavors to acquire the Christian virtues, particularly those recommended to them in the following Rules." To this end "they shall perform all their exercises, both spiritual and temporal, in the spirit of humility, simplicity and charity, and in union with those which our Lord Jesus Christ performed on earth." The Sisters were, then, "ever to remember [that] those three great virtues, like the three faculties of the soul, must animate the entire body and constitute the spirit of the Community,"

Then follow three chapters on the three vows of poverty, chastity and obedience. The last of these placed the members in their relations with those in authority over them. For this they "shall pay honor and obedience to their Institute, to the Rt. Rev. Bishop of the Diocese of Dubuque. . . the Superior General of their Society, and those whom he may direct to visit them, the Mother, and in her absence her assistant," etc., and finally, "they shall likewise obey without delay the sound of the Community bell, as they would the voice of our Lord, calling them to their regular exercises."

These directives are followed by two chapters on "Charity and union among the Sisters," and on "The means of preserving charity among themselves." Lastly, there is a listing of "Spiritual Practices," with the warning that the rules be kept "locked in their chambers," and directing that the Sisters were not to"copy them, carry them out of the house, or in any way expose them to the inspection of strangers." The general spirit of these regulations and many of their provisions are readily traceable through the subsequent revisions of the Constitutions, each approved by the Sacred Congregation and retained until the Chapter of Renewal in 1967-1968. It is worthy of note, however, that this first book of regulations made no provision for the government of the Community, since, as "Superior-General" Father Donaghoe directed all its activities, internal and external. It would remain for Mother Clarke, after his death in 1869, to supply the governmental pattern, together with the directives for the various offices of the Congregation, without which it could not have been presented to the Holy See for approbation.

The preoccupation of moral theologians of the time with dangers to the "angelic virtue" is especially evident in this first set of rules through regulations hardly consonant with an apostolic life. Restrictions

on visiting, both inside and outside the convent, the
warning not to show "too much cordiality or complai-
sance" when meeting with "persons of the other sex,"
the necessity of being "as brief as possible even when
conversing on matters of piety," all these admonitions
were aimed at safeguarding the "fragile virtue." The
personal relations between the Sisters were carefully
regulated. They were permitted, indeed, to "kiss one
another on the cheek," but only on one's vow day, for
reconciliation, or on return from a long absence, and
then never "in a public place." The Sisters were to
"carefully guard against whatever might give the least
occasion to suspect them of being in any degree inclined to the vice opposite chastity, for that suspicion alone, even were it ill-founded, would be more
injurious to the community and its holy function than
all other crimes that might be falsely imputed to
them." Then followed regulations which must have left
many school patrons and friends both puzzled and hurt:
"When passing through the streets they shall not stop
to speak to any without great necessity, and even then
they shall endeavor to satisfy their demands in a few
words, and they shall always evade by some pious remark any worldly conversation." "They shall keep their
eyes modestly cast down in the streets, in churches
and in the houses of strangers, and above all when
speaking to persons of the other sex, and even among
themselves." And again, "The Sisters are permitted
to return the salutation when persons of their own sex
present their hands, but they must never make the advance."

Leisure had little place in the philosophy of the
time, the Sisters being warned that "they shall carefully avoid idleness as the parent of all vices, particularly impurity," and "whenever their common duties allow them some leisure moments, more especially
the school Sisters, they shall faithfully employ them
in sewing, spinning, or some such work. Should they
have no work of the kind, they should ask it of the
Mother or her assistant." And for further assurance
that every moment be used well, "they shall never keep
birds, lap-dogs, or any animal that might be to them
the cause of idling away their time, which they ought
to be most scrupulous of losing, remembering that God
will demand of them a strict account of every moment."

Then there is the regulation which was the source
of unnumbered scruples on the part of generations of
novices: "Although they ought to entertain a great
love for one another, they nevertheless must carefully

guard against private friendships, which are even more
dangerous than aversions because they are generally
veiled under the cloak of charity, while in reality
they are nothing but a disorderly affection of flesh
and blood." The situation was not greatly relieved
by novice instructions on the second vow, which generally reduced a discussion of violations against it to
the simple formula: "Let them not be so much as named
among you." Fortunately, today's terminology is more
specific, and the word "friendship" means only what it
says.

Another source of scruples may well have been the
following article:

> As many serious inconveniences, even to the
> destruction of the Community, might arise
> from the Sisters disburdening their hearts
> with whomsoever they might please, they shall
> not disclose their temptations, or other in-
> terior trials to their Sisters, much less
> shall they disclose them to strangers, but
> they shall apply to the Rev. Superior, the
> Mother, the Confessor,* or the Sister Super-
> ior, but to no one else, as God having de-
> signed them for that purpose, lest by their
> disobedience God should permit them to re-
> ceive bad advice in punishment of their ob-
> stinacy. Should anyone think, however, be-
> fore God, that she stands in need of the ad-
> vice of any other person, she may ask it with
> the permission of the Reverend Superior or
> the Mother.

This regulation may well have resulted for many in
such an impasse as was once faced by a weeping eighth-
grader at the Sisters' Des Moines academy. To the
urging of a fellow student that she take her problems
to one of the Sisters, she could only respond between
sobs: "Them's my problem."

With Father Donaghoe's stress on labor[3] as a fundamental means of sanctifying oneself, it is not surprising to find the prohibitions: "They shall not on week-
days spend their time in saying any prayers but those
prescribed them by the Rule, without special permission

---

*Father Donaghoe was himself their confessor.

of the Mother, who is not to grant it if those devotions would interfere with their exterior duties, nor
shall they hear more than one Mass unless obliged to
do so by some extraordinary circumstances." Then in
a regulation which was possibly a common observance at
the time, we find the following restrictions on the
reception of the Eucharist:

> They may go to Communion on all the days spe-
> cified in the catalogue of Communion days,
> but not oftener, nor on two successive days,
> should they find it necessary for the second
> Communion to go to confession. In order to
> obviate the abuses that might arise from a
> general communion, and to add the merit of
> obedience to the grace of the Sacrament, they
> shall each time ask permission of their Mother
> or Sister Superior. As it will be proper to
> refuse occasionally even the most fervent,
> either to keep them in humility and excite in
> them a more vivid desire for the holy Euchar-
> ist, or to be at liberty to refuse permission
> to less fervent Sisters, without exposing them
> to the reflections of others; they shall when
> refused humbly submit to the privation."

We have no record of the spiritual exercises outlined for the Sisters beyond the simple horarium given
them in the little ceremony of November 1, 1833. In
November, 1849, a letter of Abbot Bruno Fitzpatrick
addressed to Father Donaghoe from Ireland indicated
that he would send fifty copies of the Office of the
Blessed Virgin by the Trappist Brothers on their coming to the States the following February. Presumably
these books were to be used in the Sisters' communal
prayer. The following schedule, found in a small
notebook in the Congregation's archives, was probably
designed for a day of recollection for some special
occasion. That it was intended for a day on which
the Sisters did not have the privilege of Holy Communion is indicated by the scheduling of breakfast
before Mass.

> 5 o'clock Rising and offering the heart to God
> 5½   Morning Prayers and Meditation
>   until 6
> 6½   Breakfast
> 7   Mass - Duties &c.
> ¼9   Five decades of the Rosary &
>   Beads for the dead
> 9   Meditation for one hour

10	Spiritual Reading for half an hour
10½	Examination of Conscience for half hour
11	Dinner Silence and Duties
¼2	Five decades of the Rosary & Beads for the dead
2	Meditation for one hour
3	Spiritual reading
3½	Private devotions
4	Examination of Conscience
5	Supper Silence and Duties
6½	Five decades of the Rosary & Beads for the dead
7	Spiritual Reading
7½	Private Devotions
8¼	Night Prayers & Meditation read

* * * * *

A shadow fell on the little Community shortly after the celebration of their public profession, when Sister M. Francis suffered a hemorrhage from the lungs. Hopeful that some weeks of quiet in the country air would restore her health, Mother Clarke, Sisters M. Catherine Byrne and Gertrude Regan accompanied her to the new log house on the prairie. Two weeks were sufficient to convince them that the remedy had come too late. On December 14, the Sisters witnessed the first death from their own membership.

* * * * *

In anticipation of opening the new boarding school, the Sisters had entered the following prospectus in the Catholic Almanac for 1846 which, however, concerns itself chiefly with the academy in Dubuque:

ST. MARY'S FEMALE ACADEMY AT DUBUQUE

This academy is under the patronage of Right Rev. Bishop Loras. Its location on the banks of the Mississippi, is healthy, and commands a beautiful prospect.

The Sisters of Charity of the Blessed Virgin will teach all the branches that are taught in the best schools of this country. The Sisters will use their best endeavors to advance their pupils in their studies, and carefully watch over their health and morals.

226

List of original land purchases, made in the names of
the early Sisters. Father Donaghoe's handwriting

<pre>
                    Terms
Board and tuition, including bed, bed-
ding and washing, payable quarterly in
advance . . . . $100.
Day scholars, in the first and second
    classes, per quarter . . . . $ 4.
Day scholars in the third and fourth
    classes, per quarter . . . . $ 3.
Fuel for the season . . . . $ 1.

                    Extra
For music and use of the piano,
    quarterly. . . . . $ 7
French language, per quarter. . . . . $ 4
</pre>

Communications should be addressed to Mother
Mary F. Clarke, the Mother Superior. There
are, besides fourteen Sisters, in the institution, seven novices, and at least sixty
pupils.

N.B. St. Joseph's Prairie, a beautiful and
extensive tract of land within a few miles
of Dubuque, is intended for the Mother House
of the Sisters of Charity of the Blessed
Virgin; a house already erected there, and
other accommodations are in progress for a
boarding school for young ladies which will
be completed in the spring.

By March, 1846, a large frame building had been
erected to serve as Motherhouse, and another as boarding school. Mother Clarke and all the Sisters not
needed at the St. Mary establishment, including the
six novices - Sisters Mary Agnes, Agatha, Xavier,
Stanislaus, Gabriel and Raphael - and the two postulants - Mary Griffin and Mary Connolly of Dubuque,
were soon busy setting things in order in their new
home. Lumber cut from their own woodland and stone
quarried from their own hillside had been turned into
other needed buildings. A rock chapel was one of the
first structures completed. Then Father Donaghoe, constituting the area about their new home into St.
Joseph parish, saw to the building of a two-story
stone structure, with full basement, for his residence
and for parish needs. He also had a log church of
ample proportions constructed nearby, In line with
the parish house there rose an adobe sheep cote, the
heavy clay for the walls having been trampled hard by
oxen. In June, the twenty-two boarding students from
St. Mary academy in Dubuque, anxious to see what their

new home would be like, enjoyed a house party at the
nearby home of Judge Lovell which had been rented for
them and from whence they inspected the buildings and
roamed the prairie.

The relief of Father Donaghoe was great when late
June brought word from Peter Snyder, his agent in
Philadelphia, that the damage suit for the fire loss
of the academy had been won, and that a deposit of
$6437.00 had been made in the bank to his credit.
There would be lawyers' fees and other costs to be met
from the amount, but it was a generous allowance, for
Snyder assured him that if it had been necessary to
sell the building "$4000.00 would have been a great
price." The suit had involved a struggle, however,
and not all because of the public authorities: the
trustees of St. Michael's, who had held the title to
the property, regarded the damages as due the parish.
Bishop Kenrick came to the rescue and induced the
trustees to relinquish, in favor of the Sisters, any
claims they might have to the awarded damages. Building plans on the prairie could move ahead with confidence now, land purchases could be paid for, and needed live stock bought. More funds would come in time
from the sale of the lot on which the academy had
stood, though there would be a second struggle with
the trustees over this. Besides, Messrs. Snyder and
McGill, ardent friends of Father and the Sisters, and
their agents as well, were making what efforts they
could to settle Sister M. Lucy Baker's affairs and
those of Sister M. Ignatius Hamelin. The former's
interests in a glassworks were shared by a sister,
Mrs. Drury, and a nephew, Edward Austin. Another
year would be needed to settle that, but the youthful
widow-religious could hope for several hundred dollars
as a return from the property. It seemed like a fortune after the Sisters' first bleak years. Another
thousand from the Hamelin estate would make them rich
indeed.

* * * * *

With building under way on the Prairie, Father
Donaghoe received a letter from Father Mazzuchelli
which hinted at the enrolling of some or all of the
Sisters under the banner of St. Dominic. The date is
not clear, but it seems to have been in early 1846.

Mt. Sinsinawa, Wis.

Very Rev. Sir
    It is probable that before the end of
this year we shall have a college, because I

hope my friends in Italy will give me some
help. In that event I shall want some Sisters for the good order of all things. To
avoid every obstacle from the part of the
Bishop of the Diocese and from the part of
the Order to which I belong, it will be ad-
visable that they should be of the Order of
St. Dominick, if possible. Should it be in
your power to help me by advice or to bring
this work about, we shall forever be indebted
to you. I have no partial feeling for any one
order, they are all the work of the Saints,
all doing the same thing and all good when
faithful to their vocation. I can dispose of
200 acres of good land with timber for the
Sisterhood. The College alone will give them
a support. You know these things more than
I do. Say nothing on all this to any one.
    Next Saturday I go to Shullsburg not to
return until the 15th inst. Nothing called
me to Dubuque this winter and I am not able
to say when I shall go there.
Your Friend in Christ
Samuel Mazzuchelli.

Women desirous of becoming religious were already helping prepare the household at the nascent Dominican
College of St. Thomas at Benton, Wisconsin, and Father
Mazzuchelli was in communication also with the Dominican Fathers in Somerset, Ohio about securing Sisters
from there. A second letter to Father Donaghoe bearing what appears to be the date of August 13, 1846 is
a more explicit invitation to the Dubuque Sisters to
put themselves at his service.

> We shall be in need of some good persons to
> keep school for the girls of this parish,
> and to do all the sewing and mending of our
> house which will be considerable this winter.
> A suitable place below the road opposite the
> church will be shortly fitted up for that
> purpose. Now, my dear Sir, if it is in your
> power to send some of your Sisters for that
> object, please to take my demand in due con-
> sideration and give me an answer soon. We
> have hired a good man to cook for the col-
> lege. The women shall cook for themselves in
> their own house. . . . My respects to the
> Sisters.

Then within a month, the Dominican priest wrote again,

this time recommending to Father Donaghoe a possible candidate who would have seemed well suited to his own purposes:

> . . . A certain Mary Fitzpatrick who lives within two miles of this place has applied to me for admittance to your sisterhood; she is truly a pious one, lately from Ireland, about 23 years old and without learning. She is healthy and strong. At present she lives with her father and brother. Should you be willing to receive her, she will go over to you without delay. . .

However, Mary Fitzpatrick shortly became Sister M. Ignatia, OP, instead, while Margaret Conway, a second candidate, became the Dominican Sister M. Clare. These were joined by two former members of the Emmits-burg Sisters of Charity, Mary McNulty - who had spent a year with Mother Clarke's Sisters as Sister M. Camil-lus - and Mary Routtan(Routtanne). These young women were permitted to resume the religious names they had held formerly, - Sisters Seraphine and Ermeline. The four formed the first little community of Dominican Sisters under the direction of Father Mazzuchelli. Sister Seraphine was soon named prioress and Sister Clara sub-prioress.[4] Meanwhile Father Samuel was planning "a small wooden house . . . for the work-women who ask to become Sisters of the Order."[5] Of the young foundation Father wrote:

> In 1846, with the authority received from the Master General, A. Ancarini in 1844, I received various pious girls of this country into our Third Order, in the hope of one day establishing a house for the education of girls.

While the two former Sisters of Charity did not per-severe, by the time of their departure a small com-munity had been formed. These would be the nucleus of the present widespread body of religious teachers. Meanwhile our Sisters, with undivided allegiance, set about acclimating themselves and their boarding schools to the life on St. Joseph Prairie.

A letter from Father Donaghoe to Bishop Loras, dated April 16, 1847, indicates a desire on the part of the Bishop to have the Sisters open another school in Dubuque, requiring the recall of a Sister from the Potosi Mission. But disaffection seems to have

persisted in Dubuque and Father Donaghoe was in no
mood to gratify the wishes of the people there for another school. Furthermore, the withdrawal
of a Sister from Potosi would lead to the closing of
that mission. Father added to his protest, "If anything good is ever to result from our poor Community,
it will entirely depend on their humble, pious and
unassuming undertakings. You know much of what they
had to suffer. I still more, but silent anguish solely belongs to them." However, some event of an encouraging nature in relation to them seems to have
occurred, for Father continued: "They unanimously and
uncalled upon declare that they enjoy more freedom to
breathe these last few days than they have since coming to the Territory. This may be too much exagerated
because their wounds are scarcely closed. It will be
my endeavor to assuage this feeling and to animate
them for new combats over a world and venomous tongues.
. . ." But others were suffering too. In that year,
with racial feeling running high, the state legislature voted the exclusion of Negro children from the
public schools. However, Loras made provision for
them - the Negro population was very small - in a one-
room school in "McCabe's yard," on Emmet street, south
of St. Mary's, where they were taught by a member of
the parish. The Potosi mission did not long survive,
probably because it was in the newly established Milwaukee diocese and Bishop Loras was concentrating his
resources within his own jurisdiction.

But, to return to the Prairie. A brook running
through the grounds at the base of the hill on which
the motherhouse was erected - the first Mount Carmel -
was dammed to keep a constant supply of water for the
cattle. Barns, milkhouse, laundry, meat house - each
would be built in its turn; later would come the
strange pyramidal structure to serve as a schoolhouse
for the children of the neighborhood. The novices
would teach in its two classrooms, one above the other. Twenty-five feet by twenty-five at its base, the
building, narrowing gradually as it rose through three
stories, was capped by a bell tower. While its bell
called the children to classes and Father's rural congregation to Mass and Vespers, a second large bell,
mounted on a sturdy scaffold and situated centrally
among the several buildings, signalled for the Sisters
the time for meals and prayers.

Gradually the land was put under cultivation. Pat
Clarke's breaking plough, drawn by three pairs of ox-
en, turning the tough sod of the prairie. The first

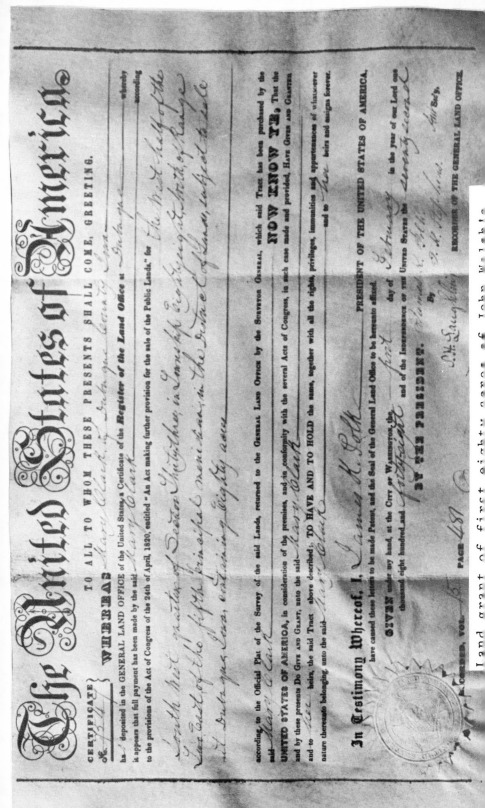

The United States of America

CERTIFICATE No. 124

TO ALL TO WHOM THESE PRESENTS SHALL COME, GREETING.

WHEREAS Mary Clark, by Subsequ County Iowa _____ hereby has deposited in the GENERAL LAND OFFICE of the United States, a Certificate of the *Register of the Land Office* at Subuque _____ according is appears that full payment has been made by the said Mary Clark _____ to the provisions of the Act of Congress of the 24th of April, 1820, entitled "An Act making further provision for the sale of the Public Lands," for the West half of the South West quarter of Section Thirteen in Township Eighty eight North of Range Two East of the fifth principal meridian in the State of Iowa subject to sale at Subuque Iowa, containing eighty acre

according to the Official Plat of the Survey of the said Lands, returned to the GENERAL LAND OFFICE by the SURVEYOR GENERAL, which said Tract has been purchased by the said Mary Clark **NOW KNOW YE,** That the UNITED STATES OF AMERICA, in consideration of the premises, and in conformity with the several Acts of Congress, in such case made and provided, HAVE GIVEN AND GRANTED, and by these presents DO GIVE AND GRANT, unto the said Mary Clark and to her heirs, the said Tract above described; TO HAVE AND TO HOLD the same, together with all the rights, privileges, immunities and appurtenances of whatsoever nature thereunto belonging, unto the said Mary Clark and to her heirs and assigns forever.

In Testimony Whereof, I, James K. Polk _____ PRESIDENT OF THE UNITED STATES OF AMERICA, have caused these letters to be made Patent, and the Seal of the General Land Office to be hereunto affixed.

GIVEN under my hand, at the CITY OF WASHINGTON, the first _____ day of February _____ in the year of our Lord one thousand eight hundred and fortyeight _____ and of the INDEPENDENCE OF THE UNITED STATES the seventysecond

BY THE PRESIDENT: James K Polk

By J. Knox Walker Sec'y.

J. N. Laughlin RECORDER OF THE GENERAL LAND OFFICE.

RECORDED, VOL. 6 PAGE 489

Land grant of first eighty acres of John Walsh's

corn planting was done by hand - five grains of corn to the hill - "one for the blackbird, one for the crow, one for the cutworm, and two to grow," as the saying went. By the second season the clumps of sod would have disintegrated, and an ordinary ploughing would blend it with the rich top soil. But hazards were many. Cinch bugs and grasshoppers, migrating ducks, prairie hens and immense flocks of blackbirds, seeking the ripe grain or the ripening fruit of the orchard; hail, drought, or a too early frost - all threatened; yet fine crops often survived them all. Prairie wolves and rustlers menaced the cattle; weasels, the ducks and chickens. Then there was always the threat of prairie fires, fed by the dry prairie grass of autumn and racing with the speed of the wind over the open plain. The pioneer farmer ran the gauntlet of them all. With livestock to be restrained there were fences to build, and these called for the felling of trees and the splitting of rails. Much of the lighter work would fall to the Sisters - cows to milk and butter to churn, pigs and chickens to feed, hay to stack for the winter, gardens to plant and tend, potatoes and turnips to dig in the fall and store in deep pits, carefully bedded in straw to save them from frost. Their assistance would be needed for thrashing, corn husking and fall butchering, sausage making, the rendering of lard, and the processing of meat for the kitchen. It was a new life for the city-bred women who had found their way to the west. A neighboring farmer, Cornelius Collins who later assisted Bishop Loras on his Table Mound farm, would tell that "One day I seen about a dozen of them Sisters coming in from the harvest fields after binding wheat,"[7] while Sister M. Michael Nihill observed: "As Rev. Father was totally ignorant either of farming or of the amount of work which ought to be required, and the older Sisters were for the most part brought up in the cities, it was consequently an unpleasant occupation for the young and the delicate. . . to inure themselves to the fatiguing tasks of farm life. Often too the men employed on the farm, seeing their docility and the inexperience of those who directed the work, allowed the Sisters to do more than their share, and that, too, of a kind not usually considered to be within the bounds of capability of a woman."[8]

Work connected with the household was also a test of fortitude in those rural beginnings. Turning the creaking windlass to draw up the water from the open well, and carrying the heavy bucketfuls for all personal and household needs; supplying wood for the

stoves in laundry and kitchen, and in the winter, for
the open fireplaces that sent much of their heat with
their smoke up the chimney - shovelling paths through
heavy snows - it was all work for the brave-hearted
and the strong. Farm help was not easy to come by,
and what men there were must be kept well-fed and
their rough clothing laundered. But most of all there
was a growing boarding school to feed and teach and
nurse and sew for. The closing of St. Philomena's in
Davenport in 1847 and Potosi in the next year brought
six more pairs of hands for the work on the Prairie,
though it was ever a matter of concern to Mother Clarke
that the pressure of such duties left the novices ill-
prepared for their later work in the classroom.

* * * * *

The fall of 1848 saw Father Cretin leaving for
Europe in the Bishop's stead, his purpose to solicit
funds and to gather recruits for the diocese - religious orders of men, German and Irish diocesan priests
or seminarians, and candidates for the Sisters of Charity. Bishop Loras' niece, Mlle. Appolline Garrant-
Loras, had been in correspondence with her uncle with
the thought of serving his mission as a religious.
Cretin visited the Loras family and discussed her plans
with the young woman. However, when her mother heard
of them, her refusal was emphatic, based on the same
considerations that discouraged many young women who
considered the possibilities: the order was quite unknown on the continent, and the hazards were many,
the greatest of them the ocean voyage. In a letter
from Montluel, France, dated November 14, 1846, Cretin
wrote Loras:

> I see great inconvenience in transporting
> young women from here. One will find some
> more easily in St. Louis or New Orleans who
> would have made good French studies and who
> would join the good Sisters at Dubuque, but
> I hesitate to propose to them to enter an
> order that they do not know.

And in a later letter: "I have found a hundred or so
in France, but the voyage!!!" However, of Jesuits,
Eudists, Marists, he could persuade none to come. The
Irish students at Paris were loathe to emigrate, and
the bishops seemed to have too strong a hold on those
in the home seminaries. As for Germans, he was able
to recruit J.J. Reffe and Alex Hattenberger, and with
these he brought the Frenchmen B.M. Poyet, J.B.
Villars, and Loras' nephew, Louis de Cailly. In a

private audience with the Holy Father, Pius IX, on
May 21, 1847, Cretin won a special blessing for his
and the Loras families, for Loras himself and all his
flock. He had declared in his letter of March 7, "I
shall ask abundant indulgences. . . for the Sisters."
In fulfillment of this promise and under the same date
there was

> granted mercifully in the Lord, through me,
> the undersigned Secretary of the Sacred Con-
> gregation of the Propagation of the Faith,
> to all the Religious women, called Sisters
> of Charity of the Blessed Virgin Mary,* who
> are dwelling in the Diocese of Dubuque, a
> Plenary Indulgence once a week on any day
> they may determine, provided they have been
> at confession and received Holy Communion
> and shall devoutly visit some church, oratory
> or chapel and there pour forth their prayers
> to God for the extension of His Holy Faith.
> The indulgence is applicable to the souls in
> Purgatory, also by way of suffrage.
> John, Archbishop of Thessalonica,
> Secretary.

Together with this there was on the same date the
grant of a perpetual indult to Father Donaghoe for a
privileged altar, the privilege to be available three
times weekly. The official documents for both remain
in the Congregation's archives.[9]

Cretin's letter to Loras, written from Rome on
April 25, 1847, contained a surprise note. He had
gone to Europe, hoping to gain candidates for Dubuque's
Sisters of Charity, but suddenly found himself with
the offer of a well-financed foundation of religious
of a highly esteemed order.

> . . . The same day that I received your last
> letter from America, I received one from the
> Visitation convent at Montluel, in which I
> was told: "We are considering founding a
> mission in America. We are easily able to
> devote to this foundation 6 good Sisters and
> 100,000 francs. Would Dubuque agree to this?
> A chaplain would accompany them." I answered
> that I would refer the matter to your Lordship.

---

* Note the use of "Mary" in the title here.

They await a response on this subject. See
what you think is best to do. The site that
you have at the side of the Protestant cemetery would be very convenient for a community.
The religious would spend the winter in Boston. They would learn a little English and
would join two American Sisters. A few
boarders would suffice for them to commence.

But there was question of the Sisters of Charity.
Would they be willing to share the field with newcomers?

The principal difficulty, I feel, comes from
the establishment already there. I have
doubted for a long time that the excellent
persons of St. Mary's are able to give a first-
rate education, and to surmount the prejudices
which their compatriots especially have
against them. Reflect, pray, and even speak
frankly with Mr. Donaghoe. The Sisters [of
Charity] will be able to make themselves very
useful as elementary teachers if they fortify
themselves in the attributes of their institution. They have made a mistake to wish to go
already too high. Within ten years this educational institution can become very useful
to religion. The upper Mississippi will be
populated, and the parents, especially from
the vicinity of St. Peter's, will find that
it is too expensive to send their children
as far as St. Louis. Besides, if one doesn't
pay attention to it, Wisconsin will have all
the religious institutions, and I think that
it is not to soon to busy oneself about it. .

Probably none knew better nor felt more keenly than
the Dubuque Sisters themselves their educational inadequacy, but the children were there to be taught
and only they were at hand to teach them. When Cretin wrote again on May 23, he had received no answer
to the above, nor to previous letters. He pursued
the subject only so far as to say:

Relative to the affair of some religious
of which I have spoken to you in my last
letter, I shall act with prudence. If
some desire to follow me, they will stop
for the winter in Boston, and if they cannot
go to Dubuque, they will easily find another
place.

No evidence remains of the Bishop's reaction to so favorable an offer, nor is there anything to indicate whether he discussed the matter with Father Donaghoe or the Sisters. It is certain only that the Visitation Sisters did not come into the Dubuque diocese until six years later, when the Reverend J.B. Villars of Keokuk accompanied a small community of them from France to establish an academy in connection with his parish.

Cretin's letter to his sister, dated January 6, 1848, sometime after his return, recalled his earlier remark about "the voyage!!!" He said in part:

> I wrote to you that we arrived at Dubuque without mishap, in spite of great dangers on land and water; a few days after our trip on Lake Michigan a steamer caught fire suddenly two miles from the coast; two hundred and sixty passengers, nearly all Hollanders, were burnt to death; only eighteen persons were saved. A number of accidents happened also on the Mississippi. A few days ago the Ohio river rose thirty feet above its normal level; Cincinnati suffered a great deal.

At his return he evidently found Bishop Loras still maintaining his distance from the Dubuque situation and Father Donaghoe occupied with problems on the Prairie, for he wrote:

> When I arrived here I discovered that I was alone to do the work; night and day I am busy visiting the sick far and near. Even at the present I have no assistant.

In spite of all the pressure of his duties in Dubuque, Cretin's thoughts and footsteps took him to the Winnebagoes at Turkey River.

> I went to see the Indians, but could remain with them only three days. The Protestants terrorize them, causing discouragement among them. I received a letter with the information that the Indians are dying in large numbers. Next spring they will be transferred to a new reservation one hundred miles from there.

Little did he think then that he would follow the Indians into the Minnesota Territory as their bishop.

It was good that with all his worries he could record
a pleasant experience:

> Shortly after Christmas I gave a brief mis-
> sion to about forty French or Canadian fami-
> lies about ten miles from here. I was de-
> lighted to hear the hymns sung in the same
> way as in France. Nearly all received the
> Sacraments. They have built a beautiful
> chapel.

He closed the letter with a personal note:

> My next visit to France may take place sooner
> than I expected. It is very difficult for
> me to travel on horseback. I am in good
> health, but I am really embarrassed at being
> so stout.[10]

* * * * *

The eccentric but not less heroic Reverend J.G.
Alleman, a former Dominican, served the Fort Madison
area of the Dubuque diocese in the forties, as missionary to Indians and whites alike. He is described
as

> a stalwart both in physical stature and
> spiritual strength. The chiefs and sachems
> of the Sacs and Foxes, among whom he labored
> as a missionary, took delight in measuring
> themselves alongside the towering, blond Al-
> satian while he might be vesting for Mass in
> their wigwams, marvelling that a paleface
> should so superbly overshadow them.[11]

His associates also included the followers of the
Prophet Joseph Smith in Nauvoo, Illinois, as well as
Smith himself, who had great respect for the "Big
Priest" and often placed his barge at Alleman's service when calls came for him from the Illinois side of
the river.[12] Alleman was interested in planting the
faith, but also orchards and vineyards. A letter to
Bishop Loras, January 26, 1847, indicated that he
would be in Dubuque soon with trees for the Bishop
and Father Donaghoe. Later he wrote again, expressing the wish that Father Donaghoe would come down to
see his supply of strawberry roots and fruit trees,
and telling that he had forwarded by boat a bag of
roots which he wished Father to dispose of among his
friends. A man of great strength and endurance, with
little concern for his own comfort, Alleman visited
his various missions, usually on foot, saw their needs

and wrote often to Loras for means to supply them, so
that his letters give an impression of a constant state
of indigence. It is interesting then to find the following document included in a communication to the
Bishop, dated August 8, 1850:

> I wish to make the following last will and
> testament if I should die before my debts
> are paid: Father Donaghoe and his community
> shall take everything belonging to me in this
> country, and what I have a right to; they
> shall pay my debts, & what is left, use it
> for the education of poor children.
> J.G. Alleman

His eccentricities grew, and on November 26, 1863, his
bishop, Henry Duggan of Chicago, having recalled him
to that diocese, found it necessary to commit him to
the St. Vincent sanitarium, St. Louis. He was then
but fifty-seven years old. Less than two years later,
on July 14, 1865, Alleman Died. His body lies in an
unmarked grave in Calvary cemetery in St. Louis,
though his memory deservedly lives on in the name of
a flourishing diocesan high school in Rock Island,
Illinois, where the Sisters of Charity. B.V.M., are
numbered among its staff.[13]

* * * * *

The winter of 1846 was severely cold on the bleak
prairie and the snow was deep. At night hungry wolves
came howling about the convent. One night when Mother
Clarke was ill, Sisters M. Magdalene and Veronica determined to be rid of "the dreadful dogs." Wrapping
themselves in shawls and taking long sticks from the
side of the fireplace, they went out into the darkness.
Striking right and left at the savage beasts, they
drove them down into the ravine, then returned, well
satisfied that Mother Clarke would have a good night's
sleep. When they told Jerry, the workman, the next
morning how they had chased the dogs away, he exclaimed,
"Dogs! My God, woman, they were wolves! I wonder they
didn't devour you!"[14] The Sisters were strangers, not
only to prairie wolves, but to snakes as well, for
while the woods and plains of Iowa held many species,
most of them harmless, they had known no snakes in
Ireland. Though the Sisters had many frightening experiences, none had serious consequences.

The Annals of Sister M. Pulcheria recount an interesting if apocryphal incident: As Father Donaghoe

was vicar to the Bishop, he was often in town. Expecting his return on one occasion, Sister M. Bernard
Murray, then the convent cook, regretted that she had
nothing tempting to offer for his dinner. She suggested to Mother Clarke that they go over to the grove
of a neighbor, Mr. Corbett, and look for fruit, although it seemed an unlikely quest in November. They
set off, nevertheless, praying as they went. In the
grove, they found a cluster of plum trees laden with
ripe fruit. After filling their aprons with plums
they turned homeward, intending to return the next
day with baskets to gather more. When they had gone
a short distance, Mother remarked that it would be
well to notice the place particularly so they could
find it easily when they returned. The Sisters re-
traced their steps and looked everywhere, but not a
plum tree was to be found. When they recounted their
experience to Father Donaghoe, he shared their wonder-
ment.[15]

Sister Mary Ursula Kenneally's father was most
kind to the Sisters, making them on one occasion the
gift of a fine cow and calf. City-bred Magdalene
Cole had the animals committed to her care, and in
order to keep the frisky young calf within bounds
while she milked the cow, she made the mistake of tying the other end of its rope about her waist. All
went well until the milk pail was half full, when the
inevitable happened. The frolicsome calf had dragged
Sister some distance before she could recover herself,
whereupon she lectured it well with a volley of mixed
German and English, to the amusement of all who witnessed her luckless adventure.[16]

As more of the local girls entered the Community,
bringing with them experience of farm life, the Sisters who had come from the East retired into the less
strenuous household duties, and the work of "minding
the boarders" and sewing for them. Human nature
being what it is, this distribution of labors did not
result in perfect harmony, though it doubtless contributed to the efficiency of both departments. Mother
Clarke was less than happy, however, in her realization that the pressure of hard labor was not only
taxing the energies of the Sisters but also robbing
them of time for necessary study and for the quiet
hours of prayer and spiritual exercises essential to
religious life. Matters had been better in that regard while they remained in Dubuque. There had been
time there for such reading as was available, they
had learned what they could of French, found courage

and strength from the instructions given by the Bishop
and Father Cretin, and enjoyed the English classes
with Denis Mahony, who was at that time engaged in
teaching in the boys' school. Later, when the Trappists came, their prior, Father Clement Smyth, a graduate of Trinity college in Dublin, would spend several two-weeks' sessions at the Prairie motherhouse,
teaching the Sisters, especially Sisters M. Joseph,
Veronica, Agnes and Agatha, and probably Michael,[17]
after which Denis Mahony "expressed much surprise at
their progress." It was this arrangement that called
forth the following elaborate greeting in a letter
written to Father Donaghoe on July 1, 1853, in which
Prior Smyth referred to his Sister-students: "Most
affectionate regards to all my good Sisters, Doctors
of Law and Letters, Professors of Astronomy, etc.,
Prof. of Belles-Lettres, harmonic combination, medical doctors, botanists and the entire faculty too
numerous to particularize, from your dear and devoted
F. Clement, Prior." But educational resources were
limited, with few books and periodicals available for
their study. Though Father Donaghoe's library, quite
extensive for the times, may have been open to them,
it was not of a kind to prepare teachers for the
class-rooms. It consisted mostly of volumes and sets
of volumes of moral, dogmatic and ascetical theology,
studies in liturgy, collections of sermons, even a
dozen or so huge tomes of the Early Fathers. Many of
the books were in French and Latin, and a few in Greek,
a fair proportion even then a hundred years or so old.
The more recent works to which the Sisters might have
looked for spiritual refreshment, were largely polem-
ical. The library as it stands today, of somewhat
over five hundred volumes, includes a few books of
devotion belonging to the Sisters, but little more
that suggests their interests or the educational resources open to them.[18]

* * * * *

It was not long after the Sisters had removed
their boarding school to the Prairie that a problem,
long brewing for the Bishop, came to a boiling point.
Mrs. Catherine O'Reilly, who had come west with the
second group of Sisters, and had taken up the duty of
housekeeper for Bishop Loras, had involved herself in
the difficulties of the parish, apparently aligning
herself with Father Healy in his insidious attack on
the authority of the Bishop. Talking more freely
than became her position, she nonetheless continued
to serve in the Bishop's household. In 1846 a spell

of illness of some weeks' duration interrupted her
services, during which time she lived with a friend,
Mary Mullony, the Bishop meeting her expenses there.
Having returned to her duties on March 1, 1847, she
wrote to Bishop Loras in response to a communication
from him, and demanded that her three BVM daughters
be returned to her. The letter, written in a strong
and practiced hand, reads:

> I received your letter of February 27th and
> if you hold yourself justified in breaking
> your promise, which as you mention, you made
> sincerely, you cannot blame me if I break
> the promise which I made at the same time,
> the intention of which was to be kept sacred
> as long as <u>you</u> would keep yours. On the re-
> ceipt of your letter I hold myself exonerated
> from all promises which I made concerning my
> Daughters and all I request is that you will
> have my three children [Sisters Mary Joseph,
> Veronica and Xavier] sent to me as soon as
> <u>possible</u>. By so doing you need not fear any
> imprudence on my part and much oblige your
> Humble Servt
> Catherine O'Riley

This was followed by a letter of Loras' addressed,
not to Mrs. O'Reilly, but to Miss Mary Mullony, dated
March 10, a rough draft of which is found among the
Loras collection of letters in the Dubuque Archdiocesan files: It reads:

> I request you to say to Mrs. O'Reilly
> 1st, that neither the Sisters nor the very
>   Revd. Mr. Donaghoe have had any partici-
>   pation whatever in the measure which I
>   have adopted last week to relieve the dio-
>   cese from paying her $8 per month during
>   her lifetime.
> 2nd, that if what I have heard of is true,
>   viz., that she is willing to employ an at-
>   torney to make noise and scandalize the
>   congregation about that business, I shall
>   not pay her the $8 which I have promised
>   on the 28th inst.
> 3rd, that if she does what is mentioned in
>   the above No.2, she will be excluded from
>   the church as a scandalous member, as well
>   as all those who shall help her in any way
>   in that work of wickedness, even Sister
>   Mary Joseph, whom I do not consider guiltless.

There seems to have been a temporary truce between
them, for Loras' account book shows regular payments
of a monthly wage to Mrs. O'Reilly until October,1847,
when Mother Clarke's accounts indicate that the Community assumed the responsibility for an eight-dollar
a month payment to her, continuing this for several
years. Meantime her daughters returned to her until
they could prove to her satisfaction that they were
not held in the Community against their will. The unfortunate woman seems finally to have been excommuni-
cated.[19] She lived until December 11, 1863, and
though in the end she refused reconciliation, this
could not be publicly revealed and she was buried from
St. Patrick church. Her body was interred in the Catholic cemetery on the bluff above the Cathedral, in
the same grave with the remains of her daughter, Sister M. Francis, who had died eighteen years before.
Eight days after the burial, Father Donaghoe wrote to
Sisters M. Joseph and Xavier, the former in Iowa City
and the latter in Davenport, giving them word of their
mother's death and burial, omitting, however, disquiet-
ing details. Sister M. Veronica had preceded her
mother in death by two years, while Sisters M. Joseph
and Xavier were to give long and able service despite
the pain-filled memories of those early years.[20]

* * * * *

Bishop Loras, visiting Europe in early 1849, returned with three French recruits, Andrew Trevis,
Philip Laurent and Frederic Jean; a German, Mathias
Michele, and an Irishman, Michael Lynch. In Waterford,
Ireland, he visited the Trappists of Mt. Melleray, offering them four hundred acres of excellent Iowa land
if a colony of them would leave their barren acres and
their famine-stricken homeland to bring the blessings
of their dedicated lives and their prayers to his
struggling diocese. He had learned from a visit by
the Trappist Brother Macarius in Dubuque in 1845 how
earnestly they had been seeking a site for a monastery
in the New World. It would be his delight to hear
that the Trappist Brother Ambrose was in Dubuque ahead
of him now, awaiting his return. And by the time the
Bishop reached Dubuque, Brother Ambrose would not be
alone, for Abbot Bruno Fitzpatrick, the Trappist Fathers
James O'Gorman and Clement Smyth, and the Brothers
Barnaby, Timothy and Joseph would have by then con-
verged on his see city to be warmly welcomed by Father
Cretin.[21] It would be a memorable meeting when Loras
returned to Dubuque, for his parlor was then the scene
of a gathering which involved a bishop, an abbot and

three future bishops: O'Gorman was to become the vicar apostolic of Nebraska, Smyth, successor to Loras in the see of Dubuque, and Cretin would shortly wear the mitre in St. Paul.[22] The monastery of New Melleray would soon be a reality.

* * * * *

The Catholic Directory of 1849[23] gave encouraging word of the Sisters' young Prairie establishment:

> St. Joseph's Female Academy is about eight miles from the city of Dubuque. The site is healthy, elevated and beautiful, and surrounded by a rich alluvial soil. The chapel and buildings are plain but neat. At a short distance stands St. Joseph's church. Its congregation is already numerous.
>
> The children of the country come early on Sunday for instructions; they are invited and cordially provided with a plentiful dinner by the very Rev. Superior.
>
> The purchase of one square mile has been made for the motherhouse of the community with funds furnished by the generous Philadelphians, as an indemnity to an unoffending society who had suffered in that city by the burning of May, 1844. ...
>
> The Very Rev. T.J. Donaghoe is the founder and director of this new order. The friends and well wishers who have heard little of this very humble community will no doubt be pleased to see the annexed privilege so graciously granted them by the venerable pontiff and head of the Church, Pope Pius IX - a plenary indulgence once a week, and to Father Donaghoe a privileged altar, March 21, 1847. . . . .

But the new home on the Prairie was soon to meet disaster. Sister M. Lucy Baker, who had died suddenly, was being waked by the Sisters in the little rock chapel the night of April 29, 1849. Sister M. Mathias, opening the chapel door to return to the motherhouse, was startled to find a man* step out of the darkness

---

*An unfortunate half-wit of the neighborhood named Kelly.

directly into the doorway. Frightened, she closed
the door in his face. The Sisters heard through the
open windows his threats as he departed. It was not
until the night of May 15 that he sought his revenge.
Mother Clarke was ill that night, and

> one of the Sisters rose to go to her, when
> she saw a bright light on the chapel side of
> the convent. She feared the sacristan had
> forgotten to extinguish the candles on the
> May altar; but what was her horror when,going
> to the window she beheld the chapel in flames.
> Nothing could be done except to call the
> Sisters and pupils and save whatever they
> could. In a few moments the chapel was in
> ruins and the convent was burning. The Sis-
> ters had not even time to dress. Some of
> them wrapped Mother Clarke in blankets and
> carried her from the burning building to a
> slight eminence at some distance where she
> was protected by trees. Others hurried out
> to the academy to save the boarders and their
> belongings. The young ladies' trunks, their
> wardrobe and some of the bedding was carried
> out of danger. . . . When morning dawned,
> there remained of their happy home only a
> heap of smoking ashes." [24]

Buildings, furniture, vestments and altar furnishings,
clothing, keepsakes, all were gone, even their precious piano. Only the Virgin's statue which they had
brought from Philadelphia, the account book which was
Mother's special care, and a heavy wooden chest in
which they had brought their belongings from Ireland
escaped the flames.

As soon as morning came, Mother Clarke dispatched
one of the workmen to town to tell the sad news to
Father Donaghoe. He came at once to the Prairie and
with him, Father Cretin, but not before the latter had
visited the bake shops of Dubuque, buying a generous
supply of bread to meet their immediate needs. Neighbors arrived with clothing for the Sisters, and, despite their losses, much merriment arose over the ruf-
fles and bustles and gaily colored garments they donned
with little regard for fit. These would serve well
enough until more suitable attire could be made.

Bishop Loras, just returned from Europe, was in
Burlington when Father Donaghoe wrote him on June 6,
telling of the disaster:

You must have heard of our fire long before
this reaches you. We telegraphed to Baltimore but you had left. Thanks be to Almighty
God, we all escaped unhurt. I had been in
town when it happened. The good Father Cretin and I went out immediately to console the
afflicted. The chapel and the front building
were entirely consumed. In a word they had
to commence housekeeping again without shoe
or stocking and barely escaped with their
lives. The boarders are now in the log
church which will be the academy, and the
Solitude is now the church and large enough.
My rooms and all that range escaped through
the united exertions of the Sisters. I lost
all the vestments, etc. The kindness of our
neighbors and people in general is above
praise. I am not in the least disheartened
and will go on with renewed energy and per-
severance. . . [24]

The "Solitude" was doubtless the parish house which
served also as Father's residence. Father Cretin's
letter of June 14 to the Bishop told of efforts to supply the needs of the Sisters:

. . . Mr. Donaghoe has estimated his total
loss at 1500 piastres. It is very possible
that the estimate is exact. I think that he
has already received more than $800. I have
written to Mr. Leopold in Galena and he has
offered $150 himself. 100 other piastres
have been received from Galena, also from the
other side of the river, and nearly 200 here.
People have sent diverse objects and money
from Davenport. Classes have not been interrupted. The boarders are lodged in the
large church. The apartment of Mr. Donaghoe
has not been damaged, and all will be re-established little by little. In the first
moment of the most pressing needs of the Sisters, such as articles of clothing, shoes,
articles of the table, I have advanced in
your name $50, well persuaded that your Lord-
ship would not disapprove of the measure. I
have given some ornaments, albs, missals, &c,
&c. . . . .

Aid came even from far away, for the Sisters of the
Visitation in Georgetown, Washington, D.C., remembered
their need with vestments and linens for the altar.

In his report to the Propagation of the Faith, for 1849, Loras said, "I have given 3000 frs. [approximately $750] to our good Sisters of Charity, who have just lost 8500 frs. during a fire that brought down their monastery into ashes."[25]

But Cretin's letter continued with other problems: "We have already four dead from the cholera, all strangers. I have ministered to them. Two others are still in danger." That summer was to see one of Dubuque's worst sieges of cholera, and both priests and Sisters were called on for heroic service. Despite the inconvenience to be expected, the academy boarders were safer from infection out of the city, and the parents were grateful when, after a brief vacation, their daughters expressed their willingness to return to the country in late June.

Meanwhile we learn from Father Donaghoe's letter of June 28, 1849 to Bishop Loras, then in Burlington or Keokuk, that he had been commissioned to buy land for the contemplated monastery.

> As soon as Brother Ambrose reached me with
> your important commission, I started for
> Dubuque, determined to fill up the measure
> of your liberality. I scarcely breathed to
> mortal until I had 4 land warrants secured
> although they had raised 50 dollars each
> within 5 days. The surveyor and Brother are
> now harnessing their buggy and I take these
> moments to write. We have a certified land
> plot which I obtained and I am now looking
> at the 16 forties within our grasp - alias
> 640 acres - alias one mile square, your 500
> & 120 bought of yr. [illegible] $250 of Br.
> Macarius' money - total 1260 acres secured.
> Glory be to God - - I am now satisfied there
> is little land in 12 miles of Dubuque that
> is not entered . . .

Then the letter turned to other matters:

> We, I mean our dear Sisters, are full of
> hope. The cholera looks us in the face at
> Dubuque. I suppose next week they will go
> to the Hospital now rented in case more of
> the inhabitants take the epidemic. A great
> many have already volunteered. It is only
> they that I will send. Indeed they are more
> ready for this than a school mission. Still

>
> we can't have the cholera just to please
> their heroic feelings. . . .

Surely the Sisters had need of hope with the evidence
of their disastrous fire still about them.

No details remain to us of the Sisters' ministra-
tions during the severe cholera epidemic of that summer, save only an excerpt from the letter of Abbot
Bruno Fitzpatrick, stricken with the disease while he
was in Dubuque. It was addressed from Ireland, November 27, 1849.

> Please tell Sister Catherine that, under God,
> she saved my life, and that my gratitude to
> her, and to the Nuns, and to the Commander
> of the Women will be as lasting as my life.
> Never can I forget the happy hours that I
> spent at St. Joseph's where all that I saw
> edified me. However, lest this remark should
> make the Humble Sisters proud, tell them for me,
> that they are not half as good as they ought
> to be, and that I say the same of all my
> flock, including in a special manner the
> Shepherd himself.

Of the Sisters' service in another cholera epidemic
in 1852 we have the following testimony, given by Sister M. Maurice Duffy in an interview with Father Kempker, Iowa church historian: [28]

> At the time, they were teaching school and
> the cholera was raging; they would go out to
> attend the sick who would send for them all
> the way out here at St. Joseph's, where there
> were only a few houses scattered here and
> there at that time. The Sisters would walk
> all that distance and teach school also.
> Sometimes they would not undress in order to
> be ready for any call, going out with the
> dawn of day and remaining all day visiting
> the patients without so much as a drink of
> water till they got home. Their rule re-
> quired them to be home before dark. Some-
> times they would find no one with the sick
> when they came, for others had fled in terror.

Classes opened again with the log church alter-
nating as dormitory and classroom until a new three-
story stone building could be erected by the summer
of 1850. The sheepfold was transformed into a chapel,

whitewashed within and without, and somewhat extended.
Wings would be added later, at the sides of the sanctuary, and in time a wooden floor would be laid. In
1854 a new stone residence for Father Donaghoe and a
sacristy would join the chapel and the parish house.
By November, 1852 a second stone structure, identical
with that built for the boarding school and wall to
wall with it, was ready to serve for motherhouse
and novitiate. In course of time, the space between the
peaked roofs of these two buildings was spanned and
the whole made into a single structure, parallel to
and some distance from the chapel, parish-house complex. But somewhat back from the line of these, and
at right angles with them, a long frame building was
erected. A two-story structure in front, the land
sloping away from the back brought the basement to
ground level. This building seems to have provided
classrooms for a time, with living quarters on the
top floor for the "working Sisters." Later, when the
boarding school was removed to the city, the classroom space served for infirmary. It was in this
frame building, at the end of the first floor corri-
dor, and facing the courtyard between the principal
buildings, that Mother Clarke lived out her days.

At the time of the fire, Catherine Butterworth
was an elementary school pupil at the academy. Her
Father, Alexander Butterworth, a widower and a business associate of Patrick Quigley, generously fur-*
nished most of the lumber for the reconstruction.

* * * * *

The Trappists did not delay long in taking possession of the lands ten miles southwest of Dubuque
and three miles from the Sisters' convent and academy
which Bishop Loras had offered them. On September 10

---

*Mr. Butterworth's death when Catherine was but
twelve years old left her an orphan, though well endowed, for he had willed her nearly forty-two acres
of what had become city land. At the age of fourteen,
she dismissed the three trustees whom her father had
appointed to care for her interests, and chose instead
Denis Mahony, whom Father Donaghoe referred to as his
"V.G." Whereupon Father Donaghoe purchased the property for the declared sum of $4,000. At the age of
15½ Catherine entered the novitiate, receiving the
name of Sister Mary Alexius.[26]The remains of Mr. and
Mrs. Butterworth now rest in the Mt. Carmel cemetery,
simple grey granite markers indicating the place of
their repose.

1849, sixteen monks left Mt. Melleray in Ireland,
bound for Iowa - a priest, Father Patrick, two choir
monks, and thirteen lay brothers, each selected for
his particular skill. Most of them were in their
twenties or thirties, young, strong and hearty. At
Liverpool they waited for a sailing vessel, the cost
of passage on it - two pounds and five shillings -
was only a fraction of the cost for steamship accommodations. This required, however, that they provide
their own food for the voyage. When they landed in
New Orleans seven weeks later, weakness from hunger
and the tainted remains of their food supply left them
easy victims to disease. The fact that the upstream
steamer on the Mississippi, the Constitution, was over-
sold necessitated their sleeping, exposed to the elements, on the open deck. Cholera was rampant at the
time, and one by one, six of the Brothers died on the
trip up the river. Together with other victims, they
were buried in shallow graves along the river banks.
When the boat reached St. Louis on November 15, the
captain decided to take it no farther lest it be
caught in the ice. Brother Bernard was able to com-
mandeer an old stern-wheeler, which, after eight days,
landed the ten remaining Trappists, in the dead of
night, at Dubuque, where for many days Brother Ambrose
had awaited their coming. No word had reached New
Melleray of the tragic journey. It was this weary
group whose arrival Brother Kieran, one of their number, described in his manuscript history of their
foundation. After spending the night in the hotel,
the entire party crowded into a hired conveyance for
their trip to the country, while their hired man loaded
their baggage into an open wagon drawn by a double
yoke of oxen, unfortunately leaving behind their bundles of bed clothing. Straw would serve for their
covering that night. Their first view of their prairie home was disconcerting: "The country at that
season had a desolate appearance. . . hilly, rugged .
. . a vast sheet of undulating prairie land, bare
surely because fire had gone over it lately." Winter had come too quickly for the arrivals to burrow
into the frozen earth to live, like their neighbors,
in dug-outs, so they suffered much from the cold.

"Our livestock," Brother Kieran wrote, with wry
humor, "was very limited - a pair of horses and an
old cow. . . made a present to the Brothers by the
Sisters of Saint Joseph convent residing three miles
east of here." Then followed a list of other bene-
factions:

It is difficult indeed to tell all the acts
of kindness them good Sisters with their
Father and founder, the Very Rev. Terrence
Joseph O'Donahue, done for our little community in its infancy, for instance, their
generous and liberal donations, the baking of
bread during the years 49 and 50. Yes and
part of the year 1851 when we made an oven of
our own. Truly as long as New Melleray exists,
the liberality of them kind hearted Sisters
should be remembered. During three years
they made and mended our stockings.

The account then told of a near catastrophe:

It can never be forgotten what they done at
the time when we had but four horses. Br.
Barnaby drove a pair of them to the convent
to bring home a batch of bread. This was in
July, 1854. They were not more than twenty
minuted in the flat-roofed shed when the
lightning struck it killing the horses in an
instant. Three of the Sisters had a narrow
escape. They were milking cows in the shed,
and had gone out of it only a few minutes
when it was knocked down by the lightning.
But then our loss was soon made all right by
Father O'Donahue sending over to our Superior
the price of a pair of horses. And what did
them good Sisters ask of us for their generous deeds? Simply our prayers, and that when
their aged Pastor was unable to celebrate
Mass for them a Priest from the monastery may
go over and officiate. ..

Brother Kieran's account failed to mention, however,
the many times the Trappist Brothers aided the Sisters
in the labors of the farm when it was impossible to
hire sufficient help.

The Trappists were not the only Brothers who came
to help the Sisters in their needs. Named by Father
Donaghoe "Protectors of the Children of Mary," there
were seven in all who shared a communal life of service at St. Joseph's on the Prairie though only five
of these persevered. Pronouncing private vows and
distinguished from the hired workmen by a religious
habit,* they were given guidance in the religious life
by Father Donaghoe, though they seem never to have

---

*An item dated October 1, 1850 in Mother Clarke's
account book reads: "11 yards flannel for Br. John's
habit."

attained canonical status. It is a matter of conjecture where the Brothers lived. The full basement of
the parish house presents a possibility, for it was
finished with a ceiling, a wooden floor and a fireplace. The first to come, Peter Kinsella, who would
take the name Brother Joseph, seems to have arrived
shortly after the fire. His sister Ellen, from Wexford, Ireland - Sister M. de Sales - had joined the
Sisters in 1847, and a niece from Waterford, Margaret
- Sister M. James - would follow in 1852. Maurice
Ahern - Brother John - was probably the next to come.
Tall, quiet and reserved, he was deeply devoted to
the Blessed Sacrament. Brother Michael Fitzgerald was
not long after. His sisters, Mary and Ellen, from
Garryowen - Sisters Mary of the Cross and Ambrose -
and his mother, Mrs. Dunn, Sister Mary Helen - whose
home had been Waterford, Ireland, would follow him to
the Prairie. Brother Bernard Carney had a daughter
in the boarding school whom he loved dearly. Brother
Anthony Grant, a small, wiry, quick-moving man, was a
favorite with the novices, enjoying their chatter as
he drove them to the fields to help with the haying
and other tasks. Then there were the two O'Sheas,
Brothers Francis and Joseph, who did not continue in
the life.

Margaret and Mary O'Shea, daughters of Brother
Francis, entered the academy in 1847 and continued
there until August, 1854. A third daughter, a young
child, Kate, enrolled in February, 1849. Of her,
Mother Clarke noted on the page of the O'Shea account
in the boarding school record, though without naming
the cause or the year: "Dear Kate departed this life
July 17th, between 12 and 1 o'clock midnight. May
all die as happy." The remains of the little girl
were laid to rest in the convent cemetery, and were
transferred many years later to the present Mt. Carmel, where her marker reads simply "Katie Shea."
Brother Francis was a gentle family man; Sundays would
find him taking long walks with his daughters, and it
was probably on these that he became aware that Sister M. Joseph, in charge of the younger boarders, was
inclined to be less motherly than he felt was for his
children's happiness. [29] Having entered the little
Community on August 9, 1851, he left it in August
to make a home for Mary and Margaret, and with him
Brother Joseph O'Shea went also.

A brief but intimate note remains to us of the
death of Brother Bernard:

Brother Bernard Carney went to the woods to
split logs for fence rails; he was not feeling well. When he came home his head ached
badly. S.M. Theresa, S.M. of the Cross and
 ?   went to do something for him. He had
his head on S.M. Theresa's breast & she was
rubbing the back of his neck when he asked
to lie down again. His head was barely on
the pillow when he died. They ran for Father
Donaghoe but Br. Bernard was dead when he
came. He dearly loved his little daughter
who was at school there & she died some time
before him. Her body was taken up so that
his coffin might be placed in the same grave.
She was dead about 6 yrs. at that time. Sister said these Brothers worked very hard.[31]

The only even semi-official record of the Brothers
in the Congregation's archives is that of their death
dates:

Brother Joseph Kinsella, October 10, 1855
Brother Bernard Carney, January 23, 1857
Brother Anthony Grant, August 13, 1873
Brother John Ahern, December 23, 1874
Brother Michael Fitzgerald, May 18, 1893.

Their remains lie in a row of graves near the hedge
and beside the Calvary group in the cemetery at Mt.
Carmel, and beside them lie those of John Mann, Mar-
garet's father, and Mrs. Jane Golden, a sister of
Father Donaghoe who spent her last years with the
Sisters at the Old home on the Prairie.

* * * * *

The rebuilding operation after the fire was still
in progress when, on October 14, 1850, Bishop Hughes,
about to sail for Europe to receive the pallium of an
archbishop, wrote Father Donaghoe, asking him to accompany him on this journey:

You have seen already what has occurred in
the Church in this country in consequence of
the last Council - New York an Archbishopric,
F.X.G. Bishop of Savannah, & c. My heart
has never experienced a moment's change
toward you, my best friend on this earth.

I am going to Europe,"near Rome" about the
middle of next month. I want you to come
with me as I go; to remain with me while I

stay; and come back with me when I return.

If you have not money for your voyage, I have.
You shall be my Chaplain. After Twenty-Seven
years of labors like yours, you are entitled
to a rest of a few months. I shall return
next May. If the Bp. of Dubuque will not
give you anything for such a respite - only
get his leave & blessing. Your purse & mine
will be one & common.

Come with me then. I count on you. Say nothing, however, about this. But be here about
12th or 15th of next month. Do not let anything, except obedience to absolute orders
prevent you.
              Your affectionate friend in Xt.
                  J. Hughes, Archbishop of N.Y.
A second letter followed quickly: "Come, I want you.
Do not tell me you have no money. I know you have
none, but my purse is yours. We have but one heart
and one soul. Now, do not answer this. The ship will
sail on November 11th. Be here to get on board. I
must go and I cannot go without you."

    What resources did Father Donaghoe have to draw on
for such a voyage? After the payment of all costs,
he had realized $4480,50 as damages on the Philadel-
phia academy. The sale of the academy lot had brought
$580.50, and Sister M. Lucy's interest in the glass-
works, $551.77, while Sister M. Ignatius Hamelin's
share in family property had amounted to about a thousand dollars. This much appears from correspondence
with the Philadelphia agents, none of it being entered
in the accounts kept by Mother Clarke. To the $800.00
which Father Cretin spoke of as contributions at the
time of the fire, Bishop Loras had added approximately
$750.00. Of these two sums, Father Donaghoe left
$164.95 with Mother Clarke for current needs. Brother
Joseph Kinsella, on entering the Brotherhood, had
turned over to Father Donaghoe $1194.50 in "silver,
sovereigns, gilders and gold,"[32] and in the course
of the year 1849, Mother Clarke had "handed over to
the treasury" $727.12 as surpluses from her accounts.
All this would have totalled approximately $10,000.00.
Large sums, of course, had gone for land, buildings,
livestock, etc. No record remains of any of this
since the accounts kept by Mother Clarke included only
receipts and expenditures which passed through her
hands. Father Donaghoe kept no accounts, or if he
did they have not survived.

At the end of October, 1850, Mother Clarke's account book shows she had no cash on hand. Her first entries under receipts for November were: "Left by Very Revd. Father when going to Europe, $475.40," followed by two smaller items, bringing her total receipts for November to $582.98.* At the end of November she had cash on hand amounting to $179.89, though $28.00 of this she had borrowed from the Bishop. Certainly her expenditures were light, considering that she was operating both a boarding school and a farm. A pencilled note at the end of her December's balanced account reads:

> Expended from Father's going to Europe, Nov. 3, 1850 . . . $495.20
> Cash in hands   227.78

What balance may have remained in Father Donaghoe's "treasury" we do not know, nor is there any indication to whom he committed its care during his absence. During his months away Mother Clarke was able to maintain a cash balance, however small, for meeting the needs of the boarding school and the wages of the farm help. It may or may not be of significance that in her November account which mentions Father's departure on November 3, she wrote the simple phrase: "A New Era."

* * * * *

Only shortly before Father Donaghoe's leave-taking, he had received word of Father Cretin's appointment as Bishop of St. Paul, an assignment to which the weary missionary did not feel equal.

---

*Sister M. Clare McGrath, to whom was committed the disposal of mementos left by Sister Rouina Lee, writes of a letter written by Mother Clarke on November 4, 1850, though she did not recall to whom it was addressed. Sister sent the letter to Mt. Carmel, and adds: "I have no copy nor did I memorize the contents, but the gist of the letter is as follows:
> Dear Sister,
> Father Donaghoe left Old St. Joseph's yesterday to accompany Archbishop Hughes on his European journey, Father took all our money except two dollars. We have two dollars and five pounds of Irish tea to face the rigors of the Iowa winter. . But God is good. . .we begin a novena of thanksgiving tomorrow.
The letter does not appear in the present file of Mother's correspondence.

Cretin had found the necessary travel as vicar general
a trial, and demands for life in the saddle would be
much greater in the untamed wilderness of Minnesota
territory. He had seen much hardship; his best years
were spent. Could he face the rigors of the north,
together with the problems of a fresh beginning under
the primitive conditions he would find there? He
would go to Rome and explain it all to the Holy Father.
So it was that Father Donaghoe and the bishop-elect
travelled in the same stage from Dubuque. Father
Donaghoe's letter of November 14, 1850, written from
New York to Bishop Loras spoke of their hurried departure and the upset of their stagecoach with its nine
occupants - a descent of ten feet into a little stream.
It was three hours before their trunks could be dragged
out of the water, but the passengers had escaped serious injury. They had arrived at the Bishop's residence the night following Hughes' famous lecture on
the "Decline of Protestantism" which, though widely
acclaimed among the clergy, was destined to arouse
much bitterness against him and the Church. Regarding the anticipated voyage, Father wrote: "We will
go on the 16th inst. by the Steamer Baltic for Liverpool, thence direct to Rome - there will be 8 of his
friends in one corner of the steamer. . . Indeed I
feel [it] that you are alone. But nothing can separate us, no, not principalities. Do pray that I may
yet do some good before I die in Iowa . . . "

A second letter from New York went to General
George W. Jones, Senator from Iowa, whose daughter
Marie was a pupil at the academy. In it he asked
that the Senator send him "the missions as reported
in '49," probably the congressional records as they
related to the Indian missions, "and whatever else
you please of public documents."

> I shall have them richly bound and presented
> to His Holiness, Pius IX, in your name, and
> I trust to obtain a distinction for you which
> will outweigh all the honors that this world
> could bestow on you. How happy shall I feel,
> and what an honor for me to introduce you to
> the Catholic Church, that is, to baptize you.
> It will be my duty to write to St. Joseph's
> Prairie, and perhaps I may have the pleasure
> of having a letter from my dear child, Marie.
> I left directions to teach her all her capac-
> ity will be able to receive - philosophy,
> chemistry and botany. Will it surprise you
> to find her learning those branches from the
> humble inmates of St. Joseph?. . .[33]

The happiness of baptizing General Jones was not to
be his, however, but was to go to Archbishop Hughes,
who administered the sacrament to the General when the
latter was about to sail for Bogota, Colombia, where
he would serve as United States ambassador.

A briefer letter to Mother Clarke, written on the
same day, committed to her the care of the Sisters in
his absence:

> . . . I have pledged you to continue faith-
> fully to discharge, as indeed you have, the
> duties to those dear children of mine, and
> at the same time to be devoted to J.M. & J.
> You know that I will revisit frequently that
> hallowed Prairie and see you engaged in the
> care of my Diamonds - & in the most holy spot
> I meet in all my travels - at the altar & in
> the Sacrifice - I shall present you to the
> Throne of God and my beloved Mother. Tell
> Sr. M. Marg. she shall be a sharer with you
> specially.

He spoke also of "the most splendid new steamer that
has been yet launched in N.Y: We expect to make the
run, as they call it, in 17 days to Liverpool."

In a long letter written from London to "Sister
Mary Joseph and all my little Pearls," Father told of
his visit with the Archbishop to the World Industrial
Exposition in the Crystal Palace in Hyde Park, London,
inaugurated by Queen Victoria, the first of the world
expositions. It was intended to commemorate the remarkable progress the nation had made as a result of
the industrial revolution. Father's letter spoke also
of visiting the new House of Lords and Westminster
Abbey, adding that

> I had the honor to dine with the now celebra-
> ted Cardinal A. Bishop of Westminster - Doc-
> tor Wiseman - I was at the Chapel of the
> Oratory where the new Puseyites live like
> the first Christians. . . . I am returned now
> from seeing the Ladies of the Good Shepherd
> and also those of the Sacred Heart.

Then his letter grew nostalgic:

> I now and again get in a word about the great
> Mississippi. . . I sang out, the far west!
> the Prairie! St. Joseph's for me. . . .I take

a peep in at you in traveling hours. There
I see the stove surrounded with my glories
and Diamonds, and then I hear outside the
well known cry of the Driver - the oxen -
Then the snow, and the chapel, and hope
brightens for I know that the whispers of my
dear children are blended with wishes for my
safety.

Returning to the London scene, he added:

I have almost closed and did not say a word
about the dear little Queen Victoria. Why, I
rode around her palace. I think I saw all
the windows, but I did not perceive one of
her seven darlings peep out. They missed it,
for I had a sweet smile prepared for them.
Well, then, I have one more in store for my
dear little children. . . .

In a private audience with the Holy Father, Pius IX,
each of the two clerics was presented with a heavily
embroidered ceremonial slipper. With his, Father
Donaghoe received a blessing for his Community and
words of encouragement for their efforts. Each also
received the body of a martyr, Father Donaghoe that
of St. Justinus, a soldier of the "Thundering Legion."
Though the relic was to remain for a number of years
without suitable housing, a matter of recurring concern to Father Donaghoe, it is encased today in a
bronze casket and reposes under the relic altar in
the rear of Mt. Carmel's motherhouse chapel.

On January 30, Father Cretin wrote Father Donaghoe
from Lyons that he was "affixed to the cross of St.
Paul," adding:

I have made my mind up to say a perpetual
farewell to my country and friends, and to
consent to so distant an exile in frozen
lands. The labors more than the honors attached to that dignity were making me shrink
from it. . . .

Then he turned to Father with a request:

Could you let me have at St. Paul, two or
three of your good Sisters? They could be
joined with two or three Sisters from France.
Which of them would you consent to give?

The answer to that question would await the return of
both men to the States. In a postscript to his letter,
Cretin wrote: "Please to present my best regards to
the Archbishop of New York. I hope he will bring
back from his next journey to Rome the Cardinal's hat."

Archbishop Hughes was the man of the hour in Rome
and other European cities, preaching to large crowds
and enjoying the entertainment of the great. Before
their return to the States, the prelate and his chaplain made a brief visit to Ireland, in late May, 1851.
Here Father Donaghoe enjoyed a few days with relatives
in Aughnacloy, the first such occasion since he had
gone to Paris to study in August, 1820. We find evidence of his visit there in brief notes dealing with
the family leases and other monetary affairs. These
indicate that he had continued to be financial adviser
to the family, and that fortunes had not greatly
changed during the years of his absence, for the two
leases secured by his father fifty years before were
still in the Donaghey name.

Although the travellers embarked for New York on
June 11, Father Donaghoe did not return to the Prairie
until a month later. Meantime there had been anxious
moments for Mother Clarke, for we find in the Loras
correspondence a letter addressed to her on January
27, 1851. The sending of it was held up by the receipt of one from her, written on the same date, and
evidently delivered by a special messenger. Bishop
Loras wrote as follows:

> Dearest Mother,
> It is with the greatest reluctance that
> for the first time I intend to interfere, as
> it were, with your peaceable community. But
> the glory of God requires it. I wish you
> would take home the good, pious, exemplary
> Sister Mary Catherine & place another one in-
> stead of her in Dubuque. I proposed that in
> vain several times to Father Donaghoe. Her
> disposition is so cold and stiff that parents
> are afraid of professing the admission of
> their children in the school, & many are de-
> prived thereby of the inestimable benefit of
> a religious education. Give me another Sis-
> ter, and in a month from now we shall have
> 130 scholars instead of 60 or 70, & I war-
> rant, an increase of tuition money. By so
> doing you will oblige, Dearest Mother,
> Your ever devoted in Christ
> Mathias Bp. of Dubuque

Mother's letter, which apparently reached the Bishop
before the despatch of his own, reads:

> Right Revd. Father in Christ
>   I am sorry for having to trouble you
> but I an truly distressed, and I have not
> known what to do. I have got the third ap-
> plication from Sister Mary Catherine begging
> of me to take them home. She is not able to
> suffer much more, and there are none of them
> happy. Therefore, I have concluded in God's
> name for them to come home, after receiving
> your blessing.
>
>   It is impossible for me to help them there.
> As they are, they are a source of annoyance
> to you, neither can they do good for their
> own souls or bodies, nor for the public, who
> is now censuring them, and calling upon them
> to know if the Sisters took to themselves
> what was said in Church yesterday. Sister
> declares that she has never yet refused a
> child who was not able to pay. Before you
> arranged with me to have the school divided,
> no person knew who paid or who did not, but
> this is only an intrusion on your precious
> time. I will have their removal arranged so
> as to give you no trouble. I beg your bles-
> sing and your prayers that I may be able to
> bear to the end my many and endless crosses.
>   I am with the greatest respect
>   your very Humble
>   Mary Clarke

The Loras file holds a third letter, apparently a
rough draft of one the Bishop sent to Mother Clarke.
Its ink has faded badly, but the following seems a
faithful deciphering:

> Dearest Mother,
>   I was about to write to you or to visit
> you in order to arrange those [illegible]
> school matters when I received your letter.
> The first idea of a select school was origin-
> ated by the Revd. Father Cretin, corroborated
> by the school commissioners and also by Sis-
> ter Mary Catherine, as far as I understood
> her. So I adopted it, believing firmly that
> it would procure them more means & increase
> the number of scholars, But I was disap-
> pointed. Many parents would neither pay nor

send their daughters to a poor school, as it
was unfortunately styled. At the same time
our Brothers came and opened their school
upon the principle of no select school, and
we succeeded in receiving 136 boys in 3
months. My ardent desire and prospect of
seeing also 136 girls under the patronage of
our good Sisters made me speak of it to Sister Mary Catherine. She took it very hardly,
and listened almost to nothing, saying that
they had better to go home.

The following Sunday I asked the people in
the church their opinion about it, showing
the advantages of no select school & requesting them to let me know what they thought of
it. Some came speaking in the affirmative,
some in the negative. I shall wait until the
letter to parents shall have been received
by them next week [illegible] to adopt a final determination on the subject.

It seems to me that all this considered cool-
ly does not authorize such a desperate resolution as to abandon the convent of Dubuque.
It seems to me D[earest] M[other], that in
fact the pious, zealous & truly exemplary
Sister M. Catherine is too weak to bear much
trouble & labour. Call her home and provide
another one in her dear place & tell me what
plans you wish that they should adopt & I
shall submit to them. Propose the condition
& I am sure that in 3 months all will be
right.

I shall visit you on Thursday or Friday next
in order to discuss the subject in full.
                    Yours respectfully and affectionately
                            in Christ,. . . .

Along with her accounts for the day, Mother Clarke
noted: "Sister M. Catherine left Dubuque Febr. 1st,
1851." Her duty as purchaser for the motherhouse on
the Prairie, as well as principal at St. Mary's, was
taken over by Sister M. Gertrude Regan, who had until
then been triply occupied at St. Joseph's - as superior of the motherhouse, assistant to Mother Clarke,
and directress of the boarding school.

                    * * * * *

During his years in Mobile, Bishop Loras had observed the work of the Brothers of the Sacred Heart
from LePuy, France, to whom he referred also as the
Brothers of Christian Doctrine. Now he sought their
assistance for the education of the boys of Dubuque.
When the first three Brothers arrived, probably late
in 1850, they found a two-story brick building near
the cathedral awaiting them. Other members came to
join them, but by 1852 they had become sufficiently
dissatisfied with the poverty and the hard winters of
Iowa, that, in order to keep them, the Bishop was
obliged to buy a farm and build on it a motherhouse.*
Even with this concession, the career of the Brothers
in Dubuque was short, for they returned to France in
1860. By that time the Sisters had been teaching in
a free school for boys near the cathedral for four
years. They now took over the building behind the
cathedral in which the Brothers had conducted an elementary and a high school, and made of it a parochial
school for both boys and girls, this notwithstanding
the rule that the Sisters "teach only young persons
of their own sex."

As for Mt. St. Bernard seminary, its fortunes under the direction of Father Andrew Trevis varied.
Its student body included, besides a number of young
men preparing for ordination, various boys from the
neighborhood who were being trained especially in
Latin in the hope that they might become candidates
for the priesthood. The exuberance of American youth
proved a disturbing experience to Father Trevis,
while his letters to the Bishop during the years 1851-
1855 suggest a restlessness on his part which did not
bode well for the permanence of the seminary. They
give confirmation to the sympathetic judgment made of
Trevis by his fellow-countryman, Father Pelamourgues
of Davenport, to Bishop Loras:

> Mr. Trevis is not satisfied to do good, he
> wants to do better, and he thinks always
> that to do better he must be at the place
> where he is not. Probably you know him as
> well or better than I do. He is a holy man,
> but to depend that he will keep long in one

---

*The mother house was adjacent to the seminary,
and Brothers and students shared the same chapel. The
Brothers called their new foundation Paradise Grove,
after their home in France.

place is out of the question.

To this he added succinctly: "He is French!"[34] In 1855 the seminary doors were closed and the students sent elsewhere for their clerical training, though there was to be use of its facilities in later years. Father Trevis, made pastor of the new St. Margaret parish in Davenport, took with him Henry Cosgrove, Peter Magne - the former Brother Jubin of the Sacred Heart order-and John Marsh, expecting to continue their training there.

* * * * *

But to return to an account of matters on the Prairie with Father Donaghoe still away. On March 4, 1851, Mother Clarke wrote Bishop Loras with regard to the prospect of opening a school in Keokuk:

> Sister Mary Margaret has delivered your mes-
> sage to me respecting the Sisters going to
> Keokuk. I am very much pleased at the pros-
> pects of a mission there. I hope God will
> be served by it.
>
> Agreeable to Father's directions, the Sisters
> have been studying all winter. I dispensed
> some of them from every other duty. As
> Father will be home in May*and the Sisters
> could not go much sooner, I wish very much
> that you would wait his arrival, as I prefer
> that he would make the selections for the
> purpose of making it a permanent mission. In
> the meantime, I will be making preparations
> and will hold the Sisters in readiness.

But these plans did not go through, perhaps because the pastor, the Reverend Jean Baptist Villars, had re-ceived the pledge of Sisters from the Visitation con-vent, Montluel, France. These Sisters arrived in 1852. They were joined by two English speaking Sisters from St. Louis from whom they quickly learned the language, and all were doing excellent work with the girls of the area. The future looked sufficiently bright for them and their pastor to cause them to engage in a construction project on a grand scale - a boarding school capable of accommodating one hundred fifty to two hundred girls. But costs being much beyond the resources of the people at that time, the ambitious

---

* He did not come until July 11.

enterprise came to an end in 1866, and the Sisters
withdrew from the city. Two years later, the work
of Catholic education was taken over by the Sisters of
Charity of St. Vincent de Paul, who soon won the
hearts of the people.

* * * * *

The late forties witnessed the efforts of the
German states to throw off the remaining vestiges of
feudalism and strive for constitutional government.
Many sought refuge from the consequent disorders in
the New World where the security of an established
republic and the hope of prosperity beckoned. Many
Catholics, chiefly from the southern states of the
loosely constituted empire, brought their hopes and
skills to Dubuque. Responding to their need for a
national church, Bishop Loras dedicated that of Holy
Trinity - now St. Mary's - for them in 1851.. The
ordination of William Emmonds in that church on December 19, 1852 gave them their first regular pastor.
From Elbenfeld, Germany, Emmonds had been adopted into the diocese in 1849, and had completed his studies
at Mt. St. Bernard. However, "he had no sooner become
pastor than he was involved in several battles with
the trustees. He discharged the lay teachers who for
two years had been conducting a school in the basement of the church, and engaged the Sisters of Charity."[35] The three assigned there were Sisters M.
Agnes Burke, Gertrude Regan and the German-speaking
Sister M. Gabriel Eisenger.* Our Sisters were to meet
Father Emmonds again several years later when he
served as pastor in Iowa City.

* * * * *

The little river town of Dubuque was growing rapidly as the stream of settlers moved steadily westward. Caravans of Conestogas and heavy wagons drawn
by plodding oxen, with flocks of sheep and herds of
cattle in tow, kept ferries busy day and night throughout the fifties. There was need for much restocking
with food and supplies before they moved on westward,
and from this the city profited. Industry was on the
rise - sawmills, factories for wagons and carriages,
farm machinery and household furnishings, were doing
a booming business. The sounds of the hammer and saw

---

*A note of Sister M. Lambertina's reads: "While
our Sisters taught at Holy Trinity, I'm not supposed
to say so, though I don't know why."

were heard on all sides as new homes went up. Along
the waterfront, warehouses and loading facilities were
in the process of construction, to care for the hides
and grain and droves of hogs waiting shipment to markets down the river. The grading of streets, the construction of culverts, and the erection of pretentious
public buildings, all spoke of progress. And in the
midst of it stood Dubuque's poor cathedral, much too
small to meet the needs of its people, its sides bol-
stered up with logs to prevent total collapse. As
early as 1849 Bishop Loras had laid the cornerstone
for a new and more adequate structure, on Main and
Eighth streets, but without sufficient funds or the
encouragement of his people, he had gone no further.
Now business houses were crowding in on that area, and
the place no longer seemed suitable. Some day the
people would be ready and time would be right. Meanwhile demands were being made for a parish in the
northern part of the city, and the Bishop granted permission for the building of St. Patrick's as an out
mission, hoping that income from it would aid in the
support of the cathedral. This, however, led to a
new battle, the Irish congregation demanding full parish status on condition of their giving any support
to the church at all. Weary of his struggle with a
fractious people, Loras brought them to heel by the
threat to withdraw all clergy from Dubuque and place
an interdict on the parish itself. Later in 1857,
with the appointment of the Prior of the Irish Trappists as coadjutor to Loras, sufficient harmony would
be restored to permit the building of a new cathedral,
beside the old one.

* * * * *

Cretin was consecrated in France by the Bishop of
Belley, January 25, 1851. On his return to America,
he brought with him five seminarians, and was soon
building quarters to serve as dwelling and church,
for the "cathedral" he found on his arrival was "worse
than a stable." Repeating his request made of Father
Donaghoe for Sisters in the interests especially of
his Indian subjects, Cretin entertained Bishop Loras
and Father Donaghoe on a tour of inspection. After
visiting the villages of the Indians and perceiving
how large a portion of their bronzed bodies was exposed to the elements, Father Donaghoe decided to
leave their souls to the French. The Sisters of St.
Joseph, a French foundation, recently established at
Carondelet near St. Louis, responded with alacrity to
Cretin's call for teachers. The little party of two

French and two American Sisters left St. Louis, October 28, 1851, running great risk by their late season departure that their boat might become ice-bound. Stopping at Galena, they stayed over night at the home of Mr. Nicholas Dowling, prosperous merchant and mayor of the city, where they were entertained by his Catholic wife who had known the Sisters in St. Louis. After attending Mass the next morning at the convent of the Sisters of Mercy, they continued on their way up the river. At Dubuque, knowing that the boat would tie up for an hour or so, they walked up the sandy bank to Third and Bluff streets for a visit with the Sisters of Charity, before heading north again.[36]

* * * * *

Not every dream had been fulfilled for the newly made Archbishop of New York on his visit to Rome. He had returned without the cardinal's hat, despite widespread rumors to the effect that it had been conferred, as we see from the following: [37]

AN AMERICAN CARDINAL

A letter from Rome in the Newark, N. J. Advertiser says it is true that Archbishop Hughes has been made a cardinal. The fact was made known to the congregation on the 10th of Oct., as the writer of the letter was assured, and the rumor is that the appointment was made against the protest of all the Catholic Bishops in the U.S.

The protest seems to have been in no way a personal one, but rather as resulting from a fear of the reactions of nativist groups in the country, already convinced that the power of Rome was growing so dangerously strong as to be threatening to their republican form of government. Father Donaghoe's letter to the Archbishop, written on the anniversary of their sailing from New York, having expressed "gratitude to you for selecting me among an hundred to accompany you to Rome," continued with a discussion of the disappointment. He said, "I was told confidentially by a priest who learned from his Bishop that before you returned from Rome, your Countrymen - the Bishops - had opposed your nomination to be Cardinal." He then named two ecclesiastics who were supposed to have been responsible, adding "Let them go to Guinea, I wad no gae a button for them a' - a man's a man'" Then he turned to his own affairs, listing for his friend his assets on the Prairie:

A word for myself. My presence at home was
useful, it gladdened all, it knocked the
rust off myself - my health has been good,
no laziness -

Then his assets:

28 good boarders, 1000 bushels of wheat,
corn & pigs ad nauseam, potatoes [?] - 25
milch cows and as many oxen & steers - horses,
wagons, ploughs, etc., 42 Sisters and 4 Protectors - a great addition, a new order -
they average the age of 40 - good intentions-
a devoted mason & carpenter & then two others
had pockets worth a searching - I believe
all are happy in the service of God, ergo I
ought to be happy . . .

His friendly closing read:

Give my love to your two good sisters, what
a treasure you have in them - they are a
balm to you, every heart wants such souls of
confidence - where else can they be found?

I am ever and devotedly
your little worth
T.J.Donaghoe, V.G.

One "Protector" whose "pocket was worth a searching"
would seem to have been Brother Joseph Kinsella whom
we recall as having turned over to Father Donaghoe
$1194.50 in cash, to which he had added the deeds to
much land in Iowa and Wisconsin. The other was no
doubt Maurice Ahern, Brother John, who had surrendered
his claim to one hundred twenty acres, the sale of
which brought the sum of six hundred dollars. This
item appears in Mother Clarke's accounts. The above
letter quoted in part contained another interesting
item:

We had the running visit of the Archbishop
of Cin. and Bp. of Pitts. It was thought by
a few of the wise that they came to examine
the competency of our ordinary - be that as
it may they intimated nothing of it to me,
yet to one or two, with due deference to
them, they were sufficiently plain. They
spent the night at St. Joseph's.

Perhaps it was a remark of Bishop Loras that led the

two ecclesiastics, Archbishop Purcell of Cincinnati
and Bishop O'Connor of Pittsburgh, to pay an unannounced visit to Mother Clarke during their brief stay
on the Prairie. On other occasions Loras had not hesitated to refer to Mother as a saint, and at this time,
he may have supported such a remark with telling details. Perhaps Father Donaghoe himself had made comments which aroused their pious curiosity. At any
rate, visit her they did, and without such previous
warning as to have allowed her the opportunity of arranging the place of the meeting. It was never her
custom to receive such visitors in her room, but rather in the parlor of the parish house; but they,
arming themselves with directions for finding her
abode, rapped, unannounced, at her door. Mother received them with composure and her usual gentle graciousness, visiting with them for as long as they
wished to stay.

The two bishops would scarcely have left without
having made a complete survey of her situation and an
appreciative study of herself. What did they observe
in the course of their visit? A quiet woman, somewhat
beyond her middle years, of medium height and slender
build, with thoughtful, deep-set eyes and ready smile,
her dress of faded black calico, a small grey shawl
pinned about her shoulders, and on her greying hair, a
white fluted cap or hood, tied beneath her chin with
a neat bow. The plain pine table at which she sat
held a candle in a simple brass holder, an open account book, a few memoranda on bits of paper, and her
writing materials. The plain board floor was bare,
in its center a small stove with a basket of chips
beside it; a simple calico-covered cot in the corner
where it would have been hidden if the door had remained open; along one wall a shelf of carefully
labelled boxes, containing community records, and on
the opposite wall, on a rude bracket, a shrine with a
crucifix and small statues of the Holy Family. It
wasn't much to look at, but it left them with ample
food for thought. When some of the Sisters expressed
regret that they had not had the opportunity of making
the room more attractive for such distinguished visitors, Mother's response was: "They were distinguished,
no doubt, but I think they will not esteem the community less for having seen my room. Maybe if the truth
were known, their own poor mothers had not a room
half so good."[36]

The Catholic Telegraph and Advocate of Cincinnati
for Saturday, November 8, 1851, contained a detailed

269

Buildings: 1, chapel; 2, chaplain's residence; 3 parish house.

and interesting account of the prelates' journeyings
through the middle west. The following is of special
interest:

> The Bishop [Loras] spends much of his time
> at the "Mound," about five miles from Dubuque,
> where his time is divided between the instruc-
> tion of four seminarians, the care of a pro-
> ductive farm, and the other duties of his of-
> fice. Though the hour was late, we determined
> to ride out to see him. We found him direct-
> ing the workmen in the field, and after pre-
> senting our respects we proceeded to Rev. Mr.
> Donaghoe's, four miles farther, where we passed
> the night. Everything connected with this
> institution gives bright hope of much useful-
> ness to Religion and Society. It possesses
> all the essentials for a seat of learning
> and Boarding School. The good founder has
> built a large house near the ruins of one
> destroyed by fire two years ago. His neigh-
> bors, of every denomination, encourage him
> in his praiseworthy enterprise.

Another glimpse into life on the Prairie was
given by the Miner's Express, Dubuque, in its issue
of October 22, 1851.

> On Sunday last, 19th inst., imposing ceremon-
> ies of being received into the order of the
> Sisters of Charity of the Blessed Virgin Mary
> took place at the Motherhouse of the Sisters
> nine miles from this place. Five young ladies
> presented themselves as candidates for admis-
> sion into that most useful order. They were
> solemnly received by the Right Reverend Bish-
> op Loras, and the sermon was preached by Rev.
> Father Clement, order of LaTrappe. The en-
> tire ceremonies were calculated to fill the
> mind with emotions far different from ordin-
> ary transactions of the world. . . .

The Sisters received at this ceremony were:

> Catherine Farrelly, of Cavan County, Ireland
>   -Sister M. Terentia
> Hanora Cahill, of Waterford, Ireland
>   -Sister M. John

```
     Mary Byrne, of Kilkenny, Ireland
                    -Sister M. Augustine
     Ann Harron, of Dubuque, Iowa
                    -Sister M. Clement
     Caroline Grenier, Montreal, Canada
                    -Sister M. Ignatius    38
```

The account of a second ceremony followed:

> On the same day and at the same place, the
> Right Rev. Bishop Loras administered the
> sacrament of confirmation to twenty-two per-
> sons, mostly children. The chapel of the
> convent was filled to overflowing, and we
> noticed an unusually large number of our
> Protestant friends there.

Of those confirmed some were boarding students, and
others were members of St.Joseph parish on the Prairie, who were served by the convent chapel. Their
own frame church would be built by Father Monaghan in
1869, shortly after Father Donaghoe's death.

* * * * *

In early 1852 the Community numbered forty-one
living members - professed, novices and postulants.
All were then situated either at St. Mary academy and
Holy Trinity in Dubuque or at St. Joseph's on the
Prairie. Of the forty-one, thirty were Irish born,
and judging from their names, eight more were of Irish
extraction. Thoughts must then have turned often to
the unspeakable sufferings that had been the lot of
those they had left behind in their famine-desolated
homeland, and of those who, thinking to escape the
pestilence which was famine's close companion, had
turned their eyes to America. Of these, shipwreck
and typhus had carried off unnumbered thousands. A
numbed bereavement was the response of those who had
survived. For Mother Clarke, whose parents had been
mercifully spared those latest years of suffering, it
had been a time of deep anxiety for the fate of her
sisters, Catherine and Martha, and their brother Edward's family. Death had claimed Edward, leaving his
wife with two small children, Mary Jane and a boy
whose name is not recorded. While Mrs. Clarke was
able to provide for her small son, the aunts Catherine and Martha undertook the care of Mary Jane. When
the aunts decided to come to America in early 1852 to
share a vowed life with their sister, they brought
their six-year-old niece with them. There was loneliness

for the little girl who would recall near the end of
a long life her happy hours of childhood play with her
little brother, by then in far-off Australia.[39]

Was it deep concern for them that caused Mother
Clarke to write on February 26, 1851: "A day of anxiety for me. No letter - resolved with the help of
God to be more resigned and bear with patience all
things as if I did not feel." A letter which came to
her on March 7, 1852 from Ireland must have given
great relief to her spirits, and renewed hope for the
long-awaited reunion with those she loved so dearly.
May 25 found them with her at St. Joseph's. Martha's
friend, the Reverend C.M. Flanagan, pastor of St.
Nicholas of Myra church, Francis street, Dublin, had
provided her with a letter of introduction to Father
Donaghoe. It read:

> Rev. dear Sir
> I congratulate you on the great acquisi-
> tion to your holy community on the accession
> of the Bearer, my old friend Miss Clarke. If
> she lives to do as much good in the new world
> as she has done in her native city, it will
> be well for those who will share in the be-
> nefit of her zeal and charity. If I had any-
> thing like a selfish feeling, I should envy
> you her possession. She has been for many
> years a most useful agent of mine, in all
> manner of charitable and religious projects.
> She possesses a rare degree of zeal and per-
> severance, and has just the dispositions and
> capabilities to fit her for a Sister of Char-
> ity. I regret that my present state of com-
> menced convalescence from a serious illness
> prevents me from enlarging as I could on the
> peculiar excellence of her character. I
> part with her with regret, wishing from my
> heart all the blessings for time and eter-
> nity that God can bestow on her.

Thirty-eight years of age when she entered, Martha
was professed on January 1, 1853, as Sister M. Josephine. Her years of religious profession were brief,
for death from tuberculosis claimed her on April 19,
1855. Her fine, quaint script, found briefly in
Mother Clarke's house account book, and in the accounts of the boarders, is unmistakable. Its presence indicated that Martha had made a brave attempt
to be of assistance to her sister. Below the half-
page of boarders' accounts, for the year 1855, in

Martha's writing there appears in Mother Clarke's hand: "N.B. In your charity pray for the soul of the writer of the above." In her house account book Mother noted: "Sister M. Josephine, 8½ o'clock this morning, feast Patronage of St. Joseph. May <u>all</u> rest in peace." A further remembrance of the gentle and retiring Martha remains in one hundred and fifty pages of carefully copied studies from St. Jerome, and St. Francis Xavier, together with "The Treasure of the Soul," and "The Ladder of Perfection," for which she named no authors, all contained in a bound notebook, and probably used for meditation.[40]

But the coming of Catherine presented quite different problems for Mother Clarke, who had often to remind her that her over-solicitious attentions were spoiling their young niece. And the irrepressible Catherine, professed with Martha and given the name Sister M. Cornelius, was in no way overawed by the superior position of her sister, whom she would admonish in her turn, even in chapter sessions. "Now, Mary Frances, you know our mother would never want you to say such things to the Sisters!" was enough to dull the edge of any correction. And when the same untamed spirit moved Catherine to laughter in the midst of a solemn chapter session, Mother Clarke restored order with the quiet command: "Sister Mary Cornelius, you may leave the room!"[41]

* * * * *

In the matter of a distinctive religious dress, Father Mazzuchelli had made a shrewd observation:

> In the Republic of the United States, the government officials, the military excepted, have no external distinction in the form or color of dress, and it does not at all accord with the taste of the citizens to see an extreme singularity in the clergy, who certainly ought to be distinguished by plainness, uniformity and simplicity of attire, but not to be rendered extravagant by reproducing the costumes of centuries ago. The venerable antiquity of a religious habit and the use of it made by the saints of the orders carries no conviction to persons in the world, for they would argue in the case under question, the garb worn by the Apostles and

our Savior Himself ought to have the preference.[42]

As Franciscan tertiaries, the members of the little Dublin community were committed to simplicity of
dress. Though they had come to be known as the "Nuns
of North Ann Street," they wore at that time no distinctive attire. However, they had noted much that
was redolent of the cloistered foundations of an earlier age in the religious habits adopted by the religious institutes whose founding they had witnessed -
flowing veils, choir cloaks and sweeping trains, for
convent wear. The elaborately starched headdress and
the voluminous folds of their dark habits for street
wear seemed ill designed for their visits to the poor
and the sick, even the plague-stricken, along the
foul, refuse-lined lanes of the city. Among a Catholic people their charitable labors brought deep respect for the garb that marked them as religious. But
when their members, like religious from the continent,
came in a missionary spirit to the Protestant domin-
ated States, they travelled in secular attire, reserv-
ing their habits for convent wear. Mother Clarke's
Sisters, finding themselves in the unfriendly atmosphere of Philadelphia, where they cannot be said to
have had a true convent, had no occasion for the a-
doption of a distinctive religious habit, nor is it
at all certain that Mother Clarke envisioned one for
her Sisters. A plain, dark dress, made with a yoke
and gathered at the belt and cuff, a shoulder cape
with a soft, attractive collar, and a "bobinet" or
lace cap, with a "wide frill prettily fluted," was a
simple and attractive attire not greatly different
from that worn by conservative women of the day. The
early dress of the novices was brown, though this
difference was no longer observed after the fire in
1849. For street wear a quilted bonnet and shawl
sufficed, with gloves or mitts as the weather dic-
tated. The reception ceremony at the time, instead
of the usual veiling, involved the conferring of the
"cap." It was this to which Father Donaghoe referred
when he spoke of giving the cap to the two "archangels,"
Sisters M. Gabriel Eisinger and Raphael Barry, in
early 1846. The following incident, however, brought
about a change.

Father Donaghoe was in his room at the Bishop's
residence one evening in late 1852, when the Bishop,
returning at ten o'clock from a sick call, rapped at
his door, and declared with some annoyance that he
would not permit the Sisters to be alone on the street

at that hour of the night. Father Donaghoe shared
the Bishop's concern, and early the next morning
strode across the yard to St. Mary academy to make inquiries and deliver the proper admonitions. Mother
Clarke was visiting there at the time, and she and
Margaret Mann were at first quite concerned, though
they were equally certain that no Sister had been out
of the house. Then Sister M. Margaret's face bright-
ened. "Father, that must have been Mrs. Corkery; she
likes the Sisters so much she tries to dress like
them." "Well, my children," was his response,"You
must have your bonnets made in such a way and with
such material that no one will wish to copy them."[43]
The commission for designing the new headdress was
given to Sister M. Catherine Byrne whose success was
complete, for the Bishop never complained again that
their garb was too attractive. A close fitting cap
with tightly crimped border, and a stiffly starched
white piece or "hood" on which a veil was worn, replaced the lace cap. For street wear, a stiff bonnet
of black cambric stretched over a pressboard and
wired frame took the place of the hood. On the bonnet the Sisters wore a long black veil, secured about
it with a narrow elastic, the veil to be dropped over
the face when the Sisters were on the street or were
returning from Holy Communion. A black shawl, and
later a full length black mantle of serge completed
the street attire. The habit itself was full about
the figure, though pleated at the waist. A cape with
a high white collar, a serge apron reaching to the
hem of the habit, wide loose sleeves extending beyond
the fingertips and worn over small, close-fitting
sleeves.-[*] A large rosary of pond lily seeds which,
Sister M. Margaret Mann noted: "I must remind the
Sisters to wear on the left side, " supported a crucifix of brass on black wood.[**] It was probably at
the time that the habit was adopted in 1853 that postulants began to wear the large white sunbonnets seen
in old photographs - the prescribed attire, not as
protection against the sun, but for chapel and parlor
wear.

---

[*]
Such was the habit as it came to be worn, with
minor adaptations, until a modified headdress was
adopted in 1962.

[**]
The black cambric bonnet would be permanently
laid aside at the time of the Eucharistic Congress
in Chicago in 1926, as a complicating factor when
travelling.

Regarding the sudden change of attire Sister M.
Lambertina's Journal recorded that "the neighbors
used to attend Mass on sunday in the convent chapel,
and when the new habit and black veils were worn for
the first time the whole congregation rose in a body
to look at the Sisters. One small boy climbed over
the back of the pew and got upon the shoulders of his
father in order to get a better view."[44] It is of
interest that for a brief time after the adoption of
the habit reception into the novitiate took the form
of a bridal ceremony. Two slight evidences of this
remain: a letter from Mrs. Libbie C. Espy Nunn of
Fort Madison, addressed to Sister M. Baptist Seeley,
on recalling memories of the school year of 1853-54,
inquired "Wasn't I your 'Bride's Maid' when you took
the veil?" The second was a clothing list in Mother
Clarke's hand, sent to a prospective postulant, which
after many years found its way into the Congregation's
archives. It is evident that Mother Clarke was scarcely au courant with the language of fashion when she
ended the list with the following: "For your reception dress you may either bring muslin, tissue, crepe,
or anything that would suit a fancy dress, a pr. of
fancy slippers, white gloves, white wreath of flowers,
4 yds. of white satin ribbon," adding: "As you may
not be received for six months you will require your
worldly clothing." Mother Clarke continued to wear
the style of dress she had worn in Dublin and Philadelphia.

When a more simplified reception ceremonial was
adopted, the postulant, holding a lighted candle,
knelt at the altar railing for the Bishop's brief
interrogation. In response to the question: "What do
you demand of the Church?" each answered: "The mercy
of God and the holy habit of the Blessed Virgin."
Then to his inquiry: "Do you of your own free will
present yourself?" the response of each was, "Yes,
my Lord." Each in turn received the bishop's blessing
and a crucifix, and on the head of each was placed
the white veil and a crown of waxen orange blossoms.
Often at the same ceremony a profession of vows and
the conferring of the black veil followed for those
who had completed their novitiate.[45]

* * * * *

From time to time Father Donaghoe shared with
the Sisters their evening recreation. On one of
these occasions he spoke of the consolation which
had come to Father Hughes and himself when pressures
were greatest during the Hughes-Breckenridge

controversy in Philadelphia. He referred to the occasion as "the night on which the Blessed Virgin made us brothers," appearing first in the room of one and then in that of the other. To this occasion he attributed that mutual regard which he held to be such that "nothing on earth can ever seperate us." 46

After the return of the two friends from Rome, Father entertained the Sisters one evening by donning his Roman cape and broad clerical hat, and strutting about the room, he mimicked encounters he had experienced in various of the European cities they had visited, interspersing his performance with ejaculations in the appropriate languages. As many of the Sisters had never enjoyed the privilege of a trip even so far as Dubuque since their entrance at the Prairie convent many years before, Father took delight in telling them of the mechanical wonders he had seen at the London exposition, and especially of the marvels of steam locomotion which he had experienced in his travels.[47]

Yet withal, Father Donaghoe had established a reputation for himself among the Trappist monks as "that terrible disciplinarian."* While few examples survive, these few are significant. One account opens with the remark: "Father Donaghoe frequently inflicted punishments in unheard-of ways." The accidental upsetting of a milk-pail in the cow barn where the novices were engaged in the evening milking had called forth an amused remark from one of them, to which others responded with a hearty laugh. It was the evening before a Communion day and when one of the more proper novices reported the infraction of the rule of silence, the novice who brought the report was deprived of Holy Communion, quite as much in reparation for the breach of the rule as for her having taken the pains to report it.[48]

However, on another occasion it was not the one who did the reporting that bore the penalty. When a novice on a very small mission was directed by the Sister housekeeper to carry a kettle of hot soup to a poor family a short distance down the street, she promptly did so without any thought of seeking out the third Sister on the mission to go the short distance with her. Her breach of the rule of companionship was promptly reported to Father Donaghoe who sent for the novice and directed her to bring her trunk home with her to the motherhouse. Here she was

---

* Letter from Brother Francis Bransfield, O.C.S.O. to Sister M. Lambertina, Dec. 28, 1911

required to lay aside her headdress, replacing it with
the cambric street bonnet, which was to be worn at all
community exercises for a month, as a means of im-
pressing upon her the rule of companionship.[49] Other
stories come down to us of Sisters called home from
the missions for one transgression or another, and
required to lay aside their habits for more or less
extended periods, wearing instead whatever apparel
might be found available.

In Father's explanation of the rules and vows,
"the slightest infringement of either he never permitted to pass unnoticed." Novices were punished for
wasting a few peas that fell among the hulls during
the shelling process, and for throwing out one or two
small potatoes with the water used for washing the
meal's supply. "A professed member was more severely
treated for a violation of poverty by waste. Every
day for a month, she and the entire Community were
obliged to go in procession to the chapel, and there
before the Most Blessed Sacrament, sing the 'Miserere'
and the antiphon 'Parce Nobis.'" (Emphasis ours.)[50]

Sister M. Magdalen Cole was required to put on a
novice veil and kneel in the Sisters' dining room
during meals for three weeks for having said she
would not go into the German school and speak German
to the children.[51] Sister M. Cassiana Griffin was
given the same penance for failing to speak at recreation, though she was at the time breaking down from
hard work. Sister was teaching at the academy and
was required to go to the motherhouse to fulfil her
penance.[52]

By way of ordinary mortification it was Father's
original intention that the Sisters should sleep on
pallets on the floor. However, when heavy colds resulted, he dispensed with the regulation.[53] In the
matter of the Lenten fast Father was probably not
more severe that Bishop Loras, who regarded it, as of
"absolute necessity."* The Bishop, having noted the

---

* Such was the Bishop's stand on the lenten fast
that it brought him into conflict with the prior of the
Trappists at New Melleray, Clement Smyth. Even the
strictness of their dietary rules and the poverty in which
they were living were not sufficient to save them from
rebuke when their hours for meals were at some variance
with the diocesan regulations for the fast.

delicate health of a young Sister as the Lenten season
was about to begin, instructed her to "put lots of
sugar" in her breakfast of a cup of coffee. He would
not permit the use of cream at all.[54] Father Donaghoe
would not allow more than a cup of coffee and a tiny
piece of bread to any of the Sisters, even those who
spent their day in manual labor. Mother Clarke, whose
frail health made her more considerate, remonstrated
with Father, telling him that the Sisters could not
stand to keep the full fast of Lent when they were obliged to work so hard. His reply was, "My Child, when
they feel too weak to stand, they may lie down, but
it is better for them to try to keep the fast." Except
in extreme cases of illness he never dispensed his
Sisters from the fasts and abstinences of the Church. [55]

After having recounted a number of the above instances, Sister m. Pulcheria concluded with the remark:
"We have given only a faint idea of the lives of penance Father Donaghoe wished his religious to live,"
adding, though providing no evidence to support her
assertion: "But his own mode of life was much more
severe."

* * * * *

In response to a question as to the probable degree of Jansenistic influence in the French seminaries
at the time Father Donaghoe made his studies, the
Reverend I. Noye of the Seminary of St. Sulpice made
the following interesting comment:

> . . . You asked me also if the rigoristic
> attitude which Father MacDonoghy took in the
> direction of the religious marked a jansen-
> istic formation. It is necessary to take
> account of the rigorism which was general in
> ecclesiastical and religious formation after
> the 1700's. The Jesuits, far removed from
> jansenism, also had severely ascetical traits.
> Austerity, which is often an influence of the
> augustinian and cistercian tradition, did not
> always signify a jansenistic theology. Ri-
> gorism in morality dominated until around in
> 1840, and it is not without difficulty that
> the positions of St. Alphonse Liguori were
> imposed little by little. (There has recent-
> ly been done a thesis by Father Guerber, S.J.,
> on the diffusion of Liguorian ideas in
> France in the 1900's). [57]

* * * * *

Life on the Prairie was harsh at best, and the narrow asceticism imposed upon the Sisters did little to soften it. Only their total dedication and self-sacrifice could do that. While some grew sharp and difficult under its strictures, many were open to the special graces of prayer and gentleness which rewarded their fidelity. Their Mother, Mary Frances Clarke shared their hardships and knew their needs, and even though she could do little to ward off the hurts that came, there was healing in the knowledge of her love and understanding.

From Mother Clarke's boarding school account book

CHAPTER V

FOOTNOTES

1. Doran Journal, p. 66.

2. Ibid. p. 67.

3. Among Father Donaghoe's notes we find a skeletal
   review of his plan for the rule. It begins with:
   "The Sisters of Charity of the Blessed Virgin:
   The end & virtues - to honor the holy Family,
   Jesus, Mary & Joseph in their hidden and labor-
   ious life by consecrating the labor of their
   hands for their proper support."
   Chapter I - "Labor - this will regard labor -
   manual & mental."
   On Poverty - "1. Plain cheap sound food. 2.fasts
   of the Church."
   On Chastity - "Industry"
   Under "Union and Charity," and "Other means of
   Union," the word "labor" is listed four times.
   An unidentified chapter: " when going to labor
   or instruct their pupils."

4. Sister Mary Paschala O'Connor, OP, Five Decades,
   History of the Congregation of the Most Holy Ro-
   sary, Sinsinawa, Wisconsin, 1849-1899,(Sinsinawa:
   Sinsinawa Press, 1954) p. 33.

5. Ibid., p. 24.

6. Ibid., p. 26.

7. Kempker Notes, Griffith Files.

8. Taken from remnants of notes left by Sister M.
   Michael Nihill.

9. On page 57 of The Early Days we read a note of
   Father Donaghoe's, dated November 2, 1847:
   "Through my application, His Holiness, Pius IX
   has granted a weekly plenary indulgence to all
   the members of our Community. I enclose a copy
   of the rescript for the same. Now let us all
   return thanks, because this favor of His Holiness is given to us in perpetuity. I also obtained an indult Mass three times a week, having
   a plenary indulgence as a personal favor. God
   and His Blessed Mother be blessed forever! Read

this for my beloved who are my joy and my crown, or in jest, my Pearls and Diamonds. God bless my dear Children." (Emphasis ours).

10. Hoffmann, Church Founders, p. 233.

11. Archbishop Dwyer, "Father John Alleman and the Mormons," Catholic Sentinel. May 3, 1974.

12. July of 1846 was to see 15,000 of his Mormon friends set out on their long trek westward, their 3,000 wagons, 30,000 head of cattle, horses and mules and vast numbers of sheep, making a mighty caravan, a journey marked by tragedy and heroism.

13. Cf. Sister M. Jean Ellen Shields, BVM, Biography of Reverend John George Alleman, Pioneer Missionary of Ohio, Iowa, and Illinois, Master's Disertation, St. Louis University, 1954)pp. 173-174.

14. McGuire, Annals, p. 142.

15. Cf. Ibid. p. 141.

16. Cf. Ibid. p. 143.

17. Doran, Journal, p.46.

18. The library referred to is a combination of Father Donaghoe's books with a number of devotional works belonging to the Sisters. To these there have been added many windfalls from other sources. It is carefully catalogued and has been made a part of the Heritage Room collection of mementoes garnered through many years by Sister Maryanita Cannon, BVM, and preserved at the motherhouse of the Sisters in Dubuque.

19. Doran Journal, p. 37.

20. When all the bodies were removed from the Bluff cemetery to the Catholic cemetery at Key West, the remains of mother and daughter, together with others in unmarked graves, were reburied in·a small area just inside the old gateway, and there they rest today.

21. Cf. M.M. Hoffmann, Arms and the Monk!The Trappist Saga in Mid-America, (Dubuque: William C.Brown Co., 1952) The writer is indebted to this work for

much of the material on the Trappist foundation.

22. Abbot Bruno wrote later to Father Donaghoe of the meeting he had had with Loras prior to this occasion: "I had the truly great pleasure of meeting Doctor Loras at dinner in Dublin. We had Dean Meyler to meet him; all who saw him, Seculars as well as Regulars, were delighted with him; his manners were admired more even than those of Dr. Murray, the Archbishop, of whom Queen Victoria said that he was the most elegant courtier she had met with. . ."

23. Catholic Directory, 1849, p. 121.

24. McGuire, pp. 149, 150.

25. Hickey collection, Griffith Files.

26. See Butterworth folder, Office of Secretary General, Mt. Carmel, Dubuque.

27. Brother Kieran Mullany, Manuscript history of New Melleray, 1849 to 1887, Trappist Abbey archives.

28. Kempker pencil notes, Griffith Files.

29. The testimony of Sister M. of the Cross, contained in the Doran Notes.

30. The marker for Jane Golden's grave reads, in error, "Mrs. Gorden."

31. The testimony of Sister M. of the Cross, contained in the Doran Notes.

32. Notations found in a small notebook in the Congregation's archives.

33. Quoted from McGuire Annals, p. 288.

34. Pelamourgues to Loras, February 14, 1857.

35. Hoffmann, Church Founders, p. 176.

36. Cf. Sister Helen Angela Hurley, On Good Ground, the Story of the Sisters of St. Joseph in St.Paul, (Minneapolis: University of Minnesota Press, 1951) pp. 22,23.

37. The Miner's Express of Dubuque for January 7, 1852, quoted this item from the Pittsburgh Commercial Journal.

38. This listing occurs in the three Community registers referred to above.

39. Pencil notes on the life of Sister M. Josephine Clarke, written by Sister M. Borgia Walsh, BVM.

40. It is interesting to share a paragraph from the very early history of the St. Nicholas church which Martha inserted at the end of the volume, characteristic as it is of the long memories of the Irish people:
    The former chapel or convent was founded by King Henry III, A.D., 1236, Ralph Leporter granting the site which was the west suburb of the city called since Francis st. St. John de Decor, the first Lord Mayor of Dublin, A.D. 1308, assisted at the Holy Sacrifice and other devotions in the former. And his successor, the great Daniel O'Connell, the veritable King of Ireland and Mayor of Dublin, was present at the dedication of the present church in in 1839.

41. Oral traditions - recounted by Sister M. Eileen Curran and St. Lucile Bruty, summer, 1974.

42. Mazzuchelli, op.cit., p. 109.

43. McGuire, op. cit.,p. 148.

44. Doran, Journal p. 68.

45. From a small black, unidentified notebook in the Congregation's archives.

46. Doran, Early Days, p. 272.

47. McGuire, p. 287.

48. Ibid., p. 289.

49. Taped interview, Sister M. Corita Slattery, March 25, 1974. The novice later became Mother Ascension.

50. McGuire, p. 290.

51. Doran, *Journal*, p. 78.
52. Ibid.
53. McGuire, p. 281.
54. Ibid.
55. Ibid.
56. Ibid.

57. Letter to the writer, dated Paris, November 5,1973.

The rigoristic spirit of the Church in the early nineteenth century can scarcely be traced to a single source. The emotionalism and pietism which marked many of the early Protestant sects had led to a de-emphasis on human emotions on the part of the Council of Trent, with its stress on the almost exclusive roles of the intellect and the will in the direction of one's spiritual life. Certainly the jansenistic spirit had its influence in the French seminaries in the period prior to the French revolution, and with the flight of the emigré clergy to England, Ireland and the States, its influence, reinforced by the theology of John Calvin, became pervasive. Consciously or unconsciously, churchmen in general absorbed the rigorism of the times, while the penitential nature of Irish spirituality, which showed itself in the severe asceticism of the early monks, lingers on even today in the pain-filled pilgrimages to St. Patrick's Purgatory at Lough Dearg. (Author's comment.)

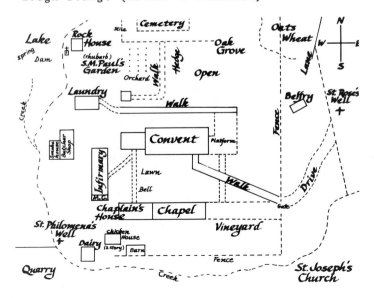

Antoine LeClaire   Margaret LePage LeClaire

Rev. J.A. Pelamourgues

Growing Pains of
The Young Community-
1853-1864

Chapter six gives us the account of a short-lived hospital opened at the instigation of the Bishop of Dubuque. It notes the rapid settlement of the lands beyond the Mississippi, the feverish building of railroads, and the consequent growth of the cities, then the temporary reversal which resulted from the panic of 1857. We are told of the appointment that year of a coadjutor to the aging Bishop, of the building of the present cathedral, and in 1858 of the death of Dubuque's pioneer Bishop. We see the priest-superior of the Sisters delaying an incorporation which would permit them to hold communal property, and his assuming control even of the household accounts, then learn of his protracted illness in early 1859 and of his consequent curtailment of farming activities. His convalescence was cheered by a visit from his lifetime friend, the Archbishop of New York. We learn of separate but unsuccessful attempts on the part of Dubuque's second Bishop to induce the Sisters of Mercy to assume responsibility for the training and the absorption into their own congregation of the Dubuque Sisters. There opened a period of rapid expansion for the Community, with the building of an academy and the undertaking of two parish schools in Davenport. To these were quickly added an academy and small schools in Iowa City, and parochial schools in Burlington, Fort Dodge, Muscatine and DeWitt, Iowa. With the growing novitiate, there came the necessity of removing the boarding school from the Prairie to the hospital site, while the outbreak of the war between the States cut off the stream of postulants from Ireland. New members thereafter would come almost exclusively from the areas served by the Sisters' schools.

Dubuque's First Hospital

Accounts of early settlements in the Mississippi
valley include many instances of illness - ague, bil-
ious fever, pneumonia, smallpox, typhoid, and cholera
being the diseases most feared. While "consumption"-
tuberculosis - was common, it would become much more
so at a later time. Accidents were frequent - steamboat collisions and burnings, injuries from runaway
horses, from accidents in the mines, in the felling
of trees, in building, and later in railroad travel.
The need for proper facilities for the treating and
care of the sufferers became apparent early. By 1846
Bishop Loras had purchased land for a hospital, [1]
content with Mother Clarke's twice repeated assurance
that the Sisters were willing for any kind of service
of which his people stood in need, and specifically
for the conduct of a hospital or an orphanage. It
was not, however, until 1852 that Loras began the
building of a three-story structure against the bluff
on an acre of ground on Fourteenth street, at the
present site of St. Joseph hall, Loras college. In
his report to the Propagation of the Faith in 1853, he
indicated that the building could be completed by
June of that year. It was, he reported in December,
to be staffed by the Sisters of Charity, under the direction of a mother superior whom he regarded as a
"real saint." During the cholera epidemic of 1849
the Sisters had cared for the patients in a building
rented by the town for hospital purposes. [2] At the
time of his writing, the Bishop himself might have
qualified as a patient if the hospital were open, for
he said: "I have just been ill for 4 months, with
trembling fever, during which I had to travel 200
leagues to plant the faith on the borders of the Missouri river, otherwise Protestantism would have taken
hold forever of these counties."[3]

General George W. Jones, Senator from Iowa, had
suggested the possibility of his securing an appropriation from Congress for the financing of the venture
as a "marine hospital."[4] However, Jones suggested
that if the building were temporarily left unfinished,
his chance for getting help to complete it would be
greater, for then he could make a plea for sufficient

funds to put it in service.

When, in late November, 1853, the Bishop proposed that the Sisters assume responsibility for its operation, he found Father Donaghoe less than willing for the venture, as we see from the following letter to Loras:

> I received your kind favor offering me the deed of four lots, on which the Hospital stands, on condition that it should be used only for the purpose of an Hospital. I gave it due consideration, and see a debt of $300, a kitchen to be erected, fence, water, furniture for an hospital &c, all to be procured &c, then to fit out Sisters for it. Then poor Father Donaghoe, as soon as he accepted the deed, at once [will have] become accountable, because all was not in immediate operation. See what I have to do - to try to extinguish all the various conflicts that agitate good Dubuque. I have always aided you in difficulties, no matter who opposed, but most undoubtedly you cannot but feel that acceptance under the present aspect of this affair would throw me into great difficulty. Under this view I most humbly do decline the undertaking, as I have already declined it.

Then Father seemed to reverse his position, for he submitted terms on which he would accept the charge. These included

> A Deed of trust of one acre, on which the building is erected, to the Revd. T.J. Donaghoe in trust for the Sisters of Charity B.V.- the trust to descend to the successor in office of the Right Revd. Mathias Loras, Bishop of the Catholic see of Dubuque.

He closed with a double negative and an unusual directive:

> Now my dear Bishop if you are not fully persuaded that it is not for the glory of God & the good of our Neighbor, do throw this letter in the fire as soon as you have read it.

Loras noted on the back of the letter: "Father Donaghoe & the Sisters refuse to accept the donation of the Dubuque hospital. Nov. 1853."

The next day Father Donaghoe wrote again, apparently in answer to a response on the part of the Bishop. This time he protested the conditions Loras was making for the transfer of the deed to the hospital and grounds.

> . . . I cannot accept a trust for the object intended, which implies a <u>dis</u>trust on the face of the deed of trust <u>to</u> me, more especially when you watch over it. . . . You will pardon me when I say that I would not accept the eight[?] acres on which the building stands with such a condition inserted that during my lifetime that either I or the Sisters would, by any fault of theirs, change the object for which it was conveyed to me in trust. . . .

Then by way of conciliation he added:

> . . . however, we can never disagree - and I do request you to burn the former letter and this note of explanation for I would not for 10,000 dollars have a word with you my Dear Bishop on this affair which I know has already cost you so much trouble with the good folks of crooked Dubuque.

Despite the protests contained in these two letters, we find the following affidavit, signed on December 1, 1853 by Father Donaghoe and witnessed by D.A. Mahony:

> Whereas, the Right Reverend Mathias Loras, the Roman Catholic Bishop of Dubuque, Iowa has this day conveyed to me one acre of land in the city of Dubuque, with the appurtenances thereunto belonging and known as the Hospital Building, now therefore, in conformity with the understanding between the parties to said conveyance, I hereby pledge myself to convey the said premises to the Sisters' Community under my charge as soon as that Community can be so recognized in law by having the same incorporated, as to be able to hold estate in its name.[5]

As to the matter of the Community's incorporation, Father Clement Smyth, prior at the New Melleray monastery, wrote to Father Donaghoe on January 9, 1855:

> I was in Dubuque on the 2nd inst., & left
> our articles of incorporation with Mr. O'Brien
> to be recorded. I wish that you had done the
> same; you would thereby secure the property
> of your community, destroy all individual
> claims on the same, & remove from weak minds
> every source of temptation which may here-
> after arise from such individual claims.

At the time, according to the receipts made out in
Father Donaghoe's name and preserved in the Congregation's archives, he was paying taxes on 1320 acres of
Iowa land, the total taxable holdings of the Community in Iowa at the time. Seven hundred twenty-five
acres of this land had originally been registered in
the name of various Sisters. The suggestion of Father
Smyth would seem then to have been highly appropriate.
However, Sister M. Pulcheria's Annals* says that "for
private reasons" Father Donaghoe preferred not to apply for incorporation. This action was to wait until
after his death, when it was taken almost immediately.

In response to the suggestion of General Jones
that the hospital building be left uncompleted, the
Bishop closed it up in its unfinished state. In a
letter of May 11, 1854, after gently chiding the General for the frequent home visits of his daughters
and their consequent absences from the Prairie academy, Father Donaghoe continued:

> You recollect when I had the pleasure to go
> in your carriage past the hospital you said
> if the Bishop had left it unfinished and
> larger, you could obtain an appropriation
> for it. There it still stands, broken win-
> dows, &c. . . . I should prefer to begin
> [as]if nothing had already been done and lay
> the foundation of one worthy of the City of
> Dubuque. . . . I am in town for the purpose

---

*Sister's account, page 305, indicates that all
the real estate belonging to the Community was held in
the names of the early Sisters. Such, however, was not
the case. All but that obtained through John Walsh
was entered in Father Donaghoe's name, and so, as far
as the land records went, was his private property.
It is not likely that the Trappist Prior was aware of
this fact.

to commence the collection - but I postponed.
All appear, and indeed are, willing. Still
it required all they could give to lay such
a foundation as I describe above, viz. $1500
or more.

A second letter, also from Father Donaghoe, found
in the Jones collection, bears the date May 23:

. . . A Committee from the City Council
called on the Sisters to know when the Hospital would be opened & how much for each patient; those were two questions the Sisters
could not answer. And since, the city has
been so healthy that no further enquiry was
made.

Again he spoke of putting off collection for the necessary funds:

Every day almost I am urged to collect in
Dubuque for the hospital. I put it off as I
want to learn from you what I can depend on.
I cannot defer it long, but it is a poor
concern as it now stands. . . .

Bishop Loras was disappointed in the matter of
government aid, for the grant which Congress made
went to Galena, not to Dubuque.[6] The hospital was officially opened September 1, 1855,[7] but before a
year was up, Father Donaghoe had received pupils
there.[8] The Congregation's account of the change from
the hospital for which Loras had deeded the property,
to the grade school, indicated complacently that
Father Donaghoe had succeeded in convincing Bishop
Loras that the Sisters of Charity had been established solely for school work.[9] That the building
functioned briefly as a hospital seems apparent, but
there is no record of the number of patients or of
the ills for which they were treated. Sister M.
Catherine Byrne acted as superior of the institute
for a time, with Sisters M. Vincent Donavan, Raphael
Barry and Martina Mullen members of its staff. When
the hospital became an elementary school under the
name of Our Lady of the Sacred Heart, Sister M. Catherine seems to have been transferred back to St.
Mary's from which Mother Clarke had removed her at
the Bishop's request. The Catholic Directory of 1859
lists her as superior there. The three other members
of the original staff remained to serve the new school.

* * * * *

The year 1854 held a day of jubilation for Father
Donaghoe, that on which Pipe Pius IX, surrounded by
the College of Cardinals and hundreds of bishops from
all parts of the world, defined the doctrine of Mary's
Immaculate Conception. The Blessed Virgin had long
been the object of his devotion, and especially under
this great privilege. On November 30, 1842 he had
written to the Sisters:

> . . . Offer now your novena with all your
> hearts in honor of the Immaculate Conception
> of the blessed Mother of God. . . . My lot
> is not yet determined .* Let this be your
> prayer and it shall be mine. The feast of
> the Immaculate Conception shall be hereafter
> our annual celebration because I hold the
> Conception is the foundation of all the
> greatness of our Blessed Mother.

There was great rejoicing when the word reached the
Prairie that the dogma had at last been proclaimed.
The Reverend Andrew Trevis and the Reverend Philip
Laurent, from nearby Mt. St. Bernard seminary, were
bearers of the news. Arriving while the Sisters were
at Benediction, they heard sung for the first time
the hymn "Hail, Star of the Morning," which Sister M.
Joseph had composed in anticipation of the event.

A question which has long called for clarifica-
tion involves the influence which Father Donaghoe may
have exercised on the action of successive Baltimore
Councils in the commemoration of the Immaculate Conception. Father Trevis, in a letter dated February
7, 1847 quoted Father Donaghoe as follows:

> I may as well acknowledge that I gave Arch-
> bishop Hughes no rest until I induced him to
> propose at the Council of Baltimore to have
> the Blessed Virgin, under the title of the
> Immaculate Conception, chosen as patroness
> of the Church in the United States.

Then the letter added a second goal:

----

*Probably the decision whether he would accompany
them to Dubuque or remain at St. Michael's.

> I want him to complete the good work by hav-
> ing the feast declared a holy day in this
> country.

John Hughes' voice in the matter would have been one
among many in the Council of 1846, for even in the
previous Council in 1843 the assembled bishops in-
voked the name of the Mother of God as the patroness
of the whole country.[13] In the matter of Father Donaghoe's second plea, Hughes wrote on May 30, 1852 with
respect to the Council just ended: "Your matter could
not be reached, and even if an opportunity presented
itself, it would not have been taken up according to
your wishes. . . ." In the ratification of the dogma,
the American Church played a significant part, but
through Francis Kenrick as Archbishop of Baltimore,
for it was he who led the discussion on the subject
and had an important role in the final act of defini-
tion.[14] John Marschall writes that as early as 1843

> Pope Gregory XVI had granted to Bishop Kenrick
> the privilege of using the titles "Immaculate"
> and "Queen conceived without original sin" in
> the liturgical prayers of December 8. And on
> May 13 of the following year the bishops at
> the Sixth Provincial Council of Baltimore
> formally petitioned the Holy See for the
> privilege of extending the devotion by desig-
> nating Mary under the title of Immaculate Con-
> ception as patroness of the United States.[15]

In 1846 this petition was granted.

In connection with the investigation of the part
Father Donaghoe may have played in all this, Sister M.
Augustina Ray, BVM, wrote on December 10, 1953 to the
Congregation's general secretary, Sister M. Michael
Flynn:

> Father [John Tracy] Ellis says that there is
> nothing in the Baltimore archives that would
> furnish any basis for an historical article
> [on the subject of Father Donaghoe's influ-
> ence]. The replies of the bishops were made
> very briefly on scraps of paper which are
> very difficult to decipher. Neither in the
> Baltimore archives nor in those of the Sulpi-
> cians at Roland Park are there any letters of
> Father Donaghoe.

A second letter, of August 6, 1955, says:

At the time I saw Father [Henry] Browne[*] in
Chicago, I also talked with Father Ellis who
assured me he had combed all the archives east
of the Mississippi and could find nothing
more than the brief notice published in the
Catholic Historical Review which we discussed
when I was at Mt. Carmel in the fall of 1953.

The brief article mentioned spoke only in the most
general way of Father Donaghoe's interest in the matter. Little as Father's influence may have been, it
was a matter of satisfaction to him to believe that
he had contributed significantly to the realization
of his hopes. His last Mass was celebrated on the
day on which the feast of the Immaculate Conception
was first celebrated as a holy day of obligation,
December 8, 1868.

* * * * *

By 1850 Davenport, occupying one of the most beautiful situations on the Mississippi river, was growing rapidly, and the need of schools was pressing.
The site of the abandoned St. Philomena academy was
by then in the center of a thriving business district,
while the area about St. Anthony church square remained
a quiet sector of the town. The church had been named
after its great benefactor, Antoine LeClaire, who was
of French and Pottawatomi descent, and a master of
several Indian languages. Serving as interpreter in
the drawing up of a number of Indian treaties, LeClaire
had won the confidence of the Sacs and Foxes.. These
tribes had endowed him with much land in and about
present day Davenport and LeClaire, Iowa, while the
Pottawatomies, in the treaty of Prairie du Chien, had
reserved for him two sections of land near Moline, Illinois. Margaret, his wife, was the daughter of
Antoine LePage, a Canadian, and on her mother's side,
the granddaughter of the Sac chief, Acoqua. Margaret
had been the beneficiary of a section of land in Keokuk.

---

[*] Father Browne was at that time writing a biography of Archbishop Hughes, which has, unfortunately,
gone unpublished. It is to Father Browne that the
Congregation is indebted for copies of Father Donaghoe's letters to Archbishop Hughes used in the present
study. Originals are, or were at that time, in the
archives at Catholic University.

Educated by religious at St. Charles, Missouri, in
the early eighteen hundreds, she may have had for her
teacher the Venerable Philippine Duchesne of the Religious of the Sacred Heart, missionary to the Indians
and superior of that mission. In 1820 Antoine and
Margaret were married in Peoria, where Antoine had been
detained for a time as a political prisoner, on the
question of his allegiance during the War of 1812.
Margaret frequently accompanied her husband in his
dealings with the Indians, and from time to time the
couple warmly welcomed and entertained visiting dele-
gations of Sacs and Foxes, sending them away with
generous supplies of corn, flour and other provisions.[16]

    The LeClaires were then, quite literally, among
Davenport's "first citizens." It is not surprising
that when the question of schools arose, they would
be among the most concerned, and that their search
would lead them in the direction of the Religious of
the Sacred Heart, for the establishment of a select
academy such as those Sisters maintained in St. Louis
and other points south. Their interest turned also
to the Sisters from Dubuque, whom they wished to see
engaged in the parish schools. Joining the LeClaires
in their efforts were the Honorable G.C.R. Mitchell,
Judge of the 14th Judicial District of Iowa, and
George L. Davenport, whose father had been one of the
founders of the town. Bishop Loras had in fact anticipated the efforts of both by writing directly to
Madame Barat, foundress of the French Religious, at
their Paris headquarters. The response to his letter,
dated October 2, 1850, came from Madame Cutts, supe-
rior-vicar for the United States, expressing the hope
that Sisters could be furnished for Davenport in 1852.
They had lost six of their members in the cholera epidemic in St. Louis in 1849, and their membership was
further reduced by the death of several of their young
religious at Grand Couteau, Louisiana, in the epidemic
of yellow fever. Further explanation of the inability
of Madame Cutts to keep her promise to Bishop Loras is
contained in an historical study of the Society:

> Reverend Mother du Rousier [visitatrix of the
> American houses in 1852] spent the spring of
> 1852-1853 in Louisiana. At Grand Couteau
> she was confronted with the problem of choos-
> ing one among three possible foundations in
> the fast developing section along the lower
> Missouri. Three appeals had been submitted
> to the Superior General. While Reverend
> Mother Cutts was visiting the Pottawatomi

Mission, Bishop Miege pleaded the cause of
Leavenworth, Kansas, where he intended loca-
ting his episcopal see. On her way from St.
Mary's to St. Louis, Mother Cutts had been
obliged to stay at St. Joseph, Missouri,
where the zealous pastor, Father Thomas Scanlan, begged her to send nuns to aid him in
caring for the children of his frontier parish. Of longer standing was the appeal of
Bishop Loras of Dubuque, but of less urgency
for he had a corps of splendid religious
workers in the Sisters of Charity of the
Blessed Virgin Mary, who had come to his diocese in 1843.

When a favorable answer came from the Superior
General regarding the appeal from Leavenworth,
preparations were begun at Grand Couteau for
the foundation. But within a few weeks an
affirmation of Father Scanlan's request also
arrived. As it was impossible to open two
new convents at the same time, Reverend Mother du Rousier decided in favor of St. Joseph,
and named Mothers Shannon, English and Gardiner
for the work.[17]

Unaware of the Bishop's efforts to meet the school
needs of the parish, Judge Mitchell and Antoine LeClaire,
in a joint letter of October 15, 1853, complained to
Loras of his supposed neglect in their regard. Father
Pelamourgues had made heroic efforts, alone and with
lay help, to hold classes for the children of the parish. However, in 1852 he had gone to France, with the
intention of not returning. Father G.H. Plathe had
been assigned to the parish to complete the construction of a stone church, and, that completed, he had
been replaced by Father McCabe. Now the latter had
been withdrawn by the Bishop. Complaining first of
this deprivation, they then spoke of the two or three
hundred children for whom a school was needed if their
parents were not to be forced to send them to the
"rank sectarian Godless schools." The letter continues:

We want & are determined to make the effort
very especially to obtain some Brothers of
the Christian Schools, (such as they have in
Baltimore) to establish a school for boys,
and some of the Sisters from near Dubuque to
establish an orphan asylum and day school for
girls. This congregation is abundantly able

to support both of these establishments &
the sooner we get them the better.

The problem of pastor was solved when word came from
Father Pelamourgues that, his aged father having died,
he was now lonely for his Davenport friends and was
returning. With the question of the Religious of the
Sacred Heart not yet settled, LeClaire wrote Loras on
December 23,

>What we want most here at present is a school
>conducted by the Sisters of Charity for the
>purpose of educating the smaller children of
>the congregation, & those whose parents are
>not able to pay high tuition fees. The Sis-
>ters of Charity will suit us admirably. Such
>a school will not interfere with the estab-
>lishment conducted by the Ladies of the Sac-
>red Heart. We must have them also.

With the new church now completed, the original building could serve for school and residence for the Sisters, so that, as Judge Mitchell put it, "the Sisters
in visiting the church which they do daily, would not
have to pass through several public streets," as they
had had to do during their brief and poverty-ridden
years at St. Philomena academy. Father Pelamourgues
returned in time to receive a visit from Madame Gallwey, and probably at that time he became aware of the
unlikelihood of the Religious of the Sacred Heart
making an establishment in Davenport. His letter to
the Bishop on February 6, 1854 was written before the
receipt of Mme. Gallwey's written decision. He indicated that his letter to the Bishop enclosed a copy
of

>the one that I had written to Father Donaghoe
>the very day that Mother Gallwey arrived at
>Davenport; by that letter you will see what
>was my opinion at that time. You will re-
>mark expecially that in the letter I do not
>ask for them to come. I think that having
>left in the way they did, I ought not to
>tell them to come. But I repeat it, if they
>come they will find always a friend in me,
>and I will try to see that there is nothing
>on my part that can prevent them to succeed
>here.

Unfortunately, no copy of the letter Father mentioned
remains, leaving us no way of deciding who was at
fault or in what respect.[18] However, there does appear

a lack of civility on the part of the Sisters in a
letter of Pelamourgues to Loras on May 1, 1847 which
read in part:

> I have here many things belonging to the Sis-
> ters which were given them by your Lordship
> or other persons. They said they did not
> want them as they did not intend to come back
> to Davenport. Please tell me what I must do
> with them.

Mme. Gallwey's long awaited decision came from St.
Louis on February 20, 1854:

> . . . I am really sorry that after so many
> liberal offers, your city should still be
> unprovided for - the good will is there, but
> want of subjects prevents the possibility of
> doing anything at this time. . . .[19]

The immigration into Iowa was at its height when
the question of the Sisters for Davenport was nearing
its resolution. The Rock Island News of May 26, 1855
described a lively scene:

> The Davenport levee presented an unusually
> stirring experience to an eye-witness on the
> opposite shore. We counted no less than
> twenty-four white-tented wagons ranged around
> near the ferry, while some twenty farm wagons
> stood here and there among a small sea of re-
> posing cattle. All the way up Brady street
> was a row of those wheeled tents, while some
> half-dozen were visible on the steamer "Dav-
> enport" just then crossing the river. All
> these, so far as we could learn, were bound
> for Iowa.

Settlers were coming into Iowa by "hundreds and thousands," steady, well-educated, industrious farmers of
New York, Ohio, Pennsylvania and other northern states,
so that Iowa was not to suffer the travail of other
states beyond the Mississippi whose history included
an era of lawlessness.

The problem of transportation had been a critical
one for the opening up of new areas, and it would be
solved only gradually, The obligation of the federal
government to secure mail delivery had moved from the
horse and saddlebag solution to the mail-carrying stage
coach. This and the necessity for moving troops for

defense had let to the construction of a few roads,
though drenching rains and deep snows made even these
at times impassable to the heavy wagons and rumbling
stage coaches that had to travel over them. The experiment with plank roads was short-lived, while the
effort to penetrate the state by way of its "navigable"
streams had led to the loss of many lives and vessels.
By 1850 the railroad fever had taken hold. Local companies undertook the building of short lines between
the more populous towns - Dubuque to Muscatine, Davenport to Iowa City and on to Council Bluffs, Burlington
to Peoria - having always in mind connection with Chicago and the East.[20] For that, a bridge was needed
to link the Chicago and Rock Island railway with the
Mississippi & Missouri road from Davenport west.[21] It
was Antoine LeClaire who turned the first shovelful
of dirt for the M.& M. railroad, which would eventually link Davenport with Council Bluffs. His residence
would be its first depot, and the celebration of its
inauguration would be held in the LeClaire House,
where "no gentleman would be admitted to table without a coat." The steel rails and the first engine,
the "Antoine LeClaire," were brought across the river
on flat boats. A blanketed crowd of Indians, come to
watch the strange proceedings, were invited to ride
its cars the first ten miles of its stretch - to Wal-
cott, Iowa, a townsite still on the drawing boards.
Though the bridge across the river was ready for traffic in June, 1855, the first locomotive to cross it -
the "Des Moines" - did not pass over the new wooden
structure until April 28, 1856.[22]

For the next year or so, activity was intense.
Over twelve hundred houses were built in Davenport in
the year 1857. The macadamizing of streets, the laying of gas pipes and brick sidewalks, the installation of street lamps, the building of a fire house,
equipped with the best in engines, hose carts and
ladders, all marked the progress of the town.

On August 17, 1855 Bishop Loras wrote Father Donaghoe that the Sisters' plans for returning to Davenport were causing great excitement, with many day
scholars and three or four boarders anxiously awaiting their arrival. He would visit Davenport on his
way to the Council, and meantime was making a promise
of "2 fine town lots at Davenport for the Sisters of
the Blessed Virgin." Then, as evidence of at least
one patient for the Dubuque hospital, he requested
Father Trevis to go from Mt. St. Bernard to St. Joseph's on the Prairie and bring Father de Cailly to

the Sisters' hospital where he would be near his doctor, adding his "hearty thanks" for the "most charitable hospitality and the tender care of the Sisters."
Father de Cailly, nephew of Bishop Loras, had met with
an accident at St. Joseph's in attempting to break a
horse to use on his missionary journeys, and was for
a time under the care of the Sisters on the Prairie.[23]
The Bishop's letter continued on an upbeat: "The first
of September ought to be memorable here for the opening of the hospital besides that of the Brothers'
school."

The Sisters assigned to St. Anthony's, Davenport,
were to reside in the home of Mr. and Mrs. George L.
Davenport until the carpenters had completed the re-
modelling of the church-school combination designed
by Mazzuchelli into living quarters and classrooms.
Father Pelamourgues would occupy rooms provided in
connection with the new stone church. It was impossible, he said, to make provision for boarding students
that first winter, but his letter of August 24 to the
Bishop dealt with other school plans:

> One of the sisters should know the German
> language, otherwise the German children will
> not come. Mr. Flammang requires that they
> should learn German in the school. I would
> like also that the Sisters should teach the
> small boys.

Father himself would continue for a time as teacher
for the older boys, with such lay help as he required.
In a letter of August 31, Father Pelamourgues assured
Father Donaghoe that he would assume responsibility
for the support of the Sisters, indicating that he
believed his and Father Donaghoe's ideas about schools
would be very much in harmony. He would need four
Sisters, of whom three would be teachers.

Sister M. Agatha Hurley, the first superior of
the newly opened St. Anthony school, preserved in her
diary many interesting details about her first years
there. Of the Sisters' welcome she wrote:

> A.D.1855, Sept. 5th, 8 o'clock A.M. arrived
> at Davenport. Was kindly received by Mr.
> Davenport - remained at his house until the
> ev'g of the 8th. After tea Sister M. Aloy-
> sius O'Leary, Str. M. Liguori Grace, Str. M.
> James Kinsella, Str. M. Dominic Sullivan *and

---

*All Irish-born..Str.M Dominic , a novice,was from Cork.

myself took possession of the house assigned
for us, day of week, Saturday. Next day Mr.
LeClaire and his lady called on us as also
several other people. Sept. 10 - Monday -
opened school - had 35 scholars. Our house
was furnished by Mrs. Davenport with the following articles. . . .

Here Sister listed the full supply of household items.
By the 18th the school had been greatly increased.
On the 22nd the Sisters went with Mrs. Davenport to
see the ten acres of land that Mr. Davenport and Judge
Mitchell were offering to the Community for the building of a boarding school. It is evident that the parish members were determined to see that the Sisters
were well provided for on this their second Davenport
venture, for Sister mentioned a steady flow of food
and other necessities. The most conspicuous gift was
a new piano, presented to them by Mr. and Mrs. LeClaire.

On December 1, the pastor wrote Father Donaghoe
that the school was going well, though it would be
larger if the poor could attend. However, he hoped
in the spring to start a free school, for he had
leased two lots on the church square at an annual rental of fifteen hundred dollars, the lease to run for
ten years. This would provide support for both the
boys' and the girls' schools. His advice to Father
Donaghoe was that he accept at once the Bishop's offer
of two lots, for they could be leased for eight hundred dollars a year, providing funds to help in the
building of the proposed boarding school. He added
that he would soon need one or two more teachers, for
those engaged in the work of the school had too much
to do. He was especially concerned that, considering
her frail health, Sister M. Agatha was working too
hard. Railroad construction, he said, was progressing at a lively rate and a train was now running
daily between Davenport and Muscatine. Within two
more weeks it was hoped that the laying of track would
be completed as far as Iowa City, allowing girls from
there to come as boarding students to Davenport where
some had already made application. The letter continued with word that the Reverend Francis X. Weninger,
S.J., had given a mission to the German people in
Davenport in which he had encouraged them to build a
church of their own. As a result St. Cunnegunda's -
later St. Joseph's - was already under construction.

On their first Christmas in Davenport, Sister M.
Agatha noted that Father Pelamourgues and "a gentleman

by the name of J. Marsh" paid them a visit, and that
the latter had sent them two loads of coal and two of
wood on Christmas eve. Sister observed that she
thought he would ba a great friend to them, as indeed
he proved to be. John Marsh, an English convert, was
studying for the priesthood under Father Trevis, who,
as newly appointed pastor, was engaged in the construction of St. Margaret church. Father Trevis had
brought with him from the Dubuque seminary John Marsh,
Henry Cosgrove, and Peter Magne, formerly Brother
Jubin of the Brothers of the Sacred Heart. He hoped
to continue the direction of their studies in Davenport. Father Marsh, in later years, as pastor of Corpus Christi, Fort Dodge would solicit the Dubuque
Sisters as teachers for his parish school. Other references in Sister's diary speak of his helpfulness
in preparing the altar for feast days and caring for
the boys on school outings. The diary continued with
the more significant events of the passing days:

the laying of the cornerstone on June 29, 1856, of
St. Margaret's - the "French church" - built on land
given by the LeClaires;

the departure of Mr. and Mrs. Davenport to be present
at the public examinations in which their daughters
would participate at St. Joseph's on the Prairie;[24]

the consecration of Bishop Smyth as coadjutor to the
aging Loras, to take place on May 3, 1857 in St.
Louis;[*]

the arrival from time to time of a letter from Father
Donaghoe or the sending of one to him;

then in July, 1857, the word of her father's serious
illness in Dubuque, with instructions from Father
Donaghoe to come. To this, Sister added brief details
of her trip: "Saturday - left on the Packet Alhambra
-Mr.Davt, procured our tickets, room, etc." That was
July 18. The next day she and her companion met the
Northern Bell at the mouth of the Fevre river near Galena, and reached Dunlieth (East Dubuque) at seven o'
clock the following morning. "We crossed the ferry -
got in an omnibus and found ourselves at the Sisters."

---

[*]To this Sister added the comment that on his
departure for the ceremonies, Father Pelamourgues had
left his twenty-one birds in her care.

home in a few minutes. . . ." She then added, "July 20 - spent the day with Revd. Father Donaghoe."

With the death of Bishop Cretin on February 22, 1857, there were rumors - and they were well-founded, for his name had gone to Rome - that Father Pelamourgues was in line for the mitre. But the good pastor had no such ambitions. He had already spoken his mind on that subject in a letter to Father Donaghoe on August 20, 1856: "I am well satisfied to be the pastor of St. Anthony's parish church. My ambitions never aspired any higher, and I am fully convinced that I am as great a man now as I ought to be and greater too." Nevertheless, on May 12, 1857 he received the bulls of his appointment to the diocese of St. Paul, and he set out immediately for Rome. On August 14, an entry in Sister's diary told that "F.P's" resignation from the St. Paul appointment had been accepted by the Pope and that he would be home in Davenport in three months. The Reverend Thomas L. Grace OP had been named in his stead. Meantime, on July 16, as Sister noted, the ground-breaking ceremony was held for the new academy.

* * * * *

Bishop Loras was growing old and was beginning to feel the effects of his strenuous life. Indeed, as early as March 31, 1852, Archbishop Kenrick of St. Louis had written his brother, the Archbishop of Baltimore, suggesting the need of a coadjutor for the see of Dubuque "whose Bishop, Mathias Loras, is "fractus tum animi tum corporis," * He went on to say that the Bishop was half blind, and therefore clearly in need of a vigorous man as coadjutor with the right of succession to the diocese.[25] By now, partially deaf and bent with age, Loras was beginning to suffer slight strokes, and he himself began to give serious consideration to his need for a coadjutor. His own choice lay with a zealous Frenchman, the Reverend August Paris of the St. Louis diocese, but in view of the attitude of the Irish toward the French clergy, that choice would scarcely have been a happy one. It seems apparent that Father Donaghoe was the chief influence in turning his choice toward Father Clement Smyth, prior of the Trappists at New Melleray. Although as early as April 3, 1856, the Abbot, on visitation from Ireland, mentioned that he feared the

---

* "Broken in mind and body."

bulls were on their way, they did not arrive from
Rome until a year later. Consecration was scheduled
for May 3, 1857, in St. Louis, and Father Donaghoe
planned to attend.

The enthusiasm of the Dubuque people over the appointment of the Irish Trappist as their new Bishop,
after all their frustrating years with Loras, resulted
in sociabilities which commanded much of his time.
Smyth hoped the novelty would soon wear off, as he
confessed in a letter to Archbishop Purcell on June
16, 1857. Between his ills and the harassments of
his office, the aging Bishop Loras had grown crotch-
ety. This, added to differences in temperament and
in national backgrounds, seems to have made the relations between the two bishops less amiable than they
might otherwise have been, for Smyth wrote:

> Our Venerable Bishop Loras remains still in
> Keokuk & this leaves me to reign alone in my
> glory. . . .Yet the absence of some is fre-
> quently a blessing. For where harmony of
> will and unity of principle do not consti-
> tute the foundation of social intercourse,
> there, friendship, however sincere and
> healthful in appearance, cannot either
> secure a happy present or promise a hopeful
> future. The Bishop is a man of extraordinary
> virtue. He is, I believe, a saint, but
> saints can try the patience of sinners. You
> well know our saintly Bishop Loras. I need
> not give you either the outline of his char-
> acter or the number and variety of his deeds.
> If a Bishop be known by his deeds, I think he
> exceeds all the Bishops of the Union in the
> number of his deeds which have incontestible
> claims in different portions of this diocese.

Later bishops would feel more kindly toward those
deeds, for they represented the acquisition of much
land and many building sites, laying the financial
basis for parish establishments and religious institutions. The pathetic reaction of the enfeebled Bishop to his own increasing infirmities seem scarcely to
have received the sympathetic understanding of his
coadjutor whose letter continues:

> Bishop Loras says that so long as he is able
> to lift his hands to heaven he will continue
> to administer the affairs of the Diocese.
> Should such be the will of God, I say, Fiat,
> fiat. . . .[26]

But the deeper bonds between the two bishops would be mainfest when, eight months later, the stricken Loras lay dying. Then, during the long night vigil, Smyth watched and prayed and sought to provide such comfort as he could to the unconscious Loras.

On July 2, 1857 the work on the new cathedral had advanced to the point of laying the cornerstone, a ceremony to which Father Donaghoe received a personal invitation. The speaker chosen for the day, Father Mazzuchelli, busy across the river with his college and the foundation of his sisterhood, had become a stranger to Dubuque. He was glad to be welcomed back. Bishop Loras was not present for the ceremony, preferring to remain in Keokuk. It was nonetheless his hope to say Mass in the new cathedral before his death, which he had begun seriously to anticipate. His wish was fulfilled; he was able, feeble and partially paralyzed though he was, to say Mass in the basement of the new structure on Christmas day, 1857.

Some months later Loras had given Father Emmonds permission for a visit to his home in Germany on condition that he would bring back young German recruits for the diocese, as the German population there was growing rapidly. On the late afternoon of February 18, 1858 Emmonds and four of his countrymen,* after crossing the river on the ice, appeared at Loras' door. He was overjoyed to receive his unexpected guests.** It was a happy moment for the Bishop, and inviting his five guests to share his dinner, he spoke of his hopes of visiting France in May. His guests, having departed, the Bishop, excited by the pleasure of the evening's visit, retired promptly. At eleven o'clock the housekeeper, hearing him moaning, called Father McCabe, who found him suffering his final stroke. Immediately summoning Bishop Smyth, Sisters M. Catherine and Agnes, and the Brothers of the Sacred Heart, Father McCabe administered the last rites, and at five o'clock the next morning Bishop Loras passed into eternity.

---

*
They were Anthony Niermann, John B. Fendrick, John Hanasch and F. Uhlenbrock.
**He had developed a great liking for the energetic young German priest, and, in fact, had entrusted him with major enterprises, to the chagrin of the older clergy. His own compatriots, especially, had become somewhat estranged from him as a result.

Whatever his limitations, Bishop Loras was a
great man, and his works live after him. One of these
works was his contribution to the Catholic colonization of the prairie states. By his efforts he sought
to draw to the cheap lands of Iowa Catholic immigrants[27]
who might otherwise have condemned themselves and their
children to continued oppression in their homeland or
wretched poverty in the slums of the eastern cities.
Letters addressed to individuals and organizations in
the States and abroad, appeals published in the New
York Freeman's Journal, and the Truthteller, the
Philadelphia Catholic Herald, and the Boston Pilot,
provided information and encouragement to those who
dreamed of contentment and of plenty for their growing families. As early as 1851, a committee of Dubuque laymen, at his instigation, established contacts
with the Irish emigrant societies of the East. Repre-
sentatives from Dubuque to the Buffalo convention in
1856 were among the ninety-five delegates from the
United States and Canada, who, together with twenty-five
missionary priests, met in Buffalo with the permission
and blessing of Bishop Timon. Their purpose was to
lay plans for informing the impoverished thousands in
the seaboard cities of the vast farmlands available
to them, and for providing assistance to those who
would respond. However, the convention largely failed
of its purpose. Archbishop Hughes was a powerful figure at the time. Pique that the convention had been
called without previous consultation with him and
dislike of its prime mover, D'arcy McGee, led Hughes
to denounce the whole affair. Initially unaware of
the full plans and purposes of the convention and of
the calibre of the personages involved, once he had
taken his stand, he would not retreat from it. Even
when Father Donaghoe sent a letter to Archbishop
Hughes to introduce Judge Corkery, who asked only the
opportunity to speak to interested groups in church
halls or basements, the Archbishop denied the request.
Yet Hughes showed much concern for the Irish poor
within the boundaries of his own archdiocese.

When Loras came into the rough, hard-drinking
young mining town of Dubuque in 1839, he promptly established societies dedicated to temperance and total
abstinence. He set the example of complete abstinence, though, as a Frenchman, he had grown up with
the use of wine as the ordinary table beverage. In
the days of rapid railroad construction in the 50's,
the largely Irish crews, laboring long hours in every
kind of weather and terrain, received much of their

pay in raw liquor, doled out at regular intervals during the day. Regarding these transients as part of
his flock, Loras sent the Reverend B. McGorrick to
minister to them, and to coax all he could to take
the temperance pledge. Loras' program of temperance,
outlined in his pastoral of 1855, so impressed the
general public as to have been largely responsible for
the Iowa prohibition law.[28]

In the course of his years as bishop, Loras established and helped finance a remarkable nunber of
churches and schools in the diocese which he had
found a wilderness. Indeed he laid the foundation
well. Others could build upon it as they would. His
work completed, he was laid to rest with due ceremony
in the sandy floor of the mortuary chapel in the basement of the partially completed cathedral.

But to return to the Prairie. There a silent
drama had been enacted at St. Joseph's - the withdraw-
ing from Mother Clarke of the handling of the household finances, which had been her limited sphere of
administration in their years on the Prairie. Henceforth even the accounts for the personal needs of the
Sisters would be under Father Donaghoe's control. He
seems to have recognized no obligation to preserve a
record of even the purchase or sale of Community properties, all of which business was transacted in his
name. Mother Clarke had kept scrupulously accurate
accounts of all moneys that passed through her hands
in Philadelphia. She took up the task again in 1847,
after the Community settled on the Prairie, though it
is quite apparent from her records that major transactions were handled by Father Donaghoe and lay outside her observation. For these, no account remains.
The purchase of the usual needs for the farm and
household, receipts from the boarding school, the
sale of farm products, the dowries of postulants, and
land rentals, appeared regularly in Mother Clarke's
accounts. Each month she struck a balance and indicated the amount of cash on hand with which to begin
the next month's business. In Mother's account book
for 1857, beginning on January 1, its entries for the
month are quite as usual - "Expenditures" on the left
page and "Receipts" on the right, as was her custom.
However, of a total of $315.75 in receipts for the
month of January, $266.50 is indicated as having been
received from Father Donaghoe, rather than from ordinary sources. Then, for the first time, we find the
balancing of the month's accounts in his hand. From
that time on, all, or nearly all, of the receipts came

in lump sums from Father, and were just sufficient to
cover the month's expenditures, the largest cash balance at the end of any month being $10.00. The last
item recorded under receipts is dated October 28,1857,
and reads: "cash borrowed, 68¢," the amount needed
to balance the total October expenses of $128.11.
There the accounts leave off. Not until January of
1869, more than eleven years later, does Mother Clarke
open her account book again - the date, that of Father
Donaghoe's death.

* * * * *

The full effects of the panic of 1857 were being
felt when Father Pelamourgues wrote Father Donaghoe
on January 5, 1859, for he said: "Times are very hard,
especially with the Irish people. Children have not
even clothes to come to school." It was certainly
not a propitious time for the opening of a boarding
school. Father introduced a personal note in his letter, suggesting that Father Donaghoe should consider
securing an assistant - possibly a successor. "I think
it will be soon time for you to ask for a coadjutor,
and to rest a little, unless you intend to wait till
you are in heaven." The advice was not untimely if
Father planned a successor, for he was quite ill when
the letter came, and remained so for five months, as
a pencilled note written by him in a tremulous hand
indicates. This illness, and the fact that the
deaths of Brothers Joseph and Bernard had robbed him
of two dedicated workmen, seem to have warned him
that he was attempting too much in the magnitude of
his farming enterprises, for an additional note reads:
"Sheep, Cattle, Horses reduced - men too, others by
the piece." Then there is the further indication of
his having entrusted to Sister M. Agatha the direction
of work in the construction of the new academy. Many
mentions of ill health appear in his letters during
the remaining ten years of his life.

* * * * *

Assuming full responsibility for the care of the
diocese after the death of Bishop Loras, Bishop Smyth
received a further burden with his appointment as administrator to the diocese of Chicago. The resignation of Bishop Anthony O'Regan on June 25, 1858 left
the see vacant until the consecration of Bishop James
Duggan on January 25, 1859. On one of his several
trips to Chicago, Bishop Smyth paid a visit to Mother
Mary Francis Monholland, then superior of the Sisters

of Mercy at Xavier academy, in what he believed to be
the interests of the Dubuque Sisters. The following account of his visit is given in the Life of
Mother Mary Monholland:

> The Sisters of Charity of the Blessed Virgin
> Mary of Dubuque, founded by Rev. T.J.
> Donaghoe of St. Michael's church, Philadel-
> phia, and Mother Mary Clarke of Dublin, Ire-
> land, were still in the first stage of exis-
> tence as a religious body. No formal rule
> had been adopted - no confirmation by Rome
> received. A certain looseness, so to speak,
> existed, or was supposed to exist.

After brief editorializing, the account continues:

> Bishop Smith, himself a strict disciplinar-
> ian, and a regularly observant Trappist,
> even on the episcopal throne, felt inspired
> to precipitate matters by introducing more
> formal conventualism among the Sisters of
> his diocese. He knew that the Order of Mercy
> was confirmed by Rome in 1840; he knew of
> Mother Francis'[Monholland]phenomenal powers
> of government; therefore, asked her to send
> some members of her community to exemplify
> the life of a confirmed order to the Sister-
> hood of Dubuque.
>
> "Oh, Bishop! how could I do that?" she ex-
> claimed, humility and justice making her
> shrink from the proposal. "There are exem-
> plary women in that congregation, which has
> not yet matured. The Foundress, a person of
> large experience, is noted for her wisdom
> and sanctity. Wait a while, and they will
> adopt a rule suited to themselves. Patience
> is all that is necessary." Bishop Smith un-
> derstood by the answer that she did not in-
> tend to reap where she had not sown; and that
> neither would she, without a positive command,
> pretend to lead to higher spirituality people
> already far advanced in the science of the
> saints, part of which science was acquired
> during the Philadelphia riots when the Know-
> nothings burned their convent to the ground.
> Disappointed, therefore, but disappointed
> like a son of Saint Bruno [sic] he pressed
> the matter no further, returned regretfully

to Dubuque, and never saw Mother Francis or
Chicago * again. His holy death occurred
September 22 [23], 1865, and Mother Francis'
prediction regarding the Sisters of Charity,
B.V.M., was fulfilled to the letter. They
have since become a flourishing community,
and have adopted a rule especially selected**
for them in Rome.[29]

Despite this first refusal, the Bishop continued to
harbor the thought of associating the Dubuque Sisters
with the Sisters of Mercy. When his fellow Trappist,
Father James O'Gorman, who had succeeded Smyth as
prior at New Melleray, was assigned in 1859 as vicar
apostolic of Nebraska and Bishop of Omaha, the new
bishop lost no time in seeking the services of the
Sisters of Mercy. When seven of the Sisters left
Massachusetts for the west in 1868, Omaha was as raw
a young town at the gateway to a new territory as
Dubuque had been for the Philadelphia Sisters in 1843,
with the added hazard of a Civil War in progress.
Traveling by boat up the Missouri, the Sisters reached
Omaha on October 21, 1864. The account reads:

No sooner had the Sisters of Mercy set their
house in order and operation than the word
of Omaha's good fortune spread to neighboring
ecclesiastical jurisdictions. Immediately
Bishop Smyth of Dubuque was contriving how
he might arrange that his diocese could share
this religious asset. To Bishop O'Gorman he
divulged plans to amalgamate his Sisters of
Charity, but recently founded, with an approved religious institution. His wandering
eye lighted upon the Sisters of Mercy. Less
than three months after the group of seven
religious arrived in Omaha to start the foundation, Bishop Smyth disclosed his ideas:

"If you have too many of those dear Irish
Sisters, I think that I could take three at
least of them this coming summer for the City

---

* Bishop Smyth was among those present for the dedication of Holy Family church in 1860.

** While Rome approved, rather than selected, the
Sisters' rule, approbation was not to come for some
years after the death of Bishop Smyth.

of Burlington, which contains about nine thousand inhabitants.

"I desire to have some of the Sisters of Mercy in my Diocese, especially those who have been educated in Ireland. I have a project in view which I hope to carry into effect, if I should survive Father Donaghoe, & it is this: I intend, Deo volente, to have our good Sisters of Charity of the B.V.M., or as Father Donaghoe calls them, 'the Sisters of the Ten Commandments,' aggregated to some society already approved by the Holy See, & thereby render them a regular religious society. I consider that the Sisters of Mercy differ the least in their customs and constitutions from our Sisters in Dubuque, & the less difference in customs the less repugnance to a union with a regularly constituted society. Had I even one house of these good Sisters of Mercy, with a superior such as your present superioress (Miss Lynch of Galway), I could then at a proper time have some of our present Sisters go through a quasi-novitiate; after one year's noviceship, have them professed & then appoint some of them to act as Superiors of other houses, already established, & require the former members of these houses to go through their canonical novitiate & have them professed as real religious."[30]

Bishop Smyth's death within the year brought that story to an end, and fortunately so, for internal problems were a source of much pain and suffering to the Sisters in Omaha, adding their burden to the physical hardships they were enduring. Sister Ignatius, the "Miss Lynch of Galway," as first superior, was herself at the heart of the problem, though her successor, Sister Josephine Jennings, apparently did not improve matters. That Father Donaghoe was unaware of the Bishop's intentions regarding the BVM Sisters goes without saying, though he may have been serving the Bishop at the time as his vicar general.

* * * * *

In a letter to Father Donaghoe on February 14, 1857, Father Pelamourgues had urged the wisdom of beginning construction of the boarding school in Davenport while the people were favorable and while Judge

Mitchell and George Davenport were well disposed. He admitted that priests from the town would not be in a position to care regularly for the spiritual needs of Sisters and students, but he thought it possible that Father Alleman might be available and willing to act as their chaplain, while Father Trevis at St. Margaret's would no doubt be happy to go for confessions. He added his own personal position: " . . .though, as you know, I prefer always day schools to boarding schools, I will try to do all I can for your Sisters who are always good, humble, obedient and willing to do good. . . ."

While the full force of the panic of 1857 had not yet made itself felt, it soon began to affect every line of activity. Iowa's - and the country's - fear of banks and banking had left it without a safe and fluid medium of exchange. Though the effects of the panic were nationwide, the result of speculation and expansion without allowance for the lag between investment and returns, Iowa had its own problems. These included the circulation of depreciated and "wild cat" currency, chiefly from across the border in Nebraska, crop losses through continued rains and floods, and low prices for such crops as were produced. The firm of Cook and Sargent, a company which had supplied many banking services in Davenport, had been largely secured by the lands of Antoine LeClaire. December 16, 1859 saw that firm close its doors, a blow which LeClaire would survive but two years.

It was, then, not the best of times for entering on a new venture. However, ground was broken in July, 1858, and the Daily Morning News of Davenport, in its issue of July 27, did its part to arouse interest in the coming institution. The "College of the Immaculate Conception," it said, was being built of brick in the "Gothic style of architecture," with sixteen-inch walls and dimensions of 72 feet by 64 feet. Its location was on Marquette street near Locust which streets were then, however, merely lines on a map. The paper added that the new institution would be "under the immediate superintendence of the Sisters of Charity, who always devote themselves with untiring fidelity to the instruction of children entrusted to their care." The ten acres of land on which the building was being constructed had been donated by Judge G.R.C. Mitchell and George L. Davenport, probably under the inspiration of their wives, the former Rose and Sarah Clarke. [31]

The prospectus issued by the Sisters declared that "The facilities of access to Davenport are un-equalled by any city in the West. . . with lines of packets running every day to St. Paul and St. Louis. ". It added: "There is direct communication by Railroad with all the Eastern and Southern states by the Chicago and Rock Island Railroad, and to the whole of the West by the Mississippi and Missouri R.R.," though the former went only as far as Chicago and the latter only to Council Bluffs. It further informed the public that the "building is located in the midst of a grove of luxuriant timber, the shady walks of which. . . are elegantly laid out." But the word "timber" could still conjure up visions of wolves and snakes, of run-away slaves and even Indians, for the memory of the Spirit Lake massacre was not yet two years old. As for studies, the prospectus listed an interesting ar-ray of subjects, with classes open to girls of all grade levels:

> Orthography, Reading, Writing, Arithmetic, Grammar, Composition, Elocution, Geography (ancient and modern), History (sacred and profane), Algebra, Book-keeping, Astronomy, with the use of Globes, Mythology, Rhetoric, Chemistry, Natural Philosophy, Physiology, Botany, the French and German Languages, Music on the Piano, Guitar, etc., Drawing in Crayons, Monochromatic and Polychromatic; also Grecian and Oriental Painting, and prac-tical instruction in Needle-work, both Plain and Ornamental.

The tuition charge for the year, "including Bed and Bedding," was $110.00, with extra charges of art, mu-sic, science and foreign languages, as well as for washing.

When the Sisters who were to staff the new academy arrived in Davenport by boat, they, together with their boxes and bundles, were loaded into a farm wa-gon, to be driven two miles into the county to their new home. There was no road, and the mud holes were many and deep. Entering the scarcely finished build-ing, they found only packing boxes for furniture. But the new faculty were not the kind of persons to be daunted. Sister M. Margaret Mann, who until then had served as novice mistress, was to be their super-ior. The others included: Sisters M. Joseph and Xavier O'Reilly, both gifted in English and the lat-ter well-versed in Latin; Sister M. Gabriel Eisenger, a teacher of German; Sister M. Cecilia Dougherty, music teacher; Sister M. Regis Colligan,[Colgan] an instructor in art; Sisters M. Clement Harron and Stella Reid, elementary school teachers; Sister M. Isidora McCarthy, an able seamstress and housekeeper; together with Sisters M. Bibiana Hynes, Mathias Connolly and Genevieve McNamee, whose specialties are not now clear.

The official opening of the academy was intended to take place on July 12, 1859. "The Sisters rose that morning at the early hour of three, and after their morning devotions, did their weekly laundry work, tidied themselves and their potential school, and awaited the arrival of carriages. The sun rose high and sank in the west without bringing them the sight of a single scholar." In the two years the Sisters remained in the country the enrollment of their academy never exceeded seven boarding students, while the location made the attendance of day pupils impossible. Even the necessities were lacking, for the nearest water supply was a pond a quarter of a mile away. A badly constructed chimney led to near suffocation when the cold weather necessitated fires. The name "Poverty Point," soon applied to it, was apt, and when Mrs. LeClaire surprised them on their first Christmas with a dinner of roast goose and trimmings, she saved them from a lonely and a hungry day. While either Father Henry Cosgrove or Father Andrew Trevis rode out ordinarily twice a week to say Mass, on Sundays Sisters and students walked the two miles in to town through weeds and briars and along mud paths for Mass at St. Anthony's or St. Margaret's.

On July 5, 1860, Father Donaghoe wrote a letter of deep concern to George Davenport:

> . . .I now deem it best to get rid of the Immaculate Conception in this way, by renting it, until it pays for itself -- In this case, I will look to you, and my honorable friend Judge Mitchell for its accomplishment. In proper time we could resume under better days our wonted duties in the beautiful mansion. ... Do not let a day slip by to relieve me of a refusal - I wish you to be my sponsors to carry out the foregoing design, as you both have been donors. ...

There would seem little hope of renting the building, considering the difficulties of distance and transportation. At any rate, the Sisters continued on at

the location, save for those who helped out in other
schools as needed, until the large Sargent residence
on Brady street became available in 1862. Here classes
soon overflowed the house, and it was necessary to re-
condition the carriage house for their use. The Sisters remained in this situation for four years, until
the elegant mansion on Eighth and Main streets, built
by the banker Richard Hill in the days of his prosperity, was thrown on the market. At that time Father
Pelamourgues purchased the original academy building
for the Sisters of Mercy who came from Dewitt to establish a hospital. With the $6000 received from it,
Father Donaghoe was able to make a down payment on
the $35,000 Hill house. Though the streets were not
yet graded or paved, other fine homes were being built
in the area. Here the academy would prosper, adding
new buildings, at first wooden, but later of brick
and stone. These were paid for through careful economy, with a narrow income from the school eked out by
returns from the making of uniforms, "calisthenic
suits," and shrouds for the dead.

Davenport had long been a resort for wealthy
southerners who came there to "ruralize," hunt, and
escape oppressive heat and the threat of the yellow
fever which carried off hundreds each year in the area
along the lower Mississippi. The LeClaire House,
built in 1839, the third year of the town's existence,
had been constructed for their accommodation at the
cost of $35,000. It was a palace in the wilderness,
for the town was then innocent even of sidewalks, and
at night pedestrians found lanterns a necessity. Now,
as war threatened, many parents from the southern and
border states, seeking a place of safety for their
growing daughters, found it at the academy. Wealth
and refinement were the lot of many of these, and their
presence gave a status to the school which marked its
after history.

* * * * *

The name Kinsella repeats itself many times in
the Congregation's early history. There was Ellen
Kinsella from Wexford, Ireland, who became Sister M.
DeSales; Margaret from Waterford, Ireland, Sister M.
James; Hanora from Dubuque, Sister M. Salome; and in
later years, Margaret from Queen's county, Ireland,
Sister M. Andrew; Eliza from Dubuque, Sister M. Mar-
cellina; and in 1897, Sister M. James' niece Mary, a
graduate of the Immaculate Conception academy in Davenport, who became Sister M. Harold, for many years a

remarkable teacher and able directress of schools.
There was also Peter Kinsella - Brother Joseph - who
by a total commitment of his life and his property,
sought to serve God and extend aid to the Sisters on
the Prairie. Then Father Michael Kinsella - though
Father Donaghoe seems to have used the name James -
who made his early studies with the Brothers in Tullow,
Ireland, was a friend of the Community during its early
trials. Located at Garryowen for a time in the 1860's,
Father Kinsella came frequently to St. Joseph's to say
Mass for the Sisters when he knew that an absence or
an illness of Father Donaghoe would leave them without the sacraments. On one occasion he gave them the
rare privilege of a retreat.

Assigned to St. Paul's. Burlington, Iowa, Father
Kinsella opened the first parish school there in the
year 1856, with Clement - later Father Clement - Lowery
succeeding a bibulous, peregrinating teacher named Sam
who had kept a school in his own casual way. Lowery
held his classes in the dank basement of the old St.
Paul church. His seventy pupils, ranging from six
years of age to twenty-one, presented many problems,
but the young man persevered in his teaching of them
until he entered the seminary. After his departure,
Father Kinsella set about securing Sisters for his
school. To raise funds for their dwelling and for a
permanent school, he sold many of his personal possessions, including a gold watch and a number of volumes from his library. In 1859, a faculty of five
Sisters arrived by boat from Dubuque. They were Sister M. Vincent Donavan, superior, and Sisters M.
Joseph O'Reilly, Antonia King, Callista Doyle and
Christina Carroll. All but Vincent and Joseph were
just trying their wings as teachers, though Christina
was a woman of mature years. The Irish band met the
Sisters at the wharf and with much fanfare conducted
them to the church for a blessing, and then to their
convent and school. Their work prospered and soon
the faculty was increased to nine Sisters. While there
was much bigotry at the time, "laying aside all religious prejudice, the schools of the Sisters were patronized by the wealthiest and most influential and
refined citizens of the city."[32] For reasons best
known to himself, Father Kinsella requested the transfer of Sister M. Joseph in 1861, and she was promptly
made superior of the Sisters at St. Agatha seminary,
Iowa City, which had been opened shortly before.

* * * * *

The year 1859 saw the transfer of the students
from the St. Joseph academy on the Prairie to the
former hospital on the Fourteenth street hill in
Dubuque. There were several reasons for the change:
the need of larger quarters for the growing novitiate,
the difficulties of travel to and from the rural academy - the heavy rains of 1859 had left the rural
population marooned for many months - and the effects
of the panic of 1857, which had left hundreds of dollars unpaid accounts on the boarding school books. A
move into the city would let some boarders become day
students thus reducing their costs. Further, the
move would make a more practical use of the hospital
structure which would now inherit the title "St.
Joseph academy." Sister M. Gertrude Regan had served
as directress to the boarding school from 1848 to
1851, when she replaced Sister M. Catherine at St.
Mary's. Transferred back to the country in 1852, on
Father Donaghoe's return, she had resumed her charge,
along with that of superior of the motherhouse and
assistant to Mother Clarke.* Now Sister accompanied
accompanied her pupils to the Hill, where she would
remain in charge until Father Donaghoe appointed her
novice mistress in 1862, a position which she would
hold for fifteen years. Apparently after her appointment to her new position, the boarding school
was phased out, for by 1863 the Hill was closed, not
to reopen until 1867, and then, because no chaplain
was available to serve it, as an out-school from St.
Raphael's

The early summer of 1859 brought Archbishop Hughes

---

*

Sister M. Lambertina's Journal carries a significant remark on page 37: "The Philadelphia Sisters were
jealous of Mother Gertrude." Entering the Community
at the age of fifteen, after some period of attendance
at the Sisters' academy, Eliza Regan, later to be
Mother Gertrude, came from an impoverished home background, and lacked the qualities of face, figure or
natural talent which might have excited a degree of
envy on the part of the Sisters. That they were jealous of her rather suggests an advantage of a different order. Father Donaghoe's consistent choice of her
for positions of authority after the removal to Dubuque
may well have been foreshadowed by earlier evidences of
his favor, given, possibly, in an effort to compensate
her for her obvious limitations. The reactions of the
other Sisters seem to have put little restraint on his
desire to see her in positions of first importance.

to the Prairie [*] on a visit to the friend of his
youth. It was a grand occasion, with an address of
welcome, a festive song in his honor, and much effort
to make his entertainment worthy of his status.
Hughes' return was by way of Milwaukee and "the cars."
On arriving home he wrote Father Donaghoe that he
would have "the pleasure of sending you by express
within a few days, the package of wintergear which I
mentioned on the occasion of my visit."

In a letter of December 13 of that year, after
having thanked the Archbishop for his welcome gift,
Father Donaghoe presented an interesting proposal to
him:

> In summer last when I wrote you from Daven-
> port, your panegyrist of the Immaculate Con-
> ception [Sister M. Joseph, who had written
> his address of welcome] had agreed to exer-
> cise her talent in poetry -- now if it meets
> your approbation, as it has mine, I rejoice,
> because my predominant bump or tendency is
> greatly enlarged by attention to the correc-
> tion of its moral as well as its doctrinal
> fitness for children -- I mean a catechism
> in verse. The questions are the same as in
> the catechism now in use, and the verse em-
> ploys every word that could be readily used
> of the answer. This may account for the
> stiffness of some of its poetry. The idea
> is taken from a catechism in verse which was
> published and approved of by the Archbishop
> of Paris and other Bishops. My Dear Arch-
> bishop, I submit to you for corrections this
> little book and when you have done the need-
> ful to it - I request as a great favor to
> give it the approbation of the ordinary, as
> written or put into verse by a religieuse.

---

[*] There is mention in J.J.Norman's obituary account
of Father Donaghoe that Bishop Hughes twice visited
him on the Prairie. The first such visit doubtless
took place in early June, 1848, for on June 8 of that
year the Bishop was in Galena, Illinois, and he would
scarcely have been so close without a visit with his
friend, either in Galena or in Dubuque. He returned
to New York directly from Galena, via Milwaukee, (Bishop Quarter's Diary continued by his brother, Very Reverend Walter J. Quarter, as administrator of the Chicago
diocese.)

Next to put it into the hands of Mr.
Dunigan or any publisher you prefer -
who may take out the copyright in his own
name. . .

The response of the Archbishop was a graceful dodge.
After many months he wrote:

. . . I still preserve the poetical catechism which you sent me December 8th, 1859.
I have read it more than once - and with very
great pleasure. The only trouble is, as I
think I mentioned to you, that the Publishing House in which I had confidence has
ceased - or rather failed. It will keep,
however, and I trust the time is not distant
when it shall appear in print, for the instruction and edification of many souls.

The following brief excerpts give some indication of
the nature of the work, the original manuscript of
which remains in the Community archives:

A Sacrament's an outward sign
of inward grace - an act divine,
of grace the mystic fountain whence
our souls imbibe its affluence.
From every one does grace accrue
if we receive with meekness due.
. . .
In confirmation by the aid
of Bishop's blessing we are made
the temple of the Holy Ghost
and soldiers of the Christian host.
The Bishop prays the sacred dove
to come to us on wings of love,
anoints our fronts with chrism divine
and o'er us makes the sacred sign.

Father Donaghoe's enthusiasm for publishing the
works of the Sisters did not extend, however, to a
request made by the textbook publishers, Payson &
Dunston. Having had occasion to observe the classic
penmanship of Sister M. Angela Quigley, they requested
that she write the models from which plates could be
made for their school copybooks. From this he withheld his consent. [33]

* * * * *

When in the late summer of 1857 Father Trevis left

St. Margaret's Davenport, for France, in the hope of
gaining relief from a severe throat ailment, it was
Trevis' former pupil, Henry Cosgrove, whom Bishop
Loras assigned to the parish. Ordained by Loras'coadjutor, Bishop Clement Smyth, on August 27, 1857,
Father Cosgrove had made his early studies in the
garret school of Bishop Loras, after which Loras had
sent him for his philosophy to St. Mary Seminary,
Barrens, Missouri. After a year there he returned to
Dubuque, where he continued his studies under Father
Trevis at Mt. St.Bernard. He was among the three
students whom Trevis brought with him to Davenport for
further study, but Cosgrove spent his final year before
ordination in the St. Louis diocesan seminary at
Carondelet. Now, not yet twenty-four years old, and
just fourteen days ordained, he began his career as
pastor for the parish that Antoine LeClaire had generously endowed.

Father Cosgrove's early interest was in a school
for the children of his parish, and his request for
Sisters brought Sisters M. Clement Harron and James
Kinsella in January, 1860. The first rectory, which
LeClaire had replaced as scarcely worthy of its function, now became the first school, while the Sisters
resided at St. Anthony's through the winter months.
They hurried home each afternoon through good weather
and bad to help Sister M. Margaret Mann prepare for
evening classes held for working girls at St. Anthony's.
Before the new school year began, the old rectory had
been reconditioned to serve as convent. Boys and
girls were taught in separate classes, held in the
convent and the sacristy of the church. While the
older boys seem to have had as their teacher the ver-
satile Michael V. Gannon, lawyer and orator,[34] Sister
M. Clement was charged with the younger boys, a task
at which she was remarkably successful and which she
continued there for forty years.

Sister M. Agatha was transferred to Iowa City in
1861, Sister M. Margaret being given charge of the
three schools; St. Anthony's, St. Margaret's and the
academy. Soon, however, at the request of Father
Cosgrove that the Sisters at St. Margaret have their
own superior, Sister M. Clement Harron was appointed
to that position. As the enrollment grew, the faculty
was increased by the addition of Sisters M. Stella,
Aloysius,Francis, Louis, Pius and DeChantal.*

---

*In 1870 Father Cosgrove undertook the erection
of the church, which, upon the establishment of the

* * * * *

On December 8, 1851, Catherine Grace, at the age of twenty-five, entered the Community from her home in Dubuque. Two years later her sister Mary Ellen, then twenty, followed her. Born in Waterford, Ireland, the daughters of Thomas and Ellen Conway Grace, they were grandnieces of Bishop Thomas L. Grace, O.P.,[36] who had succeeded Bishop Cretin in 1857 to the see of St. Paul. The father of the two girls, on leaving Ireland, had sought for a suitable home for his family on a long cruise, visiting Australia and finally settling on a plantation in the West Indies. When the climate there affected the health of family members, Thomas sold his interests, purchased railroad stock with the proceeds and settled in Dubuque with his family of three sons and six daughters. Thomas' brother Patrick, who had entered New Melleray in Ireland, was among the earliest members of the New Melleray monastery near Dubuque. That Catherine and Mary Ellen were "brought up in luxury and accustomed to the conveniences of a wealthy home"[37] may help to account for the difficulties recounted in Sister M. Lambertina's Journal:

> The first S.M.____[Liguori Grace], dismissed in 1860, complained of the food, of hardships, and of the lack of Mass and the sacraments. Fr. Donaghoe was in poor health and did not want any priest to come, was perhaps afraid of meddling that would follow. Many thought Fr. Donaghoe would not last as long as he did, and did not like to bother him. Fr. Pelamourgues said that S.M.Lig__ wanted him to write to Rome concerning the way the Sisters were left without even Sunday Mass. Some went to Bishop Smyth, but he said that Fr. Donaghoe had made him bishop and that now he would not touch Fr. Donaghoe. Fr. Kinsella

---

Davenport diocese in 1881, became its cathedral. The parish name was changed to Sacred Heart, and after the brief episcopate of the Right Reverend John McMullen, Henry Cosgrove became Davenport's second bishop. Previous to his elevation, he had completed the parish plant by the construction of a school, a convent and rectory. The Sisters of Charity, BVM have served the parish continuously from 1860 to the present. At the time of its centennial celebration in 1956, the parish could count forty-eight of its daughters as BVMs.[35]

Rev. William Emmonds   Rev. Michael Kinsella

St. Agatha Academy, Iowa City

pitied the Sisters and often came to say Mass. S.M. Lig___died insane. When with us she used to kneel on the altar steps and say that she saw Our Lord. [38]

The account continues: "Mother Clarke, in obedience to Father Donaghoe, went through S.M. Liguori's trunk and read all her letters." Among the Doran Notes, we find:

S.M. Liguori was censorious; it was deemed best to dismiss her and under the circumstances, her sister also. They went to their relative, Bishop T. L. Grace, OP, of St. Paul (1859-1897). S.M. Liguori became Sr. Symphrosia, order of St. Joseph in Minnesota. She died insane. S.M. Andrew became Mother Clare, Superior-General, Sisters of Mercy in Pittsburgh.

Mary Ellen Grace entered the Sisters of Mercy in Chicago on June 4, 1861, and after teaching for some years at Xavier academy was assigned in 1869 to found a house of Mercy at Harrisburg, Pennsylvania. Continuing as superior there, Mother Clare opened a number of daughter houses, becoming superior-general of these, with motherhouse in Harrisburg. Mother Clare continued in office until 1903, and died after a lingering illness, on June 16, 1911. Regarding the former Sister M. Liguori, the McEntee account[*] reads simply:

"Catherine was received into the St. Joseph's community at Minnesota and was given the name Sister Mary Symphrosia."[39]

* * * * *

Shortly after Bishop Loras' death, Bishop Smyth named Father William Emmonds[41] (Emonds) pastor of St. Mary church, Iowa City. Father moved quickly in the improvement of church property and in the establishment of a small parish school. To this the Sisters of Charity came in April, 1860, living and teaching

---

[*]Whatever source the McEntee account relied upon for the following, it can scarcely be given full credit, for it says: "Before Catherine had made her vows she suffered a mental collapse, and was not admitted to her profession. When Catherine was dismissed, Mary Ellen left also and both Sisters retired to the home of their kinsman, Archbishop Grace."[40]

in the "Dunkel house" north of the church. The following year, through Father Emmonds' assistance, they
opened the St. Agatha seminary at the corner of Jefferson and Dubuque streets, with Sister M. Agatha
Hurley as superior. Those who assisted her in the
opening of the mission were Sisters M. Seraphina
Short, Chrysostom Reilly, Domitilla King and Justina
O'Hagan. Father Emmonds had received from Mrs. Mary
Haberstroh, widow of Ferdinand Haberstroh, a building
which had served as the Park Hotel, prosperous in the
days when Iowa City was the state capital. When "at
the earnest pleadings and solicitation of the Very
Rev. T. J. Donaghoe, chaplain and founder of the Sisters of Charity, B.V.M., in Iowa, Father Emmonds made
the deed of St. Agatha's Seminary to the Sisters,[42]
it was on the condition that the seminary be incorporated so as to hold property in its own right. On
March 11, 1864 the eleven Sisters then in residence
at St. Agatha's - Sisters M. Joseph, Seraphine, Chrysostom, Barbara, Sebastian, Domitilla, Christine, Ann,
Ambrose, Gregory and Fidelis - "all of whom are persons of full age, citizens of the United States and
the State of Iowa,"[43] as members of the corporation,
elected as its president, Sister M. Joseph O'Reilly,
then superior of the "seminary." The Haberstroh property was then deeded to the corporation under the
condition provided by the articles of incorporation
that

> this association shall always provide a
> school, free to all scholars who may choose
> to attend, and comply with the regulations of
> the school, for which no compensation shall
> be received except sufficient to board and
> clothe the teachers.

St. Agatha's thus became a private school, and as such
was quite popular, though Father Donaghoe's letter of
October 25, 1862, addressed to Sister M. Joseph did
not sound promising:

> . . . . I permit you to receive the number
> of boarders that you asked, that is five.
> They are to bring their own conveniences
> such as bed and bedding, etc. My resolution
> is not to allow any money to be expended in
> any of our houses without my full consent.
> You would not wonder at this if you only
> knew the pain of mind as well as the sacri-
> fice of property I have had to endure in or-
> der to pay my debts. Thanks be to God I am

succeeding. You know I always have borne in
silence my sorrows even to appear cheerful
while my mind was only bearing up against
the burden. I can do this no more, my constitution suffers too much.

Requirements included a Sunday uniform for all boarding students, consisting of " a blue merino dress,
with cape of same, and plain white collar, black silk
apron and green bonnet"! Apparently the academy later
furnished the girls with bed and bedding; however,
other requirements included "four table napkins, knife
and fork, a table and a teaspoon and a glass goblet."[44]
The curriculum closely resembled that of the Davenport
academy.

While it was chiefly German parishioners who
built St. Mary's, the first Catholic church in Iowa
City, the Irish population had grown more rapidly, so
that the Germans had come to be rather an appendage
to the main body of the congregation, a situation with
which they were not at all happy. When the Reverend
F.X. Weninger, S.J., gave a mission there in 1862, he
encouraged the Germans to undertake the building of a
church of their own. The result was a simple frame
structure to serve for church and school, under the
name of St. Francis Xavier. After being served for a
year by a young Bohemian priest, it was left without
a pastor. Since Bishop Smyth could not supply another,
the congregation turned to the Franciscan Fathers at
Teutopolis, Illinois. Father Capistran Zwinge was
assigned to the church in April, 1864 on a temporary
basis. While the congregation did not care to have
dealings with Father Emmonds, they did arrange with
the BVM Sisters at St. Agatha's for teachers for their
small school, and for a time Father Capistran depended
on them to bring him his meals. After a brief time
Franciscan superiors found it necessary to withdraw
Father Capistran for missionary labors, but the people
were so greatly troubled that he was allowed to return
until June, 1865. Meanwhile many Bohemian people had
settled in Iowa City and a Bohemian priest was on his
way. Attempts to fuse the two nationalities, however,
proved futile, and gradually many of the Germans drifted
back to St. Mary's with St. Francis Xavier finally
closing in 1875. [45] Eventually the Bohemian members
built a church of their own - St. Wenceslaus.

A letter addressed by Mother Clarke to Sisters M. Justina, Seraphina and Domitilla at St. Agatha's and dated June 7, 1861, was found among Sister

Above: Sister at St.Agatha's, 1861,in first habit
M.Domitilla King   M. Seraphina Short
M. Agatha Hurley   M. Justina O'Hagan
At Right: Faculty in 1865,photographed by Father
Emmonds; Bottom row: Srs. M. Sebastian and
Bridget. Middle row: Srs. Fidelis, Joseph and
Benedict. Top row: Srs. M. Seraphina, Germanus
Vincent, Ann, Christina (or Domitilla?), Barbara

M. Domitilla's simple keepsakes after her early death in 1865. It is of special interest as the only extant letter written to her Sisters by Mother Clarke before Father Donaghoe's death. It reads:

> My dear Sisters,
>   I received your dear letters which were most gratifying to hear that you were so well and happy. I was sorry to hear that poor Sister Mary Agatha was ill with a cold. I hope she is better.
>
> Sister M. Justina, I address you first, as you are the oldest. I know you will be kind to your dear sisters, because it is in your power, from the nature of your duty, to make them happy when they are tired during their arduous duties, to have everything ready in time for them. I know also that you will get anything for Sister Mary Agatha that she can make use of during her illness.
>
> My dear Sister M. Seraphina, you have the most laborious duty, but the most profitable for time and eternity; you teach the poor of of our Lord. Do thank Him for that glorious privilege, and when you see a very poor and neglected little one, look on her with love and be kind to her, and the poor little one will be grateful and will love you. When she learns to know God, she will love Him for your sake.
>
> My dear Sister M. Domitilla, you are teaching the select school. Although your numbers are less, your duties are more arduous, as those who can pay a little will expect you to teach them everything. It is dangerous when it produces pride in the teacher, to be able to meet all their wants, and not seem deficient, but I know your good, cheerful and willing heart. You will do your best.
>
> Now for giving you a little news of home. First, our dear Father has been better this last month than I have seen him for a long time. All the healthy sisters are happy; the few delicate ones are about the same but are in good spirits as they can walk about this fine weather.

Sister Mary Gonzaga and her forces have exhausted their ingenuity and pride on the grounds. To crown all, Rev. Father has put up for them a beautiful picket fence all around. They have arrived at the height of their ambition. We have nearly all our housekeeping done. The garden looks so beautiful that it was expressed by visitors this week that St. Joseph's is the most beautiful place they have seen. I am afraid it was a dangerous remark; it will only fan the pride of the above named parties.

Now I know you will open your eyes when you see the length of this letter. It is long since I wrote one so long. I must stop now, hoping that you will be good, and do and suffer all for God, His holy mother, and for the good of those souls they love so much. Such as my poor prayers are, you shall have them that you may be truly humble. All other virtues will follow.

Your ever affectionate
Mary

The Sisters residing at St. Agatha's were, then, serving a small free school in connection with St. Mary parish, and a second small school at St. Francis Xavier, as well as conducting St. Agatha's. That all did not go smoothly is evident from comments in Father Donaghoe's letters through the years, at least until Sister M. Joseph was transferred elsewhere in 1867. How much of the problem centered in the Sisters' dealings with Father Emmonds is not clear, but he was not a man to be tampered with. While the historian of St. Mary church describes him as "irresistible, pious, learned and zealous,"[46] the Franciscan Sisters who came to Iowa City in 1875 found him "disconcertingly formidable when moved to displeasure."[47] As a pastor he was zealous, drawing his people together through the establishment of various organizations and societies, and imparting all the beauty and dignity he could to church services. In addition to performing his parochial duties in Iowa City, Father Emmonds travelled by train, ox-cart or sleigh to a number of stations in the area, often driving all night and working without rest throughout the next day. With the rapid growth of the parish, Father Emmonds undertook the erection of the present St. Mary church in 1867, and Father Pelamourgues, as vicar general, laid

its cornerstone. Two years later, on August 15·, 1869,
Bishop Hennessy performed the solemn ceremony of consecrating it, a rite permitted only to churches which
are debt-free and solidly constructed. Meanwhile
Father Emmonds was occupied with the organization of
his St. Joseph institute of advanced education, in
the teaching of which he was assisted by a lay faculty.
A man with such energy and ability would scarcely
have had great patience with persons of lesser
strength and talents.*

Mother's letter takes us back to the Prairie.
Sister M. Lambertina's <u>Notes</u> tell us,

---

*In 1872 when the Irish withdrew from St. Mary's
and established their own St. Patrick church on the
other side of the city, their pastor served as chaplain to St. Agatha's, and the girls of the new parish
attended there. Sisters went from St. Agatha's to
teach the boys in a small school in the St. Patrick
parish. In 1892, after the departure of Father Emmonds,
the St. Mary parish purchased from the Sisters the
small free school which they had conducted in accordance with the terms for the incorporation of St. Agatha's.
Sisters of St. Francis from Greenfield Park, Milwaukee
taught the parish school for a brief period, but in
1895 arrangements were made for the services of the
BVM Sisters. A corps of six teachers then took
charge of the combined grade and high school, the
latter opening in 1897.

A regulation requiring that novices complete their religious training before being sent to the mission
came at a time when parochial demands for teachers
were most insistent. This led in 1909 to the closing
of several academies, including that of St. Agatha.
Meantime, both St. Patrick and St. Mary parishes had
been provided with parochial schools taught by the
BVM Sisters, and in 1910 St. Patrick parish erected a
twenty-room convent on Harrison street to accommodate
the Sisters. In 1922, the new St. Patrick grade and
high school opened its doors. It is in this building
that Iowa City Catholic school today serves the elementary school children of all the Iowa City parishes.
The building which housed St. Agatha seminary was
sold to the University of Iowa for dormitory purposes
in 1910. In the year 1958 the new Regina high school,
built on the edge of the city made provision for all
the students of secondary level in the area. It presently serves junior high school also.

Once when S.M. Gonzaga, wearing a blue calico dress, was breaking stones in the walk leading to the gate, Fr. D. came down from the graveyard, talking to himself as was his wont when excited. As he passed S.M.G. he told her to come to his house. She went to M. Clarke for permission and was told to change her habit first. Fr. D. rebuked her for wearing a blue dress, and she said she had nothing else but her merino which she did not wish to spoil. Fr. D. Said, "I will get you a black one." He gave her a black calico, so when she is censured for wearing a black cotton habit she answers that Fr. D. gave it to her.

Father Donaghoe wrote to Sister M. Joseph of home activities about this time:

"We are cutting craut and a big wash after the corn and potato harvesting. Indeed we bless God and are united. . . ."

Again Father wrote of "the dried pork - yes and some flour you must get -- I see them rendering lard." That the corn husking was the work of the novices appears from a mention of Brother Anthony driving them out to the field in a farm wagon, the group in a holiday mood.

Sister M. Gonzaga and her sister, Sister M. Peter - Bridget and Margaret McCloskey - had come from Feeny, County Derry, Ireland, where they had been educated in the convent of the Sisters of Mercy. When in 1850 their brother John decided to come to America, they prevailed upon him to bring them with him. John bought a farm about three miles from the St. Joseph motherhouse and boarding school, but a year later he was killed while taking a piece of heavy machinery to Galena, Illinois for repairs. Bridget wrote for advice to their half-brother Patrick, for, as she said: "You have always proved yourself a father and more than a father." Patrick, who at that time was under the care of a physician in Paris, suggested their hiring a governess, though Margaret was nineteen and Bridget seventeen at the time. With no such person available, they appealed to Bishop Loras, who suggested their enrolling at the academy on the Prairie. This they did, and on September 8, 1852, Bridget entered the religious life, her sister Margaret following her on

October 10. Both were received on July 16, 1853, and professed on the same date a year later. Margaret, then Sister M. Peter, died "from a lingering illness" on December 27 of the same year, just one day before the death of Patrick in Paris. Patrick had bequeathed each of the sisters $6000.00 "to be invested in good state Stocks not transferable to the Academy nor to any other institution nor to any person or persons during their lifetime."[48] The fact that Sister M. Peter's death preceded Patrick's caused her inheritance to revert to the estate, to be divided equally among the heirs. Sister M. Gonzaga, however, "received $870.00 interest paid semi-annually from the stock held in trust - Indiana Bank Stock." For a time it was thought that Sister's mother, a widow, would join Sister M. Gonzaga on the Prairie, but there is no evidence that she did so.[49]

* * * * *

Rumblings of war seem to have been but faintly heard at the rural motherhouse, with only the rarest mention of it even in Father Donaghoe's correspondence. One exchange of letters, however, has relevance. In a letter dated November 29, 1851 and written by Archbishop Hughes, then on a mission to France to secure the neutrality of the European powers, he spoke of serious diplomatic problems that had arisen: the burning of the Harvey Birch by the Confederate vessel Nashville, the admission of the Nashville into the British port of Southhampton, and, finally, the capture of Southern commissioners on board a British vessel flying the British flag. Father Donaghoe's response on December 24 expressed his joy and relief at receiving the Archbishop's letter, for he had feared that Hughes and General Scott had been taken as hostages by the Southern forces. He wrote too of General Jones, who, on his return from Bogota, had been interned, for his communications with his longtime friend, Jefferson Davis had made him suspect. As for the war within the country, Father's cousin, General Shields[50] was on his way to take over his command, and word of battles was imminent, for the Union forces were concentrating along the Mississippi to sweep it clear of rebel forces all the way to New Orleans.

Meantime life went on in Iowa, where Bishop Smyth had become concerned about the education of the poor. His letter of February 15, 1862 to Father Donaghoe indicates that some of the girls were leaving the

Sisters' school for lack of means to meet its small
tuition charges. Having paid off a large proportion
of his debt on the new cathedral, the Bishop decided
it was time that he should give some support to the
school for girls as he was already doing for the boys'
school, especially as he regarded that the public
schools presented greater dangers for the girls than
for the boys. He therefore pledged $300.00 a year to
the Sisters "for the education of poor children in
the rudiments, such as reading, writing and a little
figures. If they or others desire to learn something
higher let them pay for it, but in a separate room
from the free children." The distinction can hardly
have been a happy one for Mother Clarke and the Sisters, who had always sought to prevent any evident
difference between the free and the paying students,
though they would have welcomed the opportunity to
serve more of the needy.

* * * * *

The city authorities of Fort Dodge, Iowa had set
aside "Seminary Square" in the hope that a religious
denomination would accept it for a school site, and
on April 18, 1862 deeded it to the Church, "on condition that the local Catholics should erect thereon
within the coming two years from the date thereof. . .
a good substantial school building."[51] The Reverend
J.J.Marsh, in whom the Sisters in Davenport had found
a friend, assumed the responsibility, contributed
$1100 of his own resources along with his labor, and
erected a two-story building with belfry. In a letter addressed to Father Donaghoe on June 23, 1862
Father Marsh suggested that he had long awaited a letter telling when he might plan for the coming of the
Sisters, in accordance with a prior arrangement. He
would come for them, but did not wish to arrive at a
time when they were not prepared. Word had reached
him, however, through Father Brazill of Des Moines,
that the Sisters were in readiness. His plan was to
leave Dubuque with them on July 9. He added the suggestion:

> I should be pleased if you could have their
> luggage brought into Dubuque, so that I may
> upon my arrival there send it off upon the
> Rail to Cedar Falls where there will be a
> team to bring it on here, so that it may
> arrive as early as they do.

Evidently everything went as planned, for Father Marsh

wrote again from Fort Dodge on the 11th telling of
their safe arrival the previous night, a day earlier
than he had anticipated. They had gone by rail to
the end of the line at Cedar Falls, and as the Sisters protested they were not too tired to go on, he
had engaged a stage coach. In this they travelled
all Wednesday night and until nine-thirty Thursday
evening, when they reached Fort Dodge "all safe, all
well, and all in good spirit." School opened before
the building was completed, classes being held in the
church. Sisters M. Michael Nihill, Regina Cosgrove,*
Cassiana Griffin and Hildegarde Whelan were the Fort
Dodge pioneers. Their mission there lasted but a
brief three years,[52] for their loved pastor died of
pneumonia on February 22, 1865. The Reverend John F.
Kempker, in notes for his History of the Catholic
Church in Iowa, wrote:

> Father Marsh, born in Wolverhampton, Eng.,
> in 1818, a man of most agreeable presence,
> genial in his ways, erudite, and scientific
> in his studies. He was a great lover of mu-
> sic, an excellent orator, and possessed a
> splendid, well-cultivated voice. Friends
> everywhere he went - his endearing friend-
> ship for his people found expression not only
> in spiritual ministration, but in timely ad-
> vice on all subjects. At the time of his
> death in the bitter cold of winter it took a
> messenger two days to reach Des Moines and
> it required Father Brazill a journey of two
> days before he could reach his esteemed fel-
> low -priest to administer to him the last
> sad duty of friendship. In 1865, his friends
> affectionately and reverently placed a precious
> monument in marble to his memory in Ft. Dodge.

* * * * *

The Reverend Philip Laurent had served for some
time as missionary in the Dubuque diocese before his
assignment to Muscatine. On one occasion he had accompanied Bishop Loras up the Missouri river to Council
Bluffs on visitation. While the Bishop returned by
boat, Laurent made the return trip on horseback, stopping at each settlement of Catholics to administer the

---

*Sister of Father Henry Cosgrove.

sacraments and give encouragement to the struggling
families. Laurent's knowledge of German, together
with his even disposition and his gracious manner,
fitted him well for the difficult task of maintaining
peace between the Irish and German factions in Muscatine. But even worse troubles for him than those of
his factious congregation lay in the bigotry of the
non-Catholic population. Badgered and insulted, he
was forced after a time to discontinue taking his
meals at the local restaurant, and he faced difficulties even in calling at the local postoffice for his
mail. Returning one day to his poor quarters adjoining the little church on Cedar street, he slipped on
the icy road and fell headlong into a ditch filled
with freezing water. An old woman passing by mocked
and taunted him, clapping her hands with joy at his
unfortunate situation. He might have drowned had not
a passerby reached a pole to him, enabling him to
scramble out. Being without a change of attire, Father Laurent had to keep to his bed without food until his heavy garments had dried out. It is not surprising that in 1862 he decided to end his missionary
labors and return to France.[54]

Father Michael Kinsella, sent to replace Laurent,
set about building a convent - the present one - to
contain two classrooms as supplement to the one-room
schoolhouse built in 1858 by a temporary pastor,
Father Peter Magne. His request for Sisters brought
Sister M. Angela Quigley as superior, together with
Sisters M. Barbara Ess, Placidus Doyle, Felicitas Carr
and Jerome Cosgrove. When the Sisters arrived in May,
before the completion of the convent, Father surrendered to them his living quarters with a German family.
He slept in a curtained off corner of the one-room
school, until on August 14 the convent was ready to
receive the Sisters. In preparation for their coming
he had held a bazaar, the proceeds of which enabled
the St. Mathias school to open free of tuition.

Father Laurent's departure from Muscatine had been
a source of grief to his parishoners and they wrote
begging him to return. Responding to their plea and
encouraged by the offer of his niece, Teresa Laurent,
to come with him, Father was soon back with his people.
Here Teresa, a capable woman and accomplished musician,
did much to make his living conditions more comfortable,
helped with the altar and the choir, and softened the
hearts of many who had formerly made his life unpleasant.[55] Meantime, Sister M. Angela became ill and returned to the motherhouse. Sister M. Agatha replaced

her as superior. In addition to the elementary classes,
the Sisters shortly opened a"select school," the predecessor to the modern high school. To it there came many
girls, Catholic and Protestant alike. Father Laurent
was a source of encouragement to the Sisters and of
support to Sister M. Agatha, especially in her double
office of superior and principal. Sister M. Felicitas
wrote many years later regarding Sister M. Agatha:
"Sister did much to have the Sisters respected here,
for it was a very bigoted place when we came here, and
if I do say so, we are highly regarded by our Protestant people and former pupils."[56]

* * * * *

On December 19, 1863, Father Donaghoe wrote Sister M. Xavier in Davenport, giving word of her mother's
death in Dubuque eight days before:

> My dear Child,
>   We have good reason to thank Almighty
> God that your Mother was attended by Rev.
> Father Francis Walsh and funeral service was
> given in St. Patrick's Church of which he is
> now the pastor. Her remains are now in the
> cemetery on the Bluff in the same grave with
> her beloved daughter, Sr. M. Francis. This
> occurred on the 11th, just two days after the
> anniversary of Sister's death in 1845. Requi-
> escant in pace. Do follow her with your
> prayers as we are now engaged also for her
> repose. I am writing to Sister Mary Joseph..

Then the letter turned to Sister M. Catherine:

> I am now sending for Sister Mary Catherine
> who is only struggling into life again. She
> was near going. I hope she will be able to
> come in the cutter. We are still in fears
> of Sister M. Philomena. In the midst of
> life we are in death . . . .

A trip in an open sleigh over eight miles of rough and
frozen roads would seem sufficiently taxing on a well
woman, yet frail Sister M. Catherine survived it. Two
years before, Father had written Sister M. Joseph
telling of the death of Sister M. Aloysius in Dubuque
and her wake and burial at St. Joseph's. To that message he had added: "Sister M. Catherine came with
the funeral - she is now lying in a precarious state.

I think she will get over it - I told her I don't like
the Dublin folk to take hint of going off. . . ." Yet
Sister was to survive for three more years, until
October 8, 1866. A part of this time she spent in
Davenport at the academy with Sister M. Margaret Mann,
doubtless a welcome change for Catherine from the Dubuque principalship for which Bishop Loras had found
her so ill-suited.

Bishop Smyth had planned an ad limina visit to
the Holy Father in 1861, but hesitated in view of the
unsettled times. When, in 1862, he saw that war was
a long term reality, he set out for Rome. On his return, passing through Ireland, the Bishop was joined,
in County Clare, by Ann and Sarah Ryan of Killaloe,
whom he had encouraged to enter the Dubuque Community.
In Philadelphia he met Mary Kelly, niece of a priest
friend of Father Donaghoe. It is possible that she
was a visitor there, for her home is listed as Joliet,
Illinois. Mary too accompanied him to Dubuque. The
coming of the Ryan sisters, who would become Sisters
M. Rosalia and Euphrasia, marked the end of what had
been a steady flow of Irish-born girls into the Community. Later recruits would be almost exclusively
Iowa-born, until the Chicago missions began to feed a
steady stream of postulants into the rural novitiate.

The boarding school which had been transferred
from the Prairie to the Fourteenth street hill in
1859 had been phased out by 1862. Sister M. Gertrude
returned to the motherhouse that fall, to begin her
duties as novice mistress, taking with her the two
Ryan sisters and Mary Kelly, postulants. Sister M.
Gonzaga had been appointed to succeed Sister M. Margaret as mistress of novices when the latter became
superior of the Immaculate Conception academy in
Davenport in July, 1859. Only three postulants entered in 1860 and none in 1861. Though numbers were
small, or possibly for that reason, Sister M. Gonzaga
did not find the work of novice mistress congenial.
Going in to Dubuque for "two weeks," she remained at
the Hill until it was closed in 1863, only then returning to the motherhouse. Two who entered in March,
1862 seem to have received their novitiate training
under Sister M. Margaret in Davenport. Sister M.
Gonzaga joined the faculty of the select school in
the Bishop's former residence in Dubuque as music
teacher. In 1873 Sister was appointed superior of
the Immaculate Conception academy.

* * * * *

In 1864, the Reverend James Scallon, pastor of St. Clement church, Dewitt, Iowa, requested Sisters for a parochial school there. Dewitt had long been a stepchild to the Church: Father McKenny, for some years pastor, had had more interest in and aptitude for farming than for ministry. Father Pelamourgues had been asked to serve it as an out-mission from Davenport. After brief experience of the situation there, he made clear his conviction that a thriving parish in Dewitt would drain from St, Anthony's many enterprising farm people who could as easily attend the Davenport church as the one at Dewitt. However, Father Scallon was now engaged in putting the Dewitt parish on a solid foundation. At his request the Sisters opened a small school there, with Sister M.Agnes Burke as superior. With her went four young Sisters, M. Louis Byrne, Antonia O'Brien, Aloysius Fennell and DeChantal O'Regan. Their accommodations were poor in the extreme, the convent, "a dilapidated little cottage," offering little protection from wind or weather.* Sister M. Antonia died there the next year at the early age of twenty-seven, and her body was returned to the motherhouse for burial. Sister M. Assisium, the former Mary Kelly, came to replace her. Though Father Donaghoe had known from the beginning that Sister was mentally unstable,[57] he had accepted her in deference to her priestly uncle. The peculiarities of her conduct were a contributing factor to the closing of the mission and led to her dismissal on August 13, 1867.[58] In regard to the closing, Mother Clarke wrote succinctly to Sister M. Margaret on June 21, 1867: "Father Scallon was here yesterday. He did not comply with the conditions of the building so he will not get the Sisters."

The Dewitt pastor then sought assistance from the Sisters of Mercy in Chicago. His cousin, the able Mother Borromeo Johnson, responded as superior of a small group of religious. Living conditions were quickly improved, and the future began to look sufficiently hopeful that Mother Borromeo considered the

---

*The biographer of Mother Mary Monholland, RSM, said of it: "The frame convent in which they lived was a shell. Rain poured through the roof. The wind rushed in at doors and windows. In winter the cold of the house was most unbearable."

erection of a boarding academy in the town. However,
being shortly apprised of the great need of a hospital
for both the physically and the mentally ill in Davenport, she turned her attention instead to the establishment of facilities there. Mother Borromeo's experience as a nurse of the ill and wounded in the
Civil War stood her in good stead. The original Immaculate Conception academy building, left vacant by
the BVM Sisters in 1862, she found to be in good condition and suited to the work at hand. Through the
services of Father Pelamourgues, it was now made
available to the Sisters of Mercy. The hospital then
established was quickly recognized as a great boon to
the city, and with the cooperation of the people of
Davenport it steadily expanded its services. An early
successor of Mother Borromeo in its administration was
Mother Mary Monholland,[59] who had earlier refused
Bishop Smyth's request for Sisters to train the Sisters of Charity in the religious life. She would now
find them friends in her new enterprise.

Sister M. Baptist Seeley was teaching in the Davenport academy when she wrote the following letter on
August 27, 1864. Sister does not identify her cor-
respondent but she does describe an interesting aspect
of community life:

> Dear Sister,
> You may remember that when I was putting
> down the fractions in your little book I
> called your attention to one particular ex-
> ample which I had never succeeded in working.
> Perhaps you have. And I am just going to tell
> you how I happen to know it now. The Sisters
> here had not seen the new edition till one of
> the young ladies brought it this summer. Of
> course she was using it during the day and we
> could not get a peep at it till the children
> went to bed. So one evening while we were on
> retreat, Sister Mary Cecilia came to me and
> said: "Sis, I have an example in the algebra
> that I can't do and Miss Keith is just up to
> it and I could not go near her tomorrow if I
> haven't it." When I looked at it I found it
> was my old customer & told her I did not think
> I could do it but I would try; so I tried till
> I was convinced I could not & went to bed.
> But Cecilia did not give up so easily. She
> went into the oratory and said the Memorare
> and told the Blessed Virgin she might do it
> or let it alone which ever she pleased, but

if she would do it she would say the Salve
nine days in thanksgiving. She took the slate
and worked it correctly without the least difficulty. When she told me she had it I
opened my eyes in astonishment and asked her
how in the world she did it. She said, "I
didn't do it. The Blessed Virgin did it for
me." I thought it showed such a kind and
sweet solicitude in our dear Mother to give
such prompt relief in such little things that
it would do you as much good to hear it as it
did myself. I think there is room for it in
the little book in its proper place so you'd
better set it down.

Then Sister wrote the following example, giving the
details of its solution:

"Ex 9th Page 202 $x\sqrt{a + x^2} = b + x^2$"

and ended with: "Love to all and pray for your own

Sister Mary Baptist." [60]

Immaculate Conception Academy
I   The first structure was more likely only
     one of the high peaked sections indicated
II   The Hill House
III A Growing Institution

FOOTNOTES - CHAPTER VI

1. Report to the Propagation of the Faith, Lyons, France, for 1846. References to these reports have for their source the Hickey collection, copies of which are available in the Griffith files, Chancery Office, Davenport, and in the archives of Loras College Library, Dubuque.

2. Cf. M. M. Hoffmann, The Story of Loras College, 1839-1939, (Dubuque: Loras College Press, 1939.) p.

3. Loras to Propagation of the Faith, February 11, 1853.

4. Correspondence, Jones Collection, Historical Library, Des Moines, Iowa, also Loras-Jones correspondence, Dubuque Archdiocesan Archives.

5. It is interesting to compare with the source material quoted the account given in the Church Founders of the Northwest, by the Reverend M.M. Hoffmann:

> Through the Sisters of Charity, Bishop Loras planned another necessary and important institution for his diocese, and that was a sorely needed Catholic hospital. He commenced the erection of a hospital building at a convenient location on a hill which is today the center of the city of Dubuque. The process of building lasted through 1852 and 1853, but when it was about completed, Loras found that Father Donaghoe, the chaplain and adviser of the Sisters' community, was opposed to taking it over. Finally after considerable argument, and after the Bishop yielded to Father Donaghoe's demand that the Sisters were to have full control or else the right of refusal, a document was signed on December 1, 1853, promising to convey to the Sisters the hospital property - a valuable piece of four lots and the building - when incorporated. But still no move was made to occupy it, and there it stood in May of 1854, unopened, with broken windows and

utterly uncared for. In this month, Senator
George W. Jones, who had already made a generous contribution toward it, introduced a
motion in the United States Congress to use
it also as a Marine Hospital, that is for the
river cases of sickness on the numerous federal and private steamers that stopped at
Galena and Dubuque. Furthermore, the Dubuque
city council commenced arrangements for the
care of city patients when the hospital should
be opened. p. 313.

The footnote on the above reads: "Letters and
documents in Dubuque Archdiocesan Archives and
in Mt. Carmel Convent, Dubuque, Father Donaghoe
letters Memorial and Art Building, Des Moines,
Iowa."

The writer has had access to all of this matter,
and has made use of it as above.

6. Hoffmann, op.cit., page 124.

7. Loras to Donaghoe, letter, August 12, 1855.

8. Doran, Early Days, p. 154.

9. Ibid., p. 154, also McGuire, p. 167.

10. Book of the Missions, p. 68 (BVM Archives).

11. Doran, Early Days, p. 265.

12. Trevis to the Sisters, December 13, 1891.

13. J.P.Marschall, Francis Patrick Kenrick, the
    Baltimore Years, Doctoral dissertation,
    Catholic University, 1965, p. 182.

14. Ibid., p. 183 ff.
15. Ibid., p. 181.
16. Unclassified notes, Griffith files.

17. Louise Callan, The Society of the Sacred Heart in
    North America, (New York: Longmans, Green & Co.,
    1937,) p. 505.

18. The Reverend M.M.Hoffmann wrote in his Church
    Founders of the Northwest, p. 235, with refer-
    ence to the Sisters of Charity in the two poverty-
    ridden years they maintained the St. Philomena

academy in Davenport: "Father Pelamourgues found himself in constant petty difficulties with the Sisters." He supplies no authorization for his statement and the present writer has found no basis for it beyond that which may be suggested by the letters quoted. However, Father Pelamourgues' remark may be interpreted as expressing his own humiliation at the conditions the Sisters faced in Davenport after responding to his urgent invitation, rather than recalling an unpleasant attitude on their part.

On page 312 of his work, Father Hoffmann speaks of Loras' desire to have the Religious of the Sacred Heart in "some cities" of the diocese, among these Dubuque. He wrote:

> While the number of schools taught by the Sisters of Charity of the B.V.M. of Dubuque had been increasing especially in Dubuque and its vicinity, Bishop Loras conceived the idea of introducing the Madams of the Sacred Heart into some cities of the diocese to conduct what were then termed "select schools." He was urged to do this principally by Father Pelamourgues, but owing to the opposition of the Sisters of Charity of Dubuque he abandoned the idea as far as Dubuque was concerned.

The present writer has found no evidence in any of the Loras correspondence to indicate any intention on his part of introducing the Religious of the Sacred Heart into Dubuque, nor of any opposition on the part of the Sisters of Charity to their introduction into any city of the diocese. However, Father Hoffmann seems to find some such evidence in the following communication of Loras, dated "in December of 1853." He does not indicate to whom the letter was addressed. He seems to find something culpable on the part of the Sisters in the Bishop's phrases "particular circumstances" and "these difficulties." The communication reads:

> The establishment of a house of the Ladies of the Sacred Heart of Jesus, a so distinguished order of the Church, has been postponed by a few particular circumstances, but I feel confident that these difficulties will soon disappear, and that the garden of our church will soon be embellished by the sweet

and brilliant flowers which bloom elsewhere in abundance under the influence of this amiable and divine heart.

Then with reference to the failure of plans for the Religious of the Sacred Heart to materialize, Hoffmann says on page 313:

> However, the entire project was later given up, and after peace was established between Father Pelamourgues and the Sisters of Charity, an academy [sic] conducted by the latter was reopened in Davenport in 1855.

The accent in all three cases is ours. When the Sisters returned to Davenport in 1855 it was to teach in the parish school at St. Anthony's, and not to conduct an academy. The question of the Immaculate Conception academy, opened in 1859, did not arise until after the Sisters had established themselves at St. Anthony's. As for peace having been established, there is no sound evidence of a war to demand the establishment of peace.

19. Bishop Loras reviewed briefly the history of his association with the B.V.M. Sisters in a report sent to the Propagation of the Faith on January 26, 1854:

> In 1843 God inspired me to appeal to the Sisters of the Holy Virgin. I went to Philadelphia and was lucky enough to persuade their worthy superior, M. L'Abbé Donaghoe, to let them come to Iowa, with the consent of Msgr. Kenrick, the bishop of that city. Five of them accompanied me at first, and a short time afterwards the rest of the community came on and with them, M. Donaghoe, who is now my vicar general. This worthy man advanced in age, did not hesitate a moment to leave the welfare of the second city of the United States where he had exercised with much fruit the holy ministry for sixteen years, to come and live in the forests and solitudes of Iowa, with these heroic spouses of Jesus Christ and beloved daughters of Mary. After many unbelievable difficulties of every sort, they came up to the number of 83. They do a lot of good to the religion in instructing children in many cities of

the diocese. They have a beautiful boarding
school three leagues from Dubuque, composed
of 36 boarders of the best families of the
country. There also is their motherhouse,
where they have at present 8 or 10 novices
who form themselves to religious virtues and
to the art of instructing under the observation of the Superior General who is a real
saint, and of the venerable Mr. Donaghoe.

20. A spirited account of the times, written at Davenport in May, 1854, gives interesting data:

. . . May we not look forward to days of prosperity? Are we not on the line of the great
thoroughfare across the State of Iowa to
Council Bluffs, Fort Laramie, to the South
Pass, Salt Lake, and to the Pacific Ocean?
Is it then to be wondered at that our town
has doubled its inhabitants in the last three
years, that four hundred houses were built
here during the last year, and as many more
anticipated; that there is not a room ten
feet square to rent in the city, and that
the public houses, and private boarding houses, cannot accommodate the people who are
emigrating to this country? Is it surprising
that real estate commands such high rates,
and that money is worth twenty per cent? . .

Twenty years ago there were less than five
thousand white inhabitants between the
Lakes and the Pacific Ocean! Now there are
nearly two million. Fifteen years ago Chicago brought her breadstuffs from Eastern
States; now she exports each year not less
than five million bushels of grain, and one
hundred and twenty thousand barrels of beef
and pork.

Seventeen years ago, I was three weeks making the journey from New York, by canal and
steamboat, to Davenport, but now it is performed in three days. . . . Six years ago
Chicago had not a foot of railroad completed,
now there are nearly five hundred miles completed within the limits of the State, and
over two thousand in process of construction.

21. There was a struggle to be made before the bridg-
ing of the Mississippi, a foreshadowing of the

war of the States, for the man who stood in its
way was Jefferson Davis, secretary of war in
President Pierce's cabinet. In 1853 he had petitioned Congress for $100,000.00 for the construc-
tion of a road from Memphis to California for
"national defense," and for a time he felt assured
of receiving the appropriation. While Government
Island #6, the site of Fort Armstrong and later
of the arsenal which featured prominently in the
Civil War, was regarded then as no longer needed
for defense against the Indians, Davis recognized
that it was one of the most advantageous sites in
the west for an armory or arsenal, and for the
manufacture of materials of war. A bridge here
would give tremendous advantage to the North in
case of hostilities. Davis sought an injunction
to prevent its construction, and a plot was soon
under way among the southern cities in further-
ance of his efforts. Nevertheless, work went on,
although even after the bridge was completed,
several attempts were made to destroy it. Iowa
Journal of History, "Jefferson Davis and the Rock
Island Bridge," Cf. Dwight L. Agnew (January,
1949,) pp. 3-15.

22. Iowa Journal of History, "Iowa's First Railroad,"
     Dwight L. Agnew, (January 1950,) p. 1 ff.

23. Doran, Early Days, p.155, ff.

24. The Dubuque Daily Herald and Express for July 1,
     1858, gives an interesting account of such a ses-
     sion as the Davenports had attended.

ST. JOSEPH ACADEMY EXAMINATION
Reverend T.J.Donahoe, Superior. Conducted by the
Sisters of Charity of the Blessed Virgin Mary.

Yesterday morning we went out to St. Joseph's
Seminary, to witness the examination of the
young ladies, pupils in this most excellent
and well-conducted institution. We found on
our arrival a great many of our prominent and
distinguished citizens present, among whom we
noticed Judge Lovell, Bishop Smith, Charles
Gregoire,Esquire, Colonel McKenney of Chat-
field and many others.

A large awning had been fixed up in front of
the building, under which the young ladies were
examined according to the program published
below. The task, or rather pleasure, of

examining was confided to the young ladies
by turns in the various exercises. We cannot speak too highly of the astonishing pro-
ficiency of the pupils, and the quick and
correct answers which were given without a
single hesitation or error to all questions
even of the most difficult character. In
English grammar we have never seen more thor-
ough and finished grammarians. The French
class in the French grammar and pronunciation
were faultless. In both exercises of memory,
oratory and poetry, they acquitted themselves
in a highly creditable manner. The program
of exercises was agreeably diversified with
comic, moral and satirical dialogues, singing,
music and dancing. Some of the dialogues
were highly amusing and instructive, and were
spoken freely and naturally. The ladies possess fine natural dramatic talents which have
been successfully cultivated. The exercises
in Geography, History, Astronomy, Chemistry,
Botany, etc., were illustrated by the young
ladies who personated the various characters,
qualities and bodies of the science in which
they were examined. Their perfect drill and
discipline in their various movements and
descriptions were astonishing, and much ap-
preciated by the spectators.

We were compelled from want of time to return
to the city at noon, but that firm and enterprising friend of education, Judge Lovell,
promised to give us a description of the afternoon, and a list of the prizes distributed,
which we shall publish again.

St. Joseph's Seminary is an institution of
which Dubuque may well be proud, and the
pleasure and satisfaction of the large and
select audience, especially the parents and
friends of the pupils, were emphatically expressed

PROGRAMME
Opening Hymn - Memorare - by Miss Dodge
English Address   by Miss O'Brien
French Address   by Miss Hoffmann
German Address   by Miss Urill
Song - Strike the Harp   by Miss O'Brien
Second Class Reading and Grammar
First Class Reading and Grammar

Dialogue   by Miss A. Gregoire
                                  and Miss F. Helm
Duette - Love Schottish - by Misses McKinney
                                  and Dodge
   French Grammar and Dialogue
                                  by Misses Hoffmann
                                  and Gregoire
                    [etc.]
It is probable that the statements regarding the
German and French accomplishments were well with-
in the range of truth, for Sister Mary Barbara
Ess of Bamburg, Bavaria, had entered just two
years before, and about the same time Sister
Mary Hildegarde Guise, from Hamburg, Germany.
The latter, however, was of the ancient French
family of Guise, exiled to Germany by the French
Revolution. Young Magdalen Guise had come to
Philadelphia with an uncle in the diplomatic ser-
vice, and came to know our Sisters there. Also
of Hamburg, Germany, and entering at the same
time as Madgalen was Sister M. Marcelline Shearer.
Eager as the Sisters were for their own improvement as teachers, they were ready pupils of the
two languages. The school at the time was under
the direction of Sister M. Gertrude, with Sisters
M. Baptist Seeley, Camillus Martin and Xavier
O'Reilly as classroom teachers, and Cornelius
Clarke, doubtless teaching music.

Pupils of the academy at this time included:
Mary and Katherine, daughters of General Dodge;
Maria and Lynn, daughters of General George Jones,
who named the states of Wisconsin and Illinois;
Olivia, daughter of Judge Hempstead; Ann and
Catherine, daughters of Senator Seeley of Wis-
consin; a Miss Clarke of Minneapolis; Helena and
Mary Ellen Shields, St. Louis; Matilda Gregoire
and Elizabeth Espey, St. Genevieve, Missouri;
Catherine, daughter of Judge Dunn of Wisconsin;
Mary, Elinor and Sue Lorimer, Ann Quigley, Margaret
O'Brien, Rose and Frances Johnson, Malvina Evans
and Josephine Scott, all of Dubuque. Ann Seeley
later became Sister Mary Baptist, and Ann Quigley,
Sister Mary Angela.

25. RACHS, "Peter Richard Kenrick, Bishop and Arch-
     bishop of St. Louis, 1806-1896," S.J.Miller,
     Vol. 84, March, June, September, 1973, p. 54.

26. Original in archives, Notre Dame University.

27. Mary Gilbert Kelly, OP, Catholic Immigrant Colonization Projects in the United States, 1815-1860, New York: U.S. Catholic Historical Society,1939, cf. p. 143, ff. also Wittke, op. cit.pp. 62-74.

28. Annals of Iowa, "Religion in Iowa - the Catholic," Charles Blanshard, June, 1962, p. 387.

29. Sister of Mercy, Life of Mary Monholland,One of the Pioneer Sisters of the Order of Mercy in the West, Chicago: J. S. Hyland & Co., 1894, p. 79.

30. Henry W. Casper, S.J.,History of the Catholic Church in Nebraska, 3 vol., Milwaukee: Bruce Press, 1960, Vol. II, pp. 75,76.

31. The writer has borrowed from her own master's dissertation, The History of the Immaculate Conception Academy of Davenport, Iowa, and of the Foundations of Catholic Education in that City, submitted to the Catholic University of America in June, 1941, under the religious name of Sister M. St. Joan of Arc. The account as given here is drawn from the research done at that time.

32. Saint Paul Church. History of the Parish and Burlington's First Church Bell, 1840-1972.n.a., n.p., pp. 35-36.

33. Doran Journal, p. 75.

34. Michael V. Gannon, native of Dublin, a popular orator, was always a warm friend of the Sisters. His daughter Ada, or "Addie," was widely known as a parliamentarian and a teacher of parliamentary law, and as such gave many courses in the Congregation's high schools and academies. She was an ardent alumna of the Immaculate Conception Academy, and on her death was waked there. Two of her sisters entered the Congregation becoming Sisters M. Cecilian and Rose Clare, or later, Rosemary. They are now deceased. Ada was on familiar terms with many of the great, including the presidential candidate, Al Smith and the Irish president DeValera.

35. Reverend Edward C.Greer, Cork Hill Cathedral, The Chronicle of St. Margaret's and Sacred Heart Parish, Davenport, Iowa, 1856-1956.(Davenport: Gordon Printing Company, 1956) pp. 236-241. The

Kempker notes in the Griffith files.)

A second cause for Emmonds' departure is suggested
by a letter of Father Laurent, dated May 10, 1892
and preserved in the Congregation's archives. It
tells of Father Emmonds' having given credit to
a bogus priest who had represented himself as a
relative to Father Laurent and an ex-missionary
from China and the South Sea Islands. Emmonds
allowed the impostor to preach, say Mass and hear
confessions for ten days, and finally to take up
a generous collection "for the missions," before
contacting Father Laurent. His humiliation at
so grave an error added to his determination to
leave the diocese. In notes dated October 21,
1918 Father Kempker reports that after some years
Emmonds returned to his home in Westphalia, where
he became a helpless imbecile, broken and penniless, and died forgotten and unmourned. To this
account Father Kempker adds the comment: "He
would have made a grand bishop."

42. Joseph Fuhrmann, History of St. Mary's Church,
     Iowa City, 1840-1916. (Iowa City: n.p. 1916)p.105.

43. Articles of Incorporation, St. Agatha's file,
     Secretary's office.

44. Commemoration booklet: St. Patrick's Church,
     Iowa City, Iowa, A Century of 1872-1972, (Iowa
     City: n.a., n.p.) p. 17.

45. Cf. Theodosius Plassmeyer, "The Church in Early
     Iowa City," Iowa Catholic Historical Review,
     February, 1936, pp. 21-37.

46. Fuhrmann, p. 43.

47. Eunice M. Mosel, OSF, They Have Taken Root. The
     Sisters of the Third Order of St. Francis of the
     Holy Family. (New York: Bookman Associates, 1954)
     p. 128.

48. Letter from Mrs. B.F. Eschleman to writer, from
     New Orleans, August 19, 1974.

49. Ibid.
50. General Shields, a cousin of Father Donaghoe,
     was an able officer in the cause of the Union.
     He had served with distinction in the War with
     Mexico. Efforts on his part to settle Irish

immigrants on land in Minnesota were sufficient
to bring on him the displeasure of Archbishop
Hughes.

51. Folder, "History of Corpus Christi School, Fort
Dodge, Iowa," taken from the diamond jubilee
booklet, The History of Corpus Christi Parish,
1932.

52. The Sisters of Mercy opened a day and boarding
school in Fort Dodge, under the Reverend T.M.
Lenihan, continuing until December 12, 1900 when
a fire destroyed the entire plant, whereupon the
Sisters left for Mercy Hospital, Iowa City. The
Sisters of Charity returned in 1902, the new com-
munity comprised of Sisters M. Agreda, Euphemia,
Casimir, Immaculata, Irene, Florina and Evelyn.
The school continues under the direction of the
Sisters of Charity to the present.

53. Griffith Files, Davenport.
54. Ibid.
55. Ibid. An account by Laurent's niece,Teresa Laurent,
in 1925.
56. Sister M. Felicitas Carr to S.M. Pulcheria McGuire,
November 24, 1903.

57. Doran Journal, p. 37."The first Sister M. Assisium
had an uncle a priest in Philadelphia. That was
the reason Father D. received her and kept her
even after it was known that she was not in her
right mind."

58. Letter, Father Donaghoe to S.M. Agatha, August
24, 1867: "Sr. Assisium is gone home and wants
back even if she should walk. Now I'd not turn
her out - the poor child - They think of sending
her to the Sisters' hospital in St. Louis."

59. Details regarding Mother Borromeo, etc., have for
their source the commemoration booklet by Sister
Mary Mark Kerin, RSM, The Relief of Suffering
Humanity, A Centennial History of Mercy Hospital,
Davenport, Iowa. n.p., n.d.

60. Account printed in The Spectator, St. Joseph
Academy school paper, Des Moines, Iowa, January,
1932, tells of an episode which had occurred in
Philadelphia many years before:
Sister M. Eliza Kelly had a surprise visitor at
the motherhouse at about this time. A young priest

introduced himself by asking if she recalled the
boy who was George Washington Jefferson's partner on their First Communion day in Philadelphia
many years before. "Oh, indeed I do remember
him," Sister exclaimed. "Are you that boy? I
thought that something good would come to him,
and now I see that the best thing in the world
is his. Thank God!" It had happened in their
Second street school where Sister's class had
included a single little Negro boy. He was an
intelligent lad and eager to learn. When the
day for the children's First Communion approached,
Sister was troubled lest the little lad be
slighted by the white children. In her instructions she tried to impress on them that all souls
were equally dear to God, yet she feared that he
would be left without a partner in the ranks.
It was then to her great relief that her caller,
John McGuigan, had stepped forward and asked the
privilege of walking with George Washington Jefferson in the First Communion procession.

St. Anthony's, Davenport, Iowa

Bishop John Hennessy. D. D.

St. Raphael Cathedral
Dubuque

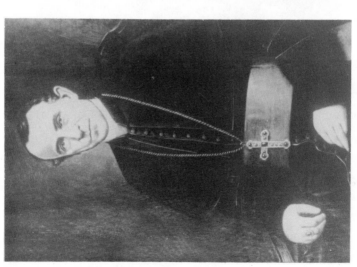

Bishop Clement Smyth, O.C.S.O.

The Man From Tyrone
Rounds Out His Years-
1864-1869

The war years, included in chapter seven, found
divided allegiances among the inhabitants of Dubuque,
yet those years added prosperity to a stable foundation of wealth. An upsurge of bigotry resulting in
the establishment of the Know-Nothing party was
largely dissipated by the response of Catholics to the
war effort and the restraint of their clergy. The
Bishop's plans for peace included an orphanage to be
conducted by the Sisters for children left ·fatherless
by the war. His death in 1865, just prior to the time
set for its opening, brought the project to an end,
for the priest-superior was unwilling to commit the
Sisters to any work other than education. That year
a group of Sisters were sent to conduct a school in
Des Moines. The vacancy in the Dubuque see was filled
in September, 1866,and in 1867 the new Bishop gave permission to the Sisters to respond to a request by the
Jesuit Fathers to serve the new Holy Family parish in
Chicago. The parish expanded at a remarkable rate and
schools were multiplied as needs arose. The account
then turns to the devotional practices prescribed for
the Community of Sisters, and the lives of those Sisters engaged in the heavy labors of household and
farm. It includes a partially thwarted attempt to
reveal something of the hidden and mystical life of
the mother foundress. It tells of serious problems
raised by the approaching death of the priest-superior
regarding Community properties, since the titles to
all save the original land purchases were recorded in
his name, and he was loathe to make a will. The command of the Bishop resulted in his signature to an
instrument conveying all Community properties to the
mother foundress who succeeded to the superiorship on
his death in January, 1869.

While Father Donaghoe had been instrumental in the elevation of Bishop Smyth to the episcopacy, little evidence remains of a close association between the two men after the death of Bishop Loras.* There is no record to indicate that the Bishop renewed Father Donaghoe's appointment as his vicar, or that Father so functioned, though he retained the title in his correspondence until his death. It would not be Father Donaghoe, but Father Brazill of Des Moines, who would administer the affairs of the cathedral parish during the interim after Smyth's death. The years 1858 to 1865 found Father Donaghoe occupied with the opening of new missions and in the care of his deteriorating health, while the Bishop was preoccupied with the duties of his office, especially his building projects.

To finance the building of Dubuque's new cathedral in the years of deep depression, it was necessary for Bishop Smyth to solicit funds both at home and abroad, while his determined flock "made their veins bleed" to see it completed. Smyth was fortunate enough to secure for its architect John Mullany, who, after an apprenticeship with his father in County Tipperary, had worked under the great architect, A.G. Pugin, in Manchester, England, and had had considerable experience in church construction in the States before coming to Dubuque. Gothic in its conception, save for the truncated tower, the soaring lines of its interior, rising above hand-carved altars and a phalanx of oaken pews, combined a serenity of spirit with a sense of stability and permanence. It thus

---

*This may have its explanation in the failure of Bishop Smyth to preserve his correspondence as Loras had done, or in the zeal of an over-efficient housekeeper or curate in clearing out files to have them in readiness for Smyth's successor. Father Donaghoe's files for those years contain almost no evidence of correspondence, in contrast to the years when Smyth had served as prior to the Trappist community.

brought to early Iowa a form of art which had its
roots in a faith and culture reaching back through
the centuries. Although Trevis' departure in 1855
had resulted in a temporary closing of Mt. St. Bernard seminary, Bishop Smyth completed the college
structure, and in 1860 twelve clerics were enrolled
as students. Smyth would say of them, however, that
probably not more than one third would persevere to
ordination. By 1864 its enrollment had increased to
twenty-five students, but not all of these aspired to
the priesthood.

The acceptance by the people of Dubuque of the
new Bishop opened up to him resources such as Loras
had never enjoyed, though the town had long been laying a solid foundation of wealth - in mining, lumbering, manufacture, the processing and transportation
of farm products, and as the source of supply for
long wagon trains of immigrants bound for the West.
The setback of the depression years was only temporary, and now war prosperity was more than supplying
for the losses. The need for the materiel of war -
heavy vehicles, provisions and ammunition - found Dubuque ready, its situation on the Mississippi being
especially fortunate for transportation. Particularly
pressing was the demand for lead. The Shot Tower,
which still looms above the city, was a busy place.
Here the molten metal, poured through screens from a
height, fell into tanks of water below to form the
much-needed lead shot. With the cathedral paid for,
Smyth took advantage of the prosperous years to build
a rectory worthy of the church it served. In simple
Georgian elegance, it rises today above its broad
lawn. Three stories in height, the interior is
marked by a gracious spaciousness, while its solid
structure and satisfying proportions reflect a perennial good taste, quite in contrast with the heavy and
more flamboyant style seen in many of the now decay-
ing mansions of the area. Both church and rectory,
preserved in their original spirit and design, are as
much a part of Dubuque's presence as of its past. The
original rectory was then remodelled and equipped to
serve the Sisters as residence and select school,
permitting them to move from the rude quarters on the
corner of Third and Bluff streets which they had occupied for more than twenty years.

The chronicle of such accomplishments would suggest an atmosphere quite at variance with the war
spirit of the sixties. The Mississippi had long been

a medium of trade and association with the South and in many of Dubuque's people Southern sympathies were strong. Democratic in politics, they were divided in their allegiance to the Union. Some resolved the conflict of loyalties by joining with the organization of Peace Democrats to protest the war, while others openly flew the Confederate flag and sent their sons to defend it. But the fifties had brought many settlers to Dubuque from the largely Protestant New England-New York area, and with them had come the spirit of abolition and republicanism. Dubuque's Irish population, Democratic in political allegiance, generally supported the Union and were willing to fight for its preservation, though certainly not for the freedom of the Negroes, whom they regarded as competitors in the labor market. Their resentment persisted against a system which left the Irish laborer on a scale below that of the Black slave who, as property, enjoyed greater security and was spared the more hazardous types of labor.

The situation was further complicated by a resurgence of the Nativist spirit in the form of a political party which came to be called the Know-Nothings. Its followers feared the growing strength of the Catholic Church in the country; convinced that its hierarchical structure endangered the democratic system, they revived all the old canards of past bigotry. Controversies over education and intemperate attacks on Protestantism by aggressive leaders, such as the widely distributed "Decline of Protestantism" lecture by Archbishop Hughes, fanned the flames. Such unwarranted remarks as that carried in the St. Louis Catholic publication, the Shepherd of the Valley, in 1851, had been clearly menacing:

> . . . the Church is of necessity intolerant. Heresy she endures when and where she must, but "if the Catholics ever gain a large majority, religious freedom in this country is at an end," - so say our enemies - so say we.

Inflammatory and irrational writings in other Catholic periodicals had provoked opposition while fighting it. The editor of the Boston Pilot wrote also in 1851:

> Whenever you find a free-soiler, you find an anti-hanging man, woman's rights man, an infidel frequently, bigoted Protestant always, a socialist, a red republican, a fanatical teetotaller, a believer in mesmerism,

> Rochester rappings. . . . You get a rather
> dirty set, you perceive, when you join their
> ranks.

That these incendiary remarks were in response to attacks can scarcely be taken as an excuse for their
tone. Counter attacks such as that published in the
Miner's Express of Dubuque on November 1, 6, 13, and
26, 1851 were equally vindictive:

> Children of Bigoted Catholic Island [sic]like
> the frogs that were sent as a plague against
> Pharaoh, have come among us. The Irish are
> to [sic] idle and vicious to cultivate land.
> In a political point of view, they are but
> mere cattle.

Before the war broke out, Smyth had expressed deep
concern lest there be a show of violence against the
Church within his diocese, but with the response of
the Catholics to the country's need, there had come a
reversal of feeling.

On the national scene, the election of the Republican Lincoln was an affront to the Irish Democrat,
and as President he became the object of constant attack in many Catholic papers. Some of these made violent protest against the Emancipation Proclamation as
an arbitrary abuse of power. Many opposed the war as
unconstitutional, and vigorously protested· the draft,
moving into a position which classified them as Copperheads. In this Denis Mahony [1] was a powerful and
persistent leader, with a strong body of followers,
not only in Dubuque but throughout Iowa. In spite of
all this, the Irish provided more than their share of
fighting men, and spirited Irish companies and bat-
talions were filling up the ranks of the Union army,
while Irish generals were proving themselves brave
and talented leaders for an heroic fighting force.

The public reaction of Catholic churchmen to the
war was muted. They had no desire to see the ranks
of the Church torn by dissension, as had happened in
the Protestant churches and in the country itself.
Regarding slavery as an institution to be tolerated
but not expanded, they maintained a pastoral rather
than a political position throughout the war. Loras'
situation, had he lived, might well have aligned him
personally with the South, for in a small way he had
been a slave-holder, though a kindly one, during his
Alabama years. Smyth, on the other hand, while

striving to keep dissension at a minimum, was strongly
loyal to the Union. His condemnation of a radical secret society propagated by Mahony, and his efforts to
restrain Mahony's anti-administration activities, had
their good effects, at least among his own flock. But
when the assassination of Lincoln shocked Smyth into
an open stand, Southern sympathizers took their revenge.

The Bishop, in the prosperous times the city was
enjoying, had purchased a fine carriage and a span of
young Morgans which he kept in a stable near the rectory. A fire set in the middle of the night destroyed
stable and contents. The act aroused the indignation
of the townspeople, Protestant and Catholic alike,
and when the Bishop left the city on a confirmation
tour, they made full reparation by providing him with
a handsome new equipage.

Through all the conflict and confusion, Bishop
Smyth had planned for peace. The departure of the
Sacred Heart Brothers from the diocese in 1860 had
left it without an order for the teaching of high school
boys. Smyth, who had once been a teaching Brother,
and who had himself conducted a school during his
years as prior at New Melleray, had been planning to
introduce the Christian Brothers into the city, and
was making preparations for a school to receive them.
But a second problem was pressing for action, one
which involved Father Donaghoe's arrangements for the
Sisters. Smyth's principal concern, as expressed in
his report of February 18, 1864 to the Propagation of
the Faith, had to do with an orphanage. The war had
left its harvest of orphans, and, in the spirit of
the times, the institutions being planned by the state
to receive them would be Protestant-dominated. With
this in mind the Bishop purchased a building with
three acres of ground immediately northeast of the
hospital site on Fourteenth street, and was involved
in reconditioning and furnishing it when he left on a
confirmation tour early in 1865. Smyth was never a
robust man. After travelling from place to place by
whatever means lay at hand - in heavy farm wagons, by
stage, through rains and high waters - he came home
suffering from a severe case of sciatica. Confined
to his bed for some months, he nevertheless wrote to
Lyons on September 4, 1865, regarding the plan for
his St. Mary orphanage: I hope to have it ready in
three weeks to give in charge of the Sisters of Charity. Peace has at length come." His report continued: "Such is the nature of my complaint or sickness

that I have to write lying down, either in bed or on a couch, and it is very painful." Despite his illness, the Bishop arranged for the dedication to take place on the feast of the Guardian Angels, October 2. Complications in his condition developed and death came quickly, on September 23.

Plans for the boys' school had partial fulfillment in the building of St. Raphael school for boys through the untiring efforts of Father O'Reilly, but its teachers would be the Sisters, not the Christian Brothers. As for the orphanage, though Father Donaghoe had shown his interest to the extent of giving a loan to the Bishop to help finance it, he did not accept responsibility for conducting it. Thus, prized projects of two bishops, undertaken on the assurance of Mother Clarke that the Sisters were willing for any service, and specifically for that of a hospital or an orphanage, had come to nothing.*

Meanwhile obsequies for the Bishop brought Kenrick from St. Louis, Bishop Duggan from Chicago and doubtless many others, with Father Pelamourgues, as administrator of the diocese, directing all. The body, clad in full pontificals, would lie in the mortuary chapel below the altar of the cathedral he had built. A vault had been prepared to receive his remains and those of his predecessor. When workmen raised the metallic casket of Dubuque's first Bishop from its sandy bed, though the body had been laid away without embalming, "the venerable and benign countenance was seen quite unchanged; his features were uninjured by decay."[2]

The diocese would be without a bishop for a year. While clerical gossip had it that Smyth's successor would be "an Irishman from St. Louis," - it proved to be the Reverend John Hennessy - Pelamourgues considered it his duty as administrator to raise a question which would not be answered until 1881 - the division

---

*As for the participation of either Father Donaghoe or the Sisters in the war effort, whatever may or may not have been the extent of it, nothing was recorded. Certainly homes bereft by war casualties or beset by illness were the objects of their charity. With encampments of soldiers in Dubuque, Davenport, and other areas in which the Sisters were engaged, many needs must have pressed upon them, and it is difficult to believe that they did not respond.

of the diocese. In a letter to the Propagation of
the Faith in December, 1865, he suggested Davenport
as the most suitable site for the see city, since it
was now the largest city in Iowa, with a population
of 17,000 inhabitants. It further boasted three Catholic churches and "the best schools in the country."
He declared also that "it excels in beauty all the
cities built along the great river."

* * * * *

The first new mission Father Donaghoe accepted
for the Sisters after the close of the war was that
of St. Ambrose, Des Moines, under its pastor, the
Reverend F. Brazill.[3] His letter to Father Donaghoe,
written from Des Moines on October 19, 1865 signaled
future problems for the Sisters:

> . . . If you calculate they would make money
> you are mistaken. If they intend to charge
> every Catholic child that would come to their
> school, in that case they would not be success-
> ful, but if no regard be paid to money unless
> from secondary standpoint, and that a remote
> one, then they would be able to effect much
> good.
>
> I have no wish that this parish should be
> embarrassed by any other burdens than its
> own; I except the motherhouse to which of
> course an annual contribution should be made.
> Now do not misunderstand me. I do not want
> those earnings to go for improvements either
> in buying furniture, property or instruments,
> and all for the permanent benefit of the or-
> der. Let whatever they buy be their own,
> but for the benefit of this place and them-
> selves. At a future date they will no doubt
> be well able to assist other places. I
> think this is fair and will give me definite
> knowledge of the terms they come on. I will
> attend to them always with respect and be
> kind to them, will give them a good dwelling
> house and school house rent free, but if I
> furnish both I expect to be paid for the for-
> mer, i.e., its furniture. Please write to
> me stating what furniture they bring, etc.,
> etc. I will be ready to go for them in two
> or three weeks. If they could bring any
> Pianos so much the better, but if they can-
> not we can I think get one or two on credit

until they can be paid for. Let me hear from
you immediately.

It seems evident from Father Brazill's letter that the
education of the parish children was to be the Sisters' burden, rather than that of the parish itself.
As for the source of the Sisters' living, that seems
not to have been his concern.

Father Donaghoe referred Brazill's letter to
Sister M. Margaret for her advice, adding: "I look
upon it as a bad beginning, because the furniture
would be a debt that we are hardly able to meet - if
music we would have to give free education, and money
must be put up in property about Des Moines or in
furniture or instruments." However, his mind was soon
made up, for a letter of instructions to Sister M.
Michael Nihill as the chosen superior, bore the date
of October 28. In it Father set down the condition
that all tuition, such as it might be, was to be paid
directly to the Sisters as some assurance of their
livelihood. To accompany Sister M. Michael were Sisters M. Baptist Seeley, Hildegarde Whelan, Ursula
Kenneally and Euphrasia Ryan, the youngest of them
twenty-five years old. Classes would be held in the
original church structure built under the direction
of the parish's first pastor, Father G.H.Plathe. A
new brick church built by Father Brazill had been
dedicated the previous May.

Accompanied by Father _____ Egan and Doctor
Smythe, the Sisters set out from Dubuque, taking the
train to Boone, since there was no railroad connection with Des Moines. A derailment in the midst of a
heavy snowstorm sent the train's rear coach, in which
the little party was riding, down an embankment and
into a pond. The cries of a mother whose child had
been hurled through the car window and into the water,
alerted other passengers. Only the infant's foot was
visible when one of the Sisters waded in and pulled
the child out of the muddy water. Three of the passengers were severely injured, while two others met
death in the accident. Dr. Smythe, caught in the
wreckage, attended the wounded as soon as he could be
released. Reaching Boone at nightfall, all sought
accommodations in the one miserable hotel. The trip
on to DesMoines was to be by stage coach. The roads
were almost impassable, and the driver could be induced to make the trip only by the payment of increased fares. As they were crossing the bottom
lands of the Skunk river, the wheels of the coach

sank deep into mud, the horses rearing and plunging
in an attempt to free them. The driver threatened to
turn back and could be induced to continue only by
additional fares. Forty more miles of wretched roads
brought them, benumbed and mud-spattered, in view of
the city lights. St. Ambrose church was a welcome
sight. Their convent was not ready on their arrival,
and Father Brazill took up a temporary abode in the
sacristy of the church, turning his rectory over to
the Sisters. School opened December 4 with one hundred fifty Catholic children.[4]

* * * * *

Dubuque's frontier days had ended by the close
of the Civil War. Untouched by its ravages and enjoying a solidly based prosperity, the young city
awaited the arrival of its new bishop, with a fine
cathedral, a spacious residence and a coach and pair,
his heritage. That he would inherit his share of
problems also goes without saying.

John Hennessy, born August 20, 1823 in the
"golden vale of Limerick," was one of the twelve children of William and Catherine Meany Hennessy. Only
nine, however, survived infancy to share in the family rosary in the evenings about the turf fire. By
his twelfth birthday, John had determined to be a
priest, and so became the favored child of the household. The presence of several master-scholars in the
area assured the soundness of his preparatory education, as it was the custom of such men to invite promising young scholars into their homes for tutoring.
By the time of his enrollment at All Hallows College,
Dublin, John was well-grounded in Greek, Latin, English and the other essential subjects. To choose All
Hallows for seminary training was to choose the life
of a missionary, since the college received its support from bishops seeking recruits for the missionary
dioceses, and they assured its students of necessary
financial aid.

At best the Hennessy family was poor. The potato
blight of 1847 which brought on the great famine meant
distress, a situation which occasioned the young seminarian's departure for America late in that year. He
was followed in time by seven of his sisters and brothers. His travels brought him directly to St. Louis,
where Archbishop Peter R. Kenrick received him and
arranged for his entrance into the St. Vincent seminary
at Cape Girardeau, Missouri, kept by the "CM's" or

Lazarist Fathers. John and seven companions were
transferred a year later to the newly established diocesan seminary at Carondelet, Missouri, near St.Louis,
for the study of philosophy and theology under two
future bishops of Chicago, Anthony O'Regan and James
Duggan. Although a seventh of St. Louis' population
died of cholera in the epidemic of 1849, the seminary
was spared its visitation. It was a year of disaster
for the young city for it was in May of that year
that the great fire had swept away a mile-long stretch
of waterfront, barely sparing the new cathedral.

Ordained on All Saints' day, 1850, in the stately
cathedral Bishop Rosati had consecrated six years before,
young Hennessy was assigned to the St. John Baptist
parish at New Madrid in the southernmost part of the
state. An old city, it had served as supply center
for Spanish troops in the days of Spain's control of
the Louisiana territory. But its prosperity had received a setback as Spanish control gave way to French.
Shortly after the entire Louisiana territory became
the possession of the United States, a succession of
severe earthquakes in the area had diverted streams,
swallowed up lands, drained lakes and formed new ones.
New Madrid had been without a priest for a year when
the young pastor assumed the care of its parish, covering 6000 square miles of sparsely populated territory. The fever-laden swamps soon put an end to Hennessy's missionary endeavors in the area, and he was
forced to return to St. Louis to recuperate. Ready
for work again, Hennessy was assigned to a small mission twelve miles from the city. By late August,
1854, however, he was vice-president and professor at
the Carondelet seminary, under the presidency of a
third future bishop and first archbishop of Chicago,
Patrick Feehan. When in 1857 Feehan was made a pastor, Hennessy advanced to the status of president. A
friendship formed during those years with a fellow
teacher, Reverend Patrick Ryan, future archbishop of
Philadelphia, would be close and lifelong.

Archbishop Kenrick's choice of Father Hennessy
to carry to Rome the decrees of the archdiocesan
synod of 1858 brought him under the observation of
Vatican officials. After his return to St. Louis, he
served for a time at the cathedral, and was then assigned to a pastorate at St. Joseph, Missouri, a
place of divided allegiance and a scene of bloody encounters. Here he served throughout the war. When
in 1865 the death of Bishop Smyth left the Dubuque
see vacant, Archbishop Kenrick proposed John Hennessy

for the office, and Rome acquiesced. The bishop-
elect chose to honor the people of Dubuque by arranging for his consecration on September 30, 1866 in the
new cathedral, Archbishop Kenrick officiating. Bishops John Henni of Milwaukee and James Duggan of Chicago assisted, while the Archbishop of Baltimore,
Martin J. Spalding, preached the sermon of the day.[5]
The diocese of Dubuque had come into its own. It was
an auspicious beginning to a reign of thirty-four years.
In time other members of the Hennessy family would
join the Bishop in the diocese. Michael, a member of
the law firm of Hennessy and Hart, resided in Davenport and served the Bishop in legal matters. Then
David, after a time in St. Paul, came to Dubuque to
assist his brother in financial affairs. A nephew,
John, entered the diocese from Ireland as a priest, to
serve there for many years, and two nieces, Maggie
and Katie Sheehy, came to manage his household.
Though Bishop Hennessy probably never renewed Father
Donaghoe's title of vicar general, Father retained it
in his correspondence, and occasionally mentioned
giving some slight service despite ill health.

Sister M. Gonzaga assigned "great credit to Bishop Hennessy for his kind words of our Community" when
a question was raised regarding the Sisters' ability
as teachers of religion at the time of his accession.
Father Brazill had succeeded * in gaining from Bishop
Smyth the status of vicar general of the diocese.
Upon the Bishop's death, while Father Pelamourgues was
authorized to act as administrator of the diocese,
Father Brazill, then pastor of St. Ambrose parish,
Des Moines, assumed the administration of the cathedral parish. He gave unusual authority to Father
James Doulin, who immediately dismissed the Sisters
as teachers of the Sunday school classes, employing
in their stead young lay men and women, for he found
the society of the young, and especially of certain
favorites, much to his liking. Father Doulin then
wrote the bishop-elect, suggesting the appointment of
priests to replace the Sisters for the teaching of
Christian doctrine in their schools. Believing himself
to have been honestly advised, the Bishop acted, but
that his action might not be too obvious in its demo-
tion of the Sisters, he appointed Father Smith to the

---

* By means which Father Laurent later spoke of as
devious.[6]

school to be taught by the newly arrived Visitation nuns.* Then he appointed Father O'Reilly to the school at the cathedral - St. Mary's - and Father Scallon to the Thirteenth street school - St. Joseph academy. Upon receiving so unexpected an assignment, Father Scallon approached the Bishop to learn the reason for it. When the Bishop told him of the message he had received, Father Scallon said: "If they - the Sisters - are not able to teach, then neither am I, for they taught me until I went to college." When the Bishop realized that he had been misled, he investigated further, learning of the Sisters' disappointment and of the growing disrespect among the children as a result of the new arrangement. Personal observation of the Sunday school situation by the Bishop led to his immediate dismissal of the young people, who, he declared had turned its sessions into a "sparking school."[8] Subsequently the Bishop spoke well of the Sisters' teaching and urged the parents to support their schools by intrusting their children to the Sisters' care.

Indications came early, however, that the Bishop was a man of moods. Hints of this occur in Father Donaghoe's letters to various Sisters through the year of 1867. Examples are:

> The Bishop is kind and distant

> I have been only once in Dubuque city since Bishop Hennesy became our Bishop. You have heard the wars there. I directed my children to be silent. They are, thank God, and enjoy peace.

> Father Cosgrove is wise and silent - all in Dubuque is quiet. I intend when the six months are up to go in.

> I write by this post to good Father Damen that I have obtained from the Bishop ample liberty to send him Sisters.

---

*Like many attempts to recall incidents after the lapse of years, the above account confuses the time element. Bishop Hennessy came to Dubuque in 1866, St. Joseph academy was opened in 1868, and the Visitation Sisters did not arrive until 1871.

The Bishop was very kind.

The Bishop pushes us hard.

I have now to go to the help of our Bishop
and indeed only hope [illegible] will
strengthen me. It will be a rugged field to
work in

There [Dubuque] I shall visit at the very
strong invitation of our good Bishop.

I will call at the Bp. to report our numbers.
He loves Catholic education.

We are still more at war at the cathedral.

In these notes we may read a foreshadowing of
things to come.

* * * * *

The year 1866 witnessed the death of Sister M.
Catherine Byrne, the first of the five original members to go. Father Donaghoe wrote on October 8 to
tell Sister M. Agatha:

> I have to announce to you the death of our
> dear Sister Mary Catherine. She spoke to me
> with a clear voice for half an hour, expressed
> her resignation to die, and she then sank
> slowly and was recollected. The Sisters and
> three priests witnessed her death. My time
> to talk with her was short, but it was a mu-
> tual consolation. 33 years in religion &
> that under my care. May God also give me a
> happy end when He wills it. She will be
> waked one night at St. Joseph's. Mother will
> feel it. She did not see her. Rosaries &
> prayer Communions in this month if you can
> for Sister.

Apparently Sister's death occurred in Dubuque rather
than at the motherhouse, since Mother Clarke could not
be with her. Sister had been at the academy in Davenport as late as May 24 when Father Donaghoe wrote to
Mother Clarke:

> The last acct. alarmed St. M. Margt that you
> were very sick. Indeed I hoped, but in the
> doubt I gave her a whole week of vacation &

Sr. M. Catherine & I will guide the helm
here at Davenport.

* * * * *

The next mission for which Father Donaghoe engaged the Sisters proved a turning point in their history. In August of 1867, the Community extended its
labors beyond the boundaries of the Dubuque diocese,
and into the young and fast-growing city of Chicago.
There it established the first of nearly forty parish
grade schools, a number of which would have high school
departments; there would follow three large central
high schools for girls, and a thriving college, and
from these would come many of its members.

The Reverend Arnold Damen,S.J., an able and dy-
namic Hollander, in the course of a mission tour
through eastern Iowa, had observed the Sisters' work
in Muscatine, at St. Margaret's in Davenport, and
probably in Iowa City, and he quickly discerned in
them possibilities for the work of his young Chicago
parish, that of the Holy Family. They were Irish, as
were most of his people, and were accustomed to missionary conditions such as were present in his rapidly expanding parish. They were unhampered by cloister,
and were dedicated, hard-working and experienced teachers. Pleased with what he had observed, he lost no
time in seeking their services.

For several years Father Damen had proven himself
and able pastor in the St. Francis Xavier church, St.
Louis, when, on the request of Bishop Anthony O'Regan
of Chicago, he and three other Jesuits gave a series
of missions in Chicago with remarkable results. The
Bishop then besought the Jesuits to establish themselves in a Chicago parish, offering them that of the
Holy Name, not then the cathedral parish. Damen, however, with remarkable foresight, chose the mudflats
of the southwest side, where land was cheapest. Immigrants were pouring into the city and already there
were small clusters of one-story frame houses in the
area. Here in 1857, at the corner of Eleventh and
May streets, he built a large church, as a mecca for
Catholic settlers. With the church attracting new-
comers there was hope of a labor force, and industry
moved in. Holy Family parish, including in its
boundaries the site where the Jesuit Father Marquette

and his party spent the winter of 1674,[*] had Polk
street for its northern limit, was bounded on the east
and south by the south branch of the Chicago river,
and extended westward without a limit. The river was
soon lined with lumber and coal yards and warehouses,
while the opening of the Armour,Libby and Klein meat
packing plant also offered employment. Dock and railroad workers, blacksmiths, draymen, brick layers, carpenters, sailors on lake steamers, built simple homes
for their large families in the area about the church.
Small businesses sprang up, for clothing, boots, and
shoes, groceries and meats, while saloons, promising
trouble for a time, found their prosperity kept within bounds by Father Damen's campaign for total abstinence.

Foreseeing, even when he built it, that the
frame church would very soon be too small for the fast-
growing congregation, Father Damen in that same year
laid the cornerstone for an immense Gothic structure.
Meantime he added wings to the frame building, to
serve as classrooms, on the one side for the girls,
and the other for the boys, employing lay instructors.
Those were the days of the deep depression following
the 1857 panic, and it was a daring man who would attempt so much. But the Irish congregation, which was
increasing rapidly, had now what they had never had
before - a home and a bit of land from which no one
could evict them, and with it, their church and the
hope of an education for their children. No sacrifice
would be too great to see the fulfillment of long
cherished dreams. Damen himself begged on all sides
for funds, visiting the camps of railroad workers and
the merchants of the city. Then, setting out to conduct missions, he spread the word of his church and
its needs, wherever he went.

---

[*] In his Prologue to the history of Holy Family
parish, Brother Mulkerins, S.J., tells of Marquette's
efforts to return to the Indians of the Mississippi
Valley. Landing at the mouth of the Chicago river on
December 4, 1674, he was too ill to go further. After
a brief encampment there, his companions drew him on a
sled down the south branch of the river to a point which
would mark the junction of Robey street and the drainage canal, where they built a cabin. They lived there
until March 19, 1675. That territory was included in
the original boundaries of the Holy Family parish.

The immense edifice was ready for dedication in late August of 1860, and its splendor sent thrills of pride through his people. Thirteen archbishops and bishops were present for the occasion, among them Dubuque's Bishop Smyth and Bishop Grace from St. Paul. Bishop Fitzpatrick of Boston was the celebrant of the Mass, with Chicago's Bishop Duggan presiding. The sermon of the day was preached by Archbishop Kenrick of St. Louis, the mother diocese of Chicago. How great must have been the amazement of those clerical visitors to see such a triumph of architecture and church art in area of mud streets, lined on both sides with deep ditches, bearing flotillas of ducks and geese - to see a herdsman on horseback gathering the neighborhood cows, even from the lot behind the rectory, and hear the clacking of chickens and turkeys in the rudely fenced back yards, even in the yard of the Jesuits themselves. But the crowds of people that filled the immense church, the swarms of children that stared in wonder at the colorful procession as it entered the church and left it, were assurance enough that the courageous missioner had not overbuilt. He had worked spiritual wonders in their dioceses; this was a wonder of another dimension.

As early as 1856, Bishop O'Regan had begged Sisters of Father Donaghoe for his Chicago diocese. A series of letters in the Congregation's files indicates that the matter had been given serious consideration, while the final negative decision suggests that Bishop Loras may have forbidden the move. The probability of this is indicated by the following unidentified memoir. It suggests the sense of frustration Mother Clarke felt at the Community's confinement within the bounds of one diocese, and the action she would have been constrained to take when the responsibility should rest on her, in case the Bishop would refuse to respond to Father Damen's request.

> We were diocesan at that time. Mother Clarke would have left Dubuque if we could not take Chicago, as we had been in Dubuque more than forty [?] years and were not getting support. We tried to get R.I. [Rock Island] but when we went to locate there, the authorities in Dubuque refused us. Mother Clarke again said we would have left Dubuque as we were so handicapped. We had been asked to take a mission near Chicago, but could not without permission of Dubuque. Taking Chicago was an accident.

The only explanation for the last statement seems to be that the request came before Bishop Hennessy had assessed the needs of his own diocese, and was caught in an expansive mood when he acquiesced, or, as we shall see later, Father Damen's oversight of the fact that the Sisters' vow formula pledged them to Dubuque.

After securing the services of the Jesuits, Bishop O'Regan next turned to Father Damen to use his influence in bringing the Religious of the Sacred Heart to Chicago. The Sisters of Mercy were at that time converting their boarding school into a hospital and that would mean that forty-five boarders were already at hand. In 1858, Madame Gallwey, with six companions, responded, occupying first a building on Wabash avenue on what is now Cathedral Square, then removing to a site on Rush and Illinois streets where they built a large frame school. When Madame Gallwey was able to purchase a twelve-acre plot on Taylor street in Holy Family parish, the frame schoolhouse was floated on a scow down the Chicago river and moved to its new location, some distance from the rising church. Here it served as a free school for the girls of the parish. A new building erected at the site on Taylor street, served as a boarding school for girls. Their establishment included also a novitiate..

The dedication of Father Damen's new church left the frame building to serve as a school for boys, to be officially named the Holy Family school, its faculty constituted of lay teachers. In 1863, Brother Thomas O'Neill, S.J., assumed charge of it, and when the old church building burned in 1864, he moved the classes into the church basement until it could be replaced. His brother, the Reverend Andrew O'Neill, S.J., came in time to supervise the construction of a new and modern brick schoolhouse on Morgan street, with a capacity of between 1500 and 2000 boys. In readiness by 1865, it came, through the years, to be referred to as the Brothers' school, although it continued to be staffed by laymen. This, with the Seminary of the Sacred Heart for girls, constituted the parish educational resources until the coming of the "Black Bonnets," as the BVM's soon came to be called. Under Father O'Neill, the parish schools were to develop into what was believed to be "the most proficient parochial school system in the world."[8] In preparation for the coming of the Sisters from Dubuque, Father O'Neill located a former chair warehouse which he had moved to a vacant lot on Maxwell street, between Jefferson and Clinton, and was readying it

Holy Family Church

Reverend Arnold Damen, S.J.

for school purposes. One area of the parish he recognized as having special needs, that between the Burlington tracks and the Chicago river, and there he
made preparations for classrooms in a one-story, two-
room frame building on West 18th street. This would
be the nucleus of a second parish which would be established in 1872, that of the Sacred Heart. It too
would be in the care of the Jesuit Fathers.

Father Damen's first appeal for Sisters was made
to Sister M. Margaret Mann during a mission he was
giving at St. Margaret parish in Davenport. The one
letter of hers which has survived helps us to realize
the educational handicap Sister suffered* and the
extent to which she was indebted to others for their
assistance with her correspondence. Dated February
11, 1867, it reads in part:

> . . . Since I wrote the above Father Damen
> come there with Father Vangoth told me to
> come to him this morning as he wished to
> speak to me. He wants our Sisters six or
> nine to teach the Paracal School. He would
> give them a house furnished and an oratory
> with Mass once or twice a week. two hundred
> and fifty Dollers a year each and if they
> teach Music and Imbroydery it will be their
> own, and the Fathers will have them under
> their own protection, and in Course of time
> if the Community wishes to buy the property,
> it will be all their own. Father Damen will
> do all He can. He would be glad to get nine
> but six will do for a beginning. I think He
> had an understanding with the Bishop about
> it. . . .

Negotiations were soon under way between Father Donaghoe
and Father Damen. The former's response to Sister's

---

*
    Conscious of her own educational limitations,
Margaret Mann sought ways to give what advantage she
could to her classroom teachers. For this she engaged
a language professor, a Mr. Werner, to teach them German and Latin. She insisted on their taking a study
hour each evening from six to seven o'clock. Sister
M. Xavier regularly taught Latin to the boarding school.
Among the other teachers were Sister M. Josephine Clarke,
who instructed in waxwork, lacework, and music; and
Sister M. Regina Cosgrove in art and embroidery.

letter, dated February 26, assured her that Father
Damen's proposition gave him much satisfaction. Since
the Jesuit was to give a mission in Dubuque in Lent
there would be an opportunity then to make definite
arrangements. He asked: "Could your health permit
you to give it a start? and would you trust your two
principals with the great burthen of the Im. Conception?" On July 10, Father Donaghoe wrote again to
Sister M. Margaret, concerning both Chicago and his
hopes for Dubuque:

> I write by this post to good Father Damen
> that I have obtained from the Bishop ample
> liberty to send him Sisters - so Chicago is
> ours, thank God. The Hill is ours - I open
> it on the 12th of August, also the free
> school along side of the Cathedral. Boys
> also we teach now. We keep all secret as
> much as possible. How and where to find
> teachers and all good ones?

Then in another vein he continued: "I will be at the
Hill when I receive your next letter. If Germanus
dies Joseph will bring her to St. Joseph's - in a
plain coffin."* While weighing the matter of Sisters
to be sent to the new mission, Father wrote Mother
Clarke, apparently from Iowa City, on July 19:

> You can tell Clotilda she goes to Chicago.
> Veronica is one and Joe or Agatha will be
> the two from here. I will give the word of
> march when I get to you for the Sisters at
> St. Joseph's. Indeed I might see them before
> they start to Chicago via Dunlieth.

Father then wrote to the Reverend Philip Laurent,
pastor at St. Mathias, Muscatine, to inquire whether
Sister M. Agatha might be spared for the new mission.
On August 5, 1867 Father Laurent made the following
generous and prophetic response:

> Your letter which was delivered to me by Sr.
> M. Agatha surprised me but gave me joy on
> account of the good news it announced. I
> think that the mission of our Sisters is go-
> ing to be revealed to them as it was revealed
> those of the Visitation.
>
> Our Sisters are called to fill a position
> which no order yet was intended for and that
> is teaching our parochial schools and

---
*The price of such a coffin at the time was $7.50.

popularizing catholicity among the masses.
I have watched them here for the last 4 years,
governed very little, criticized everything
but not sharply, rather like a kind Maecenas
and I must render them the justice that they
made themselves felt here and did good not
only among Catholics but also among protestants by the high school. I am confident
that their being called to Chicago is the
beginning of a new era for them. They will
not depend any more on only one diocese and
upon the whims and caprice of a few priests,
but they will have the Jesuits to guide them
which is saying a great deal. Thus you will
be able to say: I planted, the Jesuits wa-
tered, and God has given the increase. I
think you could not have made a better choice
that Sister Mary Agatha for that new place
and I feel assured that in a few years Chicago will speak for itself.

Sisters M. Agatha Hurley and Veronica Dunphy
were the first to go to Chicago, reaching there on
August 6, and, since their living quarters were not
yet ready for them, Father Damen sought hospitality
for them in the home of Mr. and Mrs. David Pyne, whose
two daughters would one day become Sisters M. Clemen-
tine and Ignatia, BVM. But the family was at the
point of moving to a summer cottage, and could not
then receive the Sisters. Being referred to the family of James Doran, the "flour and feed man" who
lived near, Father found a welcome for them there until their convent at 512 South Halsted street could
be put in readiness. Sister M. Agatha kept those at
St. Joseph's informed of events in their new enterprise, as Father Donaghoe's response of August 12 indicates:

Your letter gave pleasure both to Mother
Clarke and me. I trust that your accounts,
though not glowing, will satisfy me for my
ardent desire to cross the Father of Waters.
Neither you nor I can see all the advantages
of the Chicago schools for some time, but
write me your reflections. I will try to
weave and wire them into the interest of our
dear Community. . . .

Sister M. Agatha Hurley was a mature religious,
forty-four years of age, at the time of her new assignment, while her companion to the city, Sister M.

Veronica Dunphy, just twenty-four, had been a religious for only five years. Sister M. Clotilda Walsh,[11]
though forty-two years of age, had entered from Boston
just four years before. Next in age was Sister M.An-
gela Quigley, forty-one, and a religious of seventeen
years. Sister M. Zita Dunn, thirty-four, had been
professed just two days before the Sisters' departure
for Chicago. Sister M. Thomas Burke, twenty-seven,
had been in religion only seven months, four of them
as a novice. Sister M. Annunciation Hannon, just
eighteen, had been professed the year before, while
Sisters M. Scholastica McLaughlin, twenty-one, and
Cleophas Collins, twenty-two, were both novices.
Father Damen had suggested that "As Father Emmonds
does not get along well with Sister M. Joseph, I would
be glad to have her here," but though Sister was transferred from Iowa City later that fall, there is no
evidence that she went to Chicago.

Bridget McLaughlin[*] and Maggie Collins had been
school girls together on the Prairie, but when the
boarding school there closed, they had gone to the
Dominican Sisters at Benton, Wisconsin, rather than
to the academy in Davenport, because of the difficulties of winter travel there when the river was frozen.
Upon completing their schooling, Bridget had hired a
horse and buggy and the two had gone out to the Prairie to apply for admission to the religious life.
During their novice days, Sister M. Michael had put
the young Scholastica through an intensive course in
arithmetic to prepare her for the classroom. Now all
were on their way to Chicago, boarding the train at
Dunlieth - present day East Dubuque. Father Donaghoe
had put the black veil on the three novices, before
their departure, reminding them that they must not
take it to mean they were professed religious. Sisters
M. Agatha and Veronica had gone ahead on August 6, and
now a week later, Saturday, August 13, the seven arrived at the Chicago convent in the midst of a heat
wave.

While the Sisters' convent was at 512 S. Halsted

---

[*]In response to a request of Brother Mulkerins,
S.J., who was then engaged in writing the history of
Holy Family parish, Sister M. Scholastica McLaughlin
supplied him with ten pages of reminiscences. These
have served as the basis for the account given here.

street, their school was seven blocks south on Maxwell
street. The heavy week's work of preparation for
classes in the barren warehouse which was to serve as
St. Aloysius school, together with the intense heat,
had left Sister M. Agatha prostrate, so ill that the
Jesuit Father Niederkorn administered the last sacraments as the Sisters, excited and troubled, were setting out on Tuesday morning - Monday had been the
feast of the Assumption - for their first class day.

The girls of the parish had been under the direction of lay teachers during July and early August,
and the Sisters hoped that some degree of organization might have been established, but their first
problem was to find the school in which they were to
teach. In this they had little trouble, for as they
approached the general area, they were alerted to its
location by a bedlam of high pitched feminine voices,
and soon came in sight of a milling crowd of hundreds
of girls of all ages, pushing, shoving, chasing each
other about, jumping over gates and climbing over
fences. Then sudden panic struck the Sisters, for in
all the excitement of the morning, none had brought
the keys to the gate or the school doors. Sister M.
Angela quickly dispatched the young Scholastica to
bring them, so, with skirts gathered up and veil flying, she hastened back the seven blocks to the convent
while the others contemplated the possibilities that
lay before them. When the school and classroom doors
were finally opened, a throng of squirming girls
crowded in, before, beside and behind the Sisters,
each making a dash for a desk wherever one could be
found. Of necessity the Sisters would quickly learn
the arts of regimentation and command. In time the
eager pupils were sorted out and classified, and the
young Scholastica found herself with those of the
highest level, seventy-eight of them, not one of whom,
she moaned, knew long division.

Father Damen's ambition for the school was that
its pupils be "good readers, good writers, and good
at sums," Sister M. Scholastica's account continues.
"The children, like their parents, belonged to him,
so we followed his idea in all our rooms." The parents were enthusiastic in their praise of the Sisters,
and their school, much over-rating it, Sister felt, for
the reason that there were "too many in every room,

over a hundred in the first grade."[*] Sister grew quite
ill from drinking the warm, contaminated lake water,
for which action she had been reminded by one of her
pupils that if she were a Madame of the Sacred Heart
she could not have taken a drink of water without permission. "I would gladly have died," Sister wrote of
her illness, "not because of anything otherwise, but
because my scholars did not improve, though on all
sides we were praised." Meanwhile Sisters M. Veronica
and Thomas had entered upon their work at St. Stanislaus
with somewhat more assurance since the former had had a
week to arrange for their classes before the opening
of school.

On September 2, Father Donaghoe wrote to Sister
M. Joseph that the two schools had opened with 500
children and nine BVM's. He had sent Sister M. Margaret to Chicago to evaluate the situation and was
expecting her in Dubuque to give a report. "I expect a monthly account of the numbers from all schools.,"
he wrote. "It cheers our Sisters amazingly at home -
and abroad also." As for Dubuque, the schools there
had opened "with 12 childern at the Hill and 26 select,
and 25 - ½ pay also 30 boys under Sister M. Camillus."
As for himself, he wrote: "I have now to go to the
help of our Bishop. . . ." He encouraged Sister M.
Agatha to keep up hope of recovery, though Father
Damen had suggested her resignation. His letter concluded: "I'm often boasting of the 500 pearls - to
drum up ugly Dubuque."

Father Damen wrote on September 12:

> I am thankful to God that thus far the work
> of your good Sisters has been blessed by Di-
> vine Providence, although Sister Mary Agatha
> has been sick all the time. The Sisters have
> now about seven hundred children, and if we
> had room, I think that after a while they
> would have a thousand. We must hope that we
> shall be able to build a convent school for
> them. We have now in the parish schools two

---

[*]
The Religious of the Sacred Heart faced the same
problem, for their classroom pupil-teacher ratio was
75-1. (Louise Callan, RSCJ, The Society of the Sacred
Heart, (New York: Longmans, Green & Co., 1937.)
Footnote, p.636.

Sister M. Agatha Hurley, BVM.

St. Aloysius School and Convent

thousand five hundred children, boys and
girls, and we expect to bring the number to
three thousand. Is it not a glorious work
to form so many youthful hearts to virtue,
piety and religion! The Sisters are good,
humble and obedient and work with great zeal.
Thanks be to God.

And so the priests played the interesting game of numbers while the Sisters struggled with the reality.

The need of yet more Sisters at Holy Family by
mid-October brought Sister M. Agatha, now partially
recovered, to Dubuque from where she returned to Chicago with Sister M. Cortona. Chicago's need determined
Father Donaghoe to honor the request of Father Cosgrove
of Davenport for the transfer of his sister, Sister M.
Regina, from the Davenport academy. Sister M. Agnes
Burke would meet her in Davenport and accompany her.
Sister M. Agnes had been sent to fill the need for
another teacher at St. Ambrose in Des Moines, but had
found herself at odds with the superior there, and
was being recalled for the Chicago mission. Father
Donaghoe's letter of October 15 to Sister M. Margaret
gave word of the changes:

I am sending Sr. M. Agatha & Cortona today
by Br. Michael to town on their way to Chicago. . . . Father Cosgrove spoke to me that
he wishes me to remove his sister from the
Im. Conception - This is the opportunity
Chicago now offers. We must start her well.
Give her all necessary for painting, etc. He
did not explain a word of reason for the
change.

There is war between Michael and Agnes. I
will write by this post to report herself as
soon as Agnes can at Davenport. I will send
her with Regina and to no other mission -
she has to begin again like good Christians. .

As a teacher of art, Sister M. Regina, paints and all,
may well have found herself at a loss in the situation
then prevailing at both St. Aloysius and St. Stanislaus schools.

To Sister M. Joseph Father wrote on October 22:

We have now 11 Sisters in Chicago and 850
pupils in the schools of St. Aloysius and

> St. Stanislaus. God be praised. The Sisters
> are full of their mission. 150 are striving
> to get in out of the cold streets. I have
> for this to send two more Sisters for a new
> house to be taken - all is frame work - not
> painted.

His letter continued with an analysis of the Dubuque
situation:

> We are stirring up Dubuque & have nearly 300
> pupils including select school which was
> never better. The Bp. building a school
> house large on his own ground behind the
> Bishop Loras house on the other side of the
> fence - for boys. Camillus & Cyprian are
> recruiting . . .

While the number of Sisters increased at the Halsted street convent, the size of the convent did not,
as we learn from a letter of Father Donaghoe to Sister
M.Agatha shortly before Christmas: "Well, then your
house is a tight fit for 12 Sisters and the piano
graces the parlor. . .." It was indeed a tight fit.
Their little chapel, just large enough for the altar,
adjoined the dormitory, and the Sisters heard Mass and
said their prayers kneeling between the beds. But a
new note entered Father's correspondence, for Sister
M. Agatha had written of likely candidates, the first
of many to come from the Holy Family schools. His
letter continued:

> Now, my child, use your judgment with this
> decision. Our noviceship is full - but not
> too tight. Tell me if all these candidates
> could not defer until the end of January or
> the middle of Feb. 1868, as I must get a Car-
> penter and a large Heatter to keep them warm.

Sister M. Agatha only slowly recovered her
strength, and was for a time away, probably at St.
Mary's in Dubuque. She could begin to take her meals
regularly with the Sisters only on New Year's day,
1868. The young Sisters quickly learned to love her
and to feel secure under her guidance. Their table
was well provided for, and, with her in charge, the
spirit of order soon took hold in the school. The
Sisters who lived those first strenuous years were
brave women. Out of that group would come educators
of note, most conspicuous among them, perhaps, Sister
M. Annunciation Hannon, while Sister M. Agatha would

direct the foundation of many of the city's parochial
schools, serving them through many years as official
visitor. By 1870 a new St. Aloysius school had been
built at 210 Maxwell street, combining school and convent. Here the St. Stanislaus Sisters resided along
with those of St. Aloysius until, in 1878, with the
opening of Sacred Heart parish, they took up residence
at Nineteenth and Johnson streets.* Until then, Sisters M. Veronica and Thomas walked through mud streets
and over the Burlington tracks, often delayed by the
passing of long freight trains and the operations of
switch engines. Mudholes and ditches filled with water
along the roadways were bridged through the courtesy
of willing boys who carried wooden planks to permit
safe passage. The first fruit of their shcool would
be "little Mary Kane," who, entering the Community at
the age of fifteen, would become Mother M. Isabella.

Plays, choruses and other forms of entertainment
enlivened the school year, and these attained high
levels of excellence. A school band, a fife and drum
corps, and a company of Zouaves for the boys, all

----

* As the Holy Family parish continued to grow, new
arrangements were made for the smaller children
through the opening of neighborhood schools. St. Veronica's was the first of these. Opened in 1872 and
situated at Nineteenth and Van Horn, it was to be the
nucleus of the future St. Pius parish, which would be
taken over by the diocesan clergy and later by the
Dominican Fathers. The BVM Sisters continue there to
the present day. The second such school, the Guardian
Angel, was opened in 1874 on Forquer near Des Plains,
and the third, St. Joseph's, in 1877-78, on West Thirteenth street near Loomis. This was taught for a time
by the Ladies of the Holy Heart of Mary, but later by
the BVM's. The fourth school was that of St. Agnes on
Morgan near Fourteenth street, also in charge of the
BVM Sisters. Like the rest, it was under the leadership of Sister M. Agatha who acted as superior to all
the Sisters employed in the schools of Holy Family
parish. They all resided at the St. Aloysius convent-
school, and walked the various distances to their labors each day. The opening of schools for the lower
grades permitted St. Aloysius school to confine its
enrollment to the older girls - the sixth, seventh
and eighth grades and the high school. With the
great church on Twelfth street crowded for Sunday
Masses, the Masses for the children were held in the
local school halls and in the convent chapel at St.
Aloysius.

uniformed and highly disciplined, added much to the
ésprit of the Holy Family school, while the Acolythi-
cal Society kept the altar boys clad in the finest of
surplices and cassocks, with scarlet sashes and gold-
trimmed capes. Parish life was all-embracing, with
societies, confraternities, bands and choirs involving
all ages and interests and building a strong family
spirit in the ever-expanding parish. Devotions for
Lent, for May and October, novenas to Sts. Ignatius,
Xavier and others, the Nine Fridays and devotion to
the Sacred Heart, all deepened and enriched the faith
of the people. Various processions with fine silken
banners flying, and with uniformed marchers keeping
step to the martial music of the bands marked special
feasts, stirring the Irish hearts of the parishioners
and building a loyalty unique in city parishes.

While Brother O'Neill directed the boys' school,
Father O'Neill was involved in all the schools, attending rehearsals for entertainments, planning school
picnics and keeping in touch with the parents. All
found him a dedicated educator, both able and kindly,
and at home with even the smallest children. Sister
M. Agatha was a worthy counterpart. Despite frequent
illnesses, she seconded his efforts in the numerous
schools in which the Sisters taught, and cared for the
personal needs of her large household. At its height,
the total enrollment of the combined schools of the
parish reached nearly five thousand students. Out of
the thousands who passed through this school system
would come a small army of religious women.[*]

Father Damen had planned from the beginning a
complete educational system, and that would perforce
include a college - one which would some day develop
into a university that, as he put it, would "rival
Georgetown." In 1869, he began the construction of
St. Ignatius college beside the church, and its first
classes met in September, 1870. As the crowning institution of his school system, it stabilized and gave

---

[*]When Brother Mulkerins, S.J., published his history
of the Holy Family parish in 1923 he could list thirty-
four Religious of the Sacred Heart, sixty-four Sisters
of Providence, one hundred eighty-seven Sisters of
Charity, BVM, and sixty members of various religious
institutes for women, nearly all products of the
parish system of schools.

direction to the whole, raising the sights of the high school graduates and making possible for them a way into the professional world, as well as training many candidates for the priesthood.[*]

* * * * *

Although Father Donaghoe's original horarium allowed the Sisters only minimal time for prayer, as the years passed he added many devotions. The office of the Blessed Virgin was introduced with the coming of the Trappists, though its recitation seems to have been confined to Sundays and holydays. The rosary was taken for granted, and the practice of offering nine roseries for each deceased Sister - later defined as fifteen-decade rosaries - came relatively early. Elaborate May devotions with May altars, hymns and processions and the closing coronation ceremony were a delight to Father Donaghoe. There is no clear record of retreats for the professed Sisters at the motherhouse, save the one given by Father Kinsella and a rare three-day period of recollection conducted by the Trappist, Father Bernard McCaffrey, yet notes in Father's handwriting dated 1864 mention a retreat for the novices and postulants as well as for those preparing for their First Communion and Confirmation. He noted a novena for the feast of the Seven Dolors and our Lady of LaSalette, as well as hours of adoration in honor of the Blessed Virgin and St. Joseph. A notation dated "Dec. 25, 1858, Midnight Mass" gave the directive: "perpetual adoration of three hours

---

[*]By 1923 the college had had a share in the education of two hundred thirty-three priests, one hundred nine of them Jesuits. When in 1900 its president the Reverend Henry J. Dumbach, S.J., instituted graduate courses in philosophy and in 1906 a department of law, the College of St. Ignatius was on its way to becoming Loyola University. The present site for the University was purchased in 1906 in Rogers Park. While, due to changing times and neighborhoods, Damen's dream of a great school system in Holy Family parish has faded, that of a great university has found fulfillment - on its lake front campus, in its downtown school at Lewis Towers, and in the Loyola Schools of Medicine and Dentistry in the city's suburbs.

daily to the S.H. of J.M.J." in honor of the Holy
Trinity, with petitions for Catholic education. Other
devotions he noted were the Stations of the Cross on
the last Friday of every month, devotion to the Angels
for October, with prayers to the Holy Trinity in honor
of Mary Immaculate to be recited at the afternoon
visit to the Blessed Sacrament. Twelve Hail Mary's
at the two o'clock visit would honor the twelve virtues of the Blessed Virgin or the twelve stars in her
crown mentioned in the Book of Revelation. The feast
of Corpus Christi would initiate the novena of the
Sacred Heart, with adoration from two to six o'clock
each day. Then on July 17, 1867, when the question of
Sisters for Chicago was uppermost, Father Donaghoe
wrote: "I celebrated Mass at ¼4 o'clock and 7 hours
ended the adoration at 4 o'clock this morning, and
none only the Sisters marked for it knows it." Sister M. Scholastica, who, as a novice, participated in
the venture, wrote in her memoirs that Father Donaghoe
requested seven Sisters to meet him in the little parlor of his residence which adjoined the chapel, and
arranged with them for the nocturnal adoration, in-
sisting that they speak of it to no one. She added
that every Sunday during the weeks prior to the opening of the new mission he exposed the Blessed Sacrament after office until six in the evening. The Sisters in Davenport were taking adoration for the same
intention. "The morning we Sisters left for Chicago,"
Sister wrote, "Father Donaghoe said to Sister Mary
Cleophas and the writer: 'I had all that adoration
that my children might be with the Jesuits before I
die.'"

One might ask how large a proportion of the Community was in a position to share in the accumulated
devotions, for duties kept many at a distance from the
chapel and in attire which, because of the nature of
their employments, was ill suited to such assemblies.
Some of these Sisters had served for a time as house-
keepers on the missions, but when the household needs
at the motherhouse proved sufficiently pressing to
demand their services, they returned to live out their
years of labor there. One of these was Sister M.
Veronica O'Reilly, who "used to come in from the cow
yard wet half-way to her waist - a very quiet and unassuming woman and a great worker." Then there were
the two "archangels," Gabriel Eisenger from Burlington and Raphael Barry from Davenport, both of whom
had entered in 1845 at the age of eighteen. Their
duties were to keep the house and the clothing of the
workmen in order, and to cook their meals in the

basement kitchen in "Mother's house," as they called
it - the long frame building with the infirmary and
Mother's room on the first floor and sleeping quarters for the "working Sisters" on the second. Both
religious were regarded as "saints," though the black
bonnet Sister M. Raphael wore in place of her veil as
she worked made her, as the novices said, look "witchy."*

Sister Mary Terentia Farrelly from County Cavan
was the "utility man of the house," even climbing to
the roof to put out a blaze when the men were in the
fields. The lane to the cemetery with its trim hedge,
and the grass in the graveyard itself, were her special care, as well as the provision of a supply of
wood for the household's heating and cooking. After
the workmen had cut the logs into suitable lengths,
the novices and postulants, returning from their
walks, filled their arms with the firewood and delivered it where it was needed.

Teresa Fullam, having some knowledge of herbs
and a gift for nursing, spent her days at the motherhouse, after a year at Potosi, serving as infirmarian.
Sister's mother, Mrs Catherine Fullam, had come from
Ireland with her and had remained in Philadelphia when
the Sisters came west. In 1850 Father Donaghoe wrote
his agent in Philadelphia to give her the sum of
fifty-five dollars to enable her to come to Dubuque
where she made her home with the Sisters until her
death in 1854.

Sister M. Paul Scanlon, from Waterford, Ireland,
was "our meatman." After the men had butchered - usually pork - Sister presided over the meat house, reducing the heavy quarters to the cuts needed by the
kitchen, and salting, smoking, pickling and turning
into sausage the portions to be preserved. The cool-
ing system of the meat house depended on ice cut from
the river or nearby ponds, and stored, insulated with
sawdust and wood chips, in the rock house nearby.
Spare time in spring and summer found Sister busy in
her flower and vegetable garden. It would be her lot
to remain at the Old Home on the Prairie until 1904.
Then the farm would be rented, and the last of the

*Personal details given of the individual Sisters
are taken from their file folders preserved in the
office of the secretary general.

Sisters would remove to the new motherhouse above the Mississippi at Mt. Carmel. She would have seven years in which to enjoy the new home before death claimed her in 1911.

Sister M. Bernard Murray from Dublin, a "dear little soul," was "our shoemaker," for not only did she mend shoes, but she made them as well. Her cobbler's tools are among the mementoes of the past. Sister too would end her days at Mt. Carmel, in 1905, at the age of ninety-one.

Sister M. Augustine Byrne from Kilkenny was the first of three sisters to enter, Ann and Eliza following her after a number of years. Ann's life as Sister M. Louis was short, for she died after only two years, and when Eliza entered she was given the name of Louis also. Sister M. Augustine, much the oldest of the three, outlived both, for Eliza died of consumption after twenty-two years. One who as a novice had assisted Sister M. Augustine wrote later:

> You never met Sister without seeing her beads slip through her fingers. She had the care of the chicken house about half a mile from the house. Most of her day was spent there. Often when we [the novices] were on duty in the dairy, she would decide whether we joined the Community for night prayers during the summer months, or whether we went straight to bed. If it happened that the rains during the previous night made our work quite strenuous and our novice mistress would not know it, Sister M. Augustine asked that we be excused from chapel on those days. She was appointed to attend to it and we were told to obey her. During the hot season, we went down to the dairy, had our spiritual reading, supper and prayers there before we brought the cows in from the pasture. We were usually arriving home when the Community was going to the chapel."[*] On a Sunday morning in 1904, just before the last of the Sisters moved into the new motherhouse at Mt. Carmel, Sister, then eighty-two years old, was on her way to the chicken yard with a bucket of feed.

---

[*]Statement of Sister M. Louise Clarke found in the folder of Sister M. Augustine.

Reaching there she stooped to stir the food
and died as she did so. Heroic religious
that these women were, it was understood that
the Sisters engaged in such labors "never
went near the boarding school."[*]

Certainly a marked disparity existed between the
Sisters who conducted the boarding school and those
who performed the humbler tasks of house and farm.
One might well ask: What was the bond which bound together so divided a group of women in such varied oc-
cupations? What was the source of leadership and understanding that kept them close to God and to each
other? Sister M. Scholástica's brief memoirs may provide a clue:

Mother Clarke to my remembrance did not come
into the novitiate during my thirteen months
there, but I often saw her with the professed
helping to take the vegetables from the wagons
and to store them in the cellars. At the
Monday and Tuesday .wash, I was appointed in
her place to a washing machine requiring two.
It was an honor, but one of severe labor as
it required all my strength to push. My
partner had to return it to me with the same
force. Mother was not well but returned to
her old place after I went to my first mission in Chicago, August 13, 1867. . . .

At the time of Sister's recollections, Sister M.
Baptist Seeley [12] was superior of the motherhouse,
and Sister M. Gertrude Regan the novice mistress.
Mother Clarke seems to have had little need for an
assistant during those years in which she filled up
her days with manual labor. We search almost in vain
for written details of the quiet woman who so carefully guarded against any interference in the conduct
of the novitiate during those years when the direction
of the Community was in the hands of another. A fragment remains, however, in a bound diary kept by the
Congregation's secretary general of a later date, Sister M. Crescentia Markey. The entry was dated March
19, 1898. It began on page 269 and read:

---

[*] There are personal folders for only a few of the
early Sisters. For a portion of these a death notice
or a simple comment is the only earthly record of a
life of sacrifice and toil.

Sister M. Gonzaga McCloskey was here today,
and told me this about our beloved Mother
Clarke. Sister says that once when she was
a young Sister, Father Donaghoe, on his return from a walk through the little cemetery
at our old home, met her and said to her:
"My child, I have just been thinking that we
are growing old very fast. Soon all who saw
the Community in its early days will be laid
to rest up there on the hillside. There are
some things that will need explanation here-
after, though they may not be explained to
everybody just now. One of them is this:
You may have heard some of the Sisters remark,
and you yourself may have thought it strange,
that Mother Clarke receives Holy Communion
in her room instead of in the chapel with the
Community. Now I will tell you the reason
for this, but you must not speak of it until
after Mother Clarke's death. For the past
twenty-five years, Mother Clarke has never
received Holy Communion without falling into
an ecstasy, lasting for at least two hours.[*]
Her humility would conceal

The next two pages were cut out of the book, crumpled,
then apparently recovered, smoothed and reinserted.
On these the account continued:

all extraordinary spiritual favors. She is
overwhelmed with confusion at this mark of
God's predilection, and constantly begs Him
to deliver her from any and all exterior
manifestations that would in any way attract
attention. Until such time as her prayer is
answered, Mother receives Holy Communion in
her room and not in the chapel." Sister Mary
Gonzaga asked Father whether any of the

---

[*]
It is interesting to note here a passage from
The Hymn of the Universe by Pierre Teilhard de Chardin
(New York: Harper & Row, 1961, p. 154): Seeing the
mystic immobile. . . or rapt in prayer, some may perhaps think that his activity is in abeyance or has
left this earth: they are mistaken. Nothing in the
world is more intensely alive and active than purity
and prayer, which hang like an unmoving light between
the universe and God. Through their serene transpar-
ency flow the waves of creative power, charged with
natural virtue and grace. . . .

Sisters knew about the ecstasies. Father
Donaghoe replied: Yes, Margaret (Mann) and
two or three others know, but their lips are
sealed. They may not speak of them.

Confirming the account from her own observation

Sister Mary Gonzaga says that from her own
knowledge, she can state that on the day of
Communion,* Mother Clarke saw scarcely any
one. Her room was closed and the Sisters
were told that Mother Clarke did not feel
able to transact any business except what was
absolutely necessary. The day, as far as
could be, was spent in prayer and recollection. On account of the obligation to hear
Mass on Sundays and Holy days, Mother Clarke,
during the years the ecstatic state lasted,
did not receive communion on those days. She
was present in the chapel and to many it
seemed a mystery that she did not communicate.
Mother Clarke was naturally frail and delicate, and the Sisters concluded that her weak
health prevented her from fasting so long.

Sister M. Gonzaga then introduced another source of
evidence:

Reverend Patrick McCabe relates that Rt. Rev.
Bishop Loras gave Mother Clarke Holy Communion and witnessed her ecstasy. On his return
from a visit to St. Joseph's the Bishop said
to Father McCabe, "It is no wonder that they
themselves out there do flourish; their little mother is a saint." Then he told Father
McCabe what he had seen. God heard Mother's
prayer, and in later years she received Holy
Communion in the chapel without any outward
mark of special favor.

Sister M. Crescentia next took up the account:

---

* There were ninety-five such days in the course of
the year. Mother's room was on the first floor of
the infirmary building. Father Donaghoe, no doubt,
took Holy Communion to the sick there. It would not
then have been obvious to many when he included
Mother's room in his round.

The writer never knew anyone who was so
great a lover of solitude, so anxious to be
completely hidden and unknown as our dear
Mother. During her lifetime she would not
permit a line of the Community's history to
be written. To a Sister who asked Mother to
give Sister M. Joseph O'Reilly, who possessed
marked literary talents, an obedience to
write an account of the early days, she said:
"God knows it all, and that will be enough."

And from her own knowledge of Mother Clarke, Sister
began:

The writer is tempted to sketch in a few
strokes a picture she carries forever in her
heart and brain - her first visit to our venerable and beloved Mother Clarke in the summer of 1870. Here is the background: Old
St. Joseph's in the country on a perfect mid-
summer day; a large

At this point, pages 273 to 286 were cut from the
diary as if with a razor. Why? Whose was the dese-
crating hand? That will probably never be known with
certainty but later developments may suggest a possible answer. Meantime pencilled notes in the handwriting of Sister M. Lambertina Doran, secretary general from 1906 -1912, provide another insight into
the quiet woman we call Mother. Father Donaghoe is
speaking:

Many of the Srs. are grumbling because M.
Clarke does not wear a habit and go to Holy
Com. like the others & say that as she is
the Supr. she should be the model. Not long
ago when I heard this grumbling I commanded
her to get a habit & to go to Holy Com. with
the others, but the next morning I went to
her and forbade her ever to do so again. O
God, how fearfully I suffered for having
given that command.

The account adds:

S.M. Gonzaga does not know in what way he
suffered, but supposes it was of a super-
natural nature.

Once M. Clarke asked S.M.Gonzaga if Bp.

H[ennessy] had ever commented on the difference of her dress. S.M. G. said that he had not. M. Clarke said, "I'm glad, for I could never put on a habit."

A simple black calico dress with tiny white dots, gathered at the waist and the cuff, a small grey shawl about her shoulders, replaced on feast days by a white ruffled fichu matching the white lawn cap with its frill about the face, this was Mother Clarke's usual attire. To this she added a work apron on laundry days or for other duties, indoors or out.[13] Besides Mother Clarke's laundry service, there was that of caring for the heavy woollen socks of the workmen. These she washed in a wooden tub in the corner of the laundry, and after drying, matched and mended in her room. A basket of them was often beside her chair.

There is a strange note regarding Mother Clarke in a letter of Father's to Sister M. Joseph, dated July 10, 1867:

> Now Mother says she dreads her death. In that case, you and any other Sister can bring her home to lie alongside her deceased Sisters and that in a plain coffin. I think she dreads a post mortem photograph - this is the humble Mother Clarke. I gratify her earnest desire.

The directive that Sister M. Joseph "bring her home" raises questions, for there is no evidence that, after her return from Davenport more than twenty years before, Mother Clarke ever went farther from the Prairie home than in to Dubuque. It is possible that since it was vacation time, Sister was visiting in Dubuque while Mother was staying for a time in the city. The question of the photograph also is puzzling. Had the Sisters been pressuring Mother to have a photograph taken, indicating that if she did not they would of necessity have one made after her death?[14]

Apparently Mother Clarke did not yield in the matter, for the only photograph of her that exists is that made after death. It shows her clothed in the habit which she had never worn in life. An enlargement of this photograph hung for many years on the wall of every community room, as a companion picture to a portrait of Father Donaghoe. It is to Sister M. Romana Walter that the Congregation is indebted for the portrait of Mother Clarke as a living person.

From the time of her student days at Mundelein college,
when Sister attempted a portrait of her, she had studied
and pondered the features preserved by that photograph.
In 1940, when several of the Sisters who had known
Mother were still living, Sister made a second attempt,
consulting with them as the work progressed, and the
result as we have it seems to have captured much of
the spirit as well as the features of the living
Mother Clarke.

* * * * *

In August, 1867 the Hill was re-opened as an elementary school under the name of Our Lady of the
Sacred Heart, with Sisters Mary Presentation McPoland,
Zita Dunn[*] and Columba Burke in charge. The following year Father Donaghoe purchased from William E.
Wellington and his wife Eliza for the sum of $18,000
"a quarter block of the southwest corner of Thirteenth
and Main streets," on which stood a neglected mansion.
School opened there on October 9, 1868, with an enrollment of twenty-six pupils. The new school was
given the name of St. Joseph academy, and Sister M.
Ildephonse Malloy was named its first superior. However, when on January 5, 1869, just three months after
its opening, the death of Father Donaghoe left the
full burden of administration on Mother Clarke's
shoulders, her need for assistance was very real. She
immediately called Sister M. Margaret from Davenport
and assigned her to the new academy so that she might
be available for consultation and for the transaction
of necessary business in Dubuque. Sister M. Xavier
O'Reilly assumed the office of superior at the Davenport academy, and Sister M. Ildephonse was assigned
as "head teacher" to a grade school in Dubuque.

The reconditioned mansion on Main street served
as a convent and boarding school. A long frame building was soon erected at the rear of the house to provide classroom and assembly space. This would serve
for many years until more suitable quarters could be
provided. A high wooden stairway let up to the front
entrance of the mansion, flanked by a terraced lawn

---

[*]
The Book of Missions lists Sister M. Zita Dunn as
assigned to Our Lady of the Sacred Heart school, Dubuque in 1867, and at the same time to the new St. Aloysius school in Chicago. There is now no way of telling
to which she went.

which served for exhibitions of calisthenic exercises.
Both boarders and day students were accommodated at
St. Joseph academy until the building in 1881 of Mt.
St. Joseph academy, the forerunner of today's Clarke
College. The boarding students were then transferred
to "the Mount," and the girls of St. Patrick parish
joined the day scholars at the Thirteenth street
school. Meanwhile the pastor of St. Patrick's had
established a school for the boys of the parish, and
Sisters residing at the girls' school served as their
teachers.

* * * * *

Some of the Sisters still recall an incident recounted to them by a Jesuit retreat master who had
spent several years at Campion academy for boys in
Prairie du Chien, Wisconsin, directly across the Mississippi from the Iowa town of McGregor. Either he
or one of whom he spoke, had fallen into a deep depression bordering on despair. As he sat one evening,
moodily gazing across the river to the Iowa shore, he
was struck by the sight of a black cross outlined
against a golden sunset, high on the opposite bluff.
While he watched the sunlight fade, gradually the
clouds of his despondency lifted, leaving behind it a
great peace. Intrigued by the memory of the incident,
he later crossed the river and climbed the steep bluff
to a cemetery where his search led him to a cross-
marked grave at the edge of the bluff, bearing the inscription: "Sister Mary Claudia Hughes, B.V.M."
Three sisters had opened a school there in September,
1868, at the request of the Reverend B.C.Lenihan,
pastor of St. Mary church, McGregor. Sister M. Cyprian
McGrath, Bernard Murray, and Visitation Frederickson
were those assigned. Little is known of the mission's
history, save that it was short-lived, and that Sister
M. Claudia Hughes acted as superior from 1885 until
her death there on January 10, 1889. She was laid to
rest in the hilltop graveyard, and when the Community
desired to bring the remains to the motherhouse for
burial, the people of McGregor begged that they be
left, promising that the grave would never be neglected. They have kept their promise well, as Sisters who have visited there in recent years testify.

Another short-lived Iowa mission, situated near
McGregor, was that of Elkader, opened in August, 1868.
The first Sisters were Clotilda Walsh, superior, and
Sisters Loyola Rutherford, Ascension Lilly and Bene-
dict McLaughlin, all three were novices. Of it Father
Donaghoe wrote to Sister M. Agatha:

Sister M. Ildefonse took from thursday to
thursday to see Sr. M. Clotilda & Co. to
Elcader. 59* was out of himself. Sister
says it was little less than the arrival of
Columbus - 1st a Cavalcade from Clinton. One
man gave all the wood. Monday the country
turned out to halew it - Eggs, butter by the
Mothers. The girls and boys never left them
- one man saw no cream and gave them a cow -
no end to it. Fathers McGowan - Lenihan -
both staid all the time and 59 and they went
to McGregor - then crossed to Prairie du Chien.
. .

The account Father gives of Sister M. Ildephonse'
return to Dubuque in the protective custody of Father
Quigley indicates that the boat presented a merry
scene. Careful reading exonerates Sister and Father
Quigley from the possible charge of having "danced
all night," assuring us rather that Sister kept her
eyes modestly cast down or tightly closed to shut out
the worldly sights. However, she did not succeed so
well with her ears, a fault which she feared she was
obliged to confess. The letter continued:

Theres a prudent Lady Sister Ildef- aboard
the Steamer Mullywaukee - 59 came as he promised me with S.M. they danced all night
she asked me was she to confess it to F.
OReilly. She was happy when I said no - because she mortified her eyes but her ears
was not so guiltless. Lord help - So you
say we may expect Cortona & a third flower
from Chicago - about the 10th inst.

The Sisters there took in sewing, staying up
many times until midnight at their tasks. They made
the First Communion dresses and trimmed hats for the
girls, remembering that the Sisters in Dubuque had
done sewing, even making overalls for the boys, and
all by hand. The mission in Elkader closed in 1884
with no reason recorded. Chicago's "third flower"
was the twenty-six year old Margaret Scanlan, who became Sister M. Marcellus.

---

*For some reason Father Donaghoe used the number
59 to refer to the pastor, the Reverend J.J.Quigley.

Meanwhile Father Pelamourgues, in Davenport, reported that although his debts were all paid, he no
longer had "Big Antoine" to help him, and after eighteen years of faithful service had not saved so much as
a cent for himself. He had acted as administrator for
the diocese on Bishop Smyth's death but did not seem
to find it an easy matter to please the new Bishop.
Remarking that the day of the pioneer priest in the
fast-growing community was past, he left for France
in 1868. There he remained until his death in 1875,
at the age of sixty-nine. This time his Bishop had
offered him no encouragement to return. Within the
next fourteen years seven different pastors would
serve the St. Anthony parish. By then Davenport would
be a see city, and in 1882, the Reverend D.J.Flannery
would have entered upon a pastorate of more than thirty
years. As the church square came to be surrounded on
three sides by non-residential establishments, and
the north side had for its boundary the Rock Island
railroad the congregation became increasingly tran-
sient, until at last the closing of the parish school
brought to an end in 1968 one hundred and thirteen
years of continual service on the part of the Sisters
of Charity, BVM.

Writing to Sister M. Margaret at the Davenport
academy on September 2, 1867, Father Donaghoe referred
to a practice peculiarly his own, that of indicating
an appointment by handing the Sister a pinch of snuff
from the little silver box that he carried. He said
in his letter: "Sister Mary Ambrose will go down with
you. I will give her the snuff." In another letter
a year later, he wrote rejoicing over improvements in
his apartments: "It would be a comfort to look into
my three rooms - carpeted and rush bottom chairs."

* * * * *

The foundation at St. Agatha's in Iowa City had
its good times and bad. Father Donaghoe had written
shortly after its opening, to Sister M. Agatha regarding Father Emmonds:

> He will then be the only clergyman who has
> ever made the community a substantial service
> and will have a monument of his zeal at Iowa
> City. Will you not aid me then in my inten-
> tions of making the establishment the most
> useful and principal house that will belong
> to us. I believe its location is really the
> place for it, should we through God's grace

cooperate with it.

Then, with the necessity of transferring Sister M. Joseph from Burlington, Father assigned Sister M. Agatha to Muscatine and placed Sister M. Joseph in charge. While Father Emmonds was not an easy person to work with, Sister M. Joseph seems to have had her limitations also, for we read the following homely item in Sister M. Lambertina's Journal: "Even in the early days closing exercises caused strife. One Sister would not let her pupils go to another for music or vice versa. Sister M. Joseph would get mad and go to bed and stay there for days."

One set of problems seems to have arisen from Father Emmonds' photography hobby, the settlement of which called for action on the part of Bishop Hennessy. It appears that Father was taking up undue space for the display of his works, and it is likely that the display included, for the edification of the public, photographs he had taken of the Sisters. At least that seems to have been the bone of contention in 1867. In July Father wrote to Sister M. Joseph:

> I will rejoice to see Iowa City once more and all the inmates of St. Agatha's Seminary. I have no gall in me so no one need fear for I have proposed to use the things of this world as if I used them not. Give my respects to your good pastor.

But in September he wrote to Sister M. Margaret:

> The Bishop wrote to Father E to remove his photographs. Joseph's letter to my astonishment told me this. It was then I learned it from the Bishop. . . . The carpenters removed and he spoke not a word - after he vowed etc. all Diabolical - for now [he] writes regularly to me - the noises and Ghosts* - God bless us - patience.

---

*The writer recalls hearing Sister M. Renata Colvin tell of terrifying noises issuing from a stairway in the academy building, a former hotel in which a murder was supposed to have been committed. Sister resided at the academy for a number of years, going each day to teach in the St. Patrick boys' school

On December 13 his letter to Sister M. Joseph began:

> The office of this day reminds me of our be-
> loved Sr. Mary Francis. I trust that all is
> remitted her and oh! how much we have added
> to our acct. . . . The anxieties that occupy
> my mind about yourself and Sisters would make
> you shed tears plentifully.

In a final attempt to settle the problems there,
Father wrote to Sister M. Joseph on November 24, 1867:

> Dear, dear Child
>   As soon after you receive this letter go
> on to Davenport - bring with you your trunk,
> all papers and acct books and leave as much
> money as will be sufficient for house expen-
> ses. On examination I & Mother M.F. Clarke
> will know better all the affairs of Iowa
> City. You will bow to your God in thanks-
> giving for all His favors and the coming
> Feast of our Immaculate Mother will bring
> peace to your soul. Indeed all the inmates
> of St. Joseph now enjoy it here, as well as
> the New St. Joseph in the city of Dubuque.
>
> Whether in leaving or on the way say nothing
> of all you might have to complain. It is
> only God and your Superiors you have to deal
> with. This alone is enough. Creatures can-
> not give consolation. God himself can do it.
> You do believe this - act accordingly.
> Thanks be to God you have still a Father and
> a Mother at old St. Joseph's.
>   I am more than ever your devoted Father
>   T.J. Donaghoe, V.G.

After that there was no further word of troubles for
the Sisters at Iowa City.

* * * * *

Father Donaghoe's health had gradually deterio-
rated after his five-months' illness in the winter of
1858-59. His letters contained mention of serious
liver complaints, of Mother Clarke providing him with
a diet of "oatmeal gruel and charcoal," of inability
from time to time to say Mass even on Sunday. Then
anticipating a business trip to Davenport in June,
1867, he wrote to Sister M. Margaret Mann: "I will
bring two Sisters with me. One will be Sister M.

Scholastica[then a novice]. They are competent to[take]
care of me." He arranged that on his return trip, he
would be accompanied by Sister M. Joseph to whom he
wrote:

> At my request Mother Clarke wrote that you
> and Sister Germanus should come to sweet St.
> Joseph's. It will cheer her as it did Str.
> M. Benedict and Str. M. Basil who at my re-
> quest deferred their flight to their bliss-
> ful home for a few months at St. Joseph's
> Paradise. It may serve to take the cobwebs
> off yourself. In this case you might take
> charge of me home by the way of Davenport
> where they expect me.

In view of Father's condition, the monks from
New Melleray assumed charge of St. Joseph parish on the
Prairie in the summer of 1867, while Father Kinsella
from Cascade assisted them when it was possible. It
seems doubtful that the Sisters' adobe chapel continued to serve both Sisters and congregation. It
was more likely that arrangements were made at the
monastery where the monks were in charge of a small
parish and conducted a school for the boys of the area.
Immediately after Father Donaghoe's death, Bishop
Hennessy assigned the parish to Father Monaghan who
built the present frame church on an acre of land donated by Matthew Powers.15 The strange pyramidal
school house situated a short distance from the convent chapel but outside the picket fence which surrounded the motherhouse grounds, continued to serve
the girls of the parish, with the novices serving as
their teachers.

* * * * *

Father Donaghoe's sister, Mrs. Jane Golden,
spent several years in residence with the Sisters on
the Prairie. Little remains of the family reminiscences she shared with them save the word of Father
Donaghoe's boyhood devotion to the Blessed Virgin,
and the account of his mother's grief that she would
never see her son at the altar. Jane's death occurred
on April 3, 1865, while Father was in Davenport. Informed by telegraph of her death, he returned the
next day to conduct her funeral services. In the
summer of 1868, Patrick McKenna, son of Father's niece
Rose Donaghey McKenna, visited his great-uncle at St.
Joseph's. That Father involved himself in arrangements for the young man appears from two later letters

to Sister M. Agatha, the first on August 26, 1868:
"Has Patrick McKenna presented himself yet - and have
you been to fix him in college? He got humbled -
poor fellow - I think it will serve him." Then on
September 2 he wrote again to Sister: "Patrick McKenna
wrote to me from Racine. . . . Send him to school and
let him pay his boarding himself. I set him up again.
He is heartily sick of pedling [sic]. Rose asks for
her boy." Father failed perceptibly through the fall
of 1869. On November 15 he paid his last visit to the
Sisters at the motherhouse and novitiate. While he
rose every morning for the following ten days to say
Mass in the Sisters' chapel adjoining his own rooms,
on November 27 he could not leave his bed. By a great
effort he succeeded in saying Mass on the following
Sunday, but was not able to be up again until December 8, the day on which the feast of the Immaculate
Conception was celebrated for the first time as a holy
day of obligation. He was then so weak that it was
necessary for Brother Michael to support him at the
altar. This, he knew, was to be his last Mass. A
dropsical condition, together with his other ills,
caused Father to suffer acutely, despite all the Sisters' efforts to make him comfortable. Mother Clarke
scarcely left him, listening intently to all he said
that might be of some assistance to her in assuming
the burdens of the Community. A brief note of his to
the Sisters in Iowa City on December 5 remarked that
"Our Mother M.F.Clarke is midling and sat up this
week 3 nights with me. I am better." Sister - later
Mother - Gertrude related some years after, that
Father in those last days expressed his concern for
the Community in the words:

> I am going home soon. It it were God's will
> to give me two years more of life, I would
> have my dear children so situated that not a
> finger could be raised against them. But
> what I cannot do now I will do when I go to
> God. I confide my dear children to my good
> Mother who will take care of them.

Sister added: "Father Donaghoe referred to the final
approbation of the rules of his Community by Pius IX."[16]
Yet the rule as Father had written it in 1843 or 1844
contained no plan of government, an omission which he
seems never to have supplied. Without such a plan it
would have been idle to have sought approbation.*

---

* The statement, attributed to Sister M.Michael
Nihill in Sister M. Lambertina' Notes presumes a

It is difficult to reconcile with the realities
the highly colored and poetical account of those last
days as given in the Pulcheria Annals and copied almost verbatim in the Early Days. As Father grew
weaker there were serious problems to be considered.
With the Community still unincorporated, all properties save the 725 acres of John Walsh's quit claim,
which had been purchased in the names of the early
Sisters, were held in his own name. These included
the academy in Davenport, the Sacred Heart school site
and the St. Mary academy in Dubuque. In addition to
these, Father had accepted in his own name deeds for
land as follows:

1. the farm inherited from their brother by
   the McCloskey Sisters,

2. a quarter-section of land brought to the
   Community by Sister M. Regis Colgan,

3. the forty-two acres of town property
   brought by Sister M. Alexius Butterworth,
   of which Father had made a token purchase
   before her entrance into religion,*

4. and smaller parcels of land which constituted the dowries of other Sisters,

5. as well as the full section and two part
   sections in Dubuque county - plus three
   hundred twenty acres near Prairie du Chien,
   Wisconsin, all of which Peter Kinsella
   had signed over when he became Brother
   Joseph.

---

great deal. However, the remark about property seems
significant in the light of what follows:
"Fr. D. when in Rome could easily have obtained formal
approval from the Holy Fr. for the Community as Bp.
Hughes was then at the height of his power & a word
from him would have sufficed. But Fr. D. contented
himself with a blessing & oral approval. SMM says he
was deterred from seeking formal approval on account
of some property questions. Hard to tell why at this
late date. . . ."

*
   Against this property Mother Clarke was later to
borrow $30,000 for the building of Mt. St. Joseph Academy.

Without a will, all this property, legally his, would, by law, pass to Father Donaghoe's natural heirs. Yet he continued to put off making a will. During his last days Father called insistently for his nephew, - doubtless Patrick McKenna who had visited him the previous summer - while the Sisters prayed with equal insistence that the nephew would not arrive before the end.[17] Meantime, Bishop Hennessy took matters in hand, as we find among Sister M. Lambertina's Notes:

> Sister Mary Susanna Mulligan (242)* told
> this to Sister Mary Olympia Sullivan (192):
> When Father Donaghoe was near to death, Bish-
> op Hennessy together with the lawyer Mr. Drury,
> went out to Old St. Joseph's on St.Joseph's
> Prairie. They reminded Father Donaghoe that
> all the property of the Sisters was in Father
> Donaghoe's name, and that it should be deeded
> to the Sisters and that Bishop Hennessy had
> brought Mr. Drury with him to take care of
> this matter. Father Donaghoe answered, "Not
> now," and then added, "I shall attend to it
> later." Bishop Hennessy answered Father
> Donaghoe: "I have brought Mr. Drury here to
> attend to this matter and I shall not leave
> here until it is done." Father Donaghoe
> then signed the necessary papers. He then
> turned to Margaret Mann and said to her,
> "This is your work; it is just like you."

To this Sister M. Susanna added the observation:

> This was done because as Bishop Hennessy had
> said, the people had come to him about this
> matter. Father Donaghoe and Mother Clarke
> were very much unlike.

The will signed on that day - December 28, 1867 - was witnessed by Matthew Power, the farm neighbor who would shortly give the acre of land for the new St. Joseph church, and Brother Michael Fitzgerald who would outlive Father by many years. Bishop Hennessy evidently took the will to the chancery office for safekeeping, for it is there today. By it Father

---

*The Sisters received consecutive numbers on their entrance into the Community and to members these were significant, indicating roughly the time of their entrance.

Donaghoe willed to Mother Clarke, as his executrix
and sole heir, "all properties of whatever nature or
being wheresoever found within the United States of
America."

Father lingered for eight more days. On January
3, two days before death claimed him, he wrote in
pencil on a loose piece of paper the following inven-
tory of the Community's cash assets:

	Jan 3rd 1869	
Gold in round box	233.00	
In paper 2 sovereigns & 5		
dols.	20.00	
In bag	1100.00	
		1353.00
Silver in bag	180.00	
Do. small 2nd bag	21.55	
" gold piece & silver	3.50	
		205.05
20 dollar notes	400.00	
10 " "	500.00	
		900.00
		2458.05
Deposited at 6 per cent		4000.00

Then there followed a confusing itemization of the
amount on deposit. Below it all, Mother Clarke identified the accounting as "Our Father's writing. Rev.
Father wrote this Jan. 3rd, 1869, 2 days before his
death." And below this, in another hand there is written: "This last is Mother Clarke's writing."· Of the
above, $425.00 was entered into the house accounts for
immediate needs, and the rest constituted what Mother
Clarke would later refer to appreciatively as "our
little old treasury."

Many years later Sister M. DePazzi Collins wrote
regarding Father Donaghoe's last days:

> For a week before his happy death, Rev.
> Father Bernard of Melleray remained overnight
> with him in order to give him Holy Communion
> every morning at 4 o'clock. It was my duty
> as sacristan and infirmarian to rise at 3
> o'clock to build the fires and carry the
> light before the Most Blessed Sacrament.

Sister M. Pulcheria related in her Annals that

> The night of January 4, 1869, was spent by

Father Donaghoe on the cross of suffering.
Rev. Father Bernard was awakened twice during the night by voices reciting the rosary.
Thinking that Father Donaghoe had died, and
wondering why he had not been called, the
venerable Monk hastened down stairs following the sound, but when he opened the chapel
door to enter, the voices ceased, and he
found the chapel in darkness except for the
little light which burned before the Tabernacle. [18]

Sleet and snow beat against the windows on the morning of January 5, the day of Father Donaghoe's death.
Father Bernard brought him Viaticum, after which he
asked to be laid on the floor as an act of humiliation, but excessive pain soon necessitated his being
lifted into his bed again. The room was small and
only a few could be admitted. These included Mother
Clarke, Sisters Mary Gertrude, Margaret, Agatha, and
several others of the older Sisters. A few of the
many who had come from the missions during the Christmas vacation for a last visit had remained to the end.
Death came as the noon Angelus was ringing.

The body, clad in vestments, was placed in a metal casket in Father's little parlor adjoining the
chapel to which it was later removed. On Friday morning, January 8, Bishop Hennessy and the neighboring
clergy chanted the office of the dead at ten o'clock,
and at eleven, Father Bernard, assisted by Fathers
James Gaffney and M. Scanlon, sang the solemn requiem
Mass. The Bishop then pronounced the absolution and
delivered an eloquent sermon. Priests placed the
body in the grave which, in accordance with Father's
wishes, had been opened to receive it under the altar
in the little chapel. Many years later the remains
would be transferred to the Sisters' graveyard, and
the site marked by a large granite monument, erected
after the Community's golden anniversary in 1883.
That occasion would be celebrated also as Mother
Clarke's golden jubilee, and Mother Gertrude, as her
assistant, circulated among the Sisters, doubtless
with Mother Clarke's full approval, the suggestion
that any monetary gifts for the occasion be given with
the intention of erecting the monument.

Sister M. DePazzi's account did not end with the
brief statement quoted above. There followed:

During the three days that our dear Father's

corpse was exposed in the chapel, I continued
to rise at the same hour. On account of the
great number of visitors who came to pay reverence to our Father's remains, the chapel
had become very dusty. Immediately after
the funeral I carried water from the well at
some distance and scrubbed the floor. The
weather was very severe and I contracted a
cold which settled on my lungs and gave me
great pain. I told MC who sent me to bed.
During the night I do not know at what hour,
F.D.stood beside my bed, placed his hand on
my chest and the pain left me immediately. I
rose the next morning in perfect health and
I have never since had a pain in my lungs.

Then there is the account of Sister M. Agatha's repeated requests for permission to resign her position
at Holy Family in Chicago for she felt that her own
poor health was a handicap to the success of that mission. Writing to her on September 15, 1867, Father
Donaghoe had said: "You say that the doctor speaks
plainly and the Jesuit Father advises resignation.
Well, bless God, for your own Father T.J.D. gives you
hope." He had added, "I will remove you, when? when
I can, for my Blessed Mother will dispose things for
it." But Sister's health did not improve, nor was she
released from her position. When she came home during the holidays for a last visit with Father, she renewed her petition to be taken from office. Father
said: "No, I wish you to remain in Chicago. When I
go to Heaven, if there is health for you, I will obtain it." The account as given in Early Days reads:
"Father Donaghoe died on the 5th of January. From that
moment Sister's health perceptibly improved and in a
short time became perfect." [19] The last statement is,
however, scarcely to be credited, for Sister herself
recorded many later periods of ill health, and on one
occasion wrote of extreme pain in her side, a condition which had existed during Father Donaghoe's lifetime. She said that it was so severe she dreaded even
the thought of putting a pen to paper. [20] Sister was
nonetheless able to give thirty-three additional years
of remarkable service to the Congregation and to education in the Archdiocese of Chicago.

* * * * *

Thirty-six years had passed since that November
1 when Father Donaghoe assumed the role of the Community's founder, priest-superior, chaplain and

confessor, of administrator, treasurer, depository of its properties, director of its destinies and the destinies of its members. Those years had come to an end, and there was now to be another hand at the helm.

After thirty-six years Mother Clarke would now return to her position of first among many. But all was not as it had been then. For now allegiances were divided and loyalties established. She was old now, too - her best years were gone, her energies drained. Yet there were heavy burdens to be borne, and much work to be done. Well - it was all in God's hands. There were arrangements to make, and the day's problems to face. Bone-weary from much watching, Mother Clarke took from the shelf the account book closed nearly twelve years before, and wrote:

"January 5th. 1869 Dear REv. Father died this day at 12 o'clock noon.
　　　　Metallic coffin & c　　$108.00
　　　　Telegraph　　　　　　9.75.

*****
***
*

A Sister to her Foundress

Sometimes my heart goes crying
　　through the dark,
Asking a living answer to a name
Grown strangely wrapped in shadow.
　　Mother Clarke,
These have their Francis. Who can
　　blame
The soul that seeks a pattern for her
　　day—
Teresa, or the Umbrian Clare — How
　　much
It is to strive for, that the world may
　　say
"Her foundress was — She is another
　　such."
Out of the ache of silence your reply:
"Not as a glaring model shall you find
My life to you—only the strength to die
To self — a sharpened urge upon the
　　mind.
The bleeding Christ still hangs on Cal-
　　vary.
My child, you have no pressing need
　　of me."

S. M. Athanasius, B.V.M.

CHAPTER VII - NOTES

1. Denis Mahony (Dennis Mahoney), a native of County
    Cork, Ireland, came to Philadelphia at the age of
    ten years. Here he became pupil and errand boy
    for the Sisters. As he grew older he looked for-
    ward to the priesthood. Living with Father
    Donaghoe, he pursued the study of Latin under
    Father's direction. However, his mind later
    turned to law which he studied at the college of
    Charles J. Ingersoll. Marrying Catherine Hayes,
    Father Donaghoe's housekeeper, he came west when
    Father accompanied the fourteen Sisters to Dubuque.
    Here Mahony succeeded J.J.Norman as the boys'
    teacher at the cathedral in the basement of
    Loras' home, continuing there from 1843 to 1846.
    Among his students there was Daniel O'Regan who
    would become Iowa's first native-born priest.
    From Dubuque, Mahony went as teacher of the one-
    room "academy" at Garryowen where he served under
    Father Perrodin until 1848 when he was elected
    to the state legislature from Jackson County.
    Here he was made chairman of the House committee
    on schools and drafted the Public School Law of
    Iowa. Being admitted to the bar, he was again
    elected to the legislature, this time from Dubuque
    county. He became floor leader of the Democratic
    minority and showed himself an able parliamen-
    tarian and debater. In 1852 he accepted the po-
    sition of editor of the Dubuque Miner's Express,
    thus commencing a journalistic career that would
    prove increasingly stormy as the country moved
    into war. Somewhat later, together with others,
    he established the Dubuque Herald and acted as
    its managing editor until 1862. The Herald soon
    became the first Iowa daily, and exercised a
    powerful influence through the midwest. During
    these years, Mahoney served as the first presi-
    dent of Dubuque's Board of Education and as
    county treasurer.

    With the outbreak of the Civil War Mahony took a
    strong stand against the war, the policies of
    President Lincoln and his cabinet. He spared no
    invective in his condemnation of each succeeding
    move of the administration, until in August, 1862,
    a United States marshall arrested him and escorted

him under guard to Washington, where he was imprisoned for three months in the Old Capitol. A candidate at the time against the strong Republican, William B. Allison, for the United States Congress, his imprisonment effectively removed him from the race. Finding himself in the company of Southern prisoners, it was disconcerting to him to find that they were not impressed by his efforts as champion and deliverer of the South. On taking the oath of allegiance, Mahony was released, but he was only slightly chastened by his experience. His return to Dubuque was in the nature of a hero's welcome, and he was elected county sheriff against the opposition of Republicans, Union Democrats and returned soldiers. While Mahony had been on close terms with Bishop Smyth, he received no support from the Bishop in his antagonism toward the government policies, or in his organizational efforts against those who sought strength through the Unionist society. Lincoln's assassination quieted Mahony for a time, but he remained bitter to the end. Needless to say, the Sisters followed his career with interest and concern. (Sources: "Denis A. Mahony," Dubuque County History, Iowa, Iowa Writers Program of WPA, Dubuque County, 1942, pp. 56-59. M.M.Hoffmann, The Story of Loras College. p. 47 ff.)

2. A Sister of the Visitation, H.M. The Life of the Most Reverend Clement Smyth, D.D., O.C.S.O., 1858-1865. (Peosta, New Melleray Abbey. 1937.), p. 169.

3. The Reverend John F. Brazill, Irish by birth, made a portion of his clerical studies in Kingston, Ontario. There he met the Trappist, Father Clement Smyth, when Father Smyth spent some time there in the course of his search for a suitable site on which to establish a monastery. Brazill was ordained in Wheeling, West Virginia, for that diocese. However, as Father Laurent took pains to remind him many years later, he was shortly dismissed. (Letter - Griffith Files). Learning that Smyth was now Bishop of the Dubuque diocese, he applied to be received there. After two years of service in Bellevue, he was assigned to St. Ambrose parish, Des Moines, where he served from 1863 to 1881, during which time he was also vicar general of the diocese.

4. Griffith Files.

5. The source for the above biographical data on
   Bishop Hennessy prefers to remain unidentified.
   The writer is grateful for his generous sharing
   of much valuable data.

6. Letter, Laurent to Brazill, January 31, 1882,
   Griffith Files.

7. Doran Journal, page 53.

8. Brother Thomas M. Mulkerins, S.J. Holy Family
   Parish, Chicago, Priests and People. (Chicago:
   Universal Press, 1923.) p. 387.

9. Sister M. Angela Quigley was the sister of Patrick Quigley, who came to Dubuque from St. Louis
   after the Black Hawk war. He dealt in public
   lands and reared a family of thirteen children
   and one orphan. The First Mass in Dubuque was
   said in his home. Later he gave the square of
   land on which the cathedral was built. Sister
   M. Regina Lynch, who entered the Congregation in
   1889, was Quigley's granddaughter. Her mother
   was the first white child baptized in Iowa.
   (Angela Quigley file folder.)

10. Maggie Collins entered the Community from Dubu-
    que on July 24, 1866, at the age of 21. She was
    probably the daughter of Cornelius Collins, a
    neighboring farmer who gave frequent service to
    Bishop Loras on his Table Mound farm. A former
    pupil of Sister's, a Sister of Providence of St.
    Mary's of the Woods, wrote to her many years
    later:

      When I was seven years old it was my privi-
      lege to have had as a teacher at St. Aloysius
      school a Sister of Charity called S.M. Cleo-
      phas. So real was her spirituality and so
      attractive her holiness - though the children
      could not have been able to define her charm
      nor to explain it - that she completely won
      the confidence and love of her little pupils.
      Her influence over them was far-reaching and
      enduring. Under her guidance, prayer was a
      delight, little "acts" as she called sacri-
      fices, sweet and easy, and visits to the
      Blessed Sacrament were familiar talks with
      the best of friends. She inspired personal
      love for our Lord in the Holy Eucharist.
      Faith? Those children of hers did not believe;

they knew He was there.

At the beginning of each school session - morning and afternoon - just before we turned to
kneel for the opening prayer, she stepped down
from the platform to say a few words that would
lift our hearts to God and to heavenly things, and
would prepare our minds for the works of the day.
. . . Oftentimes when speaking to my mother about
Sister Mary Cleophas I said in childlike serious-
ness, "Mama, I am sure she must be the Blessed
Virgin, come back to teach us."

11. Regarding the coming of Bridget Walsh, Father
Donaghoe had written Sister M. Gertrude on November 16, 1862". . . I permit you to write to
Boston and invite Miss Walsh to come on to
Dubuque. If she could obtain from the Venerable
Father McElroy a line to say he hopes that she
has a vocation for religion I would appreciate
it very much. In relation to the outfit, etc.,
you will simply instruct her to bring on with
her all the means she possesses. . . .

12. Ann Seeley, Sister M. Baptist, the daughter of a
Wisconsin legislator, came to the academy a "bitter Protestant." The family was deeply distressed by her later desire to become a Catholic
and even more so when she decided to enter religion. It is told of her father that when he was
dying he felt the need of religion and had some
faith in Catholicism for he called out from his
bed to an Irishman passing by: "Pat, if you know
any prayers, pray like the devil, for I'm dying."
There were six other children in the Seeley family, of whom four sisters became converts. Mrs.
Sophia Seeley came to the Prairie to make her
home on June 15, 1891 and remained there until
she died on August 3, 1897. Sister had preceded her mother in death by nearly three months.
The graves of mother and daughter lie side by
side in the Mt. Carmel graveyard. Sister was a
large and handsome woman with such an expression
as to have excited the remark: "What a dear,
kind old face Sister M. Baptist has." Quiet and
gentle, Sister was never hurried and seemed never
troubled. She was a beautiful reader and was
often chosen to do the table reading and the
points of meditation. Sister was confined to the
infirmary only one day fefore her death. (File
folder, office of General Secretary.)

13. There have been circulated through the Congregation small pieces of brown checked gingham as relics of Mother Clarke. These seem to have been taken from a large work apron she wore on occasion. They could never have been a part of her ordinary dress.

14. There is recounted in the History of the Sisters of Providence of St. Mary's of the Woods, previously cited, that only after the most earnest persuasion were the Sisters able to induce Mother Guerin to have a daguerrotype taken from which a portrait was done in oil after her death. There too we have the insistence that " a likeness would be taken in any case after her death, as she well knew." (p. 692.)

15. Source - a letter and tape, Sister M. Melitta and her cousin, Sister M. Philip Fitzgibbons, of the Presentation Order, summer, 1974. Their grandmother, Mary Powers KcKeown, sister of Matthew Powers, attended boarding school on the Prairie where she was called "Father Donaghoe's candlestick" for it was her duty - and privilege - to hold the candle while Father read in the evening to the Sisters. Sister Melitta's father, Philip J. Fitzgibbons, his four brothers and three sisters all attended classes on Saturday and Sunday in which the Sisters prepared them for the Sacraments.

16. Pulcheria Annals, pp. 295, 296.

17. Sister M. Lucilla McGrath tells that as a young Sister she heard from Sister M. Aquin O'Connor that Father Donaghoe called loudly for his nephew during his last days, and that the Sisters prayed with great fervor that he would not arrive before Father's death.

18. Pulcheria, p. 297.

19. Early Days, p. 208.

20. Sister M. Agatha folder, office of Secretary General

ACKNOWLEDGMENTS OF ILLUSTRATIVE MATERIALS

The writer acknowledges with grateful appreciation illustrative materials as follows:

Frontispiece; Sister M. Romana Walter, BVM, teacher of art at Carmel School for Girls, Mundelein, Illinois. Sister's sources for her study of Mother Clarke were the post mortem photograph familiar to all older BVM Sisters, and the guidance in its production in the early 40's given her by Sisters who had known Mother Clarke.

The assemblage of Community buildings on St. Joseph Prairie: Sister M. Grace Esther Mehren, BVM. Sister used for her model a replica preserved today in the restored parish house-chaplain residence which alone remains of the original structures. The ground plan and blue prints for the replica were the work of Sister Mary Kelly, BVM, under the direction of Sisters M. Majella Kent and Nicholas Kavanagh. Sister M. James Ann Walsh, then a teacher of art at Clarke College, directed its construction, with its execution the work of Sisters M. Michail Geary, Lorraine Peper, Mary Curoe and Thomasita Ross, then novices. Restoration at the site of the old Motherhouse was begun at the friendly prodding of the Reverend Monsignor Justin Driscoll, at that time the superintendent of the Dubuque schools, and presently the Bishop of Fargo, North Dakota, who reinforced his suggestions with a generous contribution. The work was initiated by Mother M. Consolatrice (Helen) Wright, at the urging of the Sisters, and was carried out under the supervision and through the efforts of Sisters M. Phyllis Kerrigan and Roberdette, with the support of the Clarke College faculty and the Congregation's president, Sister M. Roberta Kuhn. The structure might well have been beyond reclaiming had it not been for the timely efforts of Sister M. Rosanna Darragh, now deceased, who for many years supervised the motherhouse farm.

Drawing of the ground plan of the old motherhouse: Sister M. Helen Kerrigan, BVM, teacher of art

at Clarke College, using as model a crude
sketch found in the archives.

Sketches by Sister M. Virginia Gorsche, BVM, at
present a teacher of biology at Quigley North,
Chicago Archdiocesan Preparatory School. The
sketches are adapted from the following sources:
Dublin Scene, from an old Irish print.
Doorway of Miss Clarke's Seminary, from
a recent snapshot of the entrance.
Map of Ann street area, a rough draft by
the Reverend Dermot Clarke, Dublin.
Map of Willing's Alley area, Torscher's
account of the Hogan Schism,
See Bibliography.
Log house, Dubuque's grave, and the Civil
War shot tower, Dubuque, Its History
and Backgrounds, Dubuque County His-
torical Society, 1969.
Hospital building, Loras College Spokes
man, Centennial Number, 1946-47.
Train, courtesy of Tremblay's, makers of
fine fudge, Hayward, Wisconsin, for
whom it serves as trademark.
Stagecoach, courtesy of Sister Nona McGreal,
OP, author of commemorative booklet,
Mazzuchelli.
Steamboat and canal boat.

Map of Old Philadelphia, adapted: The Philadelphia Convention and Visitors' Bureau.

Engraving of Independence Hall area: The Independence Square neighborhood. See Bibliography.

St. Mary Church and the first St. Charles Borro-
meo Seminary, kindness of the Reverend John
J. Shellem, Director of Libraries, St. Charles
Seminary, Overbrook, Philadelphia.

Xerox copy of Letter, Kenrick to Miss Clarke,
Archdiocesan Archives, Philadelphia.

Xerox copy of Letter, Mother Clarke to Bishop
Loras, Archdiocesan Archives, Dubuque

Photographs:
Bishops Conwell and Kenrick, Kirlin's History
of Catholicity in Philadelphia, See
Bibliography.

Bishops Smyth and Hennessy, Hoffmann, <u>Cen</u>
<u>tennial History of the Archdiocese of</u>
<u>Dubuque</u>. See Bibliography.

Early Dubuque, Loan from Dominican Archives
Sinsinawa, Wisconsin.

St. Agatha seminary and its Sister faculty
members, Iowa City. Photographs taken by
the pastor of St. Mary church there,
Reverend William Emmonds.

Father Damen, S.J., and the Holy Family Church
Brother Mulkerin's <u>History of Holy Family</u>
<u>Parish</u>, See Bibliography.

Photographs of the restored motherhouse on
the Prairie
Sister Mary Martens

Photographs taken in Willing's Alley, p. 92.
Sister M. Clemenze Adams

* * * * *

Cover Design
by
Mary Ullrich
Gift
of
Mildred Crisanti Thomas
OLA Academy. '37

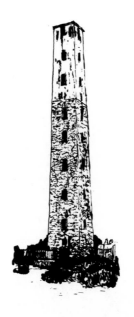

Civil War Shot Tower

Appendix

I

IRELAND - THE LAND OF DESTINY

> History is a brooding, inescapable presence in
> Ireland, a psychological burden as evident as
> the Celtic crosses marking the sites of death
> and martyrdom, ambush and retribution which
> seem to appear every few miles along the Irish
> roads. As additional reminders there are the
> ruined castles, decayed abbeys, tumbling forts
> and burned great houses of the former ascend-
> ancy.   Richard O'Connor, The Irish,
>   Portrait of a People
>   (New York: G.B. Putnams Sons,
>   1971), p. 121

Ireland, an island scarcely half the size of our
own state of Illinois, has been truly a land of destiny. The dark centuries of her tragic history sent
her children as political prisoners into bondage in
the American colonies, as slaves to the plantation
owners of the West Indies, chained in the holds of
prison ships to the horrors of Australian penal colonies. The exiled best of her manhood swelled and
officered the armies of Europe, and her dispossessed
and starving peasantry came to our shores to man our
factories, dig our canals, and build our railroads.
Then, the heavy hand of persecution lifted, Ireland
in a resurretion of her own, renewed her faith and
her devotion and went forth to carry the message of
Christ to the four corners of the earth.

Historical factors which went far toward molding
modern Europe left Ireland untouched. The Roman conquest, bringing Roman law and political order, engi-
neering and architecture, the foundation of a language common to many peoples, and the urbanity which
comes from broadened contacts, failed to extend its
control to the easternmost island of Europe. The
barbarian Norsemen came instead, ravaging and plun-
dering, though in the end founding towns and establishing foreign trade. The exposure to other cul-
tures and the enthusiasm for a cause larger than
their own which stirred the continental nations and

set them on the move in the medieval Crusades, had
few repercussions among that insular people. Instead,
the Anglo-Norman knights came to them as conquerors.
While European peoples were being roused by new dis-
coveries, fresh outlooks and a revival of classical
learning in the period of the Renaissance, the little
island was in the throes of savage conquest. In the
early nineteenth century, Ireland lay outside the ambitious dreams of Napoleon, while her own dreams lay
dead, her heroes victims of their own brave ambition
for the land they loved. In language, law and customs, the land to which St. Patrick came was stranger
to her island neighbors. In temperament, strongly
mystical, imaginative, other-worldly, there was
within her people qualities which force could not
subdue.

****

Ireland is a gentle land, its climate mild and
moist, though its western shores are rugged, yielding
a grudging living to a hardy people. Bogs cover much
of her lowland areas, as well as her plateaus and
even the tops of weathered mountains, their brownish
vegetation providing pasturage for cattle and sheep.
Its green hills and lovely lakes and streams, the
brilliance of its blossoming hillsides and country
gardens, its lush growth of ferns and flowering
shrubs, make it a fair land whose beauty none relish
more than its own Irish people.

The Druids were the wise men of pagan Ireland, its
poets, the keepers of its law and its history, and as
such their persons were sacred. The Christian poets
were heirs to their knowledge and their law, carrying
their influence into the development of the monastic
schools, into the system of Brehon law, and the content of Irish literature, giving coherence and a
sense of national unity to a people who would never
fully succeed in political unification.[1]

The early Gaels or Celts were a hardy people,
somehow akin to the great oak forests that covered
much of the land. Their life was rough and primitive.
Clan loyalty bound them in allegiance to their chiefs,
while these in turn paid homage to their local king,
and he to the ard-ri or high king, a position more of
honor than of power, its site the hill of Tara. The
bard who sat in a place of honor at the table of
chief or king sang to his harp of the brave deeds and
battles of his lord.

The stern asceticism to which the early Irish monks felt called led them to seek the solitude of rocky headlands or barren islands. To these the Holy Spirit drew many to share their lives of penance and contemplation. The love of holy learning lured scholars from across the seas, and hundreds, living in rude huts of mud and wattles, like rustic beehives, clustered around a central chapel, shared the wisdom and knowledge of the monks, their masters.

In the scriptoria of the monasteries, with ink and pen and colors of their own devising, nameless scribes of the Books of Darrow and of Kells wrought with a skill so delicate and subtle that "you will not hesitate to declare that all these things must have been the result of the work, not of men, but of angels."[2] In these silent workrooms the Latin and Greek classics were preserved, copied and passed on, through the tumultuous years of the barbarian invasions. Other monks sought exile among the Picts and Britons, the Gauls and the Franks, beyond the Pyrenees, up the Rhine and along the Po, establishing their monastic schools, some of their scholars serving the palace school of Charlemagne.

The mystic spirals and interlacing lines which marked the ancient tumulus or burial mound sculpture of prehistoric days lent inspiration to the artificers of exquisite metal and enameled work which has come down to us in altar vessels, reliquaries and ceremonial crosses, as also in the rich personal ornaments of Wicklow gold, treasures the bogs have kept safe through the ages. Evidences of these are being turned up today by archeologists in Scandinavia, the booty of the marauding Vikings. These rough seafaring people in their long, sharp-beaked ships, plundered the ancient monasteries and strongholds along the coasts in the eighth and ninth centuries, penetrating even to the heartland by way of the island's many rivers. Ravaging, burning, killing they laid waste the land, and cut short the golden age of Ireland's monastic culture. Round towers, to serve as lookouts, refuges, and repositories for their treasures, are reminders still of that far-off day. With the building of the towers came the use of stone for churches and chapels and the beginnings of Christian sculpture. Of this, the ruins of ancient monasteries and great numbers of handsomely carved Celtic crosses remain as evidence today.

By the tenth century, the Norse invaders had begun

the settlement of port towns for trading, and Wexford,
Waterford, Limerick and Dublin had all seen their beginnings. But the tide was turned against the invaders when the high king, Brian Boru, broke their power
in the battle of Clontarf on Dublin Bay in 1014,
though at the cost of his own life. Many of the
Norsemen were Christians by then, as their building
of the original Christ Church testifies. The disorders consequent on the invasions called now for reform in religion and morals. Until the eleventh century, church administration had been largely in the
hands of monastic superiors, bishops serving only in
their spiritual capacities. To St. Malachy, Archbishop of Armagh and friend of Bernard of Clairvaux,
the task of reform chiefly fell, and it was to his
introduction of the Cistercians into Ireland that
much of its success could be attributed. The division of the country into thirty-six sees, including
the archbishoprics of Armagh, Cashel, Dublin and
Tuam, was the work of the synod of Kells in 1152. A
revival of Irish learning and a marked growth in native literature followed.

Whatever reports had reached Rome regarding conditions in Ireland, Adrian IV, the only English pope in
history, thought they called for a strong hand. Acting on the mediaeval view of his universal overlordship, he conferred Ireland on the English King, Henry
II, as a papal fief. This was the Henry whose unlawful demands on the Church later led to the murder of
his former chancellor and friend Thomas á Becket,
Archbishop of Canterbury. Engaged in an effort to
hold his French possessions, Henry made no move to
claim the proffered gift until approached by Dermot
McMurrough, exiled king of Leinster, who sought aid
in the restoration of his kingdom. With Henry's permission, a band of Anglo-Norman knights under the
leadership of the Norman-Welsh Earl of Pembroke,
"Strongbow," invaded the island. Thus began the
Anglo-Norman struggle for possession of the land, in-
complete as it was to be, introducing a feudal structure without its necessary keystone, a local king.
When control seemed fairly established, Henry landed
with a large force at Waterford, asserting his overlordship. By treaty of Windsor, 1175, he acknowledged Rory O'Connor high king of the unconquered
portion of the land, while he confirmed the knights,
as his vassals, in the lands they had secured. He
reserved for himself Dublin and its hinterland.

Boundaries did not long remain secure, though in

general the Normans were content with the plains, the
coasts and the riverways, leaving the hills, the
woods and the boglands to the native Irish. On the
lands of the knights there soon arose castles and
fortresses, with native Irish to till the soil and
herd the cattle, as they had done for their chiefs.
About each castle were built the homes and workshops
of officials, artisans and retainers, a church, and
usually a monastery or a friary, for following the
settlement of the Normans there came the newly-
founded Franciscans and Dominicans, and the Augustin-
ians, and with these a new world of learning and a
reawakening of the faith. Commercial life expanded
and towns grew up under charters from the king, many
of them enclosed in walls for safety. Port towns
built their own fleets, and commerce with Britain and
the continent flourished.

It was the tyrannical King John, from whom his nobles had wrung the charter of British liberties, who
gave centralized administration to the land, built
Dublin Castle as the seat of control, and established
a coinage, the jury system and an elective parliament. A general peace settled over the lands held by
the knights, while a systematic agriculture and estate management made for progress. Lines of distinction came gradually to be blotted out, for the conquerors found the Irish language and Irish laws,
dress and customs sufficiently agreeable that they
"became more Irish that the Irish themselves." Only
along the borders between the lands of the knights
and the territories of the Irish chiefs was there
frequent conflict.

Wars in Scotland and Wales and on the continent
beckoned the restless knights, and in their absence
Irish opposition to Norman rule grew stronger. At
length the Irish called on the Scotch gallowglasses,
mail-clad and highly trained warriors, for aid, and
invited Edward Bruce, brother of King Robert of Scotland, to be King of Ireland. But, terrified by the
ravages he soon wrought on their land, they turned on
him and slew him in battle near Dundalk, north of
Dublin. The lack of a strong leader, however, prevented their uniting forces against the Anglo-
Normans. Yet even with the disorders, Gaelic literature flourished and many of the greatest books in
Irish date from this period.

The Black Death, in the winter of 1348-9, fell on

friend and foe alike, leaving Dublin and Drogheda almost completely depopulated, and spreading desolation
throughout the land.

The War of the Roses, fought between the Lancastrian and the Yorkist forces for the English crown,
found Ireland supporting the Yorkist party, a choice
which was to make her a threat to the Tudor dynasty
which succeeded to the throne in 1485. English control had shrunk to a small area about Dublin, while
the power of the chiefs, Irish in language, law and
customs, prevailed outside the shrunken Pale. The
three great earldoms, Butler of Ormond and the
Fitzgeralds of Desmond and Kildare, held independent
sway in the lands which lay in a line between Dublin
and Cork.

The policy of England from the time of the Yorkist
king Edward IV involved the suppression of the Irish
language as a step toward the subjugation of the
Irish people. All within the Pale were required to
adopt English surnames, taken from the names of
towns, of colors, or of trades. Thus we have Chester,
Sutton, Brown, Smith, Carpenter, Weaver and Cook
among the names of native Irish today. Only those
who conformed, and dropped the Irish customs, dress,
language, games and the use of the Brehon law, were
counted worthy of trading and making a living.[3] All
who clung to their own ways thereafter were regarded
as "Irish enemies."

Nor was English rule kindly to the great Anglo-
Irish earls. Those of Desmond and Kildare were accused of treason, and the former was beheaded in
1468, an action which sent a shudder of horror
through the land. Henry VII, a Lancastrian Tudor,
then sent the soldier and administrator Edward
Poynings to reduce the country to "whole and perfect
obedience." Gerald, Earl of Kildare, as viceroy, had
attained to nearly royal power through his own pre-
eminence and his connections with the other great
Irish families. Poynings was able temporarily to re-
establish the power of the king, at least in the area
comprising Meath, Dublin, Kildare and Louth counties.
Around these the Parliament of Drogheda caused a
ditch to be dug, and thenceforth these counties would
constitute the English Pale. Rule over these would
be under the direct control of the Castle. Poynings'
one lasting contribution was the so-called Poynings'
Law, which remained in effect for the ensuing three

hundred years. Under its terms, the Irish parliament was to meet only with the king's permission, and only after he and his council had been informed and had approved the measures to be presented to it.

Gerald, or Garret More, as he was also known, restored to power, ruled as viceroy to the king until his death in 1513, but by that time the young Henry VIII was king, and a suspicion of disloyalty fell on the Fitzgerald family. Garret More's son Gerald, or Garret Oge, was faced by Henry's powerful chancellor, Cardinal Wolsey, who urged Henry to take action against the "King of Kildare." When Gerald did not prove amenable to the matter of Henry's divorce he was called to London. Rule of the earldom was left with Gerald's son Thomas, known, because of his love of fine clothes, as Silken Thomas. A rumor, circulated by the unfriendly Butlers, that Gerald had been executed in the Tower of London, so enraged Thomas that he rose in open rebellion against Henry. The siege of his powerful stronghold at Maynooth followed, with Thomas finally taken. His father, who was greatly distressed over news of Thomas's rashness, did die in the Tower, though of natural causes. Thomas and five of his uncles were executed at Tyburn.[4] Henceforth the viceroy of Ireland was to be an Englishman, and until 1922 there was to be an English army in Dublin.

With the powerful Kildare Fitzgeralds out of the was, the Irish Parliament in 1536 declared Henry head of the Church and voted the dissolution of the abbeys and monasteries. Within the Pale the abbeys had been centers of English education, speech and civility, while outside it they were homes of Gaelic culture. As the Reformation advanced, the Old English or former Anglo-Normans became steadily more and more alienated from the royal policy. But the hope of order under a strong monarch appealed to many. To the Gaelic chiefs who surrendered to Henry he re-granted their lands under tenure of knightly service, and to the great Old English land-owners who would accept him as supreme in church and State he offered peerage titles. Many succumbed to these temptations. But the kings of England since Henry II had held Ireland as a fief from the Pope, and his vassals bore the title "Lord of Ireland." Having over-ridden all other claims Henry rejected that of papal overlordship and declared himself King of Ireland. The common people, to whom no compensation was made for the

losses which would accrue to them, witnessed with
deep anger Henry's destruction of the monasteries and
his sharing of the plunder with the great. A part of
the price Henry exacted of those on whom his favor
fell was their agreement to give up all that might
mark them as Irish. Their sons were to be sent to
London to be trained in English law, language and
loyalties, and the doors of Oxford and Cambridge were
thrown open to them. Marriage with the Irish was not
to be tolerated. Thus were lines drawn clear between
Henry's "English subjects" and his "Irish enemies."[6]

In his short reign, the ministers of Edward VI
tried to introduce changes in doctrine, but these
were resisted. Mary, a Catholic, restored the earldom of Kildare, but was in no position to return the
confiscated abbey lands to the Church. The determined stand of the Irish in the counties of Leix and
Offaly against English law led the government to an-
nex and partly "plant" these counties, renaming them
King's and Queen's. They were thus made part of the
Pale.[7] The eastern, more fertile half of the counties was turned over to English speculators who would
bring over colonies of English to settle there, the
west half being left to the Irish. Protracted guer-
rilla warfare was a result. Each confiscation, and
there would be many, was to leave behind it a "vag-
rant, homeless, half-savage population of beggars."[8]

Under Elizabeth,who came to the throne in 1558,
chronic disturbances, often deliberately provoked,
were made the pretext for gigantic confiscations and
brutal massacres. Acts of treachery leading to the
murder of Irish chieftains grew common.[9] The nulli-
fication of land titles, valid under Brehon law, released to the crown half a million acres with which
to reward court favorites. One of these, Edmund
Spencer, was to advise his queen: "Let the Irish be
exterminated, therefore, the priests hanged or de-
ported," and, in a somewhat different vein, "Let cor-
rupt official practices in Ireland be thoroughly
purged."[10]

The action of Pius V in declaring Elizabeth's
right to the throne invalid, and absolving her subjects from any obligation of allegiance, had the unfortunate effect of turning every Catholic into a
traitor in her eyes, and launching her on a frenetic
course of exterminating the old faith and imposing
the new.[11] The Mass was made illegal, the churches
and church revenues became the property of the now

Established Church of Ireland, and benefices were
filled with a clergy of her own making. Heavy fines
for failure to conform to the new religion, priest
hunts, rackings, and the distinctively Tudor form of
execution - that of hanging, drawing and quartering -
were introduced into Ireland as well as England.
Elizabeth's forty-five year reign had for its gory
symbol the heads of priests and Irish chieftains,
mounted on pikes on the walls of Dublin Castle, their
long hair waving in the wind. Of her rule, the
English Protestant historian, Lecky, says:

> The unspeakable horrors that accompanied
> the suppression of the Irish under Elizabeth.
> the enormous confiscations in three provin-
> ces, the abolition of the land customs most
> cherished by the people, the legal condemna-
> tion of their religion, the plantation among
> them of an alien and hostile population, ever
> anxious to root them out from the soil - all
> these elements of bitterness, crowded into a
> few disastrous years of suffering, were now
> smouldering in deep resentment in the Irish
> mind.[12]

The great earls of Ulster, Hugh O'Neill of Tyrone
and Hugh O'Donnell of Tyrconnell, had remained loyal
to the crown until the kidnapping of young Red Hugh
O'Donnell and his imprisonment as a hostage in the
Tower of Dublin Castle. His daring escape after five
years was followed by the rebellion of the two earls
and their followers, with the aid of forces from
Spain. The English multiplied their garrisons and
introduced the frightful policy of destroying crops,
burning houses, and prolonging the war into the winter. The eventual surrender of the earls was inevitable. The victorious leader of the English forces,
the Earl of Mountjoy, now went systematically about
the final subjugation of the kingdom, with devasta-
tion massacre. He then quartered garrisons at stra-
tegic points throughout the island and extended the
system of shires or counties, with sheriffs favorable to the crown. The entire land was now under
English control. Elizabeth's wars had been wars of
extermination rather than conquest. During the last
years of the sixteenth century, one-half of the population had perished. Celtic and Norman Ireland had
passed away. "A new nationality had emerged, Catholic by conviction, a blend of English and Irish in
origin, and in its upper ranks, English-speaking.

How was it to be reconciled with a Protestant government?" 13

The death of Elizabeth in 1603 brought Scotland
and England jointly under the rule of the first
Stuart King, James I. As James VI of Scotland he had
been reared under the influence of John Knox; now,
though a Presbyterian, he was to be head of the Established Church of England and Ireland. The nine
years' Ulster war had ended in a negotiated peace,
but O'Neill and O'Donnell feared treachery if they
were to appear in court to answer charges against
them. Together with more than ninety of the leading
men of Ulster, they took flight, leaving the six
Ulster counties defenseless. It was a tragic hour
for the Catholics and for the old Gaelic world. The
six counties were now open to plantation: Armagh,
Cavan, Donegal, Derry, Fermanagh, and Tyrone. Under
James the English viceroys of Ireland had been toler-
ant of religion, but the land-hungry government now
pressed for a Protestant Ulster that would provide
a safe state and furnish a population for the Established Church. Earls and nobles were accordingly
found guilty of treason and the lands of the six
counties reverted to the crown. Three million of the
three and a half million acres fell into Scotch and
English hands. While London companies were given
grants of practically all of Derry County, a large
part of the territory was to be farmed by Scottish
Protestant colonists, leaving the Irish largely dispossessed and greatly disaffected. Plantations were
then extended to north Wexford, Longford, and Lei-
trim, with the Irish tenants-at-will, that is without
tenure. Here New English colonists displaced the
Anglo-Irish or Old English Catholic aristocracy. In
response to their complaints, James pointed out that
since they gave spiritual allegiance to the Pope,
they were to him only half subjects, and as such entitled to only half privileges. 14 An embittered and
humiliated people, they only waited to strike back.
Meanwhile the Catholic countries on the continent,
and the Holy Father himself, set up a lifeline of
faith for Ireland by the establishment of some twenty
Irish colleges, at Salamanca, Louvain, Paris, Rome,
etc., to offer educational advantages especially for
young men who wished to enter the priesthood.
Bishops were appointed to long-vacant sees, and the
religious orders, Franciscans especially, recruited
members widely. The new order of Jesuits was heroic
in facing persecution, and there were many martyrs

from among its ranks in England and Ireland.

The Catholic Old English families still owned one-third of the country's land, and despite continued injustices they had remained faithful to the crown. When Charles I came to the throne in 1625, he was in need of men for his army and money for their support. In return for both, he promised relief to Catholics, but after their generous response, he quickly forgot his promises. An uprising in Ulster led a Puritan parliament to make a promise of two and a half million acres of profitable land as a reward to adventurers who would contribute £,000,000 toward putting down the insurrection.[15] The dread of confiscation and the belief that the Puritans meant to exterminate their religion sent thousands of Catholics to arms. After a bloody struggle, the cause of the King and that of the Irish was lost to the forces of Parliament. Charles was beheaded and the Commonwealth established, with the merciless Oliver Cromwell at its head.

Landing in Dublin with a Puritan army in 1649, Cromwell had determined on a mission, not only of conquest, but of revenge on the Catholics for their rebellion, and for the charge, fictitious though it was, that they had initiated the rebellion with a wholesale massacre.[16] The forces of Parliament had been sufficiently savage in putting down the rebellion, for its soldiers had been ordered "not only to kill and destroy the rebels and their adherents and relievers but to burn, waste, consume and demolish all the places, towns and houses where they had been relieved and harbored, with the corn and hay therein, and also to kill and destroy all the men there inhabiting capable to bear arms. Every cabin and cornfield in the path of the soldiers was burned, and the resulting famine was even more terrible than the sword."[17] Further,". . . the Lords Justices gave express orders that all priests who fell into the hands of the soldiers should be put to death."[18]

Yet with Cromwell there was more to come. The sieges of Drogheda and Wexford, with the massacre of thousands - men, women and children - made the name of Cromwell eternally hated in Ireland, while he piously thanked the Lord for the effectiveness of his brutality, praying that "God alone have all the glory." [19]

The war finally ended in 1652, after eleven years of fighting. Out of a population of 1,466,000 there had perished by the sword, plague, and famine deliberately produced, 616,000 persons, of whom 504,000 were native Irish and 112,000 of English extraction. [20] One could go for miles without a sight of a living thing save the savage wolves which had multiplied with frightening rapidity. Between 30,000 and 40,000 able-bodied men abandoned the country for foreign service while, under Cromwell's orders, "slave-dealers were let loose upon the land and many hundreds of boys and of marriageable girls, guilty of no offense whatever, were torn away from their country, shipped to Barbados, and sold as slaves to the planters."[21] Though their religion was absolutely suppressed, priests continued with admirable courage to move in disguise among the mud cottages of the poor, even though there was a price on their heads. The lands of ten counties were appropriated to pay land-hungry adventurers and the army. Surviving land-owners and their families were sent to impoverished Connaught, desolated by famine and massacre,[22] with promises of land there at the expense of its own starving population. The new holders of substantial areas of land were to constitute a Protestant ascendancy which would dominate the country for the next two centuries.

Restoration of the monarchy brought Charles II back from his exile in France. The Catholics who had fought for the Stuart cause now hoped for toleration and the recovery of their lands. While the King was sympathetic, the Parliament was not. Claims of a few were met, though after long delays, but most former owners received no redress. Some of these turned "tory" and took to the hills and woods, raiding the new settlers. The end of the restoration period left little more than one-fifth of the country's land in the hands of Catholics. The resentment of the dispossessed was not to be wondered at; their losses under Charles were a strange reward for their support of the Stuart cause. [23]

The trumped-up 'Titus Oates Plot' during Charles' reign, resulted in the execution of Archbishop Oliver Plunkett at Tyburn and the death in prison of Archbishop Talbot. Yet prosperity grew, despite English restrictions on Irish trade, and by the end of the reign the population had increased to nearly two million, three-fourths of them Catholics. There remained a nucleus of Catholic nobility and landed gentry, lawyers and traders, though the Protestants held the dominant positions in administration and commerce.

The hope of better times for the Catholics rose with the coming to the English throne in 1685 of James II, himself a Catholic. When more and more Catholics were given key positions in the government, Protestants began to take fright lest the land settlements be endangered. The birth of a son to James, with the resulting fear of a Catholic succession, led to the extending of an invitation by the English nobles to William of Orange, husband of James' Protestant daughter Mary, to assume the Kingship, invade England and drive out James. When the cause of James collapsed in England, he took refuge in France at the court of Louis XIV. The Catholics of Ireland pledged support to him as their king. In March, 1689, he landed at Kinsale in southern Ireland, with French money and arms. A parliament he assembled reversed the land settlement, decreed complete liberty of conscience in matters of religion, and determined that tithes were to be paid to the church of one's faith; Irish trade was to be freed of English control.

War began with a three-months'siege of Derry, in the end a failure. William's army of Dutch, Danish, German and British troops met James' Irish adherents at Oldbridge, near Drogheda, on the Boyne River. The fighting was sharp and the Irish cavalry performed well, but by the end of the day James had fled, leaving his army in full retreat. Dublin and east Ireland thus fell to William, and the followers of James withdrew to the Shannon. The siege of Catholic Limerick was long and bitter. In the end, after a bloody defeat at Aughrim, the spirited Catholic leader, Patrick Sarsfield, accepted the generous terms of William and surrendered. The treaty of Limerick, signed October 3, 1691, gave liberty and transport to France to as many Irish soldiers as wished. Some 14,000 left Ireland, the forerunners of the "wild geese" who, in the eighteenth century, made names for themselves in the continental wars. [24] But advantages of the treaty were quickly abrogated by an unfriendly parliament, and confiscations reduced the Catholic share of the land to about one-seventh. Thus ended the 'Glorious Revolution of 1688.' But for the Irish the revolution had not ended. They had again made the Stuart cause their own, and had engaged the strong force of England's greatest enemy, Catholic

France, against her. Ireland must be reduced to impotence, and for this the Penal code was to be the instrument.

During the years between the restoration of the monarchy and the coming of William and Mary, there had been peace and a relative freedom from religious persecution. Social conditions had improved rapidly and a remarkable interest in industry had arisen. Land-owners had turned to sheep-raising and the manufacture of woolen goods, and thousands found employment. In 1699, however, the commercial interests of England persuaded the British Parliament to prohibit the exportation of Irish woolen goods. This was followed by the repression of Irish fishing on the basis that it was ruining English markets,[25] "all of which made it abundantly evident that England possessed both the power and the will to crush every form of Irish industry as soon as it threatened the least competition to her own. The result was the immediate emigration of large numbers of Protestants, especially, from the industrial north, to England, America and the continent."[26]

Great distress and destitution followed the suppression of the trade in woolens, and little was done to relieve it. Marks of hunger and want were everywhere. Exorbitant rents were demanded of the wretched city dwellers crowded together under fearfully unsanitary conditions, while tithes and high rents bedevilled the peasants living in their windowless hovels of mud and straw, half-starved, and barely clad. In town and country, men were often too weak to work when work could be had. Crop failures were frequent, and three or four years of famine could be counted on in every twenty. At such times, dead and dying lay along the roadsides, so that with the accompanying fevers whole villages were laid waste. The cottiers, day laborers with only their small garden patch, depended on the potato crop, and when this failed, they died by the thousands. Yet quantities of grain and dairy products were being regularly shipped from the country to English markets.[27]

Such was the condition of the poor while behind granite walls, built by forced six-penny labor, lay the country homes of the ascendancy. Through wrought iron gateways, carriages rolled up tree-lined avenues to stately dwellings set in broad lawns and backed by handsome stables and carriage houses. Lovely sculptured gardens and walks through extensive groves of exotic shrubs and trees stretched on into great deer parks providing the pleasures of the hunt and adding zest to lives of idleness and ease. Of these, much evidence remains to this day.

By 1700 all the most illustrious names of the Irish Catholic nation had disappeared from the country, by attainder, death or voluntary exile, and the Irish parliament, now entirely Protestant, set about buttressing the Protestant ascendancy in every aspect of life. In the hope of reducing the large Catholic population to a state of total subjection, parliament enacted the notorious penal laws, to which would be added the "monstrous acts of Anne" when she came to the throne in 1702. By these, directed more toward the degradation and impoverishment of the people than toward the extermination of their faith, Catholics were deprived of all part in civil life, denied the suffrage and a seat in the Irish parliament. They were excluded from incorporated towns and cities, from the offices of magistrate, sheriff and constable and from the bar and bench. Catholics were not to possess arms; their houses were declared subject to search at any time.

Inducements were strong for the ambitious to conform to the Established Church, and many went over early in the eighteenth century. With the family's fortune, its social position and its fundamental rights as citizens and as persons, all at stake, the temptation was great, especially in view of the principle which soon came to be fixed, that "the law does not suppose any such person to exist as a Roman Catholic." The mass of the people, without legal recourse of any kind, were taught to look for redress to secret societies and violence, while "the dominant minority, flushed by success in conquest and with the means of wealth derived from confiscations, tended to cultivate the vices of the most insolent aristocracy."[28] Of the penal code, Edmund Burke says:

> All the penal laws of that unparalleled code of oppression were manifestly the effects of national hatred and scorn toward a conquered people whom the victors delighted to trample upon and were not at all afraid to provoke. They were not the effect of their fears but of their security.[29]

Another object of the penal laws was to reduce the Catholic population to the most extreme and brutalizing ignorance. The Catholic was excluded from the university. He was not permitted to keep a school, to act as tutor, to send his children to be educated abroad, or to be guardian of a child. A reward of £10 was offered for information leading to the capture of a popish schoolmaster. Furthermore, no Catholic was permitted to buy land or inherit it, or receive it as a gift from a Protestant, nor could he lease it for more than 31 years, or hold a lease the profits of which exceeded one-third of the rent paid. A Protestant who discovered a neighbor earning greater profit or secretly buying land could obtain the lease of the land by turning informer. Any Protestant marrying a Catholic was subject to all the disabilities of the code, and every such marriage, if it was performed by a Catholic priest, was declared null, and the priest subject to death by hanging. An eldest son who turned Protestant became the possessor of his father's estate, reducing his father to the position of mere tenant. An apostate wife was freed from her husband's control and entitled to a considerable portion of his property, while any child who decided to profess Protestantism was taken from his father to be reared in his new faith. Thus was wife pitted against husband, child against father.

A priest must register under penalty of banishment, and of death if he should return from banishment, whereas if he turned Protestant he was rewarded with an annuity. All members of the Catholic hierarchy were ordered to leave Ireland. To return was to be guilty of high treason, with the Tudor style of execution as penalty, a reward of £50 being offered for evidence leading to the conviction of such a person. Bishops were thus compelled to live in obscure hovels under assumed names, and to serve their people under cover of the night, frequently taking refuge in caves or among the mountains. The same situation existed for all religious priests and all unregistered clergy. Strenuous measures were enacted to enforce the law, with a fine of £100 imposed on any magistrate who neglected his duty. A Catholic of eighteen or upward could be compelled to declare when and where he had last heard Mass, who had officiated and who were present, and if he refused to answer, he was subject to a year's imprisonment or a fine of £20. To complaints of injustice, the response was: "The Catholics have no one to blame but themselves; let them

conform to the Established Church and all penal en-
actments would cease."[30] The army of spies and in-
formers resulting from the system had a demoralizing
effect on the whole social structure.

Yet the Gaelic ingenuity found means of survival,
for:

> Gentlemen's sons were sent to the sea-ports, pro-
> vided with indentures of apprenticeship to
> friendly merchants, who took care of them,
> watched for a safe opportunity, and despatched
> them, ostensibly on commercial business, to a
> foreign port, whence they made their way to the
> college in which they were to receive their edu-
> cation. Or, they got down to the remote parts of
> the coast and were taken off by smugglers, who
> anchored under the shadow of the sea-washed head-
> lands to exchange at their leisure a cargo of
> clarets and brandies for the wool which the Irish
> were prohibited from exporting to England, and
> forbidden to manufacture into saleable goods at
> home. Aspirants to the priesthood embarked with
> the "wild geese" - the recruits for the Irish
> brigade - in a like hazardous fashion; or got
> away in fishing-boats frequenting these coasts;
> and were satisfied if landed anywhere on the con-
> tinent, being fully prepared to trudge across
> mountain and plain with their faces turned toward
> Santiago or Salamanca, Lisbon or Louvain. The
> return home was effected through the same
> friendly agency. Priests, friars, and the alumni
> of the secular colleges were smuggled into their
> native island with the rest of the contraband
> freight.[31]

Cecil Woodham Smith, however, describes some of
the more sinister effects of the Penal code:

> The Penal laws brought lawlessness, dissimulation
> and revenge in their train, and the Irish charac-
> ter, above all the character of the peasantry,
> did become, in Burke's words degraded and de-
> based. The upper classes were able to leave the
> country and many middle class merchants con-
> trived, with guile, to survive, but the poor
> Catholic peasant bore the full hardship. His re-
> ligion made him an outlaw; in the Irish House of
> Commons he was described as the common enemy, and
> whatever was inflicted on him he must bear, for
> where could he look for redress? . . .

In these conditions suspicion of the law, of
the ministers of the law, and of all established authority "worked into the very nerves
and blood of the Irish peasant," and since
the law did not give him justice, he set up
his own law. The secret societies which have
been the curse of Ireland became widespread
during the Penal period, and a succession of
underground organizations, Oak Boys, White
Boys, and Ribbon Men, gathered in bogs and
lonely glens, flouted the law and dispensed
the people's justice in the terrible form of
revenge. The informer, the supplanter of an
evicted tenant, the landlord's man, were punished with dreadful savagery, and since animals were wealth, their unfortunate animals
suffered too. Cattle were "clifted," driven
over the edge of a cliff, horses hamstrung,
dogs clubbed to death, stables fired and the
animals within burned alive. Nor were lawlessness, cruelty and revenge the only consequences. During the long Penal period,
dissimulation became a moral necessity and
evasion of the law the duty of every God -
fearing Catholic. To worship according to
his faith, the Catholic must attend illegal
meetings; to protect his priest, he must be
secret, cunning and a concealer of the truth.

These were dangerous lessons for any government to compel its subjects to learn, and a
dangerous habit of mind for any nation to
acquire.[32]

All this offers a strange contrast to the native
qualities of the Irish peasantry, whose "native condition," wrote Sir Walter Scott during a visit to
Ireland in 1825, "is turned toward gaiety and happiness. Dancing for them was a universal diversion."
Groups of neighbors gathered for dancing to the fid-
dle, indoors in the winter, in "summer at the cross-
roads; wakes, with liberal potations of poteen, were
social occasions, and crowds gaily travelled immense
distances to attend market, fairs, and above all,
races." Good manners and hospitality were universal
among the poorest Irish. Scott found "perpetual
kindness in the Irish cabin; buttermilk, potatoes, a
stool is offered, or a stone is rolled that your
honor may sit down.... and those that beg everywhere
also seem desirous to exercise hospitality in their
own house. . . Irish dignity, Irish hospitality and

good manners which still charm the modern traveller
have an historic explanation. Three times, at least,
the native aristocracy was conquered and dispossessed; many fled from Ireland to exile in France or
Spain, but many remained to be forced down by poverty
and penal legislation to the economic level of the
peasantry."[33] It was eventually realized that the
Catholic clergy, if left in peace, were the best security against sedition and crime, while the hope-
lessness of destroying the faith of the people became
increasingly apparent.

Pressing demands were being made for the reform
of the Irish parliament, composed now only of members
from the Protestant ascendancy. Boroughs, each with
its seat in parliament, were being created at will by
the monarch and committed to the control of a favorite. Out of the three hundred members of Commons,
more than half were under the control of individual
patrons.[34] Bishops of the Established Church controlled many of the boroughs, and constituted half
the working majority of the House of Lords. The size
and extravagance of the administrative force, largely
absentee, placed heavy burdens on the nation, and
pensions and sinecures, passed out freely to favored
persons, added greatly to that burden. The handing
out of peerages was an effective means of control
when a vote was needed in the king's interest.[35]

The system of absentee landlordism drained from
the impoverished country during the middle 18th century a calculated annual rental of between ₤620,000
and ₤1,200,000.[36] Landholders leased great holdings
to middlemen who in turn sublet large portions. This
middleman system produced misery: the landlord rid
himself of responsibility and assured himself of a
regular income, but the tenants were handed over to
exploitation. The tenant had no permanent interest
in the soil and no security; without skill or capital,
the bit of land he held was all that stood between him
and starvation. He built his own mud hovel, planted
his own hedges and dug his own ditches, knowing that
he could be turned off the land without warning or
compensation. Exorbitant rents and forced labor left
great numbers half-starved and destitute, while
tithes for the benefit of the Established Church were
exacted from all. These the parson let to a tithe
farmer who exacted what he pleased, usually far more
than he was entitled to by law. Turning great tracts
of arable land into pasture resulted in many forcible

evictions, with no means of livelihood for the evicted to turn to, filled large areas with wanderers and
beggars, and sent numbers into the mountains where
small plots of "potato ground" became their only support. Laborers who went to England during harvest
season in the hope of employment, returned in the
fall with five or six pounds as the fruit of their
summer's labor.[37]

Workhouses were set up to clear the city streets
of vagrants and beggars. Begging children over five
years old were housed there until at sixteen they
were apprenticed to Protestants. To prevent parental
influence, children, even infants, were sent away
from their own area. The long journey, jostled together in rough carts, was fatal to many, while this
cutting of family ties in the interests of proselyt-
ism was keenly felt by Catholic parents. A "noble,
useful and truly religious undertaking of the Incorporated Society for promoting Protestant Schools"
resulted in a system of Charter Schools. Among their
"Expectations" we read:

> What an extensive and advantageous charity it
> would support, if every poor Romish family in the
> kingdom should part with one or two of their
> miserable, half-starved naked children, between
> the ages of eight and twelve years, males and fe-
> males, at the discretion of Commissioners ap-
> pointed for that purpose, and have them bred up
> in the Protestant Religion in Workhouses . . .
> as the wisdom of Parliament should direct? And
> that their parents might have no access to them,
> the children taken in one province might be sent
> to another. Could possibly a charity be better
> disposed? Or, could any Policy whatever estab-
> lish Protestant numbers with less grievance? . .
> Though the scheme may seem to carry with it some
> compulsion, it is fitted to the circumstances of
> these unhappy people, and likewise to the neces-
> sities of the Kingdom.[38]

It is of interest to compare the above with
Oliver Cromwell's address to the Dublin Council in
1657 on the matter of educating the Catholic populations:

> Whereas the poorer sorts of Irish in Ireland doe,
> as well as the rich, abound in children, and have
> for the most part noe other means to support them
> and their said children, but either by begging or

stealing or both, by which meanes they not only
prove very burthensome but alsoe unnecessary members of the Commonwealth; and whereas the said
children would (noe doubt) in time prove of excellent use if there were some course layd downe
whereby they might att the age of tenn yeares and
upwards bee taken from their Parents and bound
Apprentices to religious and honest people in
England or Ireland, that would not onely make it
their business to breede them as well principally
in the fear of God, as in such honest callings
whereby they might bee engaged, when they come
out of their apprenticeships, to gett their live-
ings by their owne industry; And whereas it is
likewise found by dailey experience that there is
a greate wante in England of labourers and servants of all sorts, occasioned partly by the late
warr and partly by carrying of both men and women
to forraigne Plantations; as also for that (noe
doubt) it would be a work most acceptable to the
Lord to have said children bred and brought up
aforesaid; That for the effecting and carrying on
of a work of soe great piety a publique Collection be appointed to be made upon a certaine day,
once every yeare, in all the respective Parishes
within Ireland.[39]

A program of Charter schools was inaugurated in
1733, intended to "rescue the souls of thousands of
poor children from the dangers of Popish supersti-
tion and idolatry and their bodies from the miseries
of idleness and beggary."[40] The Society proposed to
take the half-starving children between the ages of
six and ten, feed, clothe, and lodge them gratui-
tously, give them both a free general education and
an industrial training, apprentice the boys and provide the girls with a small dowry. The indispensable
condition was that the children be educated as Protestants.

Sir J. FitzPatrick, in a tour of inspection during which he visited twenty-eight of these thirty-two
schools in 1786-87, reported finding the children
much under-nourished, bare-footed and ragged, in un-
heated buildings, their bodies disfigured with the
itch and covered with vermin, their beds filthy, rain
coming in through roofs or broken windows. Many of
the children were unable to read and the best only
badly, while some worked hours each day, carding,
weaving, or spinning cotton, or at heavy field work.[41]

He adds that "The athleticity so strongly marked in the children of the poor in this kingdom, however shabby their clothing, is not to be found in Charter Schools.[42] "In many respects the detailed evidence of 1824-25 was more repulsive in its nature than even the dreadful statements of Howard and FitzPatrick, 1782-1787; and does not admit of being reprinted here." [43]

The passion of the Irish for learning was intense and the determination with which they maintained their hedge schools in the face of severe penalties is one of the most honorable features of their history. William Reed, in his Rambles Through Ireland, 1815, has left us an interesting description of these institutions of learning.

> A desire for education manifests itself, and very generally, amongst the lowest orders of the people. In my wanderings through the country, I found several very humble seminaries, called hedge schools. Not having any other convenience, the scholars are taught reading, writing, etc., in the open air, under the shade of some embowering hedge, or branching tree; and very often the green bank and the smooth shelves of the rock answer the purposes of the bench and the desk. There are also itinerant teachers, who become inmates of a cabin for several weeks together, and who receive only a temporary lodging and a few potatoes for instructing the juvenile inhabitants. In traveling through one of the lonely districts of the island, I met with one of these tutors. He was young, sprightly, and intelligent, and offered himself as my guide through the mountains, though he was entirely unacquainted with the comfortable equipment of hat, stocking and shoe.[44]

Of the schoolmaster, P.J. Dowling tells us:

> The principal figure in popular education during the Penal Times and till almost the middle of the nineteenth century was the hedge schoolmaster; courageous he was, rugged perhaps, independent always, possessing some knowledge, occasionally a scholar, having often an energy which made him the master of many crafts, and almost invariably possessing a great devotion to his calling. It was his school, the hedge school, increasing in number from four thousand in 1807 to over nine

thousand in 1824, which was chiefly responsible for the introduction of the State system of elementary education in 1832. But even at the end of the nineteenth century there were still priests and people . . . who preferred the hedge schools and would not allow the establishment of schools fully sponsored and partly financed by the National Board of Education in their parishes.[45]

Soon after the middle of the eighteenth century, a Catholic party began to emerge from the ghetto into which they had been driven by the anti-popery laws. Their spokesman, Charles O'Connor of Belanagare, and John Curry, a Dublin doctor, together with others, sought by their historical writings to disprove the charge of British writers that the Gaelic Irish were a barbarous people, and that the Catholics were still only waiting for an opportunity to embark on a massacre of Protestants.[46]

In the face of the crying need for reform in the land system and tithing, the year 1765 saw instead the introduction of the first coercion act, establishing a system of martial law and applying force instead of reform. Yet, in spite of admonitions, denunciations, and even excommunications by the Catholic clergy, oathbound secret societies continued to exist, and in times of distress the people obeyed the local Whiteboy[47] code instead of the law of the land.[48]

However, the American Revolution led to second thoughts on the part of parliament and the executive. The Quebec Act had kept Canada loyal with the concessions it offered to Catholics. When France declared war on Britain in 1778, and rumors of invasion began to circulate, the first relief bill for the Catholics of Ireland was steam-rollered through the Irish parliament, granting the right to long-term leases and to service in the armed forces - England had need of troops.

The American strike for freedom was a clarion call to the Irish. Their sympathy for the cause of the Colonies was all the greater because many of the colonists were emigrants from the homeland, especially from Ulster, an area already republican-minded. When France and Spain entered the war on the American side, Ireland, her garrisons stripped of troops, lay

open to invasion. In the face of this danger, landlords and wealthy professional men outfitted and
trained a formidable volunteer army. When the war
ended and external dangers had passed, the interests
of the Volunteers turned to politics, and especially
to the commercial restrictions that were the source
of many of Ireland's economic ills. The Volunteers
were a sufficiently formidable body to force the complete abolition of trade restrictions. Their next
demand was for the right of the Irish parliament to
legislate for Ireland. The leader of this movement
was the able and eloquent Henry Grattan. Cornwallis'
surrender at Yorktown had had a chastening effect on
the British parliament, and in 1782 it surrendered
its claim to control Irish legislation.

Ireland was now in appearance an independent
kingdom, sharing only a monarch with the neighboring
island. In a great flush of national pride, Ireland
established a separate postal system and founded the
Bank of Ireland. The Custom House and the Four
Courts rose in classic splendor, and Georgian elegance enclosed Rutland Square and Merrion Square and
Stephen's Green with the luxurious town houses of the
ascendancy.

The religious, social and economic disabilities
from which so large a majority of the Irish people
still suffered took on an ominous aspect as the
French revolutionary spirit spread. Reacting to its
fears, Parliament, in 1793, admitted Catholics of
Ireland to the bar, recognized their right to freedom
of worship and of education, and legalized the marriage of Catholics with Protestants. All restrictions on land tenure were removed, and admission was
granted to the national university and to military
and civil offices of the lower orders. Finally, the
franchise was extended to forty-shilling freeholders.
But there remained the check on the ambitions of a
rising Catholic middle class in their continued exclusion from the higher offices in the armed services
and from parliament. Grattan would have swept away
all such limitations but the Irish parliament did not
have the last word. Members of the executive branch
of the government - the viceroy, his council and his
staff - were subject to the appointment and the policies of the king and his cabinet, with William Pitt
as prime minister. The appointment of William
Wentworth Fitzwilliam as viceroy gave the Irish great
hope for the reform of the government and the

admission of Catholics to parliament, but when
Fitzwilliam reacted favorably to Irish efforts for
complete emancipation, he found forces of opposition
overwhelming and the anticipated support of Pitt
withheld. His recall was a heavy blow to the hopes
of the Catholics and those who supported their claims,
for many far-seeing Protestants had come to recognize
the justice of the Catholic cause.

Meanwhile, in 1791, a group of young professional
men in Belfast, stirred with the republican spirit,
had invited the indomitable Wolfe Theobald Tone to
organize them for action. The result was the Society
of United Irishmen. The professed aim of the Society
was to establish unity between Catholics and Presbyterians in the hope of gaining for them complete
religious equality with members of the Established
Church, and to bring about a reform of Parliament.
The movement, all of whose early members were Protestant, spread rapidly, with societies quickly formed
in Dublin and other centers throughout the country.

The fear of revolution which had led to the reforms of 1793 had resulted also in measures of repression. An arms act prohibited the importation or
distribution of arms, ammunition and powder, and a
convention act forbade the holding of representative
assemblies. The government attempted in 1794 to sup-
press the United Irishmen, but succeeded only in
driving the organization underground and crystalliz-
ing the determination of its leaders to set up a republic on French principles. This plan committed
them to a policy of alliance with France and complete
separation from England.

With Ireland's population so largely composed of
Catholic peasants, Tone's hope of successful revolution rested largely on a consolidation of peasant
discontent, and a cooperation of Catholics with their
Presbyterian neighbors. But the sharp competition
which rose in the southern counties of Ulster over
land leases led to the formation of the Protestant
"Peep o' Day Boys," who raided the homes of Catholics
and tried to frighten them into leaving the area. The
latter set up a counter organization, the
"Defenders," and clashes between the two groups were
frequent and sometimes fatal. By 1797 the Defenders
had been pretty well incorporated into the United
Irishmen. It was at this time that Edward Wakefield
declared that "the enormities committed by the

partisans of government ...were such as must disgrace
our annals, tarnish the character, and stigmatize the
memory of His Majesty's ministers."[50]

Pitt now made an effort to conciliate the Catholics by the foundation and partial endowment of a
college for the education of their clergy. The
French 'contagion of sedition and infidelity' threatened the continental schools, and the disorders consequent on the Revolution had caused the closing of
many of them. Madame Guillotine had already made a
bloody end to many priests and religious, and the
Irish Bishops were anxious to find a safe place for
their seminarians. Many felt it a grave mistake,
however, to confine the education of the candidates
for the priesthood to a national seminary, thus cutting them off from the broadening influence of university life, especially when that loss could not be
compensated for by the cosmopolitan influence enjoyed
in the larger training centers on the continent.

The gift of land by the Fitzgeralds [51] and the
government's subsidy, however, saw the founding of
the Royal College of St. Patrick at Maynooth, in
1795, though with the subsidy went a required oath of
allegiance to the British crown. The availability of
many French emigré priests and professors willing to
work for a competence seemed providential in view of
the college's limited resources, and posts were given
to several of these men in moral and dogmatic theology. The bishops did not realize that they were
"thereby importing a French school of thought whose
teachings so carefully . . . cultivated the spirit of
Gallicanism among the Irish clergy that the Irish
Church soon became Gallican to the core, and remained
so for nearly half a century. . . . In morals they
encouraged a repulsive rigor in the management of
consciences which rendered the following of Christ's
teachings anything but a jugum suave....The familiar
priest of the old school was a stern moralist, a man
for whom 'The Law' was a second god."[52]

When Gardiner's Relief Bill of 1782 first allowed
Catholics to open schools and educate their children
at home, the aged Dr. Keefe, Bishop of Kildare and
Leighlin, established a college at Carlow, "the first
college in Ireland in 245 years tolerated by British
law and teaching the supremacy of the Pope."[53]
Supported by the clergy and laity, it required no
oath of allegiance and was spared the crisis suffered

at Maynooth in 1798, when eighteen of its sixty-nine
students were expelled for taking the oath of the
United Irishmen. Although three of its early professors were French emigrés, it did not share the Gallican and Jansenistic tendencies of Maynooth. The able
Dr. Doyle, successor to Dr. Keefe, raised it to a
high level of scholarship and leadership, though it
never became a large institution.[54]

The establishment of Maynooth was no substitute
for emancipation, and the disaffection consequent on
the Bishops' compromise with regard to the oath drew
many Catholics into the ranks of the United Irishmen.
An unusually severe clash between the Catholic and
the Protestant peasantry in Armagh in 1795 resulted
in the establishment of the 'Orange Society' on the
part of the victorious Protestants, for the protection of their own interests and the maintenance of
the Protestant ascendancy. During the next few
months the Catholics of the area were subjected to a
violent persecution which drove thousands of them to
take refuge in Connaught. The fact that the Orange
Society was quickly joined by government officials
gave color to the belief that the government had no
intention of interfering with its lawlessness.[55]
The ranks of the Defenders grew rapidly and the
United Irishmen were quick to intensify their propaganda among them.

The arrest of a French agent in Dublin in April,
1794, involved Tone. Upon confessing his part in the
conspiracy to obtain French aid, he was permitted to
sail for America. From there, he soon went to Paris
for further negotiations. The government, in alarm
at news of the conspiracy, quickly passed an 'insurrection act,' making it a capital offense to administer an unlawful oath - members of the United Irishmen
being bound by oath - and empowering a search for
arms by which, without trial, "suspected traitors and
disorderly persons" might be sent to serve in the
fleet. The suspension of habeas corpus added to the
arbitrary powers of the government. A militia,
raised partly by conscription and consisting largely
of Catholics, was regarded of doubtful reliability,
while a new yeomanry, recruited by landlords, chiefly
from among their own tenants, was mainly Protestant.

Meanwhile the United Irishmen, having set up
military units throughout the country, formulated
plans for an uprising to be supported by the arrival
of aid from France. Sir Thomas Reynolds, who had

joined their ranks early in 1797 and had been admitted into the confidence of the leaders, decided, for a substantial price, [56] to supply the government with information. His action resulted in the arrest of the planning body at their meeting-place in the house of Oliver Bond in Dublin. Bond died in prison, while the others, including Thomas Addis Emmet, older brother of Robert, were exiled after a four years' term of imprisonment. The dashing and much-loved Lord Edward Fitzgerald, son of the Earl of Kildare, to whom the military direction of the rising had been committed, had gone into hiding with a price on his head. He managed for some weeks to avoid arrest but was finally taken on May 19, 1798, four days before the date set for the rising. He died in delirium in Newgate Prison a few days after, of a fever from a gunshot wound sustained in his capture. Henry and John Sheares, young Dublin barristers, who now took over, indiscreetly confided their plans to John Armstrong, captain of a militia unit. As an agent of the government, he accepted their hospitality and followed their every move. As a result they were shortly taken, tried and executed, while Armstrong continued to serve the government as informer.

Meanwhile a search for arms went on, and with it the seeking out of any who had administered the United Irish oath, both searches being conducted by the army, acting without restraints or limits. Quartered among a people helpless against their rapacity and cruelty, they took full advantage of their situation, ravaging, burning, killing at random, and carrying off to the fleet the innocent with the guilty. The methods used to extort information were especially vicious - floggings without limit to the number of lashes, their victims bound to the despised 'triangle'; half-hangings - repeated hanging to the point of unconsciousness; and pitch-capping - applying to the head of the victim a 'cap' lined with boiling tar. Lecky described the situation as "a scene of horror hardly surpassed in the modern history of Europe."[57] While on the one hand these methods brought forth great stores of hidden weapons, including arms and ammunition with which defecting members of the militia had supplied the people, and thousands of pikes forged by local smiths, they aroused the people to a ferocity which could lead only to disaster.[58]

In December, 1796, a French fleet, at Tone's urging, set out for Ireland, carrying 14,000 men, but

fierce winter storms scattered the vessels, and made
landing impossible for the ships that dropped anchor
in Bantry Bay. Though they held there for several
days, the people of Munster, submissive to the leadership of their bishop[59] and regarding the fleet as an
intruding army, remained loyal at that time to the
government. Wexford and Wicklow in Leinster were then
probably the most peaceful parts of Ireland, yet the
extremely short-sighted policies of the government
were to make these counties the scenes of the blood-
iest and most bitter fighting of the rebellion, the
only mercy of which was its brevity.

The Castle, fully informed of plans, had rendered
Dublin rebels helpless through terrorist methods and
the consequent seizure of arms. It had also anticipated the capture of the viceroy and the members of
his privy council in their homes on the night of May
24 - an action which was to initiate the rising. A
full military force, supplemented by well-armed members of the ascendancy, poured into the streets of
Dublin, and the leadership of the rebellion there
melted away. Officers outside Dublin mustered their
troops and awaited orders that never came.

Ulster, where Tone's greatest hopes lay, had been
quickly and brutally disarmed, while the bloody excesses of the revolution itself cooled the enthusiasm
of the Ulsterites for French revolutionary principles.
Battles and skirmishes were isolated events, save for
the savage fighting which Wexford and Waterford were
to witness, with the final tragedy played out on
Vinegar Hill. It was a motley army, mostly peasants,
armed with pikes, scythes, pitchforks and such guns as
they could capture from local garrisons, that faced
the combined forces of the enemy - regulars, militia,
and yeomanry, well-armed, uniformed and provisioned.
Goaded to desperation and maddened by rumors fed them
of threatened Orange massacres, this peasant army,
born almost overnight, fought with complete abandon-
ment and the utmost bravery. While other members of
the clergy looked on with horror at the excesses,
Fathers John and MIchael Murphy and Philip Roche were
caught up in the desperation of their flocks and
proved themselves men of remarkable leadership and
military skill. Barbarities there were, but though
Father Roche made every effort to restrain his people
from the worst of these, he was hanged later for his
part in the struggle.

It was all over by mid-August save for the signs

of havoc and the penalties that were to follow. The belated arrival of a small French fleet in Lough Swilly on October 12, with Wolfe Tone on board the flagship in the uniform of a French officer, resulted in his arrest and courtmartial. Found guilty of treason, he cheated the hangman by taking his own life.

Vengeance was to fall on the government's most helpless subjects, with senseless executions, the consigning of hundreds, without trial, to the fleet or to confinement in the holds of prison ships. Hundreds more were transported half around the world under unspeakable conditions of wretchedness to the horrors of England's newly-established penal colonies in Australia where, without limit of sentence, they were to suffer hardships and brutality which knew only the limits of human endurance.[60] All this in-inflicted wounds that would fester through the years.

The "Red Harvest of '98" was over. The rebellion had provided Pitt with the climate needed for advancing his plan for the union of the Irish Parliament with the British Parliament, The aroused fears of the great landlords and the need they felt for the protection of British military power played into his hands. While bribery in the form of sinecures, peerages and direct money grants had long been common in the Irish parliament, never had it been more flagrant. Pitt's purpose was accomplished by the passing of the Act of Union late in 1800, so that in January 1801, Ireland was incorporated into the United Kingdom.[61,62]

Many of the Catholic hierarchy, under the leadership of Archbishop Troy of Dublin, had lent their support to the plan for union, depending on the prospect held out to them of complete emancipation. A part of the price to be paid for that emancipation was surrender to the king of the right to control by veto the papal appointment of bishops[63] and to supervise all correspondence of the Irish hierarchy with Rome. The government proposed further to assume responsibility for payment of the Catholic clergy. Disputes over these concessions were to sharply divide the clergy, give rise to angry protests from the people as a surrender to a new and galling bondage, and complicate relations with Rome for twenty years, until Rome finally rejected the agreement.

A tragic anti-climax of the Rebellion of 1798 was an abortive attempt at insurrection in 1803 under the leadership of the brave and daring Robert Emmet. Induced [64] into an uprising which it was hoped would reveal to the government any latent leadership among the remnants of the United Irishmen, he unfortunately confided his plans to the barrister, Leonard McNally. Long a government informer, McNally had played the double role of government informer, and of counsel to the early leaders of the United Irish movement, among them Robert's brother, Thomas Addis Emmet. Surrounded as he was by a network of spies, Emmet's every move was known.[65] Months of patient planning and the elaborate forging and stock-piling of pikes and ammunition in the very heart of Dublin ended in a fiasco when government agents circulated contradictory directives among his followers. When the signal was given on the night scheduled for action, Emmet found himself with a mere handful of frightened pikemen of the lower order. "I expected other resources and found myself entangled with a rabble."[66] Their senseless killing of Lord Kilwarden, returning with his niece from a quiet evening in the country, at once alienated the sympathies of Kilwarden's close friend, John Philpot Curran. As a skilful lawyer, Curran had saved many an Irishman from the gallows, exposing suborned witnesses and insuring fair trials. Further alienation resulted when Curran discovered that Emmet was the secret suitor of his daughter Sarah, a fact revealed when he was arrested at Harold's Cross, Dublin, where he had gone in the hope of a farewell visit with her. Emmet's all-night trial ended with an impassioned plea in the cause of freedom. This and his public execution - his hanging from a rude scaffold, followed by his beheading - which took place in front of St. Catherine's church on Thomas Street, fixed his memory deep in the hearts of the Irish people. [67] "By 1809 more than 600 different offenses had been made capital - a state of law unexampled in the worst periods of Roman or oriental despotism."[68]

Only a leader of Daniel O'Connell's gifts of mind and body could have raised again the hopes of the Irish people and girded them as a nation to new efforts. [69] O'Connell was a huge man, well built and powerful, a master of eloquence, with a deep understanding of the Irish mentality and a sympathy with the aspirations of his people. He was equipped with a resonant voice responsive to every mood and passion, yet powerful enough to reach out to the farthest edge

of the mighty crowds which his personal magnetism
drew to him.[70]

Ireland's most fundamental problem was that of
the land. As long as the great estates remained intact, there was simply not enough land left to feed
all those who were trying to live from it. The population was increasing rapidly, the result of early
marriages among a prolific people, and the tendency
of the small farmer to subdivide his limited acreage
to provide home sites for his married sons left large
numbers dependent on plots much too small to provide
for growing families. Potatoes were the one staple
food, and their failure meant disaster. Competition
for land was sending rents ever higher, while farming
methods cried out for improvement.

To the growing middle class, however, the griev-
ance most deeply felt was the fact that Catholics
were still debarred from all the more important offices of the state. They could not sit in parliament,
serve as judges, as colonels in the army, captains in
the navy, or ministers in the government, or hold any
except the most junior offices in the civil service.

Early agitation for emancipation had come to nothing. True, it could have been had for a price,
probably as early as 1799. That price included
still: assigning to the English king the right to
veto papal appointments to Irish sees, allowing commissions to control all correspondence with Rome, and
accepting the payment of the Irish clergy by the
government. The issue was not brought to a focus until 1808. It then caused a permanent rift between
Grattan, who had long sought justice for the Irish
and who regarded the arrangement as just and equit-
able, and O'Connell, who saw it as a new and invid-
ious attempt to enslave the Church. The resulting
division was to delay political emancipation for many
years. A number of the Irish bishops and wealthy
Catholics, as well as their influential Protestant
friends, were favorable to the compromise, and Rome,
grateful for England's part in the defeat of Napoleon
and the delivery or Rome from his control, had agreed
to the terms. It was O'Connell who rallied the
clergy and people to fight to keep the Irish Church
free from royal domination, thereby incurring for
himself the enmity of many government leaders, but
winning the loyalty of a Catholic nation. But the
fight for emancipation was still to be made.

The real struggle began with O'Connell's founding of the Catholic Association in 1823. Its activities depended upon the leadership of the Catholic clergy, aroused for the first time into concerted action, and the total participation of the people. This latter he effected through the "Catholic rent," a monthly contribution of a penny a family, an amount so low that even the poorest could pay. The result was a remarkably large working capital and with it the psychological effect of involvement among the thousands of contributors. The possibilities it presented for trouble were not lost on the government, despite O'Connell's policy of non-violence.

A new vitality was not long in being felt. Up to then the Catholic vote had been controlled directly by the landlords, who had encouraged the extension of the franchise to all forty-shilling free-holders since by it their own political influence was augmented. But by concerted action the general election of 1826 had resulted in success for candidates acceptable to the Association in many counties. In organized bands and with great fanfare the Irish went to the polls when O'Connell, at their urging, stood for the Clare election. Success would win for him a seat in the British parliament and they were determined to see that he got it. Winning with a vote double that of his opponent, he refused the oath presented to him. The situation was too critical for Parliament to hold out longer. An Emancipation bill introduced in March, 1829, passed rapidly through both houses. Emancipation was at last a reality, and when, under the new law, O'Connell again stood for election, he entered in triumph a law-making body that would never be quite the same again.

While the victory brought great joy to the Irish people, the reaction in England was one of profound indignation. O'Connell met the hostility of many of the most powerful men in both houses. They demanded as concession the suppression of the Catholic Association, the disfranchisement of the forty-shilling free-holders, and the extinction of all male orders of religious in the United Kingdom through a law forbidding the admission of new members into their ranks. While the last of these measures was never seriously put into effect, it proved a deterrent for some time to the growth of these bodies. The grant of representation in Parliament had had its price.

At last, however, Emancipation had been achieved, and now O'Connell's battle for the repeal of the union was to occupy his enormous energies, involving mass meetings of remarkable proportions and good order, while, the land problem unsolved, and with industrialization in England rapidly undermining Irish hand manufacture, [71] Ireland was moving inexorably to a terrible depopulation through the Great Hunger of 1847-48, under the very eyes as well as the rule of the world's most affluent nation.

APPENDIX - NOTES

1. Cf. <u>Encyclopedia Britannica</u>, Vol. XII, p.599, 1963 ed.

2. <u>Proceedings of the Royal Irish Academy</u> (52, c.4 1940) cited by Katherine Hughes in "The Golden Age of Early Christian Ireland," in <u>The Course of Irish History</u>, F.W. Moody and F.X. Martin, eds. (Cork: Mercier Press, 1967), p. 88.

3. Cf. Alice Stopford Green, <u>The Making of Ireland and Its Undoing</u> (London: Macmillan & Co.,1908) p. 134.

4. Cf. <u>Encyclopedia Britannica, loc.cit.</u>, p. 605.

5. <u>Ibid.</u>, p; 606.

6. Cf. Green, p. 282 <u>et passim</u>.

7. Cf. <u>Encyclopedia Britannica, loc. cit.</u>, p.606.

8. William Edward Hartpole Lecky, <u>A History of Ireland in the Eighteenth Century</u> (London: Longmans, Green & Co., 1892) 4 vol. Vol I, p.19.

9. Cf. <u>Ibid.</u>, pp. 3, 5, 18.

10. Edward M. Hinton, <u>Ireland Through Tudor Eyes</u> (Philadelphia: University of Pennsylvania Press, 1935), p.44.

11. E.A. D'Alton, <u>History of Ireland from the Earliest Times to the Present Day</u> (London: the Greshman Publishing Co., n.d.), Vol. III,p. 59.

12. Lecky, Vol. I, p. 26.

13. Encyclopedia Britannica, <u>loc. cit.</u>, p.607, 1963 ed.

14. <u>Ibid.</u>

15. <u>Ibid.</u>

16. Cf. Lecky, Vol. I, p. 46 <u>et passim</u>.

17. <u>Ibid.</u>, pp. 83-84.

18. <u>Ibid.</u>, p. 96.

19. Ibid., p. 102.

20. Ibid., p. 104.

21. Ibid.

22. Ibid., p. 105.

23. J.G. Simms, "The Restoration and the Jacobite War," The Course of Irish History, p. 205.

24. Cf. Lecky, Vol. I, p. 141.

25. Ibid., pp. 177-179.

26. Ibid., pp. 179-80.

27. Cf. Ibid., pp. 184-188.

28. Ibid., p. 147. Of the penal code, Edmund Burke says: "All the penal laws of that unparalleled code of oppression were manifestly the effects of national hatred and scorn toward a conquered people whom the victors delighted to trample upon and were not at all afraid to provoke. They were not the effect of their fears but of their security." (Lecky, Vol. I, p. 144).

29. D'Alton, Vol. Iv, p. 472.

30. S.A., p. 51.

31. Cecil Woodham Smith, The Great Hunger, Ireland, 1845-9 (London: New English Library, 1962) p. 21 et seq.

32. Cf. Ibid., pp. 19-21.

33. Cf. Lecky, Vol. I, p. 185.

34. Cf. Ibid.

35. Ibid., p. 213.

36. Cf. D'Alton, Vol. IV, pp. 471-475.

37. Lecky, Vol. I, p. 232.

38. Corcoran, p. 49,quoting from Dublin Pamphlet of 1735, Haliday Collection, R.I.A., Vol. 121.

39. Corcoran, T. S.J. The Clongowes Record 1814-1932, (Dublin: Brown & Nolan Ltd., n.d.) p. 26.

40; Lecky, Vol. I, p. 233.

41. Corcoran, p. 60.

42. Ibid.

43. Ibid., p. XXVII.

44. Quoted in T. Corcoran, S.J. , Education Systems in Ireland from the Close of the Middle Ages. (Dublin: Department of Education, University College, 1928).

45. P.J. Dowling, A History of Irish Education: A Study in Conflicting Loyalties (Cork: The Mercier Press, 1971), p. 99.

46. Maureen Wall, "The Age of the Penal Laws," in The Course of History, p. 227.

47. The Whiteboys, so called from their custom of wearing white shirts in their nighttime activities, were a secret society constituted largely, though not entirely, of Catholic peasantry. Their leadership was something of a mystery, for some were well clad and well mounted. Their set purpose was retaliation for wrongs done the peasantry by the landowners. These included the enclosing of common pasture lands, forced evictions, forced labor and personal cruelties. Their methods were brutal, and included the breaking down of enclosure fences, the maiming and crippling of cattle, arson, and even murder. Secret societies of the kind in other parts of the country assumed various names, but the terms 'whiteboy' and later 'ribbonmen' were loosely applied to all. Their activities added to the problems of absenteeism, for many landowners fled the country from fear of them.

48. Wall, p. 229.

49. Cf. J.C. Beckett, The Making of Modern Ireland, 1603-1923 (London: Faber & Faber, 1966), pp. 253-254.

50. G. Lecker Lampson, Ireland in the Nineteenth
    Century (London: Archibald Constance & Co.,
    1907), p. 49.

51. The present Sister M. Denis (Geraldine) Gregory,
    BVM, had for her maternal great, great, grand-
    mother, Kate Nagle, the famous Irish beauty who
    was immortalized in Edward Lysaght's song, "Kate
    of Granavillo." Kate was of the same family of
    Nagles as Nano Nagle, foundress of the Presenta-
    tion order, and was a cousin of Edmund Burke,
    M. P. Sister is descended from the Leinster
    line of Geraldines, or Fitzgeralds. Leinster
    House, built by the Earl of Leinster, father of
    the Irish hero of 1798, Lord Edward Fitzgerald,
    is now the seat of the Dail Eireann, or the
    Parliament of the Irish Republic.

52. Sean O'Faolain, The Irish (Great Britain:
    C. Nicolls & Co., 1969), pp. 95-96.

53. Peter Guilday, Life and Times of John England,
    First Bishop of Charleston, (1786-1842), 2 vol.
    (New York: America Press, 1927).

54. The part played by the thousands of emigrés who
    sought refuge in England, in amelioration of
    prejudice against the faith, is inestimable, and
    England's relief of their situation is among her
    noblest acts of charity. Cf. Guilday, ibid.,
    p. 65.

55. Beckett, p. 257.

56. Through the years, Reynold's rewards for his
    services to the government, granted in the form
    of cash payments, pensions and sinecures, to-
    talled £45,740. Richard Robert Madden, United
    Irishmen, Their Lives and Times 12 vol. Vol.XI,
    p. 216. (New York: Catholic Publication Society,
    1916).

57. Lecky, Vol. IV, p. 265.

58. Cf. Thomas Pakenham, The Year of Liberty, the
    Story of the Great Irish Rebellion of 1798.
    (Englewood Cliffs, N.J.: Prentice Hall, Inc.,
    1969).

59. "Dr. Moylan's Pastoral of 1796, to his flock in
    Cork, who were then rejoicing in the appearance

of the French Fleet in Bantry Bay, had placed him foremost amongst those in Ireland who were determined to uphold the King's power in England." (Guilday, op. cit., Vol. I, p. 74).

60. Cf. T. J. Kiernan, Irish Exiles in Australia (Dublin: Glonmore & Reynolds, Ltd., 1954).

61. "It seems very improbable that it [the Act of Union] could have passed by bribery alone; it was necessary that the Unionists should be able to point to a bloody and apparently dangerous rebellion, drawing therefrom the moral that nothing short of union could secure property and protestantism (but especially property) from the return of a like danger.

"It follows that the Rising was not unwelcome to the Unionists; and indeed there is ample evidence that it was nursed, guided and timed by the Castle authorities." Maurice Craig, Dublin, p. 266 (London: Cresset Press, 1952).

62. ". . . that avowed fact which is now a part of history, that the rebellion itself was fomented and encouraged in order to facilitate the Union . . . . the real cause of the Union lay deeper, but is quite obvious. It is to be found in the religious dissensions which the enemies of Ireland have created . . . and seek to perpetuate among ourselves; . . . they separated the Protestant from the Catholic and the Presbyterian from both; they revived every antiquated cause of domestic animosity and they invented new pretexts of rancour; but above all, my countrymen, they belied and calumniated us to each other, and they declared that we hated each other, and they continued to repeat the assertion until we came to believe it; they succeeded in producing all the madness of party and religious distinctions; . . . they plundered us of our own country, and left us to recover at our leisure from the horrible delusion into which we had been so artfully conducted." O'Connell to a meeting of freeholders in Dublin, September 18, 1810. P.S. O'Hegarty, A History of Ireland Under the Union, 1801 to 1922, (London: Methuen & Co., 1952) p.63

63. Archbishops Troy of Dublin and Moylan of Cork "were to travel hand-in-hand up to 1815, during the intense period of the Veto agitation. Both . . . were imbued with the Continental philosophy of the divine right of kings, and with the policy of passive obedience to the enemies of Irish freedom. . . . They were out of sympathy with the movement for independence from the outset. . ." (Guilday, Vol. I, p. 73).

64. "Had William Pitt, as Sir Bernard Burke told Dr. Thomas Addis Emmet of New York in the 1880's, really suggested that a messenger be sent to Paris to induce Robert Emmet to return to Ireland and start a new rising? Besides Sir Bernard's word several circumstances seem to support that claim. . ." There follows a detailed account of the operations of a certain William Putnam McCabe which seems to point to the government's use of him for that purpose. Helen Landreth, The Pursuit of Robert Emmet (London: McGraw-Hill Book Co., 1948). p. 118.

65. This view is rejected by D.A. Chart, Ireland from the Union to Emancipation (London: J.M. Dent & Sons, Ltd., 1910) and by others who claim the government was taken quite by surprise, a view hardly to be credited.

66. Dublin Historical Record, Vol. IV, p. 92.

67. Cf. Helen Landreth, The Pursuit of Robert Emmet (previously cited), a detailed and carefully documented account of the rising under Emmet.

68. National History of Ireland, Vol. IV, p. 309.

69. Gladstone said of O'Connell:" He was the greatest popular leader whom the world has ever seen. . . . He was really the first political agitator. . . the father of the Nationalist Movement in Ireland. He called into active operation the forces and passions of race, the visions and ideals of love of country . . . He was the first to arouse into activity the enormous political power which lay dormant in the people, and to organize it on constitutional lines. He was the inventor of popular agitation as it is now practiced in all constitutionally governed countries - that system by which the will of the people in the making of

laws, the removal of abuses, the granting of
reforms, finds expression in political, social
and trade organizations with scattered branches
under a central executive, and members sub-
scribing to a common fund; in the registration
of voters, and in meetings and demonstrations
and processions, with bands and banners. He
brought the people, the democracy, the crowd,
into the political arena, dictating policy by
their weight of numbers and determined will to
kings and parliaments. Great indeed is the
world's debt to O'Connell for the orderly progress of liberty. . . . In Ireland the people
loved him almost to adoration. They followed
him with unbounded trust and devotion. He was
thoroughly Irish in nature, in temperament, in
manner. . . . He was in a word the incarnation
of a nation." Quoted by Michael MacDonagh in
"O'Connell, the Tribune, Clare Election, and
Repeal Meetings," Catholic Emancipation Centenary,Rev. Myles V. Ronan,ed. (Dublin Colm
O'Locklainn).

70.   Cf. Wm. E. H. Lecky, Leaders of Public Opinion,
Vol. II, "Daniel O'Connell," (New York:
Longman, Green & Cp., 1903).

71.   " The economic effects of the Union were disastrous, as they were intended to be. The system referred to by Pitt, of keeping Ireland
poor and miserable, had, perforce, to be abandoned in 1782 when the Irish Parliament made
its declaration of independence, but it was at
once re-established when the Act of Union gave
England power to re-establish it."(O'Hegarty,
p. 380.) The study from which the above is quoted speaks of the abolishing of protective duties at a time when industrialization was progressing rapidly in England where an ample supply of capital and of coal gave so marked an
advantage to English manufacture that one industry after another was wiped out in Ireland,
save that of linen in Belfast. With unemployment general in the cities and populations
swelling as a result of rural evictees seeking
refuge there, conditions of poverty became unspeakable even before the horrors of the great
famine. Cf. O'Hegarty, 380 et passim.

Data From Community Register As Kept by Mother Cecilia Dougherty

TABLE

No.	Name	Residence		Entrance	Age	Profession	Death
1.	Mary Frances Clarke	Dublin	Ireland	11/ 1/33	30		12/ 4/87
2.	Margaret Mann	Dublin	Ireland	11/ 1/33	25	8/15/45	8/25/73
3.	Rose O'Toole	Dublin	Ireland	11/ 1/33	24	8/15/45	3/10/90
4.	Eliza Kelly	Dublin	Ireland	11/ 1/33	25	8/15/45	4/21/81
5.	Catherine Byrne	Dublin	Ireland	11/ 1/33	24	8/15/45	10/ 8/66
6.	Mary Lawlor (Alphonse)	King's Co.	Ireland	6/16/35	25	8/15/45	7/29/59
7.	Maria Lalor (Clare)	King's Co.	Ireland	8/15/37	21	8/15/45	5/ 3/1901
8.	Bridget O'Leary (Aloysius)	Dublin	Ireland	6/21/39	35	8/15/45	12/ 8/61
9.	Francis O'Reilly	Cavan Co.	Ireland	6/24/39	17	8/15/45	12/14/45
10.	Catherine Murray (Bernard)	Dublin	Ireland	8/14/39	25	8/15/45	2/21/1900
11.	Eliza O'Reilly (Joseph)	Cavan Co.	Ireland	3/19/40	24	8/15/45	5/ 7/87
12.	Eliza Fullam (Theresa)	Moate	Ireland	6/26/40	30	8/15/45	2/23/75
13.	Eliza Mullen (Philomena)	Philadelphia,Pa.		8/16/40	15	8/15/45	9/13/54
14.	Ann Caniff (Patrice)	Galway	Ireland	9/ 8/41	21	8/15/45 Dismissed 1/6/61	
15.	Eliza Regan (Gertrude)	Philadelphia,Pa.		9/24/41	15	8/15/45	6/ 2/1919
16.	Sarah Cole (Magdalen)	Philadelphia,Pa.		1/ 1/42	30	8/15/45	7/22/76
17.	Adele Hamelin (Ignatius)	Philadelphia,Pa.		6/ 2/42	35	8/15/45	6/ 5/51
18.	Catherine O'Reilly (Veronica)	Cavan Co.	Ireland	12/ 8/42	18	8/15/45	11/ 1/61
19.	Julia Donavan (Vincent)	Cork	Ireland	12/24/42	19	8/15/45	1/12/92
20.	Mary Baker (Lucy)	Shropshire,	England	11/11/44	30	8/15/46	4/29/49
21.	Elizabeth Sullivan (Bonaventure)	Cork Co.	Ireland	11/11/44	21	8/15/46	4/ 8/70
22.	Letitia Burke (Agnes)	Galway	Ireland	12/ 4/44	21	8/15/45	4/24/1904
23.	Ellen Hurley (Agatha)	Cork	Ireland	12/10/44	21	8/15/45	5/ 5/1902
24.	Jane O'Reilly (Xavier)	Cavan Co.	Ireland	8/15/45	16	12/15/47	3/10/99
25.	Rosanna Griffin (Stanislaus)	Dubuque	Iowa	8/29/45	18	10/ 1/47	8/16/64
26.	Barbara Eisenger (Gabriel)	Burlington	Iowa	9/ 1/45	21	10/ 1/47	1/25/08
27.	Joanna Barry (Raphael)	Davenport	Iowa	9/ 3/45	18	10/ 1/47	4/22/01
28.	Mary Griffin (Cassiana)	Dubuque	Iowa	3/19/46	17	5/ 8/47	1/ 8/60
29.	Mary Connelly (Mathias)	Dubuque	Iowa	3/25/46	24	5/ 8/47	4/25/03
30.	Ellen Kinsella (deSales)	Wexford Co.	Ireland	9/18/47	25	1/29/49	2/27.88
31.	Catherine Colligan (Regis)	Dubuque	Iowa	9/18/47	18	1/29/49	11/29/86
32.	Mary Nihill (Michael)	Clare,Cavan Co.Ire		6/29/48	17	3/25/51	9/21/12
33.	Margaret Mulligan (Francis)	Dubuque	Iowa	5/10/49	15	3/25/51	3/30/95
34.	Ann Quigley (Angela)	Dubuque	Iowa	1/11/50	24	9/29/51	7/23/85

Table Continued

No.	Name	Residence		Entrance	Age	Profession	Death
35	Ann McDonnell (Lucy)	Kilkenny	Ireland	6/ 1/50	36	9/29/51	1/24/09
36	Mary Scanlan(Paul)	Waterford	Ireland	9/ 3/50	36	12/ 8/54	8/10/11
37	Catherine Farrelly (Terentia)	Cavan Co.	Ireland	5/ 8/51	21	1/ 1/53	2/11/06
38	Hanora Cahill (John)	Waterford	Ireland	5/11/51	35	12/ 8/54	9/23/86
39	Mary Byrne (Augustine)	Kilkenny	Ireland	6/16/51	29	12/ 8/54	9/25/04
40	Ann Harron (Clement)	Dubuque	Iowa	6/27/51	15	1/ 1/54	4/14/19
41	Caroline Grenier (Ignatius)	Montreal	Canada	7/ 2/51	18	1/ 1/54	9/17/77
42	Mary Tench (Borgia)		Ireland	9/ 8/51	25	1/ 1/54	8/21/86 60
43	Catherine Grace (Liguori)	Waterford	Ireland	12/ 8/51	25	1/ 1/54	Dismissed 12/26/
44	Mary J. O'Hagan (Justina)	Derry Co.	Ireland	12/15/51	20	7/16/54	4/11/01
45	Martha Clarke (Josephine)	Dublin	Ireland	5/25/52	38	1/ 1/53	4/29/55
46	Catherine Clarke(Cornelius)	Dublin	Ireland	5/25/52	43	1/ 1/53	10/12/62
47	Margaret O'Brien (Joachim)	Waterford	Ireland	7/ 4/52	35	7/15/54	5/15/65
48	Margaret Kinsella (James)	Waterford	Ireland	8/ 5/52	24	7/16/54	7/27/01
49	Bridget McCloskey (Gonzaga)	Derry Co.	Ireland	9/ 8/52	18	7/16/54	1/20/15
50	Margaret McCloskey (Peter)	Derry Co.	Ireland	10/10/52	20	7/16/54	12/27/54
51	Martha Mullen (Martina)	Derry Co.	Ireland	10/20/52	28	7/16/54	8/18/87
52	Catherine Seery (Monica)	Dublin	Ireland	10/21/52	30	7/16/54	1/15/92
53	Ann Seely (Baptist)	Elk Grove	Wisconsin	3/ 1/53	24	12/24/54	6/19/97
54	Bridget Collins (dePazzi)	Limerick	Ireland	5/ 1/53	22	12/24/54	12/28/15
55	Ellen Grace (Andrew)	Waterford	Ireland	6/11/53	20	12/24/54	Left 12/26/60
56	Mary Fitzgerald(...Cross)	Garryowen	Iowa	7/ 2/53	18	12/24/54	3/11/14
57	Ellen Cosgrove (Regina)	Dubuque	Iowa	9/ 8/53	15	12/ 8/55	2/18/89
58	Lucy Reilly (Ildephonse)	Galena	Illinois	9/ 8/53	15	7/25/55	7/25/55
59	Ann Foley (Scholastica)	Garryowen	Iowa	11/ 1/53	20	7/25/55	4/25/66
60	Mary A. O'Reilly (Chrysostom)	Dubuque	Iowa	11/21/53	18	7/25/55	11/ 3/66
61	Catherine McCarthy (Benedict)	Cork Co.	Ireland	11/21/53	15	7/25/55	9/21/67
62	Ellen Fitzgerald(Ambrose)	Garryowen	Iowa	12/23/53	26	7/25/55	8/20/07
63	Henrietta LaCroix (DeChantal)	Albany	West.Va.	12/23/53	18	7/ 2/56	11/ 2/60
64	Bridget Roach (Anthony)	Garryowen	Iowa	3/13/54	20	7/ 2/56	2/ 5/93
65	Annie Walsh (Philomena)	Philadelphia	Pa.	3/19/54	16	9/ 8/55	5/ 4/64
66	Annie Ryan (Louis)	Kilkenny	Ireland	5/10/54	20	7/ 2/56	7/16/56
67	Elizabeth Keneally (Ursula)	Dubuque	Iowa	5/24/54	22	7/ 2/56	12/20/04

TABLE continued

No.	Name	Residence		Entrance	Age	Profession	Death
68	Ellen Mulgrew (Anastasia)	Garryowen	Iowa	8/15/54	18	7/ 2/56	12/ 4/87
69	Catherine Cosgrove (Jerome)	Cavan Co.	Ireland	8/15/54	34	7/ 2/56	3/23/82
70	Frances Sullivan (Dominic)	Cork Co.	Ireland	9/ 8/54	25	9/ 8/56	9/ 8/86
71	Julia Kelliher (Ann)	Cork Co.	Ireland	9/13/54	24	10/ 5/56	4/10/11
72	Catherine Reilly (Gregory)	Garryowen	Iowa	10/15/54	20	10/ 5/56	6/ 6/76
73	Teresa Byrne (Bridget)	Muscatine	Iowa	11/19/54	18	10/ 5/56	5/28/76
74	Ellen Martin (Camillus)	Galena	Illinois	2/ 2/55	18	10/ 5/56	3/ 3/11
75	Eliza McCarthy (Stephen)	Cork Co.	Ireland	2/ 2/55	22	3/19/57	Dismissed 8/9/61
76	Catherine Reid (Stella)	Elkader	Iowa	5/30/55	19	3/19/57	11/25/14
77	Catherine Kiernam (Claude)	Meath Co.	Ireland	5/30/55	25	3/19/57	2/13/98
78	Helena Hynes-(Bibiana)	Dubuque	Iowa	5/30/55	18	3/19/57	4/ 5/97
79	Bridget Quinn (Martha)	Kilkenny	Ireland	5/30/55	20	3/19/57	9/ 2/09
80	Catherine Butterworth (Alexius)	Dubuque	Iowa	4/29/55	15	3/19/57	5/14/06 63
81	May McNamee (Genevieve)	Dubuque	Iowa	4/29/55	15	12/ 8/57	Dismissed 4/26/
82	Margaret Courtney (Sebastian)	Garryowen	Iowa	10/ 7/55	20	12/ 8/57	7/ 9/06
83	Margaret Short (Seraphina)	Dubuque	Iowa	10/ 7/55	15	12/ 8/57	9/ 4/25
84	Cathy McCarthy (Isidore)	Cork Co.	Ireland	4/29/55	24	12/ 8/57	2/ 1/05
85	Mrs. Dunn (Helen)	Waterford	Ireland	12/ 3/55	55	12/ 8/57	2/18/75
86	Mary Dougherty (Cecilia)	Garryowen	Iowa	2/ 2/56	18	12/ 8/57	9/ 7/19
87	Rose Carroll (Christina)		Ireland	5/ 1/56	38	3/19/58	10/15/99
88	Mary A Ess (Barbara)	Bamburg	Bavaria	5/27/56	20	3/19/58	5/ 1/15
89	Sarah O'Keefe (Basil)	Garryowen	Iowa	7/26/56	17	3/19/58	8/ 6/67
90	Mary Malloy (Ildephonse)	Davenport	Iowa	9/ 8/56	19	3/19/58	9/14/71
91	Bridget Carr(Felicitas)	Dubuque	Iowa	9/24/56	18	3/19/58	2/13/11
92	Elizabeth Phelan(Petronella)	Abbey Felix	Ireland	10/28/56	22	12/15/58	7/ 2/11
93	Magdalen Guise (Hildegarde)	Hamburg	Germany	10/28/56	25	12/15/58	11/25/59 62
94	Magdalen Shearer (Marceline)	Hamburg	Germany	10/28/56	29	12/15/58	Dismissed 1/10/
95	Margaret Hurley (Peter)	Waterford	Ireland	11/22/56	25	12/15/58	12/ 2/85
96	Catherine Savage(Laurence)	Downpatrick	Ireland	10/31/56	65	12/15/58	2/11/82
97	Margaret O'Regan (Calista)	Dubuque	Iowa	3/25/57	17	12/15/58	5/ 9/07
98	Elizabeth Doyle (Perpetua)	Dubuque Co.	Iowa	5/10/57	22	12/15/58	4/11/91
99	Mary Doyle (Placidas)	Dubuque Co.	Iowa	5/10/57	18	7/ 1/59	
100	Mary O'Brien (Antonia)	DAvenport	Iowa	8/29/57	19	7/ 1/59	

TABLE continued

No	Name	Residence		Entrance	Age	Profession	Death
101	Catherine King (Domitilla)	Galway	Ireland	9/ 8/57	19	7/ 1/59	12/14/65
102	Joanna Ryan (Evangelist)	Garryowen	Iowa	9/15/57	22	7/ 1/59	3/29/10
103	Eliza Byrne (Louis)	Kilkenny	Ireland	10/ 7/57	18	7/ 1/59	7/ 6/79
104	Catherine McLaughlin (Fidelis)	Carlow	Ireland	2/ 2/58	27	9/ 8/59	12/12/12
105	Mary J. Clarke (Josephine)	Dublin	Ireland	8/ 6/58	14	5/10/61	6/22/18
106	Catherine Mullaney (Alphonse)	Liverpool	England	5/15/59	26	5/10/61	5/ 4/75
107	Ann Devlin (Cassiana)	Dubuque	Iowa	1/ 1/60	25	11/21/61	3/12/27
108	Mary E. Regan (DeChantal)	Dubuque	Iowa	7/16/60	18	5/24/62	1/23/22
109	Mary A. Whelan (Hildegarde)	Garryowen	Iowa	10/ 7/60	21	7/ 2/62	3/ 8/83
110	Margaret Dunphy (Veronica)	Burlington	Iowa	3/ 62	19	8/15/62	1/15/17
111	Jane Fennell (Aloysius)	Davenport	Iowa	3/31/62	25	8/15/62	8/28/74
112	Mary Kelly (Asissium)	Joliet	Illinois	10/29/62	23	2/23/64	Dismissed 8/13/67
113	Ann Ryan (Rosalia)	Killaloe,Clare, Ire.		10/29/62	24	2/23/64	8/17/95
114	Sarah Ryan (Euphrasia)	Killaloe,Clare, Ire.		10/29/62	22	2/23/64	10/10/03
115	Isabelle O'Connor (Alcantara)	Dubuque	Iowa	12/27/62	19	2/23/64	Dismissed 1866

Register kept by Mother Cecilia from 1862 to Father Donaghoe's death in 1869

Entrance	Name	Age	Residence	No.	Rec'd	Name in Religion	Prof.	Left
4/12/63	Alice Finley	19	Burlington,Ia.	116	2/23/64	Cortona	6/ 7/65	
4/12/63	Mary Bopp	21	Muscatine,Ia	117	2/21/64	Germanus	5/ 7/65	
4/16/63	Bridget WAlsh	38	Boston,Mass.	118	2/23/64	Clotilde	5/	
5/24/63	Mary McGrath	22	Dubuque,Ia.	119	2/23/64	Cyprian	5/ 7/65	
5/24/63	Johanna Kenealy	18	Dubuque,Ia.	121	2/23/64	Damian	5/ 7/65	
5/24/63	Mary Rogers	22	Dubuque,Ia	120	2/23/64	Eugenia	5/ 7/65	3/11/73
6/ 9/63	M.A. Corrigan	33	Jersey City,N.J.	122	2/23/64	Eulalia	5/ 7/65	
9/10/64	Abbie Wallace	21	Garryowen,Ia.	123	7/25/64	Anselm	12/23/66	
11/13/64	Eliza Keas	25	Muscatine,Ia.	124	7/25/65	Stanislaus	1/ 4/67	
12/ 8/64	M.A. Gandolfo	22	Holy Cross,Ia.	125	7/25/65	Philomena	5/10/66	
4/ 4/65	Ellen Moore	20	Davenport,Ia.	126	7/25/65	Loretto	8/12/66	11/ 8/71
8/15/65	Mary J. McPoland	18	Dubuque,Ia.	127	12/ 8/65	Presentation	12/23/66	
8/15/65	Kate Duffy	18	Dubuque,Ia.	128	12/ 8/65	Maurice	12/23/66	
8/31/65	Kate O'Connor	17	DeWitt,Ia.	129	12/ 8/65	Theodore	12/23/66	
8/31/65	Margaret Blessington	16	DeWitt,Ia.	130	12/ 8/65	Conception	12/23/66	2/27/73
9/ 6/65	Fannie Linehan	19	Davenport,Ia.	131	12/ 8/65	Incarnation	12/23/66	11/19/74
9/ 6/65	Mary Fitzgerald	21	Iowa City, Ia.	132	12/ 8/65	Joachim	12/23/66	9/27/11
11/12/65	Elizabeth Small	22	St. Teresa's Ia.	133	12/ 8/65	Assumption	12/23/66	
12/14/65	Annie O'Donnell	23	Davenport,Ia.	134	3/19/66	Cosmas	1/ 1/68	9/ 5/96
12/14/65	Kate Dunn	32	Davenport,Ia.	135	3/19/66	Zita	8/11/67	
12/16/65	Kate Hannon	16	Dubuque,Ia.	136	3/19/66	Annunciation	8/11/67	
2/ 2/66	Mary McDonnel	20	New Melleray,Ia.	137	3/19/66	Purification	8/11/67	
7/27/66	Bridget McLaughlin	20	New Melleray,Ia.	138	9/16/66	Scholastica	8/15/68	
8/24/66	Maggie Collins	21	Dubuque,Iowa.	139	9/16/66	Cleophas	8/15/68	
8/24/66	Kate Tobin	16	DeWitt,Iowa	140	9/16/66	Antonia		6/20/67
8/ 8/66	Lizzie Lawlor	17	DeWitt,Iowa	142	9/16/66	Cornelia	1/ 1/68	
8/ 8/66	Lizzie Noonan	15	Fort Dodge, Ia.	141	9/16/66	Philomena	3/25/68	
8/26/66	Mary Swift	19	Iowa City,Ia.	143	9/16/66	Nativity	3/25/68	
8/26/66	Maggie Iten	15	Davenport,Ia.	144	9/16/66	Dolorosa	1/ 1/68	
1/ 1/67	Jane Burke	27	Garryowen,Ia.	145	4/12/67	Thomas	8/15/68	
1/ 1/67	Annie Burke	24	Garryowen,Ia.	146	4/12/67	Columba	8/31/68	Died12/6/74

Entrance	Name	Age	Residence	No.	Rec'd	Name in Religion	Prof.	Left
9/12/67	Mary Frederickson	24	Davenport,Ia.	147	11/10/67	Visitation	3/19/69	
9/12/67	Emily Motie	15	Davenport,Iowa	148	11/10/67	Henriette	3/19/69	
9/12/67	Mary Healy	21	Iowa City,Ia.	149	11/10/67	Basil	3/19/69	
9/12/67	Mary Brady	17	Davenport,Ia.	150	11/10/67	Patrick	3/19/69	
10/22/67	Alice Rutherford	26	Muscatine,Ia.	151	11/10/67	Loyola	8/ 8/69	
10/31/67	Katie McLaughlin	23	New Melleray,Ia.	152	1/27/68	Benedict	3/19/69	
11/ 1/67	Hanorah Kinsella	26	St. Joseph's,Ia.	153	1/28/68	Salome	3/19/69	
11/ 1/67	Kate Keas	22	Dubuque,Ia.	154	1/27/68	Polycarp	3/19/69	
11/20/67	Crissie Sturdevant	19	Davenport,Ia.	155	1/27/68	Chrysostom	3/19/69	Dis.8/16/69
12/ 9/67	Johanna Haw	22	New Melleray,Ia.	156	6/19/68	Hyacinth	11/19/69	
10/13/67	Louisa Lilly	22	Burlington,Ia.	157	6/19/68	Ascension	8/ 8/69	
1/ 3/68	Kate Hays	26	Garryowen, Ia.	158	6/19/68	Kotska	12/10/69	
1/12/68	Sarah Savage	20	Prairie Creek,Ia	159	6/19/68	Pauline	12/10/69	
5/ 7/68	Mary Burns	20	Waukoma, Ia.	160	8/31/68	Felix	12/10/69	
5/ 9/68	Catherine Conron	19	Chicago, Ill.	161	8/31/68	Borromeo	12/10/69	
5/27/68	Ellen Forman	22	Chicago,Ill.	162	8/31/68	Winifride	12/10/69	
6/ 7/68	Mary Sullivan	23	Prairie Creek,Ia.	163	11/ 1/68	Lucian	7/25/71	
6/27/68	Agatha Hiberger	20	Muscatine,Ia.	164	11/ 1/68	Germanus	8/11/71	
8/17/68	Kate Healy	22	Muscatine,Ia.	165	11/ 1/68	Cyril	8/11/71	
9/21/68	Mary J. Mullen	20	St. Teresa's, Ia	166	9/ 8/69	Antonia	11/16/69	6/19/71
10/ 3/68	Margaret Scanlan	26	Chicago, Ill.	167	3/19/69	Marcellus	12/30/70	
11/ 3/68	Eliza Harding	26	Chicago, Ill.	168	3/19/69	Celestine	8/13/71	

APPENDIX III

THE CONGREGATION'S SOURCE MATERIALS

USED IN THIS VOLUME

The originals of all the following materials are contained in the Congregation's archives:

1. All letters addressed to Father Donaghoe and all but a small fraction of his letters to members of the Congregation. That small fraction are in typescript.

2. All letters of Mother Clarke save those addressed to Bishop Loras, and all letters addressed to her.

3. Annals written by Sister M. Pulcheria McGuire, in typed form - a 404 page study. Referred to as McGuire Annals.

4. Journal - a collection of episodes and recollections communicated to Sister M. Lambertina Doran by others, many of them by Sister M. Michael Nihill. Referred to as Doran Journal.

5. Diary, kept by Sister M. Cresentia Markey - a recounting of incidents as they occurred during her years as general secretary. It includes also recollections shared with her by early Sisters. Referred to as Markey Diary.

6. Diary, kept by Sister M. Agatha Hurley during her early years at St. Anthony School Davenport.

7. Notes, pencilled notes kept by Sister M. Lambertina Doran, supplementary to materials included by her in her early history of the Congregation, In the Early Days.

8. Household account books kept by Mother Clarke on the Prairie, beginning in 1847 and continuing almost to her death in 1887, with an interruption from late 1857 to early 1869. Also several small notebooks containing accounts of the boarders as kept by her.

9. Large account book from the Philadelphia years, and loose leaves from an account book kept by Father Donaghoe there.

10. Two small note books and loose memoranda kept by Father Donaghoe.

11. Copies of the Congregation's publication, Our Herald, 1913 to 1957.

12. Journal of Events - a chronological listing of occurrences in the history of the Congregation.

13. Mission Book, containing skeletal accounts of the missions in the order of their opening, giving name of pastor, list of pioneer members and occasional pertinent comments.

14. Community Registers, the earliest of which are discussed in the text.

15. Record of Postulant Wardrobes, listings of items postulants brought with them on entering the Congregation.

16. Book of Statistics, including mortuary list, with causes of death, etc., as kept by Sister M. Lambertina Doran.

17. Tax Receipts beginning in 1846.

18. Folders containing historical data relating to various early missions.

19. Individual folders containing such personal data as remain regarding the early members.

20. Fragmentary memoirs kept by early Sisters.

21. Manuscript copies of Father Donaghoe's and Mother Clarke's first rules.

22. Unpublished Master's dissertations: Sister M. St. Joan of Arc (Jane) Coogan, History of the Immaculate Conception Academy of Davenport, Iowa, and of the Foundation of Catholic Education in that City. Catholic University of America, 1941.

    Sister M. Anna Rose Callan, The Sisters of

Charity of the B.V.M. and Their Schools in Chicago, 1867-1940. Submitted to Loyola University, Chicago, 1941.

* * * * *

The following data are offered for the sake of simplifying footnotes:

1. All letters addressed to Bishop Loras quoted in this work are contained in the Archdiocesan archives, Chancery office, Dubuque Iowa.

2. All letters of Father Donaghoe to Archbishop Hughes are contained in the Hughes collection at the Catholic University of America. Those quoted are photo copies received in 1953 from the Reverend Henry Browne, then engaged in the writing of a biography of Archbishop Hughes, which has, unfortunately gone unpublished.

Bibliography

BOOKS - IRELAND

Akenson, Donald H. The Irish Educational Experiment, The National System of Education in the Nineteenth Century, London: Routledge & Kegan Paul, 1970.

Akenson, Donald H. The Church of Ireland, Ecclesiastical Reform and Revolution, 1800-1885 New Haven: Yale University Press. 1971.

Beckett, J.C. The Making of Modern Ireland, 1603-1923. London: Faber and Faber, 1966.

Brennen, Rev. Martin, M.A. The Confraternity of Christian Doctrine in Ireland: 1775-1835. Dublin: Browne and Nolan Limited, 1934.

Carleton, William. Traits and Stories of Irish Peasantry. London: 1836, 3 vol.

Chart, D.A. Ireland from the Union to Catholic Emancipation. London: J.M. Dent & Sons, Ltd., 1910.

Chart, D.A. Litt. D. Medieval Towns: The Story of Dublin. London: J.M. Dent and Sons, Ltd., 1932

Connell, K. H., Irish Peasant Society, Four Historical Essays, Oxford: Clarendon Press, 1968.

Connor Cruise O'Brien Introduces Ireland, Owen Dudley Edwards, Ed. New York: McGraw Hill Book Co., 1969.

Corcoran, T., S.J., Litt,D. Education System in Ireland from the Close of the Middle Ages. Dublin: Department of Education, University College, 1928.

Craig, Maurice, Dublin, 1660-1860. London: The Cresset Press, 1952

Cullen, L. M., Life in Ireland, London: B. T. Batsford, Ltd., 1968.

472

Cullen, L. M. Six Generations, Life and Work in
    Ireland from 1790. Cork: The Mercier Press
    Ltd., 1970.

Paul Cullen and His Contemporaries with their Letters
    from 1820-1902. Vol. I. (Bishop of Armagh 2 vol)
    Kildare: Leinster Leader Ltd., Naas, Co., 1961.

D'Alton, Rev. E.A., L.L.D; M.R.I.A. History of
    Ireland from the Earliest Times to the Present
    Day. 6 vol. London: The Gresham Publishing
    Company, n.d.

De Blacam, Hugh. The Saints of Ireland, The Life-
    Stories of SS. Brigid and Columcille. Milwaukee:
    The Bruce Publishing Company, 1942.

Dowling, P. J. Hedge Schools. Cork: Mercier Press
    Ltd., 1968.

Dowling, P. J. A History of Irish Education, A Study
    in Conflicting Loyalties. Cork: The Mercier
    Press, 1971.

Edwards, R. Dudley, and Williams, T. Desmond, Ed.,
    The Great Famine, Studies in Irish History,
    1845-52. Dublin: Brown & Nolan Ltd., 1956.

Emmet, Thomas Addis. Ireland Under English Rule, or
    A Plea for the Plaintiff. Vol. II. 2 vol.
    New York: G. F. Putnam's Sons, 1909.

Fitzgibbon, Constantine. Out of the Lion's Paw,
    Ireland Wins Her Freedom. London:
    MacDonald & Co., 1969.

Fitzpatrick, Rev. Br. J.D. Edmund Rice, Founder and
    First Superior General of the Brothers of the
    Christian Schools of Ireland. Dublin: M.H. Gill
    & Sons, Ltd., 1945.

Fitzpatrick, William John, J.P. Life and Times of
    Contemporaries of Lord Cloncurry. Dublin: James
    Duffy, 1855.

Fitzpatrick, William John, J.P. Life and Times and
    Correspondence of the Right Rev. Dr. Doyle,
    Bishop of Kildare and Leighlin. 2 vol.
    Boston: Patrick Donahoe, 1862.

Gerard, Francis A. Some Fair Hibernians. London: Ward & Downey. 1907.

Glynn, Anthony. High Upon the Gallows Tree. Tralee: Anvil Books Ltd., 1967.

Green, Alice Stopford, The Making of Ireland and Its Undoing. London: Macmillan & Co., 1908.

Hale, Leslie. John Philpot Curran, His Life and Times. London: Jonathan Cape, 1958.

Harvey, John. Dublin, A Study in Environment. London: B.T. Batsford, Ltd., 1949.

Hay, Edward, Esq. History of the Irish Insurrection of 1798. Boston: Patrick Donohoe, n.d.

Hinton, Edward M. Ireland Through Tudor Eyes. Philadelphia: University of Pennsylvania Press., 1935.

Hogan, James Frances. The Irish in Australia. London: Ward & Downey, 1887.

Hutch, William, D.D. Nano Nagle, Her Life, Her Labours, and Their Fruits. Dublin: McGlashan & Gill, 1875.

Hutton, Arthur Wollaston., ed. Arthur Young's Tour in Ireland 1776-1779. 2 vol. London: George Ball & Sons, 1892.

Johnson, Charles. Ireland Historic and Picturesque. Philadelphia: The John C. Winston Co., 1902.

Kiely, Mary. O'Donel of Destiny. New York: Oxford University Press, 1939.

Kiernan, T.J. The Irish Exiles in Australia. Dublin: Clonmore & Reynolds, 1954.

Lampson, G. Lecker. Ireland in the Nineteenth Century. London: Archibald Constance & Co., 1907.

Landreth, Helen. The Pursuit of Robert Emmet. New York: London: Whittlesey House, McGraw-Hill Book Company, Inc., 1948.

Lecky, William E. H. A History of Ireland in the
    Eighteenth Century. New Ed. 5 Vol. London:
    Longmans, Green & Co., 1892.

Lecky, Wm. E. H., Leaders of Public Opinion,
    Vol. II, "Daniel O'Connell," New York:
    Longmans, Green & Co., 1903.

Lee, Grace Lawless. The Huguenot Settlements in
    Ireland. London: Longmans, Green & Co., 1936.

MacIntyre, Angus. The Liberator, Daniel O'Connell
    and the Irish Party, 1830-1847.
    London: Hamish Hamilton, 1965.

MacManus, Seumas., The Story of the Irish Race.
    New York: The Irish Publishing Co., 1921.

Madden, Richard R., The United Irishmen. Their Lives
    and Their Times. New York: The Catholic Publi-
    cation Society of America. 1916. 11 vol.

Magdalena, Sr. M. Some Aspects of the History of
    Mother McAuley's Times. Dublin: Unpublished.

Maxwell, Constantia. Country and Town in Ireland
    Under the Georges. London: George G. Harrap &
    Co., Ltd., 1940.
Maxwell, Constantia, Dublin Under the Georges.
    1714-1830. London: Faber and Faber, Ltd. 1946.

Moody, T.W. Moody, & Martin, F.X. O.S.A. eds.
    The Course of Irish History. Cork:
    The Mercier Press, 1967.

Moore, Thomas. The Life and Death of Lord Edward
    Fitzgerald. Boston: Patrick Donahoe, 1860.

Murray, Robert H. Helps for Students of History
    Ireland, 1714-1829. Dublin: n.d.

O'Brien, Ven. Richard Baptist. Life of Catherine
    McAuley. New York: D & J Sadlier & Co., n.d.

O'Connor, Elizabeth P. Herself, Ireland.
    New York: Dodd Mead and Company, 1919.

O'Connor, Richard. The Irish, Portrait of a People.
    New York: G.P.Putnam's Sons, 1971.

O'Faolain, Sean. The Irish. Harmondsworth,
    Middlesex, England: Penguin Books, 1972.

O'Hegarty, P. S. The History of Ireland Under the
    Union. 1801 to 1922, London: Methuen & Co.,
    Ltd., 1952.

O'Mullane, Brigid. The Huguenots in Dublin."The
    Little Green." Vol. VIII: No.4, Sept-Nov.
    Dublin Historical Record.1946.

Pakenham, Thomas. The Year of Liberty, The Story of
    the Great Irish Rebellion of 1798. Englewood
    Cliffs, N.J.: Prentice Hall Inc., 1969.

Pritchett, V. S. Dublin, A portrait.
    New York: Harper & Row, 1967.

Ronan, Rev. Myles V. An Apostle of Catholic Dublin,
    Father Henry Young. Clonskeagh:
    Browne & Nolan Limited, 1944.

Ryan, Rev. John, S.J. Irish Monasticism, Origins and
    Early Development. London: Longmans, Green and
    Co., 1931.

S. A. Mary Aikenhead, Her Life, Her Work and Her
    Friends, Giving a History of the Foundation of
    the Congregation of the Irish Sisters of Charity.
    Dublin: M.H. Gill & Son, 1882.

Savage, Roland Burke, S.J. Catherine McAuley the
    First Sister of Mercy. Dublin: M.H. Gill
    & Sons, Ltd., n.d.

Savage, Roland B. A Valiant Dublin Woman, A Story of
    George's Hill, 1766-1940. Dublin: M.H.Gill &
    Son, Ltd., 1940.

Smith, Cecil Woodham, The Great Hunger, Ireland,
    1845-49. London: New English Library, 1962.

Sutherland, Hugh. Ireland Yesterday and Today
    Philadelphia: The North American, 1909.

Those Splendid Sisters "The Irish Sisters of Charity
    and Mercy, Reformers of Hospitals." compiled by
    James J. Walsh, New York: J.H. Sears & Co. 1927.

Tuathaigh, Gearoid O. Ireland Before the Famine, 1798-1848. Dublin: Gill & Macmillan, 1972.

Yee, Chiang. The Silent Traveler in Dublin. New York: The John Day Company, n.d.

BOOKS - UNITED STATES

Andreas, A.T. Illustrated Historical Atlas of The State of Iowa, 1875. Chicago: Lakeside Building, n.d.

Barton, George. Walks & Talks About Old Philadelphia. Philadelphia: Peter Reilly Co., 1928.

Billington, Ray A. The Protestant Crusade, 1800-1860, A Study of the Origins of American Nativism. Chicago: Quadrangle Books, 1964.

Bolton, W.H. The Pageant of Transport Through the Ages. London: Sampson Low, Marston, & Co., Ltd., n.d.

Brann, Rev. Henry A.,D.D. Most Reverend John Hughes, First Archbishop of New York. New York: Dodd, Mead & Co., 1892.

Brown, Sister Mary Borromeo. History of the Sisters of Providence of Saint Mary of the Woods. Vol.I. Chicago: Benziger Bros. Ind., 1948.

Burt, National. The Perennial Philadelphians. Boston: Little & Brown Co., 1963.

Callan, Louise, The Society of the Sacred Heart in North America. New York: Longmans,Green and Co., 1937.

Canfield, Walden. Making of Modern America. New York: Houghton Miflin, 1950.

Carey, Sister Mary Helen. The Irish Element in Iowa up to 1865. Master's Thesis, unpublished, Catholic University of America, 1944.

Casper, Henry W., S.J. History of the Catholic Church in Nebraska. 3 vol. Milwaukee: Bruce Press,1960. The Church on the Northern Plains, 1838-1874.(1960)

The Church on the Fading Frontier, 1864-1910.
(1966)
Catholic Chapters in Nebraska Immigration
1870-1900. (1966)

Sadlier's Catholic Directories, 1833 - 1869

Conroy, Rev. Joseph P., S.J. Arnold Damen, S.J. A
Chapter in the Making of Chicago. New York:
Benziger Brothers, 1930.

Crepeau, Soeur Rosemary, OP,Un Apotre Dominicain Aux
Etats-Unis, Le Pere Samuel Charles Gastan
Mazzuchelli, Paris: n.p., 1932.

Davis, Allen F., and Haller, Mark H., Ed. The Peoples
of Philadelphia, A History of Ethnic Groups and
Lower-Class Life, 1790-1940. Temple University
Press Philadelphia: 1973.

DeCailly, Rev. Louis, Memoirs of Bishop Loras, First
Bishop of Dubuque, Iowa, and of Members of His
Family from 1792 to 1858. New York: Christian
Press Association Publishing Co., 1897.

De Courcy, Henry. The Catholic Church in the United
States. Translated and enlarged by John Gilmary
Shea. New York: Edward Dunnigan and Brother.
1857.

Diary and Visitation Record of Rt. Rev. Francis
Patrick Kenrick. 1830-1851. Translated and edited
by Most Rev. Edmond F. Prendergast, 1916.

Donaghy, Thomas J., F.S.C. Philadelphia's Finest, A
History of Education in the Catholic Archdiocese,
1692-1970. Philadelphia: The American Catholic
Historical Society. 1972.

Donnelly, Eleanor, C. A Memoir of Father Felix
Joseph Barbelin, S.J. Philadelphia: n.p, 1886.

Doran, Sister M. Lambertina, B.V.M. In the Early
Days: Pages from the Annals of the Sisters of
Charity of the Blessed Virgin Mary. (1833-1887)
U.S.A. 1911.

Dougherty, Hurley, Daly, Coyne, et al. Sisters of St.
Joseph of Carondelet. St. Louis: B. Herder Book
Co., 1966.

Driscoll, Justin A., With Faith and Vision, Schools
of the Archdiocese of Dubuque, 1836-1966.
Dubuque: Bureau of Education, Archdiocese of
Dubuque. 1967.

Dubuque County History, Iowa: Iowa Writers' Program
of WPA, Jessie M. Parker, State-wide Sponsor;
Joseph F. Flynn, Sponsor, Dubuque County, 1942.

Duff, John B. The Irish in the United States.
Belmont California: Wadsworth Publishing Co.,
1971.

Eleanore, Sister M. On the King's Highway.History of
the Sisters of the Holy Cross of St. Mary of the
Immaculate Conception, Notre Dame, Indiana.
New York: D. Appleton & Co., 1931.

Ellis, John Tracy. American Catholicism. Garden
City: Image Books - Doubleday & Co., 1965.

Ellis, John Tracy. Documents of American Catholic
History. Vol. I. Chicago: Henry Regnery Co.,
1967.

Ellis, John Tracy, ed. Documents of American
Catholic History. Milwaukee:
Bruce Publishing Co., 1956.

Ellis, John Tracy. Perspectives in American
Catholicism. Benedictine Studies.
Baltimore: Dublin: Helicon, 1963.

Erskine, Marjory. Mother Philippine Duchesne
New York: Longmans, Green & Co., 1926.

Eskew, Garnett Laidlaw, The Pageant of the Packets,
A Book of American Steamboating. New York:
Henry Holt & Company, 1929.

Evans, Mary Ellen. The Seed and the Glory, The
Career of Samuel Charles Mazzuchelli O.P. on the
Mid-American Frontier. New York: McMullen
Books, Inc., 1950.

Faherty, Rev. William B. S.J. Dream by the River -
Two Centuries of St. Louis Catholicism, 1766-
1967. St. Louis: Piraeus Publishers, 1973.

Fisher, Sidney George. Diary of: 1834-1871.
   Philadelphia: Historical Society of Philadelphia,
   Philadelphia, 1967.

Franzwa, Gregory M., The Old Cathedral, St. Louis:
   Archdiocese of St. Louis, 1965.

A Full and Complete Account of the Late Awful Riots
   in Philadelphia, Embellished with Ten Engravings.
   n. a. Philadelphia: John B. Perry, 1844.

Garraghan, Gilbert J. The Jesuits of the Middle
   United States.Vol. III. New York:
   America Press, 1938.

Greeley, Andrew M. That Most Distressful Nation: The
   Taming of the American Irish. Chicago:
   Quadrangle Books, 1972.

Greer, Edward C., Rev. Cork Hill Cathedral, The
   Chronicle of St. Margaret's or Sacred Heart
   Parish. Davenport Iowa; 1856-1956.
   Davenport: Gordon Printing Co., 1956.

Guilday, Peter. History of the Councils of Baltimore
   (1791-1884). New York: The Macmillan Company,
   1932.

Guilday, Peter. Life and Times of John Carroll.
   New York: The Encyclopedia Press, 1922.

Guilday, Peter. Life and Times of John England,
   First Bishop of Charleston (1786-1842). 2 vol.
   New York: America Press, 1927.

Gue, Benjamin F. History of Iowa from the Earliest
   Times to the Beginning of the Twentieth Century.
   New York: Century History Co., 4 v.

Hassard, J.R.G. Life of Most Reverend John Hughes.
   New York: D. Appleton & Co., 1866.

Havighurst, Walter. Upper Mississippi, A Wilderness
   Saga. New York: Rinehart & Company, 1944

Havighurst, Walter. Voices on the River, The Story
   of the Mississippi Waterways, New York:
   Macmillan Co., 1964.

480

Healy, Kathleen, RSM, Frances Warde: American
     Founder of the Sisters of Mercy. New York:
     Seabury Press, 1973.

Hennrich, Kilian J. OFM Cap. "Comparative Study of
     Third Order Rules," Franciscan Studies.
     March 1944.

Henry, Sister Gertrude, H.M., The Life of the Most
     Reverend Clement Smyth, D.D., OSCO, Second Bishop
     of Dubuque, 1858-1865, Peosta: New Melleray
     Abbey, 1937.

History of Dubuque County. Ed. Franklin T. Oldt.
     Chicago: Goodspeed Historical Assn., n.d.

Hoffmann, M.M. Antique Dubuque, 1673-1833.
     Dubuque: Telegraph-Herald, 1930.

Hoffmann. M.M. Arms and the Monk! The Trappist Saga
     in Mid-America. Dubuque: Wm. C. Brown Co., 1952.

Hoffmann, M.M. Centennial History of the Archdiocese
     of Dubuque. Dubuque: Columbia College Press,1938.

Hoffmann, M.M. The Church Founders of the Northweat:
     Loras and Cretin and other Captains of Christ.
     Milwaukee: Bruce Publishing Co., 1937.

Hoffmann, M.M. The Story of Loras College, 1839-1939.
     Dubuque: Loras College Press, 1939.

Holland, Sister M. Ildephonse, RSM. Lengthened
     Shadows, A History of the Sisters of Mercy,
     Cedar Rapids, Iowa. New York: Bookman
     Associates, 1952.

Hurley, Sister Angela. On Good Ground, The Story of
     the Sisters of St. Joseph in St. Paul.
     University of Minnesota Press, 1951.

n.a., The Independence Square Neighborhood,
     Philadelphia: Penn Mutual Life Insurance
     Co., 1926.

Johnson, Gerald W. Andrew Jackson, An Epic in
     Homespun. New York: Minton,Balch & Co., 1927.

Johnson, Gerald W. Pattern for Liberty: The Story
     of Old Philadelphia. New York;
     McGraw-Hill Book Co., Inc. 1952.

Kane, John Joseph. Irish Immigrant in Philadelphia.
PhD. Dissertation. University of Pennsylvania.
Filmstrip, 1950.

Kelly, Sister M. Gilbert, OP. Immigrant Colonization
Projects in the United States, 1815-1860.
New York: U.S. Catholic Historical Society, 1939

Kenrick, Francis Patrick. Diary and Visitation
Record of - 1830-1851. Trans. and ed. Most Rev.
Edmond F. Prendergast. n.p. 1916.

The Kenrick-Frenaye Correspondence, 1830-1862.
Selected, arranged and annotated by F.E.T.
Philadelphia: Wickersham Printing Co., 1920.

Kirlin, Joseph L.J. Catholicity in Philadelphia from
the Earliest Missionaries Down to the Present
Time. Philadelphia: John Jos. McVey, 1909.

Lewis, Henry, The Valley of the Mississippi.
St. Paul: Minnesota Historical Society, 1967.
(Published in Germany, 1854).

Logue, Sister Maria Kostka, PhD. Sisters of St.
Joseph of Philadelphia: A Century of Growth and
Development 1847-1947). Westminster, Md.:
Newman Press, 1950.

MacLysight, Edward. Guide to Irish Surnames.
Dublin: n.p., 1964.

Mahony, D.A. The Prisoner of State, New York:
Carleton, Publishers, 1865.

Marschall, J.P. Francis Patrick Kenrick, 1851-1863:
The Baltimore Years. Doctoral Dissertation, unpublished. Catholic University of America, 1965.

Maynard, Theodore. Great Catholics in American
History. New York: All Saints Press Inc., 1957.

Maynard, Theodore. The Story of American Catholicism.
New York: Macmillan Company, 1941.

Mazzuchelli, Samuel Charles, O.P. Memoirs, Historical
and Edifying, of a Missionary Apostolic. trans.
by S.M. Benedicta Kennedy, OSD. Chicago:
W.F. Hall Printing Co., 1914.

McGrath, Sister Albertus Magnus, What a Modern
    Catholic Believes about Women, Chicago:
    The Thomas More Press, 1972.

McGreal, Sister Mary Nona, OP. Samuel Mazzuchelli,
    O.P. A Kaleidoscope of Scenes from His Life.
    n.p.n.d.

McGill, Anne Blanche. The Sisters of Charity of
    Nazareth Kentucky. New York: The Encyclopedia
    Press, 1917.

Melville, Annabelle M. John Carroll of Baltimore,
    Founder of the American Catholic Hierarchy.
    New York: Charles Scribner's Sons, 1955.

Minogue, Anna Catherine. Loretto, Annals of the
    Century. New York: America Press, 1912.

Montay, Sister Mary Innocentia, CSSF, M.A. History
    of Catholic Secondary Education in the Arch-
    diocese of Chicago, Doctoral Dissertation,
    Washington: Catholic University of America
    Press, 1953.

Moretti, Girolamo. The Saints Through Their
    Handwriting. London: Collier-Macmillan Limited,
    1964.

Mosel, Sister M. Eunice, OSF, They Have Taken Root,
    The Sisters of the Third Order of St. Francis
    of the Holy Family. New York:
    Bookman Associates, 1954.

Mulkerins, Brother Thomas M., S.J. Holy Family
    Parish, Chicago, Priests and People.
    Chicago: Universal Press, 1923.

n.a. Pages from a Hundred Years of Dominican
    History: The Story of the Congregation of
    St. Catherine of Sienna. Cincinnati:
    Frederick Pustet & Co., 1921.

Nolan, Hugh J. The Most Reverend Francis Patrick
    Kenrick, Third Bishop of Philadelphia 1830-1851.
    American Catholic Historical Society of
    Philadelphia, 1948.

O'Brien, Mother Gabriel, RSM. Reminiscences of
    Seventy Years. Chicago: Fred.J. Ringley Co.,
    1916.

O'Connor, Sister Mary Paschala, O.P. Five Decades,
    History of the Congregation of the Most Holy
    Rosary, Sinsinawa, Wisconsin, 1849-1899.
    Sinsinawa Press, 1954.

O'Connor, Frederico M., S.J. Reaction to the
    Community Life of Active Women Religious.
    Doctoral Dissertation, 1971.

O'Donnell, George E. St. Charles Seminary, Overbrook,
    1832-1943. Philadelphia: Jeffries & Manz, 1943.

O'Shea, John J. The Two Kenricks, Philadelphia:
    John J. McVey, 1904.

Parker, George F. Iowa Pioneer Foundations, Vol. I.
    Iowa City: State Historical Society of Iowa,
    1940.

Petersen, S.J. Steamboating on the Upper Mississippi,
    the Waterway to Iowa. 1637-1833. Iowa City:
    State historical Society of Iowa, 1937.

Ray, Sister M. Augustina, BVM. American Opinion of
    Roman Catholicism in the Eighteenth Century.
    New Your: Columbia University Press, 1936.

Reck, Franklin M. The Romance of American
    Transportation. New York: Thomas Y, Cromwell
    Company. 1938.

Repplier, Agnes. Philadelphia, the Place and the
    People. New York: The Macmillan Company, 1925.

Rosenberg, Morton M., Iowa on the Eve of the Civil
    War, A Decade of Frontier Politics, Norman:
    University of Oklahoma Press, 1972.

Rothensteiner, Rev. John. History of the Arch-
    diocese of St. Louis, 1673-1928. 2 vol.
    St. Louis: Blackwell Wielandy Co., 1928.

Sage, Leland L., A History of Iowa. Ames:
    Iowa State University Press, 1974.

Schlesinger, Arthur M. Jr. The Age of Jackson.
    (abridged). New York: A Mentor Book,
    New American Library. 1945.

484

Shambaugh, Benjamin F., The Old Stone Capitol
Remembers. Iowa City: State Historical
Society, 1939.

Shannon, William, V. The American Irish
New York: Macmillan Company, 1963.

Shea, John Gilmary. The Catholic Church in Colonial
Days, 1521-1763. New York: Edward O. Jenkins'
Sons, 1886.

Shea, John Gilmary. History of the Church in the
United States. New York: n.p. 1856.

Shields, Sister M. Jean Ellen, BVM, Biography of
Reverend John George Alleman, Pioneer Missionary
of Ohio, Iowa and Illinois, Master's Dissertation, unpublished. St. Louis University, 1954.

Sister of Mercy. Life of Mary Monholland, one of the
Pioneer Sisters of the Order of Mercy in the
West. Chicago: J.S. Hyland & Company, 1894.

Sister of the Visitation, H.M. The Life of the Most
Reverend Clement Smyth, D.D., OSCO, Second Bishop
of Dubuque, 1858-1865. Peosta: New Melleray
Abbey, 1937.

Smith, George Winston, and Judah, Charles. Life in
the North during the Civil War, A Source History,
Albuquerque: University of New Mexico Press,
1966.

Some Schools of Catholic Spirituality, Jean Gautier,
Ed., Kathryn Sullivan RSCJ, trans. New York:
Desclee Co., 1919.

Spaulding, J.L., D.D. The Religious Mission of the
Irish People and Catholic Colonization, New York:
Catholic Publication Society, 1880.

Spalding, M.J. D.D. "The Philadelphia Riots: The
Native American Party." Miscellanea. Louisville:
Webb, Gill & Levering, 1855.

Spencer, J.W., Burrows, J. M.D. The Early Days of
Rock Island and Davenport, Chicago:
Lakeside Press, 1942.

Schauinger, Joseph Herman. Cathedral in the
Wilderness. Milwaukee: Bruce Publishing Co.,
1952.

Sweeney, David F. O.F.M. The Life of John Lancaster
    Spalding, First Bishop of Peoria, 1840-1916.
    New York: Herder & Herder, 1965.

Thomas, Sister M. Evangeline, Ph.D. Footprints on the
    Frontier. Westminster: Newman Press, 1948.

Thurston, Herbert, S.J. The Physical Phenomena of
    Mysticism. London: Burns Oates, 1952.

Tourscher, Francis, E., OSA. The Hogan Schism and
    Trustee Troubles in St. Mary's Church.
    Philadelphia: The Peter O'Reilly Co., 1930.

United States Documents in the Propaganda Fide
    Archives. A Calendar, First SEries, Volume Three
    Ed., Finbar Kenneally, OFM., Academy of American
    Franciscan History, Washington, D.C., 1971.
    (Notre Dame University Archives).

White, Rev. Charles I. Mother Seton, Mother of Many
    Daughters. Garden City: Doubleday & Co., Inc.,
    1949.

Wilkie, Franc B. Davenport Past and Present: Includ-
    ing the Early History and Personal and Anecdotal
    Reminiscences of Davenport. Davenport:
    Luse, Lane & Co., 1858.

Wittke, Carl. The Irish in America. Baton Rouge:
    Louisiana State University Press, 1956.

Youle, Estelle LePrevost. History of Clinton County
    Iowa to 1946. n.p., 1946.

ARTICLES FROM HISTORICAL JOURNALS.

From Records of American Catholic Historical Society.
RACHS.

Auld, Helen. "Critical Years of the Catholic church
    in the United States." Vol. I, March, 1939.pp.1-21.
Chandler, Charles L. "Catholic Merchants of Early
    Philadelphia," Vol. 64,June, 1953, pp. 94-103.
Flintham, Lydia Stirling, "The Sisters of Charity of
    the Blessed Virgin Mary." Vol. XV, March, 1904,
    p. 46.

"Full Particulars of the Late Riots: a Contemporary
    Pamphlet," LXXX, 1969, p. 24.

486

Griffin, Martin I.J. "Church of St. John the Evangelist." XX. 1909, pp. 350-405

Griffin, Martin I.J. "Life of Bishop Conwell." XXIII-XXIX. Running serially, beginning with Vol. XXIII p. 17, 1912, ending with Vol. XXIX. p. 384,1918.

Griffin, Martin I.J. "Marc Anthony Frenaye." XXXVIII. p. 132-143, 1927.

Griffin, Martin I.J. "The Story of St.Mary's." X,1899.

Guerrieri, Dora. "Catholic Thought in the Age of Jackson." LXXIII, pp. 77-91, 1962.

Guilday, Rev. Peter. "Concerning Trusteeism." LIV, 1943.

Hindman, Jane F. "The Irishman Who Developed American Culture." LXXI, June 1960,pp. 23-30.

Jackson, Joseph. "Catholic Burial Grounds in Philadelphia." June,1945,Vol. LVI, pp. 70-81.

"Diary of Patrick Kenny." Vol. IX, 1898 et seq.

Kenrick, Francis Patrick. "Report on the Condition of the Church of Philadelphia Made to Our Holy Father, Pope Gregory XVI, June 1, 1838." Vol. 38, 1927, pp. 207-217.

Kite, Elizabeth S. "Joseph Bonaparte, Ex-King of Spain." LIII, Sept. 1942, pp. 129-151.

Love, Very Rev. Thomas J. S.J. "The Evolution of St. Joseph College." LII, 1941, pp. 161-173.

Mallon, Edw. A. "Reverend William Loughran," Vol. 54, March, 1943, pp. 78-79.

Maier, Rev. Eugene. "Matthew Carey, Publicist and Politician, 1760-1839." June, 1928, Vol. 39, pp. 71-154.

Margaret Patricia, Sister, S.N.D. "White Servitude in the American Colonies." XLII, 1936,p. 12.

Maria Alma, Sister, "Catholic Sisterhoods." LII, March, 1941, p. 24-61; June, 1941-88-109. Sept. 1941, 174-184; Dec. 1941, 219-241 &c.

McAvoy, Thomas J., CSS. "The Irish Clergymen in the United States." Vol.75, March 1964, pp. 6-38.

McCall, John. "Jottings on the Kenrick Family." IX, 1898.

McCarthy, Rev. Charles F. "Episcopal Nominations in the Catholic church." XXXVIII, December 1927, pp. 297-309.

McDevitt, Rt. Rev. Msgr. "How Bigotry Was Kept Alive by Old-time Textbooks." Vol. XXIII,1912. pp. 251-261.

McNally, Rev. Wm.F. "The Sulpicians in the United States." Vol. 28, 1917, pp. 126-130.

Meyers, Mary Ann. "The Children's Crusade: Philadelphia Catholics and the Public Schools." 1840-1844. LXXV, 1964, pp. 103-130.

Miller, S.J. "Peter Richard Kenrick, Bishop and
Archbishop of St. Louis, 1806-1896."
Vol. 84, No.1-3, 1973.
Moriarity, Thomas F. "The Truth Teller and Irish
Americans of the 1820's." LXXV, 1964, p. 39-52.
Murphy, Jos. J., Rev. "Mother Seton's Daughters,"
Vol. 28, 1917, pp. 131-134.
Nolan, Rev. Hugh, J. "Philadelphia's First Diocesan
Synod." LIV. 1943, p. 28-43.
Norman, J.J.E., and Middleton, Rev. Dr., OSA,
"The Very Rev. T.J. Donaghoe" Supplement 14.

O'Reilly, Isabel M. "One of Philadelphia's Soldiers
in the Mexican War, A Life Sketch of Brev. Major.
John P. J. O'Brien, A.D. 1818-1850,"
Vol. XIII, 1902, pp. 127,257, 411.
"San Domingo Refugees in Philadelphia." June, 1912.
p. 97-125 &c.
Schmandt, Raymond H."A Selection of Sources Dealing
with the Nativist Riots of 1844."
LXXX, 1969. pp. 68-200.
Stokes, William. A., Archibald, Randall, et al.
"Address of the Catholic Lay Citizens," a Con-
temporary Pamphlet." LXXX, 1969, pp. 134-147.
"The Truth Unveiled, A Contemporary Pamphlet by a
Protestant and Native Philadelphian."
LXXX, 1969, pp. 148-175.
"Selections from the Correspondence of the Late Mark
Anthony Frenaye, from A.D. 1834 to 1856, (Auto-
biography of M. S. Frenaye). v. XIII, 1902,
pp. 454-486.
"Marriage Registers at St. Joseph's Church, Philadel-
phia, Pennsylvania from 1824-1836," From the
Originals by Francis X. Reuss, XX, 1909,p.290.
"Index of Historical Pamphlets, " 1902, Vol. XIII,
pp.60-119.

From the Iowa Catholic Historical Review, ICHR

Hoffman, M.M. "The First Native Iowans of the
Priesthood." November, 1930, p. 23ff. ·
Hoffman, M.M. "The Oldest College in Iowa,"
May, 1935, Vol. VIII, pp. 1-14.
Hoffman, M.M. "Clement Smyth, Second Bishop of Iowa,"
Volume IX, February, 1936, pp. 1-20.
McEvoy, E.L. "Beginnings of the Catholic Church in
Northwest Iowa, with special reference to Emmets-
burg and Palo Alto County." May, 1935,
Vol. VIII, pp. 15-37.
Martin, M.J., "The Patronal Relic of Iowa,"
June, 1934, Vol. VII, pp. 47-51.

488

Plassmeyer, Theodosius, OFM, "The Church in Early
Iowa City, A New Light on the First Franciscan
Father in Iowa and on Bishop Clement Smyth,
1864-1865." February, 1936, pp. 31-37.
Bray, Elizabeth. "In His Own Right." June, 1934,
Vol. VII, pp. 1-11.
Mullin, F.A., "The Chronicle of New Melleray Abbey,"
April, 1934, Vol. VI, pp. 14-20. June, 1934,
Vol. VII, pp. 23-32.
Hoffmann, M. M. "Loras in Alabama," April 1933,
Vol. VI, pp. 29-37. June 1934, Vol. VII,
pp. 30-39.
Stuart, Anne Meysembourg. "History of the Catholic
Press of Iowa." October 1932, Vol. V, pp. 11-38.
Hoffmann, M. M. "Europe's Pennies and Iowa's Missions."
October, 1932, Vol. V. pp. 39-48.
Hoffmann, M. M. "An Epic of Early Iowa: Father Trecy's
Colonization Scheme." October, 1931, Vol. III,
pp. 1-13.
McBride, Sara. "Beginnings of Catholicity in Des
Moines," Octover, 1931, Vol. III, pp. 14-24.
Hoffmann, M. M. "Davenport's 'First' Cross," October,
1931, Vol. III, pp. 30-34.
Kessler, W.G. "Sources in Early Iowa Catholic Church
History." November, 1930, Vol. II, pp. 27-34.
Griffith, C.R. "H. V. Gildea: Pioneer Church
Builder," January, 1930, Vol. I, pp. 14-25.

From the Iowa Journal of History. IJH

Johnson, Hildegarde Binder, "German Fortyeighters in
Davenport," January, 1946, pp. 3-53.
Petersen, Wm. J. "Beginnings of Journalism in Iowa."
July, 1947, pp. 261-289.
Bergman, Leola Nelson, "The Negro in Iowa,"
January, 1948, pp. 3-90.
Agnew, Dwight L. "Jefferson Davis and the Rock
Island Bridge," pp. 3-14.
Gallagher, Ruth A. "This Iowa," January, 1941,
pp. 3-51.
Petersen, Wm. J. "Wolves in Iowa," January, 1940,
pp. 50-93.
Palett, Frank. "Farm Pests in Pioneer Iowa,"
April, 1943, pp. 176-205.
Jackson, W. Turrentine, "Army Engineers as Road-
builders in the Territory of Iowa,"
January, 1949, pp. 15-33.
Agnew, Dwight L. "Iowa's First Railroad,"
January, 1950, p.1 ff.
Petersen, Wm. J. "Diseases and Doctors in Pioneer
Iowa," April, 1951, p. 97 ff.

Rutland, Robert. "The Copperheads of Iowa: A
Re-examination," January, 1954, p. 15 ff.

From the Annals of Iowa

Blansard, Charles, "Religion in Iowa, the Catholics,"
Summer, 1962, p. 387.
Colton, Kenneth E. " The Stagecoach Comes to Iowa,"
Winter, 1960. pp. 161-186.
Lenehan, Rev. B. C. "Right Reverend Mathias Loras, D.D.
First Bishop of Iowa," January, 1899, p.579 ff.

From the Journal of History and Politics. JHP

Pelger, Louis, "Iowa City: A Miniature Frontier of
the Forties." January, 1931. pp. 3-26.
Lorch, Fred W. "Iowa and the 1849 Gold Rush,"
July, 1932, pp. 307-376.
Petersen, Wm. J. "Some Beginnings in Iowa,"
January, 1930, pp. 3 ff.
Wilson, Ben Hur. "Abandoned Railroads of Iowa."
January, 1928, p. 3 ff.
Gallagher, Ruth A. "Money in Pioneer Iowa, 1838-
1865." January, 1934, pp. 1-59.
Petersen, Wm. J. "Population Advance to the Missis-
sippi, 1830-1860," October, 1934,pp. 312-353.

From Miscellaneous Sources

Griffith, C.F., "The Erection of the Diocese of
Davenport." Mid-America, April, 1952, Vol. III
No. 4.
Heffern, Brother Colman, OCSO. "Clement Smyth,(1816-
1865): A Founder of New Melleray and Civil War
Bishop." Reprint from American Benedictine
Review, n.p., n.d.
Holweck, Rev. F.G."Contribution to the Inglesi
Affair," St. Louis Catholic Historical Review.
Vol. V, 1923. pp. 14-39.
Griffin, Martin I.J. "History of Old St. Joseph's,
Philadelphia: ICBU Journal, 1882.
O'Connor, Thos. F. "Catholic Archives of the United
States." Catholic Historical Review, XXXI, 1920.
O'Reilly, Isabel M. "One of Philadelphia's Soldiers
in the War of 1812." Catholic Historical Review,
XXIX, 1918.
Rothensteiner, Rev. J.E. "Archbishop Kenrick's First
Years." St. Louis Catholic Historical Review.
Vol. V. 1923, pp. 205-229.
Shaun McCarty, S.T., "Touching Each Other at the
Roots. " Review for Religious Vol. 31, No. 2.March 1972

COMMEMORATIVE BOOKLETS AND PAMPHLETS

Boyle, Rev. William J. The Story of St. Michael's 1834-1934. Philadelphia: Jeffries & Manz, 1934.

Donnelly, Kenneth P.M., A History of St. Patrick's Parish, Iowa City, 1872-1972. Commemoration Booklet, Iowa City: n.p. 1972.

Fuhrmann, Joseph, History of St. Mary's Church, Iowa City, 1840-1916. Iowa City, n.p. 1916.

Griffith, C.F. Saint Peter's Parish, Keokuk, Iowa, 1832-1929, Iowa City: Iowa Catholic Historical Society, 1929

Centennial Booklet p Saint Patrick's Parish, Garryowen, Iowa, 1843-1943. n.a., n.p.

Diamond Jubilee Booklet. The History of Corpus Christi Parish.1932. Folder, "History of Corpus Christi School, Fort Dodge, Iowa." n.a., n.p.

The College Spokesman, Iowa Centennial Number, November, 1946- January, 1947. Dubuque: Loras College, 1947.

Kerin, Sister Mary Mark, RSM, The Relief of Suffering Humanity, A Centennial History of Mercy Hospital Davenport, Iowa. n.p., n.d.

Saint Paul Church - History of the Parish and Burlington's First Church Bell, 1840-1972. n.a., n.p., n.d.

Souvenir of the Centenary of St. Michael's Parish, Galena, Illinois, 1832-1932, Compiled by Rev. J.T. Donohue, Galena Gazette, 1932.

Se Centenaire de la Maison Loras, Lyon, n.p., 1940 A Pamphlet.

Moore, Justin E. The Warnings of Thomas Jefferson: or a Brief Exposition of the Dangers to be Apprehended to our Civil and Religious Liberties from Presbyterianism. (Philadelphia: Wm. J. Cunningham, 1844) Pamphlet.

Smith, John S. St. Anthony's 1837-1935.Davenport: n.p., n.d.

Index